THE DEMOCRATIC IMAGINATION IN AMERICA

The Democratic Imagination in America

Conversations with Our Past

Russell L. Hanson

PRINCETON UNIVERSITY PRESS

In Memory of
REGINA ANN GEISE HANSON
1930–1978

CONTENTS

WHEN I first proposed the thesis that became this book to my dissertation committee, one of its members advised me not to pursue it because he did not think that I would complete it in my lifetime. I was determined to prove him wrong and spent the next five years writing my dissertation and preparing this volume. However, as I view the "finished" product of my efforts I now comprehend the full import of his warning (which I should have realized when it was issued, since I greatly respect this man's opinion). With the publication of *The Democratic Imagination in America: Conversations with Our Past* my life's work has only just begun. I have barely scratched the surface of American democratic thought, and even if I were to spend the rest of my life reflecting on its development, no definitive reading of the democratic imagination would be forthcoming. At best a deeper appreciation of its complexity and variegation might grow, calling for still further efforts to understand the tradition of which we are unavoidably a part.

In that sense there can never be a "finished" interpretation of American experiments with democratic living, unless we stop experimenting with democracy. I do not regard my inability to accomplish this end as a failure, though I am painfully aware of the shortcomings of this work. Instead I shall rest content if those who read my work will disagree with it, so that we will all be led to reexamine the democratic imagination in America and search for a better understanding of it. If this work helps stimulate such a discussion I may yet live to see my project completed, even if my "thesis" is never finished!

If so, I cannot and will not take sole credit for this accomplishment. I have incurred many debts along the way; though I may never be able to repay them all I want to acknowledge them here. While I was at the University of Minnesota, both the Graduate School and the Department of Political Science provided financial assistance to me. That assistance was indispensable during the time at which I first began to think about the issues discussed herein.

I also appreciate the cooperation of my colleagues in the Department of Political Science at Indiana University, especially Professor Elinor Ostrom, who let me pursue this in my own time. That show of confidence did far more to encourage me to complete my thesis than other forms of encouragement given to ABDs laboring in the academic world, and I am extremely grateful for it.

My greatest intellectual debts are to Professor Terence W. Ball of the Department of Political Science, University of Minnesota, from whom I learned about political theory, and especially about the relationship between language and politics. I also gained from Terry an appreciation for graceful writing, although my own efforts compare poorly with his accomplishments in that area.

Professors L. Earl Shaw, Jr., and Edwin Fogelman of that department also served on my committee, as did Professor David W. Noble, of the Department of History, and Professor H. E. Mason, from the Department of Philosophy at the University of Minnesota. All raised significant questions and made helpful suggestions concerning the project.

Chapter One benefited from the insightful criticism of Terence Cornelius, and in a later form from comments by D. Christi Barbour, James Farr, Keith Fitzgerald, W. Richard Merriman, Maria Papadakis, Daniel Sabia, Larry Spence, and Elizabeth Trousdell.

Portions of Chapter Twelve were read in another incarnation by D. Christi Barbour, Fred Dallmayr, Keith Fitzgerald, R. Booth Fowler, W. Richard Merriman, and Elizabeth Trousdell—all of whom made useful recommendations.

Sanford G. Thatcher and Gretchen Oberfranc of Princeton University Press have my sincere gratitude for seeing this project through to its completion and guiding me through the intricacies of the modern publishing world. Sandy also engaged two exceptionally fine reviewers, William Connolly and Jennifer Nedelsky, both of whom read the manuscript twice, once in its original version, and again in revised form. They provided me with perceptive criticisms and helpful suggestions for improving my argument, and if it still remains unconvincing it is not because they failed to do their job, but because I was unable to meet their high expectations.

Bruce MacGregor edited the manuscript, which was typed by Marcia Pickett, Jerilee May, and Terry McArtor. I am grateful to Bruce for his gentle assistance in preparing a "cleaner" manuscript. All authors should be so lucky as to have an editor like him.

Two people deserve special mention. D. Christi Barbour helped me prepare the final manuscript, though the word "helped" grossly underestimates the care and effort she devoted to matters of accuracy, style, and format. Moreover, my discussions of American political thought with Christi and Dick Merriman have significantly shaped my thinking in these matters, not least because of our differences of interpretation.

Constance Jean Hanson is the one person on this long list of friends, helpers, and critics who was with me from the beginning to end of this project. She has read it almost as many times as I have, always offering sound ideas about matters of content, organization, and style. Most importantly, she always insisted that I "say what I mean."

Connie also offered the support and encouragement I needed to carry on my writing. She understood the weaknesses of an author who does not write easily, and she suffered all of the attendant inconveniences as deadlines approached. All too often, my early mornings and late evenings became her early mornings and late evenings, and my domestic and parental responsibilities became hers, yet she bore them willingly and with grace and humor. Hers was truly a labor of love, which I shall endeavor to return in kind.

JUNE 30, 1984
BLOOMINGTON, INDIANA

THE DEMOCRATIC IMAGINATION IN AMERICA

I

THIS IS A HISTORY of the origin and development of democratic ideologies in the United States. It tells the story of democracy in America from the Founding period until the Great Society and a little beyond. Like all stories, this one is told from a particular point of view, one that I would like to make explicit from the outset, since it is in the way I tell this story that any claim to originality lies.

In the first place, I reject what might be called objectivist accounts of the history of democracy in America. Such treatments either explicitly or implicitly use a transhistorical ideal of democracy to evaluate political institutions and practices from our past. Conclusions are then drawn about whether or not "progress" has been made in the struggle to achieve democracy. The so-called Progressive historians, e.g. J. Allen Smith, Charles and Mary Beard, and Vernon L. Parrington, once practiced this sort of historiography, but historical accounts of particular ideas, institutions, movements, and the like continue to be written as if current manifestations of the subject in question are the result of developmental processes that seem to advance in a positive direction. Thus, the history of democracy in America is often told as the history of the *advance* of democracy in America, wherein the imperfectly realized democracy of the Revolutionary period is shown to have been completed in the great waves of reform that occurred at generational intervals between then and now (Pole 1967). The same might be said of subjects other than democracy, but the tendency seems especially pronounced in this case, perhaps because it involves a fundamental part of our own political self-conception and is therefore susceptible to friendly revision (Fitzgerald 1979).

Less friendly critics of this sort of historiography provide an important corrective to this tendency, insofar as they question the direction of historical development. They often see defeat where others see victory for democracy, and so they are not inclined to assume that history unfolds in a progressive fashion. However, many of these revisionists reach their conclusions by applying conceptions of democracy that are just as transhistorical as those employed by progressive historians. The conclusions are different, but the objectivist method is the same.

Objectivism is truly an antihistorical attitude, however, for it denies the problematic nature of making historical comparisons and judgments altogether. The resort to an ideal of democracy denies the integrity of historical conceptions of democracy by subordinating them to the truth of a "timeless" conception, which upon inspection usually turns out to be a projection of contemporary prejudices about democracy. It is simply not possible to step outside of our history in order to view our place in history; those who try to do so become not objective, but objectivist.

Nor are historians the only ones who are guilty of this. The same attitude can be found in many political scientists' work on democracy in the United States. Although they have not been as preoccupied with the problem of progress as have historians, political scientists often betray an objectivist attitude in their treatment of the relationship between democracy and "critical realigning elections." To cite a current example:

Historically, realignments have affected the nature of government leadership, the realms in which government action is appropriate, and the directions which government policy output takes. *If democracy means that voters have control over government, a critical realignment is the voters' most significant instrument of that control.* The change in party support resulting from realignment enables the government to produce those policies which complete citizen control. (Campbell and Trilling 1980, 3–4; my emphasis)

According to this view, realignments prove that democracy really works in the United States. The potential for popular control, defined as "voters' control over government," is *always* present, though it is realized only at crucial moments in American history when realigning elections take place. Hence, realignments are the corrective devices by which governments are kept from straying too far from the sovereign will of the people.

Here, too, the implicit assumption is that the *meaning* of democracy is timeless, while its *practical realization* is episodic. It is precisely from this premise that Campbell and Trilling argue that realigning elections are important democratic moments in American history. Yet it is quite apparent that ideas about democracy need not be stable. In fact they, no less than ostensibly democratic practices, show considerable variation over time. Consequently, the achievement of democracy, conceived as a narrowing of the gap between "the democratic ideal" and its practical realization, is much more problematic than indicated by this sort of account.

One of the reasons that ideas about democracy are not stable is that the meaning of "democracy" itself is a matter of political dispute. Precisely because democracy has become the ultimate standard by which we evaluate and judge our political institutions and practices, the meaning of democracy is not, nor can it be, a matter of political indifference.[1] The struggle to control the definition or meaning of democracy in

---

[1] Even the traditional enemy of democracy, the aristocratic class and its political allies, now concedes that "democracy is the worst form of government except for all the rest that have been tried from time to time," as Churchill (1947) put it. Ironically, as the leader of the Conservative opposition Churchill was instructing the Labour party members of Parliament on the virtues of democracy, and admonishing them to be true democrats!

order to legitimate (or criticize) institutions and practices "in the name of democracy" is, therefore, one of the most important aspects of American political history—one that is trivialized by objectivist accounts that focus on progress toward some transhistorical ideal of democracy.

Hence, the first step in coming to understand the meaning of democracy is to concede the normality and perhaps even inevitability of disagreements over the meaning of this potent political symbol. Disputes over the meaning of democracy are to be expected, insofar as the meaning of democracy is strategically important in political affairs. Nothing less than the power to decide what counts as democratic is at issue. The history of democracy in the United States must therefore be the story of these disputes as they unfolded in time.

This suggests that significant changes in the rhetoric of democracy ought to be especially interesting to historians of democracy, for it is in rhetoric that ideas and action are indissolubly linked. Rhetoric is itself action, and at the same time its main purpose is to persuade people to act, by accepting or rejecting the rhetorician's arguments on behalf of, or against, a certain conception of democracy. This persuasion involves the giving of reasons for the plausibility of the rhetorician's celebrations or condemnations of existing political practices. In American politics the plausibility of such proffered reasons depends on their anchorage in conceptions that are central to Americans' collective understanding of themselves as political actors. Because democracy is one of these concepts it should come as no surprise that the rhetoric of democracy has always played a prominent role during periods of political change in America. Consequently, a study of changing rhetoric seems a particularly auspicious way of examining the history of democracy in the United States.

II

AT THIS POINT we may anticipate the story that is to follow. The history of democracy and its achievements in the United States is well told in the unfolding rhetoric of democracy. In this book I shall reconstruct that history by examining the ways in which "democracy" has been used at various times by various groups, with the intention of showing how and why these usages figure in the historical evolution of "democracy" in the United States.

It will be evident that my interest goes well beyond "mere words," however. If I concentrate on words and their usage it is because I am convinced that certain "keywords" like democracy unlock whole formations of meaning by revealing the connections between political practices and the beliefs that inform them (Williams 1976). This is most obvious when meanings change. Because ideas about the meaning of democracy partially constitute "democratic" practices, changes in the former cannot be independent of the latter. When ideas about democracy change, so do the practices of democracy. Similarly, when practices change, that implies that ideas have also changed. Conceptual revision and political reform are, therefore, but two sides of the same coin (Connolly 1974).

This means that we must think of realignments not only as changes in the practice of politics, but also as realignments in beliefs and ideas about politics as well. Insofar as these changes bear on democracy we must be alert to the way in which they embody an interplay of conceptual revision and political reform that together make up an experiment in democracy. Thus, one of my primary objectives is to show how changes in political rhetoric may be linked to changes in underlying patterns of economic and political development. Such linguistic changes are, I submit, an intergral part of the process by which newly emergent structures of power and influence are established and legitimated. As such, these changes perform important ideological functions in more general processes of social reproduction and change.

This is particularly evident in the evolution of democratic rhetoric in American politics. That evolution is the result of a long struggle between rival conceptions of democracy. For the most part this struggle has been relatively invisible, as first one, and then another, conception of democracy enjoyed a significant competitive advantage over its rivals. From time to time, however, this struggle has been quite visible and intense as the reigning interpretation of democracy has come under increasing attack and has eventually been replaced by one of its competitors, whereupon the cycle begins anew.

One of the main arenas in which this contest has been waged is in the rhetoric of American politics. The successive displacements of one conception of democracy by another are recorded in the changing language of party platforms, campaign slogans, and political manifestoes. By analyzing these, it is possible to reconstruct the fundamental struggle to control the meaning of an extremely potent political symbol.

This struggle must be understood in terms of underlying patterns of political and economic conflict. Historically, the displacement of one interpretation of democracy by another has been associated with the displacement of one dominant economic group by another. As new groups have gained political and economic ascendancy, so too, have new conceptions come to the fore—conceptions that quite naturally were more congenial to the interests of these groups. In the process, the abstract principles of democracy have come to receive diverse interpretations as their custodianship, to use Parrington's (1954) term, has changed hands.

The major reformulations of "democracy" occurred at key points in the development of the American economy involving the transitions from mercantile to competitive capitalism, from competitive to monopoly capitalism, and from monopoly to state welfare capitalism. These transitions were tied to the emergence of newly dominant forms of capital and, by implication, new class structures. These developments found expression in, for example, partisan realignments, changes in the balance of state and federal power, altered relations among legislative, executive, and judicial branches of government, and—above all—changes in the role of the state in the economy. As new forms of capital and new constellations of class interests emerged, the role of the state in the accumulation process also changed. At times this necessitated fairly radical reorientations of state economic activity, e.g. from intervention to nonintervention, and back again. The persistent need to justify the use of state power on behalf of an economic system predicated upon the private accumulation of wealth became particularly acute at such times. The redefinition of democracy and the reshaping of institutions and policies were important means by which compromises between classes were established.

Of course this is quite consistent with Marx's and Engels's dictum that "the ruling ideas of every age are the ideas of the ruling class." Insofar as newly emergent classes or class fractions have been able to establish the hegemony of their particular conception of democracy, they have been able to institute new practices and legitimate them. This does not mean, however, that ideas about democracy and its practice are in some sense "determined" by underlying economic forces. Vulgar Marxists who try to make this sort of argument forget Marx's criticism of the "contemplative materialism" of Ludwig Feuerbach, who failed to see that the circumstances that determine consciousness are themselves a social product. It is human beings who make—and remake—the circumstances of their existence, though not, to be sure, just as they please.

Ideological changes, then, are not caused by economic transformations, for economic changes are themselves the product of humanly wrought changes in the social relations of production. Since the latter are practices informed by ideas and beliefs, in short, consciousness, the process is clearly dialectical or interactive. Hence, it would be more accurate to say that economic transformations are the *occasions* of significant ideological shifts, but not their causes.

By implication democratic belief systems are not simply masks or weapons used by certain interests against others, nor are they cultural mechanisms for managing social and psychological strain, as most conceptions of ideology imply. They are instead structures of symbolic action in which the meaning of important and problematic areas of social life is established and modified (Geertz 1964). Belief systems are the medium in which men and women become aware of their interests and struggle to achieve them, as Marx so aptly put it in the Preface to his critique of political economy.

The importance of decisive periods in the development of the American economy for the project at hand lies in their significance as occasions for a more extended discourse on democracy. Because these periods in American history were times when ruling ideas about democracy were vulnerable, rival conceptions of democracy sprang forth and elicited responses. During the course of these exchanges actions were criticized, practices legitimated, and institutions reconstituted, all in the name of democracy. Hence these were times of democratic vitality in which the rhetoric of democracy flourished.

III

ONCE WE ADMIT that the meaning of democracy is an ideological affair, a new problem arises. Given the proliferation of meanings of democracy that attends such disputes as those mentioned above, is there any way to evaluate their relative merits so that we might be in a position to determine whether or not the replacement of one dominant interpretation by another represents "progress"? Or must we concede the relativity of the matter, having abandoned the use of "objective" ideas of democracy as our point of reference?

The latter recommendation is especially common among political scientists, who wonder if the anarchic results once expected from democratic politics have not manifested themselves in language instead. Most contemporary treatments of democracy begin rather despairingly with the observation that democracy is everywhere approved, though its true meaning is almost nowhere understood. The tremendous popularity of democracy has invited appropriation by movements of every stripe, and in the process, we are told, "democracy" has been transformed into little more than a "hurrah" word with very little meaning of its own. Consequently, we are advised, "democracy" is no longer a very useful concept for political evaluation and ought to be abandoned in favor of more precise concepts, e.g. "polyarchy" (Dahl 1956), or at the very least refined into a more scientifically useful concept (Oppenheim 1971).

It is extremely unlikely that a more refined concept of democracy will enhance our understanding of democracy. The gains in precision that allegedly accrue to those who adopt more scientific concepts, e.g. polyarchy, are achieved only by withdrawing from the ongoing debate over the meaning of democracy. Scientific objectivity, in this as in other instances, requires detachment from the "real world of democracy." Conceivably this detachment might permit a greater consensus on the meaning of democracy within the scientific community (though even this has not transpired), but it cannot tell us very much about what we want to know about democracy and the meaning it holds for those who practice politics. The further our science is from the world in which we live, the more it can say in a technical vein, but the less it has to tell us in a practical sense.

Then, too, the detachment of science is never really achieved. In the case of democracy, it is evident that political science has not removed the confusion surrounding this concept. If anything, it might be argued that political scientists have merely added to that confusion by promulgating still more definitions of democracy. This is unavoidable, since political science can neither escape the confusion of "democracy," nor dispel it via some sort of linguistic legerdemain. So long as political scientists claim to have anything to say about the real world of democracy, they must concede their status as participants—and hence partisans—in the ongoing debate over the meaning of democracy.

This need not imply that political scientists have nothing distinctive to contribute to this debate. Although they cannot resolve the debate once and for all, political scientists may at least recognize it as a *political* dispute of the first order and try to characterize it as such. The political-*cum*-conceptual dispute is not merely "about words" or "merely verbal" and therefore solely of semantic interest. It is through and through a political dispute, and merits investigation for that reason alone.

Thus, if we are now confused about the meaning of democracy, as some say we are, it is not simply because we disagree about what it means. Such disagreements have always surrounded democracy, because of different groups' willingness to use the openness of language in self-interested ways. Unless we want to conclude that these and all other instances of disagreement over the meaning of democracy are due to confusion on the part of the disputants, there must be something peculiar about contemporary disagreements that sets them apart and leads to the heightened sense of confusion evidenced by those who bemoan the politicization of "democracy."

As a matter of fact, there *is* something unusual about current disputes over the meaning of democracy. Although they incorrectly attribute this problem to an unfortunately high degree of "semantic variability" in ordinary language, observers who fear that democracy has become little more than a "hurrah" word are right to suspect that our present condition is different from apparently similar periods in history when disagreement over the meaning of democracy was very widespread indeed. The difference lies in the nature of present disagreements over democracy, as compared with previous episodes in the history of "democracy." Specifically, I contend that whereas previous disputes were underpinned by a shared understanding of the issues at stake in them, contemporary disputes are not. The participants in past disagreements over the meaning of democracy at least agreed about the source of their differences; the problem to which they applied different solutions was therefore a unifying force in their discussions. This is not true of contemporary disputes, which lack this underlying unity or closure. Present disagreements involve different solutions to different problems, as it were, and so the interpretations of democracy that are offered in them are incommensurable in a way that past notions of democracy were not. As a result, contemporary disagreements about liberal democracy lack coherence—they *are* confused.

More concretely, contemporary discussions about liberal democracy have become incoherent largely because they avoid the central focus of traditional liberal democratic discourse, or what Ackerman (1980) calls "power talk." The identity of liberal democracy as a distinctive form of power talk has always been related to efforts aimed at reaching an accommodation between liberalism and democracy, without sacrificing one to the other. The defining feature of liberal democratic discourse involves the simultaneous embrace of liberalism and democracy, and the history of this kind of discourse is in large measure the result of successive efforts to reconcile their contradictory implications in practice.

That some sort of accommodation is necessary was never doubted by earlier generations of liberal democrats because they recognized that liberalism and democracy addressed somewhat different aspects of the problem of political power and its place in society. Liberalism was concerned with the proper scope of political power, and liberals were therefore preoccupied with questions about the proper limits on political power and their effective location, so to speak. Democracy, on the other hand, focused on popular sovereignty or the ultimate source of rightful power, and by implication the exercise of that power by agents of the people. In short, democracy established the *identity* of the sovereign in society, whereas liberalism defined the *limits* on sovereign power, regardless of who exercised that power.

Thus, there was nothing intrinsically democratic about liberalism, nor was there anything especially liberal about democracy. Nondemocratic liberal regimes, e.g. constitutional monarchies, were conceivable and in fact prevalent. Nonliberal democracies were also imaginable, although they were not very common at all, owing to the widespread distaste for unrestrained democracy or "mobocracy."

Nor were liberalism and democracy simply different; they were potentially incompatible. According to democratic doctrines, the people or their legitimate agents ought to rule, and any restraints upon that rule were undemocratic, unless they were self-imposed. That guarantee was not strong enough for many liberals, who opposed absolute power in any form, but especially where it was exercised by the democracy. Indeed, if forced to choose, they most often favored absolute monarchy to absolute democracy as the lesser of two evils. If class rule was unavoidable, better it be by the class best suited to rule, and not the unwashed commons or "demos." Hence, the search for reliable limits on the exercise of political power pointed away from democracy, just as the struggle for popular rule was often directed against liberal regimes.

The historical convergence of liberalism and democracy in England was therefore a remarkable phenomenon, as Macpherson (1977) notes. This convergence made for a distinct version of power talk in which the main topic of conversation involved the establishment of justifiable limits on popular sovereignty, particularly where these limits served to protect private property. Resolutions of this problem were, of course, highly provisional and subject to renegotiation. As a result different versions of liberal democracy, each associated with a different conjuncture of historical "discussants," are now discernible.

The same is true of the United States. Here, as in England, the clash of interpretations often coincided with economic class distinctions, so that in one way or another liberal democratic power talk involved discussions about the proper relationship between the public power of the democracy and the liberty of wealthy people.[2] More to the point, these dis-

---

[2] In the United States this clash was not between liberals and democrats, as it often was on the continent, but among liberal democrats of various

cussions centered on the boundaries of public power as exercised by the democracy or its appointed agents, and on the rights of property owners against the exercise of that power.

Naturally, the particular issues varied from period to period; at the time of the founding the corruption of politics by the commercial spirit was the principal issue, while the Monster Bank, the Robber Barons, the Trusts and the System embodied later concerns. Nevertheless, the common lineage running throughout each of these conversations on the meaning of liberal democracy may be traced to more or less conscious efforts to reconcile liberal and democratic doctrines. The apparent absence of that lineage in contemporary liberal democratic discourse implies, therefore, that we have forgotten the main topic of conversation in liberal democratic power talk, and that is why we are so confused about the meaning of liberal democracy in the present age. Our disputes over the meaning of liberal democracy lack closure or coherence because there is no longer a well-defined and widely shared sense of what is at issue, namely, the mutual accommodation of liberal and democratic principles. Our conversation has degenerated into a veritable babel in which all participants speak past, rather than to, one another.

IV

If THIS DIAGNOSIS of the current crisis of democracy is correct, then we must ask how this state of affairs came to pass. Why is there no longer any closure to our disputes, as there has been in the past? What explanation for this can be offered, and does it permit us to imagine conditions under which closure may be reestablished?

---

persuasions (Hartz 1955). Therefore, recounting the history of liberal democracy in this country does not entail a blow-by-blow description of some titanic struggle between the representatives of two traditions. Rather, it involves an interpretation of the internal process by which liberal democrats explored the practical meaning of "keywords" in their culture. That is, this history is a study in the constitution of meaning, which is always a collective endeavor, though not always a peaceful or rational one.

That, in fact, is my chief concern in this matter, and most of this book is devoted to showing how the closure that made liberal democratic power talk coherent was gradually eroded during the course of American history. The current state of confusion surrounding the meaning of liberal democracy reflects the cumulative impact of past turns in our historical conversations on liberal democracy. As each successive dispute over the meaning of democracy in America unfolded in history, the topic of conversation was further deflected from the problem of reconciling liberalism and democracy, so that in the present age the problematic nature of liberal democratic power talk is all but forgotten. The cumulative effect of historical reinterpretations was to liberalize democracy so thoroughly that any tension between liberalism and democracy was almost completely sublimated.

In this way periodic reinterpretations of liberal democracy allowed chronic "legitimation crises" to be resolved without ever requiring any fundamental alteration in the underlying political economy of American capitalism. By virtue of political reinterpretation at the hands of powerful groups in American society, "democracy" was domesticated and made safe, so much so that it no longer seems necessary to remember that democracy was once considered a radical notion, and for that reason was viewed with suspicion and even downright dismay.

This taming of democracy has profound implications for our present situation because it seriously limits *our* capacity for reinterpreting liberal democracy in appropriate ways. The manner in which past crises of legitimacy were resolved effectively reduces our room for maneuver; that is, we can no longer interpret and reinterpret liberal democracy in certain ways because of the way in which our predecessors defined it and bequeathed it to us. In that sense, "the tradition of all the dead generations weighs like a nightmare on the brain of the living," as Marx well knew.

The extent of this amnesia is betrayed by the ease with which we now drop the "liberal" modifier in "liberal democcracy" and simply refer to "democracy," as if there were no question about the topic of conversation. This way of speaking implicitly denies any tensions between liberalism and democracy and so enables us to avoid important—and divisive—issues in our political discourse. It has even gotten to the point where nonliberal varieties of democracy are now incomprehensible to most of us, although Macpherson (1966) has tried to show us that they have a pedigree at least as democratic as ours, and perhaps more so.

The significance of this becomes apparent once we recognize that we are now experiencing a "crisis of democracy" and that this crisis will not be resolved until we are able to arrive at a new interpretation of liberal democracy capable of supporting legitimate political institutions. For some, e.g. the "neoconservatives," this crisis is the result of too much democracy: our ability to govern ourselves in an age of scarce resources is far exceeded by democratically justified claims on those resources (Crozier 1975). For the critics of the neoconservative position, the crisis stems from too little democracy: the limits on governability have less to do with an overabundance of democratic claims than they do with certain intrinsically undemocratic features of modern capitalism (Steinfels 1979). Both sides agree, however, that we have reached one of those proverbial "crossroads in history," and that the road we follow will decisively alter the nature of democracy in America.

Thus, the current crisis of democracy centers on the meaning of democracy for us and those who come after. The meaning of liberal democracy has been called into question and so is open to interpretation and reinterpretation in new and unusual ways. However, we apparently lack the ability to discover a meaningful way out of this crisis because we are no longer able to generate new ideas about liberal democratic ways of governing ourselves. Our old conceptions of liberal democracy are inadequate for our current situation, but no new conceptions have emerged to take their place. That, in fact, is why we face a crisis today—it is a time when the old is dying, but the new cannot yet be born.

All of this is argued at much greater length in the chapters that follow. Chapter One presents in more systematic form my argument about the degeneration of liberal democratic discourse in the United States. This argument establishes the narrative framework in which Chapters Two through Eleven move. Essentially these chapters provide more detailed expositions of the key episodes in the semantic history of democracy in America. However, Chapter Twelve is in many respects the most important part of the book because it is there that I discuss the implications of my analysis for the future of liberal democratic power talk in this country.

My point in telling this story, after all, is not really to improve upon our knowledge of the past, although I am certainly not opposed to that worthy goal. Much of what I write is not new; I do not present heretofore undiscovered facts about American history. The events I describe and the people whose work I discuss are well known to lay readers as well as professional historians. Indeed, I suspect that the latter will find my account inadequate, particularly if they specialize in one of the eras that I can only briefly characterize in this book. Because I look at a span of history that covers more than two hundred years, I simply cannot satisfy the specialist's curiosity, nor meet the exacting requirements for entrance into the ranks of experts on, say, Jacksonian democracy.

I admit all of this in advance because my interest in the past is ultimately future-oriented. As I explain in Chapter Twelve, the purpose of this historical analysis is to illuminate the possibilities for reinvigorating liberal democratic discourse. By showing how and explaining why we are confused, I hope that it will become apparent that we must return to the original problem that animates liberal democracy, namely the tension between liberalism and democracy.

In turn this will require something of a "democratization of liberalism" in order to undo the stultifying effects of the liberalization of democracy that has already occurred. In addition to resuscitating democracy, this may very well entail a reinterpretation of liberalism so as to make it safe for democracy, as Macpherson (1977) suggests. I am inclined to agree with Macpherson (1973) and Bell (1976) who, despite their obvious differences, conclude that this reinterpretation must emphasize certain ethical aspects of liberalism that have heretofore been repressed by liberal commitments to market institutions that no longer serve these ends as well as others might.[3]

This does not mean that this radicalized discourse cannot be "liberal" in orientation, however. Indeed, it must be liberal in some sense in order for us to understand it, let alone judge its outcome as progressive or degenerative, for those terms are relative to the liberal tradition. But it does mean that to be liberal "in some sense" involves a commitment to liberal democratic principles of political argumentation, even if that requires us to abandon our allegiance to liberal democratic institutions and practices that no longer, or perhaps never did, embody those principles very well. That is, we must remain committed to liberal democracy as an open discourse in which substantive conclusions are not predetermined, but are uncovered in the process of argumentation itself. The challenge, then, is not to defend liberal democratic *institutions*, but to uphold the liberal democratic *principles* that inform and partially constitute the institutions that ostensibly embody them. Where these institutions can no longer be shown to do so, they must be abandoned in order to remain true to liberal principles of discourse.

[3] Liberalism, too, is an historical concept; its meaning has changed considerably over the years, as both Bell (1976) and Macpherson (1977) make clear. The possibility of democratizing liberalism is in fact predicated on this, as it implies a reversal of certain self-destructive tendencies in the liberal tradition itself. The chapters that follow explain what those tendencies are and analyze their effects on democratic ideas. Chapter Eleven reviews this "liberalization of democracy," while Chapter Twelve discusses possibilities for democratizing liberalism. For now it is sufficient—and necessary—to note that "liberalism" is no less historical than "democracy."

Not all readers will be convinced by my arguments on this point, I am sure, and in some respects I hope they are not. There is something vital and important about disagreements over the meaning of liberal democracy, *if* those disagreements reflect a common engagement. Indeed, I suspect that such disagreements are the mainspring of whatever progressive forces there are in history, because they cause us to entertain the possibility that existing ways of conducting our political affairs are neither necessary nor necessarily democratic. Disagreement over the meaning of democracy makes criticism a permanent possibility, and from that comes the inspiration to do better or make progress in our efforts to live democratically.

For this reason it does not matter if my own interpretation of what liberal democracy means in the present day and age meets with something less than universal acceptance. I am not propounding a definition of liberal democracy that will silence the babel that symbolizes the current crisis of democracy, for I do not believe that would constitute progress. As I shall argue in the next chapter, progress in liberal democratic discourse does not consist in winning the debate, but in extending the discussion in a meaningful fashion by arguing well. This involves a willingness to engage in a collective effort to clarify the problematic relationship between liberalism and democracy. When that happens progress is made and we all emerge winners, insofar as we are able to reach an accommodation by reasonable means.[4]

Hence, I shall rest content if this history helps us remember what question animates liberal democratic discourse (insofar as it is *both* liberal and democratic at the same time) and so makes it possible for us to engage in coherent power talk once again. In that sense, liberal democracy has no

[4] My claim here, which will be redeemed in Chapter One, is that progressive discourses *on* liberal democracy can be identified, even if progressive interpretations *of* liberal democracy may not. My earlier criticism of objectivist historiography was directed against its method, not its aim, which, as should be evident from these last few paragraphs, I share.

meaning other than what we give it during the course of our struggle to find some sort of practical accommodation between liberalism and democracy. That, I submit, is the proverbial lesson of history, and also what must be done now and in the future if liberal democracy is to remain viable.

The Rhetoric of Democracy

I

IN ORDER TO DETERMINE whether or not liberal democracy is still a viable tradition in the United States, we need to know what the appropriate vital signs are, and where to look for them. Both needs may be satisfied if we construe liberal democracy as a rhetorical tradition, the progress or decline of which is reflected in political arguments about the meaning of liberal democracy.[1] This will allow us to gain some perspective on the current crisis of democracy, which is but the most recent expression of this tradition, and on the likely outcome of this crisis.

To speak of liberal democracy as a *rhetorical* tradition may seem a bit odd. We are more inclined to think of it as a philosophical or perhaps ideological tradition on the one hand, or a specific set of institutional arrangements on the other. However, that way of construing it has the singular disadvantage of reducing liberal democracy to a set of ideas that seem to exist apart from or independently of the political institutions and practices they inform. Against this tendency MacIntyre (1981, 58) is surely right to argue that a unified history of ideas and practices is needed, since there are not two pasts, one populated by ideas, the other by institutions and actions. The fact that ideas about democracy are at least partially constitutive of what are called democratic practices

[1] By rhetoric I mean "action on minds by means of discourse" in situations where logical demonstration is not possible (Perelman and Olbrechts-Tyteca 1969). That is, rhetoric refers to the classical art of persuasion, of which sophistry was only a perversion. Ordinary usage now treats rhetoric and sophistry as identical, but I want to resist that tendency here.

means that a democratic tradition must be viewed as a unity
of ideas and practices unfolding in relation to one another,
and not as an abstract philosophical system moving through
history.[2] For that reason it seems especially appropriate to
concentrate on rhetoric when analyzing the vitality of the liberal democratic tradition, since it is in rhetoric that the relationship between liberal democratic ideals and practices is
most clearly revealed. Ideas about liberal democracy find
practical expression in the course of arguments over the desirability of particular institutions and practices. Similarly,
the beliefs that inform and constitute liberal democratic institutions are made explicit during the course of debates over
their standing within particular political communities.
Hence, the conceptual link between ideas about liberal democracy and the political practices implied by them is forged
in political rhetoric.

A *tradition* of liberal democratic rhetoric exists insofar as
the rhetoric of one generation of members in a historical political community is related in some way to the rhetoric of
other generations. This rhetorical continuity across generations is not simply a matter of shared ideas or institutions,
however. To define the unity of a rhetorical tradition in this
way would only recapitulate the sort of historiography of
which MacIntyre is rightly critical. Rather, we need to think
of "tradition" in a way that allows the particularity and
uniqueness of the rhetorical linkages between the theory and
practice of each and every generation to be visible, while
preserving an intelligible continuity between them. We need
a "tradition" based on family resemblances, to use Wittgenstein's analogy, not ideological or institutional identities.

Once again MacIntyre is quite helpful in this regard, for
he suggests that a tradition "is an historically extended, socially embodied argument, and an argument precisely in part

[2] That is to say, ideas and practices are conceptually, not contingently,
related, though that need not imply the two are identical. Hence the locution
"partially constitutive."

about the goods which constitute that tradition" (1981, 207). That is, *vital* traditions embody continuities of conflict over the meaning of the central ideas in those traditions and the proper institutional and practical forms constituted by them. By implication, a rhetorical tradition of liberal democracy is an historically extended argument over the practical meaning of "liberal democracy." The generational continuity of which I spoke earlier is one of shared contestation over the meaning of liberal democracy. That continuity is therefore rhetorical in a double sense: it is expressed *in* rhetoric, and *by means of* rhetorical arguments for and against particular interpretations and instantiations of liberal democracy.

We can sometimes see this continuity in arguments and argumentative styles when we compare different moments in the history of a tradition. This is especially true when rhetoricians of one period self-consciously borrow the arguments of their political ancestors. Many political traditions originate in the experience of founding a polity, and so it is not unusual to see later generations return to that founding for inspiration and guidance during times of crisis. For that reason, particular arguments and claims are passed down from generation to generation and seem to exemplify the continuity of the tradition in which they exist.

However, this continuity is superficial; it is possible to speak of continuous traditions even in the absence of any such similarity in the content of different generations' rhetoric. That is because the underlying unity of tradition consists of a common discursive *activity*. It is a common action that binds generations to one another and identifies them as different moments in the same political tradition. The specific arguments that are the product of this activity may or may not show signs of continuity. They are incidental to the activity itself, and it is the activity that constitutes a tradition.

In the case of the liberal democratic tradition, this is a problem-solving activity. It centers on establishing a practical relationship between liberalism and democracy. As we have seen, this relationship is problematic; no natural or logical connection between the two exists. Otherwise there would be no need to argue about potential solutions and there would be no liberal democratic tradition, as that is understood here, since no power talk or argument about the meaning of liberal democracy would be necessary.

The accommodation of liberal and democratic principles must be achieved at a concrete level. Even though no general resolution exists, particular interpretations of liberal democracy, i.e. particular resolutions of the tension between liberalism and democracy, may be appropriate in particular communities at particular times. Indeed, the arguments over the meaning of liberal democracy that constitute the liberal democratic tradition are arguments conducted in communities as they seek to understand the practical meaning of liberal democracy as it applies to them and their situation.

The connection between the moments that compose a tradition is therefore a practical one. Each moment represents an argument over the meaning of liberal democracy appropriate to that moment. It is this common effort to establish the problematic meaning of liberal democracy that constitutes the family resemblance that runs through each and every generation in a political tradition.

Thus, what Collingwood (1939, 62) said of the history of political theory may also be said of historical traditions: They do not consist of different answers given at different times to one and the same question. Rather they represent efforts to solve a problem that is more or less constantly changing, as are the solutions to it. Rhetorical traditions such as liberal democracy are always being constituted and reconstituted in the process of political argumentation. They depend for their existence on more or less continuous disputation (which does not, of course, rule out the possibility that some disputes are historically more important than others). Any assessment of the present and future viability of liberal democracy must therefore inquire into the origins of rhetorical conflict over the meaning of liberal democracy in order to determine whether or not this tradition is or can be a "live" one.

II

ARGUMENTS OVER the proper relationship between liberal
and democratic principles as they apply to particular circumstances are essentially debates about the meaning of liberal
democracy for historically situated political communities.
They are efforts by those communities to resolve something
that is problematic, but which must be settled, at least provisionally, in order for politics to proceed.

These arguments over the meaning of liberal democracy
may take place on more than one level. For instance, they
may focus on whether or not certain policies or practices are
consistent with liberal democracy. Such disputes usually proceed within fairly well-established and widely recognized
rules of argumentation, and so their resolution is reasonably
straightforward. The various arguments are made and
weighed according to prevailing norms of argumentation, and
a decision is reached that settles the issue.

Other arguments, however, may focus on the way in which
arguments are conducted and resolved. These are just as
much arguments over the meaning of liberal democracy as
those previously mentioned, since liberal democratic power
talk is as much distinguished by the ways in which arguments
are settled as it is by specific arguments about the proper
relationship between liberalism and democracy. Indeed, it
may even be true that these argumentative practices are actually what distinguish liberal democracy from other forms of
power talk, insofar as they constitute the specific identity of
this way of talking about power in society.

The liberal democratic commitment to the "consent of the
governed" is especially important in this connection, for it is
this ideal that informs all liberal democratic discourse insofar
as it *is* liberal democratic discourse. This commitment speci-
fies the basic rule of all liberal democratic argumentation,
namely, that legitimate decisions must be the result of a discussion in which participants reach an agreement that is
freely given. Differences are therefore resolved by persua-

sive, rather than coercive, means, so that arguments are fairly concluded—from which it may be inferred that the governed have given their consent to the actions implied in the resolution of an issue.

In principle, the consent of the governed implies that a rule of unanimity prevails in political discourse. Arguments do not end until all parties have agreed to end them, and so have given their consent to a settlement. In practice, of course, procedures like majority rule, in various forms, are invoked to close debate before unanimous agreement has been secured. Such practices may be necessary, since actions may have to be made before unanimity prevails, especially in cases where unanimity is unlikely to be achieved. However, the legitimacy of these practices depends on the extent to which they resemble the rule of unanimity: majority rule is preferred to, say, minority rule, as a way of closing debate because it more closely approximates the rule of unanimity, especially if provisions for extraordinary or concurrent majorities are included.

Even this example shows, however, that the argumentative practices that constitute liberal democratic discourse, and identify it *as* liberal democratic discourse, may become a matter of dispute, and properly so. Commitments to principles like the "consent of the governed" require interpretation in order to have practical application in specific situations, and for that reason arguments over the meaning of the "consent of the governed" often arise and are perhaps unavoidable. Hence, disagreements over the justifiability of majority rule, and on the need for special majorities on certain issues that are considered fundamental in some way, are to be expected.

Disputes over the practices that govern argumentation seldom arise on their own. They usually grow out of lower-order disagreements over the compatibility of certain policies or actions with liberal democracy. These disputes often begin amidst a consensus on the rules of the game, but, where the issues are highly significant and the stakes of the game are substantial, they may escalate to arguments over the rules for deciding the issues themselves. The chapters that follow provide numerous examples of this phenomenon of argumentative contagion, in which "small" disputes over the meaning of liberal democracy become full-fledged debates about the meaning of liberal democracy, in which the constitutive principles of argumentation are at issue.

Such generalized arguments are especially important in the historical development of traditions like liberal democracy, because their outcomes often change the course of argumentation in fundamental ways. By changing the way in which arguments are decided, these disputes profoundly influence the types of arguments that may be presented and, most importantly, the types of arguments that may be *successfully* presented. Indeed, that is why the practices that govern arguments themselves become the object of disputation. The fundamental identity of liberal democratic power talk is at stake, and the struggle to control or define that identity by stipulating the meaning of liberal democracy is what animates these debates.

For that reason, these disputes may be called "essential contests," and I now turn to a discussion of their key features.

III

BECAUSE LIBERAL DEMOCRACY is a rhetorical tradition, its vitality depends on the persistence of disputes and arguments over the meaning of liberal democracy for particular communities at particular times in their history. Within that tradition, it would seem that liberal democracy is an "essentially contested concept," a phrase introduced by W. B. Gallie (1955–1956) to describe concepts the proper use and meaning of which are the subject of considerable disagreement. According to Gallie, an essentially contested concept like democracy is used quite differently by various groups of people to describe particular political practices. Moreover, each group, while recognizing the existence of competing usages, insists that its particular way of using democracy is the correct use of the term. And each group offers what it takes to be convincing arguments, evidence, or other forms of justification in defense of this claim (ibid., 168).

What sets essential contests apart from other linguistic squabbles, however, is the fact that each group's arguments on behalf of its usage of democracy have merit. Indeed, it may even be said that the various groups' arguments have more or less *equal* merit, and that no group's usage of democracy is self-evidently superior to any other group's usage. This is because no general principle for evaluating the usages of an essentially contested concept exists. Essentially contested concepts have a uniquely "open" texture that invites conflicting usages and claims. They are distinguished from other concepts by the fact that they involve the partisan application of multiple criteria, the relative importance of which is unsettled and open to dispute, in the appraisal or evaluation of complex achievements. Since various groups may attach different significance to the criteria involved, it is possible, even likely, that they will arrive at different conclusions regarding the praiseworthiness of a given accomplishment.

Gallie insists that such contests are sustained by rational arguments, even though they do not admit of rational resolution. They do not, in other words, reflect mistaken or confused uses by some participants in the contest. If they did, the dispute presumably could be resolved by showing what the "real" or "true" meaning of democracy is. However, such efforts would only expand the contest, according to Gallie, for there is no universally agreed-upon usage of democracy, nor can there be one.

Neither do the various uses in an essential contest over the meaning of democracy reflect incommensurable interpretations, according to Gallie, for that would imply that such disputes were not even sustained by rational arguments. In the absence of any common ground the contestants would not really be arguing about the same thing at all, and the "dispute" would in fact consist of a misunderstanding rather than an essential contest, as described by Gallie.

John Gray (1977) suggests that essentially contested concepts are themselves symptomatic of more encompassing differences of opinion in society. According to Gray, "essentially contested concepts find their characteristic uses within conceptual frameworks which have endorsement functions in respect of definite forms of social life" (ibid., 332). Hence, the use of essentially contested concepts typically "involves assent to definite uses of a whole range of contextually related concepts of a no less contestable character" (ibid., 332). Since this combination of usages generally coheres around worldviews connected with specific forms of life, Gray conjectures that "essentially contested concepts occur characteristically in social contexts which are recognizably those of an ideological dispute" (ibid., 333).

If different interpretations of liberal democracy are ideologically informed, however, the argumentative practices that constitute an essential contest over the meaning of democracy are clearly rhetorical (Garver 1978). They are exercises in persuasion, oriented toward establishing agreement in situations where demonstrative logic has no force.[3] In that sense, "the meaning of an essentially contested concept contains arguments about its meaning, and *that* is the sense in which the proper use of an essentially contested concept involves endless disputes about its proper use" (ibid., 164; my emphasis).

The disputes are endless insofar as rhetorical arguments are never conclusive, unlike scientific, dialectic, or atechnical arguments. As such, they may be characterized in the following way:

> As opposed to science, rhetorical arguments are rarely necessary; the ideal of a rhetorical argument is to construct not an invulnerable argument but the best argument possible

[3] Recall Lewis Carroll's account of "What the Tortoise Said to Achilles," wherein Achilles' claim that "Logic would take you by the throat, and FORCE" the tortoise to accept Achilles' conclusion is defeated by the tortoise's stubborn refusal to accept the premise from which that conclusion was derived.

in a particular situation. As opposed to dialectic, rhetorical arguments are never final; the ideal of a rhetorical argument is not to silence the opposition forever but to take the opinions of one audience in one situation and make those opinions lead, as best one can, to a particular verdict. Finally, as opposed to sophistical or atechnical argument, rhetorical arguments keep the controversy centered on the arguments themselves; the ideal of rhetorical argument is not victory as such and at any cost but doing the best in the situation by means of argument. (ibid., 159)

Consequently, the openness of rhetorical disputes about the meaning of liberal democracy is an essential feature of the liberal democratic tradition, and the source of its argumentative vitality.

IV

IF ESSENTIAL CONTESTS are radically open, in the sense that no definitive resolution is conceivable, why do they persist? What motivates the contestants to continue arguing when the possibility of victory is apparently removed?

There are, of course, other options open to them. Gallie himself discusses the possibility that the various parties to an essential contest might, upon recognizing it *as* an essential contest, resign themselves to the relativity of the matter and simply withdraw from an argument that, because it cannot be rationally resolved, seems pointless. If essential contests over the meaning of liberal democracy are ideological disputes, and are seen as such, what motivates the participants to continue in their search for closure?

It seems likely that in the case of democracy, at least, the admittedly high stakes involved, namely the control of a potent political symbol, might keep the parties interested, especially if individual participants feared that by withdrawing their interests would be neglected altogether. In this case, "not losing" might replace the goal of winning as a sufficient inducement to continue arguing.

Precisely because the stakes are so high, however, it is conceivable that one or more parties to the debate might decide to close the contest unilaterally. They might decide to "damn the heretics and cut the cackle," and abandon the force of the better argument in favor of more dependable weapons in the political struggle to control "liberal democracy" (Gallie 1955–1956, 194).

Against these possibilities, Gallie (1964) hoped that once contestants recognized that democracy was an essentially contested concept they would also recognize that rival uses of it were not only logically possible and humanly likely, but were of "permanent potential critical value" to their own uses and interpretations. They would continue to dispute the meaning of democracy because they saw in the process of disputation itself a means of promoting democratic progress.

This underlying commitment to arguing well does not preclude the possibility that certain interpretations of liberal democracy might prove decisive for particular communities. Kekes (1977) and, to a certain extent, Garver (1978) argue that this hope of finding what Care (1973) and Dekema (1981) refer to as a "practical closure" motivates participants to engage in essential contests. Even though they may concede that no general resolution of the problem of liberal democracy is possible, participants in an essential contest may argue that their interpretation is best for their community at this time and for certain issues. In this conjecture of particularities, a provisional interpretation of liberal democracy might be established, one that other disputants might even concede is preferable to their own, so long as circumstances do not change.

However important this consideration may be, it must be subordinated to the commitment to argue well, according to Gallie's line of reasoning. Gallie's participants are not motivated only or even primarily by the desire to win their particular contests. They are committed to extending the argument in optimal ways. To borrow from MacIntyre (1981, 175), the practice of arguing well involves a coherent and complex form of socially established cooperative human activity through which goods internal to that form of activity are realised in the course of trying to achieve those standards of excellence which are appropriate to, and partially definitive of, that form of activity, with the result that human powers to achieve excellence, and human conceptions of the ends and goods involved, are systematically extended.

The fact that one or another interpretation proves to be at least temporarily superior is incidental to the pursuit of excellence, though that does not make this occurrence unimportant.

The commitment to arguing well is a *virtue* in MacIntyre's sense of that term: it is "an acquired human quality the possession and exercise of which tends to enable us to achieve those goods which are internal to practices and the lack of which effectively prevents us from achieving any such goods" (1981, 178). Without this commitment certain "external" goods may accrue to particular individuals: they may win an essential contest and so be able to define "democracy" for their community. However, that victory will not necessarily contribute anything to the development of the liberal democratic tradition and may even contribute to its decline, at least insofar as it is oriented toward winning, and not excellence in argument.

In other words, the commitment to arguing well is a necessary condition for the persistence *and development* of a historical tradition. Without this commitment, the extended argument over the meaning of liberal democracy will not progress in a way that enlarges upon past accomplishments and will in fact come to an end.

Thus, the participation of commited liberal democrats in an essential contest has a specific purpose. It is oriented toward *improving* the argumentative tradition in ways relevant to that generation.[4] Disputes over the meaning of liberal de-

---

[4] I reexamine the liberal democratic commitment to progress via contestation in Chapter Twelve.

mocracy arise because past interpretations become problematic under new historical circumstances. Indeed, it could not be otherwise. Past solutions are only solutions to past problems. It is precisely because they no longer work or have become problematic in some way that new contests are generated. The participants in these contests do not seek past remedies, but instead they try to recapture the exemplary mode of problem-solving of their founders and the other glorious forebearers of their political community (Shumer 1979).

Consequently, contemporary arguments represent "a commentary upon and response to the past in which the past, if necessary and if possible, is corrected and transcended, yet corrected and transcended in a way that leaves the present open to being in turn corrected and transcended" by some future generation (MacIntyre 1981, 137). Present disputes over the meaning of liberal democracy represent historically situated attempts to make a particular tradition relevant to the solution of specific problems that characterize that situation. They result in reinterpretations that are never definitive, because historically situated, but which help constitute anew the tradition involved.

V

AS ENVISIONED by Gallie, essential contests resemble philosophic or forensic disputes. That is, they are assumed to be situations in which only arguments come into play. The unspoken assumption is that each of the contestants enjoys a relatively equal standing in the contests, and that the only legitimate way of resolving a particular dispute is through the "force of the better argument." It is not, in other words, a situation in which coercion plays a prominent role, for that would violate the free and unrestrained give-and-take of truly genuine debates.

Indeed, it is this presumption that allows us to conclude that continued participation in essential contests is rationally motivated. The possibility of arriving at a provisional resolution through persuasion is what induces participants to participate, rather than forsake the dispute altogether or seek to "damn the heretics." If this condition is not met, then the very idea of progress through rational contestation is called into question, since the outcome of particular disputes' may depend less on the arguments offered than on the ability of one or more of the contestants to force their position on others.

Where "debates" are forcefully organized and prosecuted, "la raison du plus fort est toujours la meilleure," or "the reason of the strongest is always the best," according to La Fountaine (Parenti 1978, 136). However, it is only in *genuine* contests that progress through contestation is a sensible notion. In contests that are not genuine, i.e. where winning has replaced the pursuit of excellence as the primary purpose of argumentation, no progress may be expected. Instead, the various stratagems for winning are likely to bring about degeneration, especially where they involve coercive means that contradict the whole notion of "consensual agreement."

This coercion need not involve the use of naked force; it may involve much more subtle, but no less effective, mechanisms of coercion. In such instances it may be extremely difficult to tell, on the face of it, whether a contest is truly genuine or only appears to be so. For coercion may not even involve an agent coercing another (Ball 1978). It may be "structural," residing in the organization of discourse itself, or rather in the rules by which discourse is organized and conducted. Such subtle coercion, even though it remains invisible and anonymous, undermines the prospects for progressive development just as surely as brute force.

Habermas (1975) refers to contests like this as instances of "systematically distorted communication," in which the outcome of a dispute *seems* to be the result of a rational discourse in which only the "forceless force of the better argument" holds sway, but which in fact reflects a mobilization of bias within discourse itself. This mobilization of bias, to use Schattschneider's (1975) term, systematically distorts the course of an argument so as to skew the outcome of political discourse in ways that typically render the legitimacy of existing forms of social organization unquestionable. Existing modes of collective decision-making are taken as given in discourse, which necessarily shifts to marginal considerations.

These distortions may be traced to the underlying patterns of domination in which communicative processes are embedded. Systematic distortions of communication introduce a "mobilization of bias" into the organization of political discourse by surreptitiously incorporating relations of power and influence into the symbolic structures of speech and action. In so doing they organize certain questions, e.g. those bearing on the nature of political and economic domination, out of political discussion, thereby contributing to the reproduction of the patterns of domination from which they arise.

The effectiveness of systematic distortions in concealing the nature of domination, and in producing an apparent consensus on fundamental questions of social organization by restricting the range of debate, depends in very large measure on their relative invisibility and appearance of objectivity. Their ability to produce an apparant consensus on fundamental questions of social organization, i.e. to surreptitiously incorporate relations of power into the organization of discourse itself, is a function of their unobtrusiveness. To the extent that they become visible and are recognized for what they are, their potency is reduced.

Thus, when assessing the vitality of the liberal democratic tradition in terms of the essential contests that sustain it, it is imperative that we be able to distinguish genuine from pseudo or distorted contests. The mere presence of contestation is not sufficient for this task because it is possible to have contests over the meaning of liberal democracy that do not proceed democratically. A more positive criterion is needed for making this distinction.

The nature of such a criterion becomes obvious once we recognize that the assumptions made by Gallie and others about essential contests are *counterfactual*. As we have just seen, the motivation for participating in an essential contest consists of the expectation that only the force of a better argument carries weight. Otherwise, there is little or no inducement to enter into the discussion, since any "understanding" that is reached will be inauthentic. It will have been achieved by force, and not by persuasion. Essential contests are, therefore, oriented toward the possibility of reaching an unforced agreement.

To be sure, this possibility is seldom if ever realized during the course of actual contestation. Nevertheless, it provides the underlying rationale for all essential contests, the existence of which depends on the participants' belief that an unforced agreement is within their reach. According to Habermas, this counterfactual assumption, upon which "unavoidable fiction rests the humanity of intercourse among men who are still men," anticipates an ideal speech situation in which only the force of the better argument reigns (McCarthy 1973, 140).

Hence, the genuineness of a dispute is a necessary condition for progressive development to occur. It ought to serve as the standard for discriminating between genuine and pseudo contests. Unless disputes are true disputes, in which only the force of argument reigns, the life of exemplary achievements cannot be prolonged or emulated.

VI

ANY ASSESSMENT of the authenticity of democratic discourse must assume an ethical vantage point from which judgments about exemplary achievements may be made. I shall now describe an ideal of democratic discourse in which power plays no role. Only rational persuasion determines the outcome of such a discourse. To the extent that particular discourses on democracy are themselves democratically organized, they will anticipate this ideal state of affairs in which reason rather than power carries the day. By implication, when a historical sequence of discourses shows evidence of becoming more democratically organized, that sequence may be called progressive. When it does not it may be called degenerative.

Thus, progress consists of movement away from discourses organized by power, and toward those organized by reason, i.e. by what Habermas (1979a) terms the "forceless force of the better argument."

This formal conception of democratic discourse is not arbitrary. It is derived from a priori conditions for communication and is therefore grounded in a communicative ethics that is in some sense objective, without being ahistorical (Apel 1980; Habermas 1979a). Thus, the notion of an ideal discourse is partially constitutive of all communication, and particularly democratic communication, which cannot be reduced to "communiqués" (Freire 1970). Ideal discourse is not something that exists apart from reality, but is instead present in reality as the anticipation of successful communication. Consequently, it is not a transhistorical ideal against which the progress of history might be measured. It is an immanent ideal by which the practices it informs may be evaluated and criticized.

Ideal speech situations are characterized by a mutual orientation toward reaching an understanding on the part of participants who enjoy equal standing in the discussion, and who have equal chances for selecting and employing various arguments on their own behalf (McCarthy 1973). These formal conditions of discourse are connected with the conditions for an ideal form of life in which coercion is absent, and all communication is governed by a communicative ethics oriented toward the force of the better argument.

Obviously, this form of life and the speech situations sustained by it are ideal, and even utopian (in the sense of "nowhere" achieved). Nevertheless, it is the *anticipation* of this ideal in every speech act situation that motivates participants to engage in discussions in order to resolve their differences.

The effective presence of this ideal speech situation in ordinary discourse is most evident when breakdowns in communication occur. For it is then, when understanding cannot be taken for granted, that efforts to reach an understanding or accommodation take place. These efforts toward reaching

an understanding ultimately presume an ideal speech situation in which agreement is reestablished only by the force of
a better argument.

Habermas' claim in this regard is based on a theory of universal pragmatics, or communicative competence, which involves the

> systematic investigation of *general structures* which appear
> in *every possible* speech situation, which are *themselves*
> *produced through* the performance of specific types of *lin-*
> *guistic expression*, and which serve to situate pragmatically
> the expressions generated by the linguistically competent
> speaker. (McCarthy 1973, 136–137)

Or, in simpler language, this universal pragmatics concerns
the conditions under which successful communications of any
sort are produced.

According to Habermas (1979a) all human communications—or speech acts, if you prefer—are oriented toward the
achievement of understanding.[5] Their success as communications depends on achieving the desired understanding
among the desired group of people. This in turn depends in
the first place on the mutual comprehensibility of utterances.
Unintelligible utterances cannot, by definition, achieve mutual understanding. Thus, a general condition of understanding is that utterances be intelligible, a need that is typically
fulfilled during a speech act as speakers attempt to clarify
their utterances by making them (more) comprehensible.

However, the success of an utterance also depends on how
well situated it is vis-à-vis external reality (the world of perceived and potentially manipulable objects), normative reality
(the realm of socially recognized expectations, values, rules,
and so on), and inner reality (the arena of actor's intentions).[6]
That is, pragmatically well-situated utterances are those that

[5] For Habermas, successful communication is the paradigm for all human
action. Various kinds of action may therefore be understood as derivative
forms of communication (Habermas 1979a, 40, 209).

[6] Cf. Held (1980).

involve *true* propositions about the world, *sincerely* uttered in the *appropriate* context.[7]

Normally, these considerations seldom surface, as it is usually assumed that utterances are true, sincere, and appropriate (as well as intelligible). These assumptions form a background consensus that informs social interactions and renders them more or less unproblematic. When this consensus breaks down, or when it can no longer be taken for granted, social interactions become problematic. In order to restore their smooth functioning, actors must identify which of the assumptions has apparently been violated, and they must work toward reaching a new understanding by showing that the assumption in question has not, in fact, been violated, or that its violation can be rectified.

If the source of the disturbance lies in the unintelligibility of a communication, this may involve little more than efforts to clarify the utterances in question. And if it lies in the insincerity of certain speakers, that will be revealed as the communicative action unfolds, and "what they do" contradicts "what they say."

If, on the other hand, the disturbance concerns utterances whose truth or appropriateness is called into question, then understanding can only be reestablished through discourse, i.e. a situation in which the constraints of action are removed, and the discursive validation of "truth" or "appropriateness" takes place.

When the truth of a speaker's utterance is in question, the discourse is said to be theoretical. Speakers have an implied responsibility to show their statements are true by providing an explanation as to why they are true. Their utterances must, in theoretical discourse, be supported by an explication in which, say, the causes of a particular event are described,

[7] This is true of all speech acts; hence the universality of this pragmatics. Speech acts are also institutionally situated, and their success will depend on institutional rules of production, as well as pragmatic considerations.

the general law that links cause and event is stated, and the theory from which that law derives is invoked.

Speakers are also obliged to provide a similar account of the correctness or appropriateness of their utterances when that is questioned. This is done in practical discourse, wherein speakers must justify the appropriateness of utterances by referring to the grounds for their claims, which in turn may be related to more general moral principles, and ultimately to a conception of the good or just life.

In either of these discourses, the validity of an utterance may be immediately redeemed by reference to an underlying consensus on what is "true" or "right". However, if no such consensus exists, the truth or rightness of a particular utterance must be established by recourse to the force of the better argument. This progression to ever more fundamental levels of argumentation must be freely permitted if the ensuing resolution or understanding is to be justifiably termed genuine or rational. And once this resolution is achieved, the possibility of normal interactions is restored, and action proceeds apace.

Thus, speech itself, insofar as it is oriented toward understanding, anticipates an ideal speech situation in which only the force of the better argument carries weight. Ideal speech is prefigured in all speech, for it represents the minimal set of conditions that are ultimately required for successful communication to occur.

VII

THE CONCEPT of an ideal speech situation may be used to distinguish between genuine contests over the meaning of liberal democracy and those that only appear to be genuine, when in fact they are systematically distorted. Such distorted situations represent pathological variants of undistorted communication, i.e. ideal speech, and they may be identified with reference to an ideal speech situation.

However, this does not mean that we simply compare ideal to real discourse and measure the extent of distortion.

Rather, it requires that we reconstruct a historical discourse in order to arrive at some understanding of how that particular discourse *would* have proceeded in the absence of systematic distortions. The orienting question in this reconstructive effort is this:

> How would the members of a social system, at a given stage in the development of productive forces, have collectively and bindingly interpreted their needs (and which norms would they have accepted as justified) if they could and would have decided on organization of social intercourse through discursive will-formation, with adequate knowledge of the limiting conditions and functional imperatives of their society? (Habermas 1975, 113)

Thus, the notion of ideal speech cannot be applied in unmediated form. It must first be translated into concrete form, i.e. a form within history. Once this counterfactual situation has been created, it is then compared with the actual discourse as it took place. To the extent that the actual discourse diverges from the reconstructed discourse, systematic distortions are presumed to be operating. Thus, ideal speech does not serve as a positive construction of some utopian conception of democracy, but as the regulative principle by which counterfactual discourses may be developed and tested against concrete discourses.

To dismiss the concept of ideal speech as unrealistic or wildly utopian is therefore to mistake Habermas's project altogether. He is not offering ideal speech situations as blueprints for the Good Society. Instead, he is trying to establish a principle for assessing the legitimacy of the outcome of disputes between competing conceptions of the good society (White 1980). The whole point of Habermas's theory is to deny the possibility of a general theory of emancipation and to insist on the historicity of organizational and strategic considerations on emancipation (Schroyer 1973).

J. Donald Moon (1980) rightly notes that ideal speech situations may not produce a consensus at all, insofar as participants in such a discussion may not be able to develop arguments that persuade other participants of the superiority of certain forms of social organization over others. For this he faults Habermas, claiming that the indeterminacy of discourse under ideal conditions can be eliminated only if participants share common interests, by which he apparently takes Habermas to mean substantive interests. Moon finds this to be an objectionable way of breaking the "deadlock of democracy," since it seems to deny the plurality of interests that exist in human societies.

This objection misses its mark, however, because ideal speech is *always* a counterfactual situation. It is not something that can ever be realized, nor is it even something toward which we strive, at least not in the same way that other, substantive utopian notions dictate we do or ought to do. Rather, ideal speech is something that is implicit in the act of speech itself, and so it permits us to ask if an existing consensus on social organization is genuine, i.e. uncoerced. It allows us to evaluate the democratic claims of existing forms of social organization that do produce consensual outcomes, or at least outcomes that appear (or are claimed) to be consensual. The real danger, then, is not that ideal speech may lead to a deadlock of democracy, but that without a notion like ideal speech we will not be able to distinguish a genuine from a false consensus.

Ideal speech is especially useful for criticizing the democratic claims of pluralist societies, which Moon ultimately takes as models for democracy. Indeed, Habermas has tried to show how liberal democracies have made criticism—and legitimation—impossible by equating apparent consensus with real consensus. They do so by associating democratic decision-making with particular forms of organization that are presumed to be "essentially democratic."

The best example of this is the liberal notion of the social contract, which Rousseau identified as the source of political legitimacy. At the same time, Rousseau confused this principle for evaluating the legitimacy of political institutions with the form those institutions ought to assume. The same is true of contemporary democratic theorists who identify democracy exclusively with certain institutions, be those competitive elections or schemes for workplace democracy (Habermas 1979a).

The seriousness of this error lies in the fact that concrete institutions are likely to incorporate systematic distortions of communication, insofar as they exist in societies that are not free from domination. When democracy is identified with particular organizational forms, any chance of criticizing those forms and the distortions they embody is eliminated. Legitimacy becomes an accomplished fact.

In the case of the social contract, the liberal anticipation of consensual decision-making is rendered uncritical by the identification of consensus with the outcomes of particular decision-making procedures. Because these procedures are believed to be essentially democratic, they are presumed to produce essentially democratic results. The legitimacy of this conclusion depends, however, on the prior acceptance of certain procedures as democratic, which the social contract theorists establish by *definition*, rather than demonstration. In presenting social-contract democracy as self-justifying, they systematically distort the course of argumentation by protecting the original premise, which concerns the democratic quality of certain institutions and procedures, from critical scrutiny.

This has significant political import. Habermas (1979a) argues that this refusal to examine the basic premise of the argument in favor of social-contract democracy conceals the patterns of domination implicit in the procedures represented in the social contract. In particular, it conceals the existence of a class structure that is founded on power rather than reason. The de facto consensus on organization that appears to underlie liberal democratic conceptions of democracy is, therefore, only de facto, and not genuine. It is a consensus shaped by power and not rational discourse.

By insisting on the difference between the organization of

democracy and its legitimating ground, ideal speech refuses to incorporate unacknowledged relations of power into the ideal of democracy. It does not prejudice the case by favoring certain organizational forms over others, but remains critical, although it is tempered by the particularities of a given historical situation. What is democratic in a given situation must itself be decided "democratically"—that is the only proviso.

VIII

FOR HABERMAS the critique of systematically distorted communication begins with the presumption that all historical discourses on politics are necessarily distorted by virtue of their being embedded in a social context of domination. In particular, general interests tend to be suppressed in favor of the narrow, special interests of ruling elites, who may of course present the satisfaction of their interests as necessary for the satisfaction of societal needs.[8] This situation may be identified, and of course criticized, by reconstructing a historical discourse as it would have proceeded in the absence of distortions.

This reconstruction involves an *empirical* assumption to the effect that the constellation of interests involved in a suspected instance of distorted communication coincides sufficiently with the set of interests that would have to find expression in a situation free of distortion. Furthermore, it requires the *methodological* assumption that it is meaningful and possible to reconstruct "the hidden interest positions of involved individuals or groups by counterfactually imagining

---

[8] Cf. the various "trickle down" theories that have been advocated in recent years. Such theories present the satisfaction of business entrepreneurs as requiring special attention, so that the expected benefits of entrepreneurial activity might then trickle down to those who ride the coattails of business leaders.

As Przeworski (1980) notes, the logic of this argument *is* inescapable, but only insofar as the status quo is taken for granted: in a capitalist economy, the needs of business really must be satisfied before "prosperity" will be shared by other members of society. However, this presumes the desirability of capitalist relations, and that is the sense in which distortions take place.

the limit case of a conflict between the involved parties in which they would be forced to consciously perceive their interests and strategically assert them" (Habermas 1975, 114).

In other words, we must begin with existing conflicts, ascribe interests to the participants in them, and then imagine the limit case of conflicting interests. To the extent that this limit case of conflicting interests fails to find expression in actual discourses, interests are being suppressed and distortions are obviously at work.

The logic behind these assumptions is far from being clear. Habermas (Thompson and Held 1982, 256) concedes that the research program implied by his theory is still in its infancy. Hence, we must look elsewhere for concrete models of undistorted communication. I suggest that situations involving essentially contested concepts may provide such models. The discursive nature of these contests is, as we have seen, quite similar to the essentials of Habermas's notion of ideal speech. They may therefore prove quite useful in analyzing certain instances of systematically distorted communication.

As an illustration of this strategy, consider the case of liberal democracy. This concept is obviously relevant to the legitimation process. During the past two hundred years it has become one of the most important standards by which political power and influence are legitimated and criticized. If we assume that distortions are most likely to occur in language regions that impinge on the progress by which structures of domination are legitimated, then democracy and its rhetoric are prime candidates for the infiltration of systematic distortions.

However, these distortions are subject to periodic breakdown, as old structures of domination and their associated distortions are challenged and eventually replaced by new ones. Such breakdowns involve essential contests over the meaning of democracy and its application to existing political and economic institutions. They may therefore accompany the legitimation crises that attend fundamental social change.

Since essential contests over the meaning of democracy occur at times when old distortions are decaying, but when new distortions have not yet taken root, I would argue that they constitute examples of *relatively* undistorted communication. They are not completely free of distortion, because they very seldom involve contestants of equal strength and influence. And they tend to reflect the contest between ruling elites, rather than broader contests involving all interests in society. Consequently, elements of power and influence inevitably come into play. Nevertheless, these intrusions are likely to be far less systematic during periods of transition from one structure of domination to another.

On the other hand, the unequal nature of essential contests over the proper use of democracy ensures their eventual resolution. The contest will therefore be periodic rather than continuous. Hence, the semantic history of democracy will not consist of one long contest between rival conceptions of democracy. Instead it will consist of a series of contests separated by relatively long periods of quiescence during which particular conceptions of democracy enjoy hegemonic influence. By reconstructing that history, we may be able to trace the ebb and flow of systematic distortions in language regions relevant to legitimation. We may even be able to determine if the distortions are becoming more virulent, and longer-lived. This, of course, would shed considerable light on whether or not the liberal democratic ideal in America is likely to remain viable now and in the near future.

The advantage of this kind of historical analysis is that it reveals the stark contrast between periods of contest and quiescence, thereby illustrating the power of systematic distortions to produce one-dimensional patterns of thought and action. At the same time, it illustrates the limitations of this power and reveals its vulnerabilities. Hence, it offers a potentially important contribution to a critical theory of domination, when applied to a particular historical tradition.

IX

BOTH REASON and power figure prominently in the dynamics of rhetorical change. This is especially true of discourses on democracy, which are themselves concerned with problems of social organization. They are discourses on organization, carried on within particular political communities on particular occasions, and they center on the legitimacy of existing patterns of organization vis-à-vis alternative modes of collective action. At this level, then, discourses necessarily involve questions of organization—the questions posed by communities themselves as they struggle to organize themselves along democratic lines.

It is here that the role of reasoned argumentation is especially likely to be visible. Yet, this should not lead us to overlook the role of power in shaping these discourses on social organization. The organization or structure of a discourse delimits what can be said, about what, and by whom in that discourse. This "mobilization of bias" rules certain questions of organization out of order, so to speak, thereby restricting the range of criticism that may be intelligibly and legitimately leveled at existing political institutions.

It should be noted that my concern here is not with discursive constraints per se. All discourse is constrained by rules that make meaningful communication possible. However, not all such constraints are subject to the scrutiny of participants in a discourse, and when these constraints skew the outcome of a discussion in favor of some interests and against others, it is reasonable to suspect that they are supported by power, rather than reason.[9] It is, after all, unreasonable to expect that people would engage in rhetorical exchanges if they knew their case was lost from the start. Other courses of action, e.g. violence or withdrawal, would seem more appropriate in such situations.

Hence, as historical observers with an interest in assessing the progress of liberal democracy, we must determine where the restrictions on discourse lie, whence they arise, and ultimately, whether they have become more or less relaxed

[9] The distortion of discourse by power is also what makes that discourse ideological. It is not the content of a discourse, but its organization, that is ideological.

during the course of our history. This last consideration is fundamental to any judgment on the progress of democracy. Since we cannot make such judgments on the basis of the content of any discourse without becoming objectivistic, we must concentrate instead on the discursive conditions under which proposals for democratic reorganization have been advanced. In other words, we must ask ourselves if discourses on democracy have themselves become more democratically organized, so that in some sense progress in history might be discerned. We must situate individual discourses on democracy, including our own, on the horizon of our history so as to chart their progress.

To raise the issue of progress in this connection need not imply a return to progressive historiography, for the notion of progress involved here is very different. It involves shifting our attention away from considerations about progress *toward* some universal conception of democracy, in order to focus on progress *away* form some less-than-ideal state of affairs. The less-than-ideal state of affairs is, of course, any systematically distorted discourse on democracy. To the extent that the power of organization determines the outcome of reasoned discourses on democracy, that outcome cannot be considered fully democratic, whatever its substance. To the extent that the role of power in discourses on democracy has declined in our history, then we may say that progress is discernible.

Progress, then, depends on replacing undemocratic rules of discourse with more democratic ones. It involves the recognition of the power of rules in discourse, and their role in regulating what can and cannot be said. The possible distortion of discourse by undemocratic rules must therefore become a subject of discourse itself in order for progress to be made. Discourse on democracy must proceed reflectively in order to advance democratically.

Thus, essential contests appear to be significant moments in the life of a rhetorical tradition like that of liberal democracy. When the organization of contests over the meaning of democracy itself becomes a matter of discursive investigation, discourse becomes reflective. Participants then consider not only what democracy means, but the manner in which collective judgments about the comparative merits of various interpretations of democracy are or might be made. Such contests are about the relative roles of power and reason in political argumentation and involve questions of progress and its conditions.

I would like to designate these contests as involving "problem-shifts," wherein *modes* of collective problem-solving, and not just individual solutions, are at issue. That is, they involve considerations of the rhetorical practices that govern contests over the partisan interpretation of democracy, and the relationship between those practices and liberal democratic progress. When discourse on democracy becomes reflective, I want to say that a rhetorical problem-shift has occurred and that this shift may be characterized as progressive or degenerative.

My purpose in calling this sort of development a problem-shift is to emphasize some of the logical similarities between assessments of scientific progress and rhetorical improvements. Recently, Laudan (1977) has argued that *scientific* research traditions can be evaluated as either progressive or degenerative on the basis of their actual or potential capacity for solving outstanding puzzles or problems. Those traditions that are better "problem-solvers" are progressive, at least insofar as the solutions they promise or provide do not contradict or compromise the underlying assumptions and methodological prescriptions that inform them, and indeed constitute their identity *as* a distinction research tradition.

By analogy, we might argue that the progress or degeneration of *rhetorical* traditions depends on the success with which the argumentative practices they embody prove able to solve the political problems that attend rhetorical conflict, especially those having to do with tolerance and the necessity of choosing among different interpretations. That is, a rhetorical tradition like liberal democracy "gets better" to the extent that successive generations are able to improve its practices, without perhaps ever perfecting them. To improve liberal democracy in this context means to solve, at least provisionally, problems that arise out of disputes over collective organization. It is to decide how to decide what liberal democracy means in a particular context, and what political institutions and practices attend that meaning.

Not just any solution will qualify as a progressive one. In the case of scientific research programs or traditions, neither *ad hoc* solutions nor those that violate the "negative heuristic" of the tradition in question count as progressive solutions. Rather, they represent degenerate moments in the life of a particular line of inquiry, insofar as they involve merely terminological adjustments on the one hand, and an outright repudiation of key tenets of a program or tradition on the other.

By implication, progressive problem-shifts in the rhetorical tradition of liberal democracy must be distinguished from "solutions" that usher in degeneration and decay. In particular the resolution of historically situated essential contests over the meaning and practice of liberal democracy may not contradict the hard-core assumptions of liberal democracy without causing a degenerate problem-shift, at least for the *liberal* democratic tradition. Specifically, this means that a necessary, though perhaps not sufficient, condition for rhetorical progress to occur is that the provisional resolution or closure of essential contests must conform to the basic principles of argumentation that inform the rhetoric of liberal democracy.

The chief rhetorical principle of liberal democracy is of course the commitment to consensual decision-making. Popular consent and sovereignty are indissolubly linked in the pantheon of liberal democratic ideas, and the most cherished liberal democratic institutions, e.g. representative legislatures, are valued because they are said to embody these ideals. Hence, the notion that collective decisions must be based on the consent of the governed lies at the center of the hard-core or negative heuristic of liberal democracy.

Consequently, the *progressive* resolution of essential contests over liberal democracy requires that the collective answer of a given generation to the question "what does liberal democracy mean for us?" must itself *be* the result of consensual decision-making. The possibility of rational discourse depends on this proviso, because it is this openness that motivates contestants to participate in political debate. What is democratic must be decided democratically, if the progressive development of the liberal democratic tradition via contestation is to occur. Similarly, when the outcome of essential contests is not decided democratically, i.e. in accordance with the basic commitment to consensual decision-making, then a degenerate problem-shift in the rhetorical tradition of liberal democracy takes place.

X

AN ESSENTIALLY contested argument or rhetorical tradition will develop in a *progressive* manner to the extent that its particular moments, or disputes, evidence successively weaker forms of systematic distortion. That is, it will be progressive to the extent that the force of the better argument *alone* determines the outcome of particular disputes. Where power rather than persuasion distorts the argument by dictating its outcome, that argument is degenerative.

This means that if we should discover that our own discourses on democracy are more severely constrained than past discourses, we must concede the possibility that we are in danger of forgetting how to govern ourselves democratically. For it is not just in what we now say about democracy, but also in how—and even whether—we say it, that the future of democracy lies. Insofar as open discourses are vital stimuli for a vivid democratic imagination, they keep alive democratic possibilities. Should our discourses, and hence our imaginations, become impoverished, so too do democratic vistas as they recede beyond our ability to recall them.

I am afraid that something like this has already begun to occur in the United States. As the following chapters will show, our ideas about democracy have come to be identified with a particular kind of discourse on democracy, one that unfortunately reserves a disproportionate role for power vis-à-vis reason in deliberations on collective action. The role of power is not immediately apparent, however, because it forms part of the invisible structure of discourse itself and does not show itself in more obvious proposals for collective action on behalf of certain identifiably partisan interests. At the same time, the one-dimensionality (Marcuse 1964) of our democratic imagination, which equates this discourse with democracy, prevents our seeing and criticizing this tendency.

The story that follows is not therefore an altogether happy one. It is a story about the decline of democratic possibilities in the United States. Nevertheless, the end of the story is not yet written, for in the course of telling what has so far transpired we may yet rediscover that which is in danger of becoming irretrievably lost. If so, anamnesis may overcome amnesia. That at least is my hope, and my reason for telling the story in the way I do.

CHAPTER TWO

Republican Rhetoric
in the Founding Period

I

IN THIS CHAPTER I examine the influence of republican ideology on the politics and rhetoric of the Founding period. It is my contention that republicanism provided an ideological framework common to nearly all of the various factions of this period, and that the successive clashes between these factions occurred within the context of a shared commitment to republican principles. Initially, this consensus was founded on a traditional interpretation of republicanism, which held that a virtuous citizenry was necessary to republican survival. However, the difficulty, if not impossibility, of sustaining virtue in an extended republic gave rise to an alternative interpretation of republicanism that attempted to remedy this defect by institutional means. The last fifteen years of eighteenth-century American politics may be seen as an internecine struggle between this new republicanism, espoused by the Federalists, and the older, more traditional republicanism, to which the Antifederalists, Democratic-Republican Societies, and Jeffersonian Republicans were successive heirs. Most of this chapter will be devoted to a reconstruction of this contest between divergent interpretations of republicanism, a contest that is recorded in the extraordinarily rich rhetorical exchanges of this period.

Before turning to this task, however, I shall contrast my interpretation with others that have been suggested. In the first place, my account should be distinguished from those interpretations that assert the nonideological and pragmatic nature of political conflict during this period. Roche (1961), for example, describes the Founding Fathers as consummate politicians who, inspired by their practical experiences rather than their philosophical inclinations, managed to hammer out a pragmatic compromise on the proper structure and functions of the new government. It is evident that such explanations presume the existence of an ideological consensus within which a practical politics might operate, and to that extent they resemble my proposed interpretation. However, they deny the existence of significant ideological conflict *within* that consensus. In what follows I will show that such conflict did in fact occur during the Founding period, and that it quite properly may be considered ideological, even though it was situated within an overarching universe of republican discourse.

I should add that my interpretation is incompatible with those studies that characterize this period in terms of some titanic struggle between the forces of democracy and aristocracy (landed or otherwise). I include in this group those studies, e.g. Parrington (1954a), that see this struggle as a clash between philosophical traditions, as well as those, e.g. Beard (1965), that see it as a struggle between economic classes.[1] Nor do I find useful any distinction between those, e.g. Brown (1968), who believe that democracy triumphed, and

[1] I leave aside here the question of the relative importance of ideology and material interests in determining the politics of this period. As I noted in the Prologue, this way of posing the question neglects the constitutive nature of ideology, which acts as the medium in which men and women become conscious of their interests. Interests and ideologies are therefore conceptually related, not casually connected.

More recent "economic interpretations," e.g. those advanced in the essays collected by Young (1976), display a greater sensitivity to this connection between ideology and interests, but they still do not sufficiently appreciate the wisdom of Marx's contention that it is in ideological forms that men become conscious of the conflict between class interests and "fight it out" (Marx and Engels 1968, 183). They too easily associate particular ideologies with particular classes, without discussing values held in common. Geertz (1964) resists this reduction of ideologies to "masks and weapons" and emphasizes the collective dimension of disputes that occur within a mass belief system.

those who assert that it either lost to or was subverted by aristocracy. These explanations are certainly not congruent with the self-understandings of the men involved, who vigorously opposed their opponents' attempts to describe their actions and philosophies in these terms. They become plausible only via the imputation of democratic or antidemocratic motives to actors on the basis of twentieth-century conceptions of their actions.[2] In fact, this imputation of motives is quite plainly anachronistic, as neither "democracy" nor "aristocracy" enjoyed widespread popularity during this period of American history. Both were terms of derogation and were used to defame opponents rather than support a philosophical position that was identifiably "democratic" or "aristocratic."

It is therefore inconceivable that a struggle between them could dominate the politics of a nation for over a decade and a half, precisely because the *ideal* of democracy possessed little normative force during this period. While it is true that the idea of democracy was well known to colonists at a very early date, and that certain practices that have since come to be associated with democracy did exist during this period, there were very few men willing to call themselves "democrats." Most preferred to call themselves "republicans," or perhaps "democratic-republicans," thereby denoting which brand of republicanism was being articulated.

The reason for this was, quite simply, that "democracy" and "democrat" were generally used and understood by eighteenth-century Americans as terms of political derogation (Palmer 1934; Shoemaker 1966). Democracy referred to a specific order or class of society, the commons, and to the form of government in which the commons exercised an inordinate (or even absolute) preponderance of power over the aristocratic and royal orders of society. It was a form of class rule in which the interests of the many prevailed over the interests of the few. It was also a form of government in which

[2] Even Sheldon Wolin (1981a) succumbs to this temptation in his discussion of "the people's two bodies."

the interests of the many prevailed over the general interests of all, for the interests of the many were no less particular than the interests of the few, since the many were all members of the same order of society.

Thus, democracy violated the principle of mixed government, which was thought to be the bulwark of individual liberty. A smoothly functioning democracy, in which the commons' interest supplanted the common interest, was to be avoided, just as absolute forms of monarchical or aristocratic rule were to be avoided.

A badly functioning democracy, or ochlocracy, was to be feared even more than a smoothly functioning one.[3] As Madison put it in *Federalist 10*, "Democracies have ever been spectacles of turbulence and contention; have ever been found incompatible with personal security or the rights of property; and have in general been as short in their lives as they have been violent in their deaths." Only "theoretic politicians" who failed to understand that democracy was particularly susceptible to the mischief of faction recommended its adoption (Rossiter 1961, 181).

This understanding of democracy was still quite prevalent during the Founding period, although the Democratic-Republican Societies and the Jeffersonian Republicans did suc-

---

[3] Ochlocracy = *ochlos* (mob) + *kratia* (rule), or "mob rule." Barker (1975, lxv–lxvi) reports that *demos* was originally used to refer to countryside dwellers, the people of *agros*, as distinct from city dwellers, the people of *asty*. With the reforms of Cleisthenes (c. 509 B.C.), which involved the reorganization of the Athenian community into a new system of tribes based on the *demes* of the countryside, *demos* came to embrace the people of *asty* as well as the people of *agros*.

Ochlos, on the other hand, was used to refer to crowds in the market place, or to the mob of oarsman in Athenium triremes. Hence, it carried commercial and occupational connotations, rather than residential ones, as did *demos*. This is important insofar as commerce and occupation fall into the realm of economics, not politics. Ochlocracy, then, represents the invasion of public affairs by private interests, and therefore the corruption of politics. The same corruption of virtue by commerce is the principal theme of republican discourse in the Founding period, as will become evident.

ceed in neutralizing some of the more odious connotations of the term. Nevertheless, democracy did not assume a place of preeminence among American political ideals until well into the nineteenth century, as the following chapter will show. Consequently, the Founding period cannot be characterized appropriately as a struggle between democratic and antidemocratic forces. Instead it must be seen as a struggle among republicans for custody of the republican ideal, a struggle that remained within the universe of republican discourse even as it expanded its limits.

II

HAVING REJECTED both nonideological and counter-ideological explanations, let me proceed to defend my claim that the Founding period is best understood as a contest between a traditional republicanism and its revisionist offspring.

There has been a growing appreciation, among historians at least, of the importance of republicanism in the political culture of late eighteenth-century America (Shalhope 1972). The initial impetus for this realization was provided by Caroline Robbins's work (1947; 1968) on the influence of English libertarian thought in America. It gained momentum with the analyses of Kenyon (1955) and Adair (1957), which suggested the existence of an ideological framework common to Federalists and Antifederalists alike. Richard Buel (1964) combined these insights and suggested that this common framework had its roots in the seventeenth-century dissenting tradition in England. This suggestion was extensively developed by Bailyn (1967), who showed how this dissenting tradition made its way to America and was subsequently transformed in light of American experiences with self-government.

This line of historiography emphasizes the disproportionate influence of English libertarian thought on the political culture of pre-Revolutionary America.[4] However, this influence

---

[4] This interpretation has been challenged recently on two fronts. Wills (1979; 1981) claims that the primary influence was Scottish, while others, e.g. Lutz (1980), argue that the roots of American constitutionalism are indigenous, stemming from covenant theology.

does not appear to have crystallized into a self-consciously republican philosophy until about 1776. Kenyon notes that

> before 1776, the prevailing opinion in America had been that the ends of government—liberty, justice, happiness, and the public good—could be secured within the framework of monarchy. . . . After 1776 [the colonists] tended to associate all the characteristics of good government with republicanism, and with republicanism only. (1962, 166)

And Jefferson himself observed that Americans "seem to have deposited the monarchical and taken up the republican government with as much ease as would have attended their throwing off an old and putting on a new suit of clothes" (Wood 1972, 92).

The rhetoric of the Revolutionary years is replete with evidence of this republican ascendancy. Prior to 1776, "republic," "republicanism," and "republican" were most often used as defamatory clichés to stigmatize critics of the existing order (Adams 1970). These terms conjured up the horrors of the Commonwealth period and indicated a willingness to subvert the balance of the English constitutional order. But this began to change with the publication of Paine's scorching critique of that constitution, which he alleged to be an amalgam of monarchical and aristocratic tyrannies. "Republicanism" began to acquire respectability as it came to symbolize the justness of the colonists' cause against this corrupt rule. In the space of a very short time, it became the rallying cry for independence from the corrupting influence of English politics on American politics and society.[5]

---

[5] The crystallization of political discourse around republican themes was hastened by widespread opposition to the Crown, rather than a positive consensus on the meaning of republicanism. Recent investigations have shown that several different strains of republican thought coexisted during this period, some of which enjoyed a local or regional hegemony, while others were peculiar to certain socioeconomic groups. Nevertheless, republicanism offered a universe of discourse in which particular interpretations of the meaning of republicanism might be tested and amended.

Shalhope (1982) provides an excellent summary and analysis of the burgeoning literature on varieties of republicanism, which is too broad to cite

In this context, the term "republic" came to refer to the characteristic aim or purpose of government, rather than to a specific form of government. Republican government was distinguished by its pursuit of the general welfare, as Paine noted: "The word *republic* means the *public good*, or the good of the whole, in contradistinction to the despotic form, which makes the good of the sovereign, or of one man, the only object of government" (Wood 1972, 55–56). Indeed, the etymological roots of "republic" imply this: republic is from the Latin *res publica*, meaning "of the public," or more gracefully, the commonweal, whence commonwealth.

Given this characterization of the aim of republican government, the colonists refused to identify republicanism with specific institutions or types of regime.[6] The only qualification on what was to count as a "republican" regime was that it must rest upon a balance of social interests or orders, i.e. a balance between royal, noble, and popular interests. The notion of "mixed government," which identified this balance with the commonwealth was, of course, the specific contribution of Roman historians, e.g. Cicero and Tacitus, and the Greek Polybius, all of whom figured prominently in the thought of the Founders (Colborne 1965).

In England this balance was secured in a regime that mixed kings, lords, and commons in a constitutional monarchy.[7] It

---

here. The essays in Young (1976), and the works of Nash (1979), McCoy (1980), and Isaac (1976) deserve special mention, however, for their careful analyses of the *dynamic* qualities of republican thought, which they trace to the conflict between divergent interpretations of the meaning of republicanism.

[6] Indeed, John Adams could claim with some justification that "technically, or scientifically, if you will, there are monarchical, aristocratical and democratical republics," each capable of realizing republican principles (Bailyn 1967, 283). Given the colonists' experience with self-rule, and the absence of royal and aristocratic orders in America, the new republic was destined to be "democratical," i.e. wholly popular. It was nevertheless considered a republic, and not a democracy.

[7] This balance of orders was only imperfectly reflected in a functional separation of powers. The conflation of balanced *interests* and checked *powers*

was the perception, by the colonists and their "Country" tutors in England, that this balance had been upset by the usurpations of the Crown. The consequent corruption of English politics referred, therefore, to a corruption in the body politic, and not to the vices of private individuals (Shumer 1979). It pointed to an imbalance of interests that threatened liberty and hence the commonweal.

The Country politicians and publicists from whom the colonists drew their inspiration were eighteenth-century radical writers and opposition politicians who were united in their criticism of "Court" and ministerial power in England.[8] They were, as Bailyn puts it,

> the Casandras of the age. . . . [who] refused to believe that the transfer of sovereignty from the crown to the Parliament [by the Glorious Revolution] provided a perfect guarantee that the individual would be protected from the power of the state. . . . They insisted, at a time when government was felt to be less oppressive than it had been for two hundred years, that it was necessarily—by its very nature—hostile to human liberty and happiness; that, properly, it existed only on the tolerance of the people whose needs it served; and that it could be, and reasonably should be, dismissed—overthrown—if it attempted to exceed its proper jurisdiction. (1967, 46–49)

---

has led, Wills (1981) argues, to a lack of appreciation for the significance of bicameralism in the Constitutional arrangement of powers.

[8] Kramnick (1982) has recently challenged the "republican" interpretation of the Country opposition in England, arguing that Pocock and others have underestimated the influence of Locke on Country ideologists. By highlighting the "liberal" dimension of the opposition in England, Kramnick implicitly challenges those who see the roots of American *republicanism* in the Country party.

Kramnick has little to say about the implications for American thought of his finding. Appleby (1982) does, however; she concludes that significant liberalizing influences were at work on the republican tradition in America. This is also McCoy's (1980) main point, although Appleby disagrees with his characterization of Jefferson as a classical republican struggling to sustain virtue by promoting agriculture.

The Country opposition in England saw in the Walpole administration ample evidence of nefarious government. Pocock summarized their suspicions as follows:

> But the executive possesses means of distracting Parliament from its proper function; it seduces members by the offer of places and pensions, by retaining them to follow ministers and ministers' rivals, by persuading them to support measures—standing armies, national debts, excise schemes—whereby the activities of administration grow beyond Parliament's control. These means of subversion are known collectively as corruption, and if ever Parliament or those who elect them—for corruption may occur at this point too—should be wholly corrupt, then there will be an end of independence and liberty. (1965, 565)

For this reason the American Revolution was much more than an act of rebellion against the Crown. It was a rebellion against the corruption of republican politics by the Crown, a corruption that was not confined to England but which extended to her colonies, for they were after all part of the body politic. And it was an act of restoration by which virtue, the foundation of republican politics, would once again be made possible in the cycle of "revolution."

Steeped as they were in the classical republican tradition, and reinforced by the disproportionate impact of the Country ideology of opposition, the perpetrators of the American Revolution were committed to a classical conception of citizenship. Citizenship required virtue, and virtue involved a commitment on the part of each individual to value the commonweal over his own selfish interests, and to place his specific virtues, e.g. courage, wisdom, a talent for leadership, and so on, in service to the community (Skinner 1978; Pocock 1975). Consequently, virtue provided the ultimate protection against the two most serious threats to the republic's existence, namely, invasion and faction. Against the former, virtue insured the existence of a patriotic citizenry able and ready to defend itself against acts of aggression. And against the latter, it implied a willingness to rise above the particular interests of faction in order to promote the common good. In that sense, civic virtue was synonymous with the love of liberty, for it stood ready to oppose domination by outside or inside interests.

Liberty, too, was public, not private. Liberty in republican politics did not refer to civil liberty. That was to come later, with the "liberalization" of republicanism. Instead it referred to the liberty to participate in public affairs, and especially to the common interest of all in a public sphere of participation in which there was no domination, i.e. no imbalance of interests (Shumer 1979).

Hence, the virtuous republic was one in which the specific virtues of the citizenry were organized in such a way as to protect the commonwealth.[9] In the classical tradition specific virtues were often associated with each of the classes or orders of society. These orders were expected to practice their specific virtues and defer to the virtues of other orders. This structure of deference actually *constituted* the republic, insofar as it was a surety against factionalism. The appearance of factions was, therefore, a sign that the structure of deference was corrupted.

The men of the revolutionary generation were sympathetically inclined toward this view of republican virtue, although their understanding of it had been significantly altered by their liberal and revolutionary experiences (Pocock 1975; Yarbrough 1979a). They believed that American virtue was being corrupted by its affiliation with monarchical rule in England (Bailyn 1967; Wood 1972). The act of revolution was, therefore, imbued with a special significance. It was to be the purifying action by which the corrupt influence of England was removed, moral regeneration achieved, and a virtuous republic once again made possible.

[9] Interestingly, this sense is retained in Cicero's translation of Plato's *Politeia* as *Res Publica*, since *Politeia* was an investigation into the proper arrangement of the virtues of courage, wisdom, and moderation under the more sublime virtue of justice (Bloom 1968, 440–441).

Given this understanding, it is not surprising that the apparent absence of virtue and self-restraint that seemed to plague the years immediately following the Revolutionary War caused considerable disillusionment among American republicans. The self-sacrifice and patriotism of the war years had given way to greed and profiteering, and as William Bingham said, "Private Interest seemed to predominate over every Consideration that regarded the public weal" (Wood 1972, 415–416).[10] Factional strife within the thirteen states and the impotence of the Confederal Congress caused men to fear for the health of the body politic, and to consider possible remedies for the "diseases most incident to republican government."

In searching for these remedies, however, significant ideological differences over the nature and ends of republican government began to emerge.[11] The prevailing republican consensus, based as it was on broad and moralistic sentiments, buttressed by a shared aversion to monarchical rule, began to polarize around competing interpretations of republicanism, as we shall see in the next section.

III

THE FIRST CLASH over the nature of republican government occurred during the Constitutional Convention and the period of ratification immediately thereafter. This dispute between Federalists and Antifederalists grew out of dissatisfac-

---

[10] Forrest McDonald (1958; 1965) has analyzed the process by which "selfish" regional and state parties and economic groups came to dominate the politics of the Confederation. Wood (1972) also presents a detailed description of the chaotic and disillusioning nature of this period in American politics.

[11] Shalhope (1982) and Appleby (1982) both stress the religious aspect of some republicans' thought, as distinct from purely political considerations, which I emphasize here. The convergence of "evangelical" and "secular" versions of republicanism in New England produced a potent civil millenarianism directed against the decline of deference in politics, i.e. the "corruption of virtue." It also established the foundation for an unyielding Federalism in that section of the country. Cf. Hatch (1977).

tion with the Articles of Confederation, which the Federalists alleged failed to provide the Confederal Congress with sufficient authority to pursue the common good in foreign, commercial, and economic affairs. A Constitutional Convention was convened in Philadelphia during the summer of 1787 for the "sole and express purpose of revising the Articles of Confederation" in light of these deficiencies.[12]

The "revisions" that subsequently emerged from this convention amounted to an entirely new governmental framework, a framework whose republican credentials were not obvious to all concerned. In the course of trying to justify it as republican, on the one hand, and to vilify it as antirepublican, on the other, two distinct interpretations of republicanism evolved. Both employed the traditional categories of republican thought, e.g. virtue, corruption, and the commonweal, and both claimed to represent the Revolutionary interpretation of those categories. However, they differed in their assessment of the extent of post-Revolutionary corruption, its primary causes, and the permissible range of truly republican remedies for that corruption.

The interpretation most familiar to later generations was that articulated by the Federalists. However, it is important to remember that the Federalists were espousing a "new science of politics" based on a conception of republicanism that was ostensibly more "realistic" than that of earlier republicans.[13] That is, it was the Federalists who challenged the prevailing interpretation of republicanism. This has been obscured by the fact that the Federalists were organized, at the

[12] Congressional resolution of February, 1787.

[13] Many of the Federalists, and Madison in particular, were strongly influenced by the Scottish Enlightenment and its passionate theory of human interest (Adair 1957; Wills 1979). Washington's belief that "we have, probably, had too good an opinion of human nature in forming our confederation" led the Federalists to search for a sounder, more realistic basis for political design, which they found in this theory of interest-inspired behavior (Wood 1972, 472). Hirschman (1977) provides a fascinating account of "how interests were called on to counteract the passions" in the moral sciences of the Enlightenment.

national level at least, before the Antifederalists, whose interpretation of republicanism was actually much closer to the
prevailing wisdom. No doubt the victory of the Federalists
also contributed to this state of affairs; history is after all written primarily by and about winners.

Be that as it may, the emergence of the Antifederalists in
response to the Federalist challenge represents an attempt to
articulate a republican tradition that had gone largely unquestioned. Consequently, I shall begin with the Antifederalist presentation of the prevailing wisdom, and then proceed
with the Federalist challenge to it. This will highlight the
Antifederalists role in the founding of the Constitution, for
which they deserve to be counted among the Founding Fathers, inasmuch as the new nation was "founded" in discourse
between them and the Federalists (Storing 1981).

The interpretation of republicanism to which the Antifederalists gave expression was grounded in the notion that republican government over an extensive territory was impossible. Following Montesquieu, proponents of this tradition,
e.g. Agrippa, held that "no extensive empire can be governed
upon republican principles, and that such a government will
degenerate to a despotism, unless it be made up of a confederacy of smaller states, each having the full powers of internal
regulation" (Kenyon 1966, 132–133). This conclusion was
based on the assumption that a republic must be composed
of a population that is reasonably homogeneous in its customs
and concerns in order for a unitary public good to exist.[14]
Large territories, insofar as they encompassed a greater variety of interests and concerns, were far more likely to suc-
cumb to faction, in which the collective welfare would be

[14] Farry (1984) shows how this concern over the social diversity of an extended republic informs the Antifederalists' demand for a bill of rights to
protect them from an overly energetic government. At the same time, the
existence of social diversity also explains some of the differences among the
Antifederalists themselves over the need for—and contents of—a bill of
rights.

sacrificed in the clash of what Cato called "interests opposite and dissimilar in nature" (Wood 1972, 500).

As evidence for the proposition that republican virtue was possible only in republics of small territorial extent, the Antifederalists cited numerous examples of successful and long-lived small republics, and of course the ill-fated Roman attempt to establish a republican *empire*. Hence, Agrippa was convinced that the "idea of an uncompounded republick, on an average one thousand miles in length, and eight hundred in breadth, and containing six millions of white inhabitants all reduced to the same standards of morals, of habits, and of laws, is in itself an absurdity, and contrary to the whole experience of mankind" (Kenyon 1966, 134).

The Federalists were well aware of the strength of this popular belief. For that reason, both Hamilton and Madison felt compelled to address the problem of the "extended republic" in the *Federalist Papers*. Hamilton's argument in *Federalist* 9 defended the proposed Constitution as one for a confederal republic, which Montesquieu had explicitly recognized as a solution to the problem of extended territory. And he neatly turned the Antifederalist argument back upon its proponents by noting that it logically implied the dismemberment of those states already sufficiently large as to include a diversity of interests. This was, of course, politically unacceptable to the Antifederalists and the constituency to which they tried to appeal with their argument. Thus, Hamilton's argument blunted the force of this objection to the proposed Constitution.

But Madison's argument was far more important, for it indicated the extent to which the Federalists were willing to deemphasize the importance of virtue as the foundation of republican politics. In *Federalist 10* Madison disputed the claim that small republics were more likely than large ones to be free from the mischief of faction. He argued that factions were "sown in the nature of man," and that small republics and democracies were particularly susceptible to oppression by a majoritarian faction. Large republics, on the other hand, offered a solution to the problem of majoritarian factions:

> Extend the sphere and you take in a greater variety of parties and interest; you make it less probable that a majority of the whole will have a common motive to invade the rights of other citizens; or if such a common motive exists, it will be more difficult for all who feel it to discover their strength and to act in unison with each other. (Rossiter 1961, 83)

From this, Madison concluded that a coalition of the majority of society in the extended republic "could seldom take place on any other principles than those of justice and the general good" (ibid., 325).[15]

This was not the only safeguard of the general good, however. An extension of the sphere of government necessarily meant that the actual governance of the republic must be left in the hands of elected representatives. But it also enhanced the likelihood that virtuous men would be selected as political leaders:

> as each representative will be chosen by a greater number of citizens in the large than the small republic, it will be more difficult for unworthy candidates to practise with success the vicious arts by which elections are too often carried; and the suffrages of the people being more free, will be more likely to center on men who possess the most attractive merit and the most diffusive and established characters. (ibid., 82–83)

The cumulative effect of representation over an extended sphere, Madison hoped, would be the refinement and en-

---

[15] Adair's (1957) essay on *Federalist 10* demonstrates that Madison borrowed this argument on the extended republic from Hume, who believed that Montesquieu's arguments were much more applicable to the founding of an extended republic than to its preservation. Madison, of course, turned this on its head and made the extended republic the bulwark of preservation for republican politics.

largement of public views as a result of "passing them through the medium of a chosen body of citizens, whose wisdom may best discern the true interest of their country and whose patriotism and love of justice will be least likely to sacrifice it to temporary or partial considerations" (ibid., 82).

That Madison was not a "pluralist" should be apparent. He did not equate the public good with the outcome, whatever that might be, of factious struggle, or with the resultant of the parallelogram of social forces. Rather, as Wills (1981) rightly observes, Madison hoped that factions would neutralize one another, providing a "space" in which public spirited men might not only perceive the public good, but pursue it. Proper representational arrangements, then, would ensure that the wisest citizens would rule, while the extended republic ensured that they would have latitude to do so.[16]

The Antifederalists did not dispute the need for, or desirability of, representation, but they strenuously objected to the large electoral districts preferred by Madison. The proposed Constitution stipulated that the first House of Representatives be composed of sixty-five members, and that thereafter the ratio of representatives to citizens should not exceed one to 30,000. The Antifederalists feared that these provisions would make the lower house of Congress, which was the only branch of the new government directly accountable to the people, inadequately representative. The number of representatives was simply too small to adequately reflect the diversity of interests and opinions included in an extended republic. As Richard Henry Lee put it,

> a full and equal representation is that which possesses the same interests, feelings, opinions, and views the people themselves would were they all assembled—a fair representation, therefore, should be so regulated, that every order of men in the community, according to the common course of elections, can have a share in it—in order to allow

[16] This "space" was a public space, akin to that provided by a properly balanced arrangement of orders in a mixed regime.

professional men, merchants, traders, farmers, mechanics, etc. to bring a just proportion of their best informed men respectively into the legislature, the representation must be considerably numerous. (Kenyon 1966, 209)

The problem of inadequate numbers was aggravated, the Antifederalists believed, by the likelihood that those few seats that were provided for in the new Constitution would be captured primarily by men of conspicuous military, popular, civil, or legal talents, i.e. the "natural aristocracy."[17] Melancton Smith argued that

if the elections be by plurality,—as probably will be the case in this state,—it is almost certain none but the great will be chosen, for they easily unite their interests: the common people will divide, and their divisions will be promoted by the others. There will be scarcely a chance of their uniting in any other but some great man, unless in some popular demagogue, who will probably be destitute of principle. (ibid., 384)

Given the absence of requirements for frequent, even annual, elections and limitations on tenure in office, the Antifederalists were convinced that the electoral bias in favor of the "natural aristocracy" would degenerate into a tyranny in which the interests of the middle and lower classes would be consistently ignored.[18] Therefore, Madison's hope for an en-

[17] The frequent rhetorical use of "aristocracy" and "democracy" as terms of derogation may well be responsible for some historians' inclination to see ratification as a struggle between aristocratic and democratic forces. When such rhetoric is placed within the context of the argument over the true principles of republicanism and representation, this confusion is removed. This demonstrates the danger of accepting rhetorical labels at face value, without first gaining an appreciation of the context in which they occur, and the argumentative functions they serve.

[18] Kenyon (1955) describes the Antifederalists as "men of little faith" whose theory of representation reflected a profound distrust of elected officials. Frequent elections and limited tenure were seen as important mechanisms for controlling corruption among these representatives, and for ensuring that at any given moment they reflected the immediate views of their constitu-

largement and refinement of public views via the medium of elected representatives was, ironically, not realistic, according to the Antifederalists, who saw Madison's argument as disingenuous.

Madison himself acknowledged the possibility that "men of factious tempers, of local prejudices, or of sinister designs" might gain office in a representative system of governance (Rossiter 1961, 82).[19] Consequently, he did not rely solely, or even primarily, on virtuous rulers to guarantee the safety of the republic. Instead, he relied on "auxiliary precautions" to hold rulers in check:

> In the compound republic of America, the power surrendered by the people is first divided between two distinct governments, and then the portion allotted to each subdivided among distinct and separate departments. Hence, a double security arises to the rights of the people. The different governments will control each other, at the same time that each will be controlled by itself.[20] (ibid., 323)

Madison's concern for the proper design of political institutions, and in particular his "policy of supplying, by opposite and rival interests, the defect of better motives," was interpreted by some Antifederalists (and many later commenta-

---

encies. For the same reasons, delegate instruction was also popular with some of the Antifederalists. Thus, the Antifederalists stood *for* "actual" representation (Storing 1981), at least in an extended republic in which they saw no possibility of a general interest on which "virtual" representation might rest.

[19] Madison thought larger republics were less vulnerable than smaller ones, however.

[20] For a highly persuasive account of the different functions served by extending the republic, on the one hand, and compounding it on the other, see Carey (1978). The extended republic was invoked as a protection against majority tyranny, while the compound nature of the republic was a surety against governmental tyranny. Carey reminds us that bicameralism was an important aspect of this compound design because it acted as an internal check on legislative encroachments on executive and judicial authority, which is a danger often overlooked in the so-called "age of the imperial Presidency."

tors) as an attempt to do away with virtue as the foundation of republican politics (Rossiter 1961, 322). For that reason, Wood (1972) claims that the Constitution of 1787 involved a repudiation of the principles of republicanism of 1776. This repudiation, according to Wood, signalled the end of the classical republican conception of politics, which saw the individual as an active citizen, directly participating in the affairs of the republic, and the emergence of a liberal conception of politics in which the individual appeared as cognizant chiefly of his own interests, and participated in public affairs only to the extent that such involvement was essential for the realization of those interests.[21]

Too much can be made of this apparent abandonment of virtue, however. The Federalists talked both as if virtue were to be restored, and as if it were to be replaced by a more reliable basis for understanding human action (Pocock 1975). They were skeptical about the virtue of men and their capacity for self-denying actions, but then so were the Antifederalists, who were "men with little faith" in their fellow citizens (Kenyon 1955). However, the Federalists were more confident than their opponents that virtue could be incorporated as a *systemic* feature of republican politics. In this they followed Machiavelli, who turned increasingly from a consideration of the individual virtues of *The Prince* to a discourse on the collective virtue of the citizen body as a whole (Skinner 1978, 1:176). The Federalists saw in the decline of deference to leaders by citizens, especially in the states, evidence that collective virtue was crumbling. True to their heritage, they saw this as a constitutional problem, but they gave it an apolitical, even antipolitical, interpretation, and this was at odds with more traditional accounts of republicanism.

The hold of classical republicanism over the Federalists was

[21] Cf. Pocock (1975) for a summary and critique of Wood's claim in this regard. See also Ball (1983). Barbour (1980) accepts Wood's contention in this regard and suggests that the procedural emphasis of much of American social policy since the Founding has its ideological origins in this triumph of liberalism over republicanism.

after all somewhat attenuated. They were by and large a younger generation than their Antifederalist opponents. More importantly, they had been schooled in the new science of moral enlightenment espoused by men like Hutcheson and Hume (Wills 1981). The influence of Hume was especially important in this regard, for in Hume's philosophy individuals appear as dangerous egoists driven by passion and self-interest. They threaten to destroy the very possibility of society, let alone commonwealth politics, unless virtue can be enlisted to restrain their actions.

But Hume's virtues, wrenched from a context of communal life, are a far cry from those of the classical republican tradition. As MacIntyre (1981) shows, virtues are no longer treated as excellent practices in Hume. They are reduced to rules, obedience to which constitutes virtue. At the same time, the new science began to simplify the catalogue of virtues. Virtues associated with particular kinds of practices receded in the face of virtue writ large, which increasingly came to be seen as a moral concept. This "simplification" and the treatment of virtue as rule-following made it possible for Hume to ensconce Fame, or rather the pursuit of Fame, as the political virtue par excellence.

It was left to the Federalists to translate this into practice. Whereas constitution-making was traditionally conceived as a practical exercise in organizing particular virtues, Madison began to treat it as a science of rule formation. Hence, the inculcation of virtues no longer required a practical education, though of course a willingness to obey rules was still a minimal condition for political success. Hamilton found this willingness in the desire of individuals for fame. This was not so much the glory that animated classical republicans, as it was vainglory. However, it did provide a reliable motive for obeying the constitutional rules and pursuing the common good.

The impact of liberalizing tendencies on republican thought is quite evident here. Nevertheless, the categories of analysis, and even the political problem against which they are deployed are recognizably republican. In this respect it seems more accurate to see the Federalists as transitional figures, rather than first-generation liberals. They were men whose beliefs were both republican and liberal, and the tension between these two conceptions of politics was resolved differently by different individuals. For example, John Adams, one of the older Federalists, believed quite strongly in the classical interpretation of virtue and its place in republican politics.[22] Madison was convinced that at the very least a republican citizenry must have sufficient virtue and intelligence to select wise and able leaders.[23] And Hamilton felt certain that proper institutional arrangements, where they failed to recruit virtuous men to begin with, would promote virtuous deeds by making men's interests and duties coincide.[24] Only Noah Webster and William Vans Murray seemed willing to publicly entertain the notion that a well-designed republic might dispense with virtue altogether (Wood 1972).

Indeed, the very fact that the "new science" of the Federalists was preoccupied with "supplying the defect of better motives" indicates the extent to which it was imbued with a

[22] For an account of Adams's reactions to the apparent decline of republican virtue in America, see Howe (1966).

[23] "No theoretical checks—no form of government, can render us secure. To suppose that any form of government will secure liberty or happiness without any virtue in the people is a chimerical idea. If there be sufficient virtue and intelligence in the community, it will be exercised in the selection of [leaders]. So that we do not depend on their virtue or put confidence in our rulers, but in the people who are to choose them" (Madison 1900–1910, 5:223).

[24] "This position will not be disputed so long as it is admitted that the desire of reward is one of the strongest incentives of human conduct; or that the best security for the fidelity of mankind is to make their interest coincide with their duty. Even the love of fame, the ruling passion of the noblest minds, which would prompt a man to plan and undertake extensive and arduous enterprises for the public benefit, requiring considerable time to mature and perfect them [could be so harnessed]" (Rossiter 1961, 437). See also Adair (1974) and Stourzh (1970) for discussions of Hamilton's views on fame. Notice Hamilton's use of self-interest to counteract passions that run counter to the dictates of virtue (Hirschman 1977).

concern for virtue. From this perspective, the Constitutional provisions advanced by the Federalists were not simply substitutes for a waning civic virtue. They were also means of promoting virtuous actions among men who were not virtuous to begin with (Yarbrough 1979b). They were designed to induce the most talented and ambitious men to seek political office, and to direct their talents and ambition toward public-spirited service. The compound republic was a means for making men's interests and duties coincide, and for limiting the harmful effects that might result from any disjuncture between interest and duty. The "new science" was therefore a new science of virtue, and not a new science of human nature or politics.

Thus, the Federalists were—*pace* Wood—concerned with the problem of virtue. However, their emphasis on a virtuous elite was unmistakably at odds with the Antifederalists' reliance on the genius of the people. It was this failure on the part of the Federalists to consider political means for promoting virtue amongst the citizenry that made their proposals both politically and theoretically suspect. Yarbrough (1979a) argues that the Federalists failed to perceive that the violence and destruction that they associated with popular participation under the Articles was characteristic of the founding of a new political order, and not a necessary consequence of political activity in general. As a result, they were led to a rather narrow view of the importance of political action in promoting and sustaining virtue in the citizenry. This was in turn reflected in their attempts to weaken the power of state and local units of government, and in their decidedly Burkean view of representation (Yarbrough, 1979b).

This, of course, made them politically vulnerable to Antifederalist charges that the Constitution was a thinly disguised plan for implementing an aristocratic tyranny. The Federalists responded by denouncing the "democratical" (and later, "jacobin") tendencies of their opponents. As always, both sides laid exclusive claim to a "republicanism" between the unbalanced extremes of government in the interests of the few, and government in the interests of the many. But in the long run the Federalist strategy of denouncing the "democracy" was self-defeating, given the decline of deferential politics and the hierarchical society on which it was based (Pole 1966).

The Federalist failure to provide participatory opportunities was deficient in another way as well, for it hastened the decline of civic virtue. In limiting popular participation to the selection of leaders, the Federalists consigned the population to a state of civic lethargy, in which citizens failed to develop a sense of moral and political responsibility that, according to classical republican theory, accompanied civic involvement. Citizens failed to acquire those minimal insights that would have allowed them to choose wise and able leaders. And they failed to learn to love liberty, i.e. to love and pursue the public good in politics. Thus, the Federalists' "realistic" assessment of the decline in virtue in America turned out to be a "gigantic self-fulfilling prophecy" once it found institutional expression in Constitutional arrangements that made scant provision for civic involvement (Jacobson 1963; Yarbrough 1979a; 1979b; Ball 1983).

Madison eventually became aware of this error on the part of the Federalists. His later insistence on the need for a vigilant citizenry as the ultimate defense against an overly energetic government led him to consider means by which the enervating effects of representation over an extended sphere might be overcome. He concluded that

> whatever facilitates a general intercourse of sentiments, as good roads, domestic commerce, a free press, and particularly *a circulation of newspapers through the entire body of the people, and Representatives going from, and returning among every part of them*, is equivalent to a contraction of territorial limits, and is favorable to liberty, where these may be too extensive.[25] (Madison 1900-1910, 6:70)

[25] For the same reason, he applauded the plan to build a strong system of public education in Kentucky as a model for the nation: "A popular Govern-

For these reasons, Madison opposed Washington's condemnation of the Democratic-Republican Societies, and he even lent qualified support to the idea of competing parties as a means of incorporating popular activities in government (Hofstadter 1969).

As we shall see in the next section, however, these suggestions met with considerable opposition in the Federalist camp, leading Madison to withdraw his support of the Federalist cause.

IV

ALTHOUGH THE FEDERALISTS did succeed in winning approval for their Constitutional proposals, they did not succeed in establishing their interpretation of republicanism as definitive. The bifurcation of American republicanism, which originated in the Federalists' dispute with the Antifederalists over the nature and functions of representation in the extended republic, continued to characterize American politics during the 1790s.

To be sure, the context in which this bifurcation developed was substantially different from that whence it emerged. In vanquishing the "anti-rats" the Federalists had both criticized the Articles of Confederation and defended the Constitution on republican grounds.[26] They had successfully challenged an existing political order and its underlying republican ideology by promulgating an alternative republican vision.

Once in power, however, the Federalists themselves were

---

ment, without popular information, or the means of acquiring it, is but a Prologue to a Farce or a Tragedy; or perhaps both. Knowledge will forever govern ignorance: And a people who mean to be their own Governors must arm themselves with the power which knowledge gives" (Rutland 1983, 24).

[26] Elbridge Gerry, citing the unfair rhetorical advantage obtained by the nationalists through their appropriation of the label "Federalist," suggested that "rats" and "anti-rats" would be more accurate names for those favoring and opposing ratification, respectively. Cf. Zvesper (1977). See also Wood (1972) on the successful and, according to him, disingenuous rhetorical strategy of the Federalists. Pocock (1975) disagrees with Wood's claim in this regard since he is willing to grant the Federalists' claim to republican status.

challenged by groups, e.g. the Democratic-Republican Societies and the Jeffersonian Republicans, which sprang up in opposition to their policies and practices. The roles of challenger and challenged were, therefore, reversed, but with one crucial difference. The later opponents of the Federalists were men who for the most part had favored ratification. They shared a commitment to classical republicanism, and an aversion to the "new science" of republican virtue. However, this ideological position required them to be a loyal opposition. Banning makes this point well:

> Once ratification was a fact, however, most Antifederalists found themselves on different mental terrain. The classical-republican foundations of American constitutional thought taught that a constitution, once established, changed only for the worse. The accepted task for friends of liberty was neither counterrevolution nor reform. It was to guard against social and political degeneration, to force a strict adherence to the original principles of a government, to see that things became no worse. (1978, 113)

Consequently, they represented a loyal opposition, whereas the Federalists, in their role as challengers, had been a more subversive lot.

The opposition groups were loosely bound together by an un-Federalist republicanism that sprang from the same soil as Antifederalism, newly enriched by the diffusion of the French Enlightenment in America. This alternative republicanism was highly critical of the energetic government advocated by the Federalists, and deeply suspicious of the motives and inclinations of representatives elected under the auspices of the federal Constitution. Hence, it embraced many of the same issues and concerns that animated Antifederalist thought and may therefore be considered the direct descendant of a republicanism that had been superseded by Federalism.

The philosophical basis of this alternative republicanism was elaborated in Paine's *Rights of Man*, which was first published in America during 1791–1792, when Paine was still highly respected. Paine argued that men were naturally social, though not political, creatures. This natural sociability was rooted in the common interests which all men have in cooperative efforts to satisfy natural wants and was augmented by a natural inclination toward social affection which, while not necessary for human survival, was essential to human happiness. The resulting harmony acted as a kind of republican virtue and rendered government

> no further necessary than to supply the few cases to which society and civilization are not conveniently competent; and instances are not wanting to show that every thing which government can usefully add thereto, has been performed by the common consent of society, without government. (Paine 1942, 151)

Paine's arguments were intended as a response to Burke's condemnation of the French Revolution, but they were readily adapted to American circumstances by the Democratic-Republican press. Jefferson himself, in a note to Madison, welcomed the *Rights of Man* to America, saying "I am extremely pleased to find it will be reprinted here, and that something is at length to be publicly said against the political heresies which have sprung up among us. I have no doubt our citizens will rally a second time around the standard of 'Common Sense' " (Chinard 1939, 258).[27]

The publication of Jefferson's remarks as an introduction to the *Rights of Man* touched off a spirited pamphlet debate between Publicola (J. Q. Adams), on the one hand, and Agricola, Brutus and Philodemus, on the other, over republican principles articulated by Paine and supported by Jefferson. The relative weakness of the Republican press in the capital became apparent during this exchange, causing Jeffer-

---

[27] The heresies to which Jefferson referred were being circulated by Adams in his "Discourses on Davila," which defended the superior ruling qualities of the natural aristocracy, and bemoaned the unreliability of elections as means for ensuring their utilization.

son and Freneau to found the *National Gazette* in order to
remedy that weakness.[28] Among the first and most prestigious
contributors to the *National Gazette* was James Madison, who
had broken with Hamilton over the latter's aggressive commercial and fiscal policies.

In a remarkable series of seventeen unsigned essays in the
Gazette, Madison expressed his alarm at the antirepublican
implications of those policies, and his concern for a citizenry
ever-jealous of governmental encroachments on its liberty.
The concern of *Federalist 10* and *51* over the problem of governmental tyranny pervades these essays, but Madison's emphasis on a virtuous citizenry, as opposed to institutional arrangements, to provide a solution for this problem stands in
marked contrast to his earlier thought. There then followed,
in 1793, his *Letters of Halvidius*, in which Madison refuted
Pacificus' (Hamilton's) arguments in favor of a strong and energetic federal executive by pointing out the imperialistic and
expansive nature of unchecked grants of power.

The Republicans were united in their belief that the Federalists' program for achieving the common good relied too
heavily on an energetic government driven by men's passion
for fame, and insufficiently on virtuous tendencies in society
itself. This was particularly evident in their opposition to economic policies designed to transform America into a commercial empire. Hamilton was determined to use the powers of
the federal government to establish the fiscal and monetary
foundations for a mercantile economy similar to that of Great
Britain. The various elements of his program, which included
the creation of the Bank of the United States, the assumption
by the federal government of all outstanding state and national debts, and a revenue system, were all designed to provide a favorable climate for the increase of manufactures and
trade. Hamilton also called for a strong army and navy to

[28] Freneau published excerpts from the *Rights of Man* in the *Gazette* and
published a poem lavishing praise on Paine in his *Daily Advertiser*: "Roused
by the REASON of his manly page, Once more shall PAINE a listening world
engage" (Freneau 1929, 124).

protect American economic interests from foreign interference (Stourzh 1970).

Republicans were horrified by Hamilton's proposals. The older republicanism was essentially anticommercial in spirit, for commerce represented the antithesis of public-minded participation in the affairs of the republic. Commercial activity was private activity, and to the extent that men preferred its rewards to those of public service, the virtuous foundation of the republic was seriously endangered. The withdrawal of the best men from politics, and the attempts by others to use positions of authority to further their own economic ends, were the likely consequences of this commercial inclination.

The fact that governmental policies were explicitly intended to encourage this type of behavior particularly offended Jefferson and Madison, neither of whom had gone as far as Hamilton in rejecting virtue as the cornerstone of republican politics.[29] Jefferson especially was concerned with Hamilton's apparent willingness to encourage the growth of commerce at the expense of agriculture, for he believed that agricultural pursuits instilled a particularly valuable kind of republican virtue. Consequently, he opposed policies that threatened to destroy the preeminence of agriculture and agrarian virtue. At the same time, Jefferson vigorously pursued policies designed to stimulate agriculture, including agricultural commerce, i.e. trade. This, as Appleby (1982) has shown, reflected his belief that an expansion of agriculture was synonymous with the cultivation of virtue, so long as it proceeded by increasing the number of independent freeholders. Hence his opposition to primogeniture, and his expansionist land policies.

In this way, Jefferson sought to identify republican virtue

[29] On Hamilton's replacement of virtue with self-interest in republican theory, see Stourzh (1970) and Pocock (1975). Yarbrough (1979a) points out that Hamilton's theory may be seen as encouraging a different kind of virtue, rather than supplanting virtue altogether. Personal, rather than civic, responsibilities are emphasized, and their contribution to the public good is applauded.

with a certain kind of commerce, namely, that oriented toward increasing access to land.[30] For this purpose, government was useful, but where government energetically pursued other ends, it was dangerous, and even antirepublican. Hamilton's vision of an American commercial republic modeled along the lines of Great Britain and promoted by action of the national government did not square with Jefferson's image of the yeoman republic.

These philosophical differences over republican principles found concrete expression in numerous disputes over domestic and foreign affairs. On the home front, Hamilton's funding system, the establishment of the Bank, the assumption of debts, and Madison's proposals to reduce American dependence on British trade all touched off heated disputes between the Federalists and their Republican opponents. The Republicans attacked Hamilton's policies, which, they alleged, had "greatly encreased the spirit and enterprize of speculators, and occasioned in this way the most detestable and enormous frauds, and promoted a depravity of morals and a great decline of republican virtue" (Zvesper 1977, 146). They looked forward to the time when the Federalists' hold on Congress, which they were certain resulted from the biased and corrupt system of representation, would be broken, and the offending measures repealed.

The Federalists responded by noting that "under the severely republican Constitution, enterprize has enlarged its sphere, and explored new regions of profit, that our country, everywhere presents the charms of creative cultivation and diffuse opulence," and that Hamilton's efforts had much to do with this state of affairs (ibid., 151). And they impugned the loyalty and motives of their detractors. In Hamilton's words—

It is a melancholy truth, which every new political occurrence more and more unfolds, that there is a description

---

[30] Paine went even further than Jefferson in this regard, wholeheartedly embracing commercial development, so long as it was "natural," i.e. not aided and abetted by government policies (E. Foner 1976).

of men in this country, irreconcileably adverse to the government of the United States; whose exertions, whatever be the springs of them, whether infatuation, or depravity or both, tend to disturb the tranquillity order and prosperity of this now peaceful flourishing and truly happy land. A real and enlightened friend to public felicity cannot ob-
. serve new confirmations of this fact, without feeling a deep and poignant regret, that human nature should be so refractory and perverse; that amidst a profusion of the bounties and blessings of Providence, political as well as natural, inviting to contentment and gratitude, there should still be found men disposed to cherish and propagate disquietude and alarm; to render suspected and detested the instruments of the felicity, in which they participate. (ibid., 142–143)

Hamilton was, in effect, accusing the Republicans of bad faith, for they were enjoying the fruits of prosperity even while condemning the husbandry most responsible for it. But it seems more likely that the Republicans were victims of bad conscience, rather than actors in bad faith (ibid., 124–131). They were willing to concede the inevitability, even desirability, of economic growth, but they hoped to avoid the corruption of politics that accompanied that growth. Since they believed that this corruption was the result of a (corrupt) governmental sponsorship of commerce, they were led to conclude that growth without corruption was possible only if society were left to follow its own "natural" course.

V

THE IDEOLOGICAL differences between Federalists and Republicans over the compatibility of virtue and commerce were greatly intensified by the two sides' reactions to the unfolding French Revolution.[31] Initially, American enthusi-

---

[31] The French Revolution, in the words of Colonel Higgenson, "drew a red-hot ploughshare through the history of America as well as through that of France. It not merely divided parties, but molded them; gave them their demarcations, their watchwords, and their bitterness. The home issues were

asm for the popular revolt against the *ancien régime* was widespread, but with the assumption of power by the Girondists, and the subsequent rise of the Jacobins, the Federalists began to withdraw their support for the revolutionary cause. Reports of the "violent excesses" of the new regime only confirmed Federalist suspicions about the intemperate nature of democratic rule. The Genêt affair, and the "seditious" activities of the Democratic-Republican Societies in its wake were seen as evidence that the democratic contagion had made its way to America, and the Federalists moved quickly to contain it. Their press railed against these "self-created" societies that claimed to speak for the people. Attacks such as that on the Kentucky Democratic Society were not uncommon:

> But in Kentucky you have a Democratic Society—that horrible sink of treason,—that hateful synagogue of anarchy,—that odious conclave of tumult,—that frightful cathedral of discord,—that poisonous garden of conspiracy,—that hellish school of rebellion and opposition to all regular and well-balanced authority. (P. Foner 1976, 27)

Beneath this colorful verbiage there lurked a profound distrust of extra-Constitutional means of popular expression. The Societies, stated Oliver Wolcott, Jr., were "unlawful, as they are formed for the avowed purpose of a general influence and control upon the measures of government" (ibid., 24). By resorting to popular agitation as a means of influencing legislation and administrative policy, they undermined the authority and legitimacy of those duly elected officials who were supposed to act as a medium for the refinement and enlargement of public views. A truly virtuous people would not engage in these activities, which threatened to undo the Constitutional arrangements upon which the stability of the republic depended.

---

for a time subordinate, collateral; the real party lines were established on the other side of the Atlantic" (Parrington 1954a, 1:327).

The Societies defended their actions by pointing out that

> under a Constitution which expressly provides *'That the
> people have a right in an orderly and peaceful manner to
> assemble and consult upon the common good,'* there can be
> no necessity for an apology to the public for an Association
> of a number of citizens to promote and cherish the social
> virtues, the love of their country and a respect for its Laws
> and Consitutions; nor can it be derogatory to Freemen *in
> America* to declare their attachment to *Universal Liberty*
> and openly to profess a sacred regard to the great princi-
> ples of *Natural Equality.* (ibid., 25)

Far from apologizing, the Societies took pride in exercising
their right and duty to "watch with the vigilance of a faithful
centinel" the actions of their government, lest it pass beyond
the bounds of permissible authority (ibid., 25).

The Federalists attempted to discredit the Societies by denouncing them as "democratic," hoping thereby to associate
them with the excesses of Jacobinism.[32] At the same time,
they laid plans to capture the republican label for their own
use. Fisher Ames, in a letter to John Rutledge, emphasized
the need to "wrench the name *republican* from those who
have unworthily usurped it. . . . Names and appearances are
in party warfare arms and ammunition. It is particularly necessary to contest this name with them now" (Morantz 1971,
145.)

In order to wrest the republican name from their opponents, the Federalists launched an intensive campaign to educate the public on the differences between democracy and
republicanism, and on the evils of the former and the virtues
of the latter. Ames argued that "our sages in the great con-

---

[32] Many of the clubs gladly obliged the Federalists in this matter. Of the
forty-two societies listed in Link (1942), and the four additional clubs mentioned in P. Foner (1976), sixteen used "Democratic" in their official titles,
sixteen used "Republican," two used "Democratic-Republican," and four
preferred labels such as "Committee of Correspondence" and "French Society."

vention intended our government should be a republick,
which differs more widely from a democracy, than a democracy from despotism" (ibid., 11). Ames's views on the differences between a democracy and a republic were well known:

> A republic is that structure of an elective government, in
> which the administration necessarily prescribe to them-
> selves the general good as the object of all their measures;
> a democracy is that, in which the present popular passions,
> independent of the public good, become a guide to the
> rulers. In the first, the reason and interests of society gov-
> ern; in the second, their prejudices and passions. (Ames
> [1854] 1971, 21)[33]

These sentiments were echoed in a more partisan way by
Noah Webster in a famous letter to Joseph Priestly, in which
he explained American usage of these terms:

> By democracy is intended a government where the legis-
> lative powers are exercised directly by all the citizens, as
> formerly in Athens and Rome. In our country this power
> is not in the hands of the people but of their representa-
> tives. The powers of the people are principally restricted
> to the direct exercise of the rights of suffrage. Hence a
> material distinction between our form of government and
> those of the ancient democracies. Our form of government
> has acquired the appellation of a *Republic*, by way of dis-
> tinction, or rather of a *representative Republic*.
>   Hence the word *Democrat* has been used as synonymous
> with the word *Jacobin* in France; and by an additional idea,
> which arose from the attempt to control our government
> by private popular associations, the word has come to sig-
> nify a person who attempts an undue opposition to or influ-
> ence over government by means of private clubs, secret
> intrigues, or by public popular meetings which are extra-
> neous to the constitution. By *Republicans* we understand

[33] As summarized by James T. Kirkland, Ames's close friend and president
of Harvard (Ames [1854] 1971, xxiv–xxv).

the friends of our Representative Governments, who believe that no influence whatever should be exercised in a state which is not directly authorized by the Constitution and laws. (Webster 1953, 207–208)

The extent to which the Federalists were willing to pursue this strategy is dramatically illustrated by the case of the Pennsylvania Federalists, who were generally known as the Federalist-Republicans. After their defeat in the election of 1800, they promptly dropped the Federalist prefix and began calling themselves Republicans, and their opponents Democrats (Morantz 1971, 145).

Initially, the Federalists' strategy seemed well taken. The Whiskey Rebellion of 1794, which was widely attributed to the subversive activities of the Societies, made plausible the Federalists' dire predictions of democratic distemper. It brought the immense prestige of Washington to bear against the Societies and the principles for which they stood.[34] But after a brief respite during the deliberation of the highly unpopular Jay treaty (1794), which they had opposed from the start, the societies began to wither under the continuous attacks of the Federalist press. The notorious XYZ affair, and the passage of the Alien and Sedition Act of 1798, then signalled their demise.

In the long run, however, the Federalists' strategy misfired. In trying to show that they were the sole and rightful heirs to the republican tradition of the Revolution, the Federalists attempted to identify republicanism with a particular set of institutional arrangements, as Webster's letter suggests. To the extent that their educational program succeeded, republicanism came to be associated more with a particular in-

[34] Because of the enormous influence of the *Rights of Man*, Link (1942, 104) says that Paine "deserves credit for fathering the democratic societies." Ironically, Paine dedicated that work to Washington with the following words: "Sir, I present you a small treatise in defence of those principles of freedom which your exemplary virtue hath so eminently contributed to establish . . ." (Paine 1942).

stitutional form of government, and less with the characteristic purpose or aim of government, as it had been during the
Revolutionary years. And in becoming more concrete, as it
were, it lost some of its moral force, even as it became more
vulnerable to criticism by those who were dissatisfied with
the constitutionally provided avenues of representation.

"Democracy," on the other hand, was proceeding in the
opposite direction. Whereas it had referred previously to a
particular form of government, it began to acquire more abstract and positive connotations. The Democratic-Republican
Societies and the Jeffersonian Republicans succeeded in neutralizing the more odious connotations of "mob rule" through
their counter-educational efforts, and their "responsible" opposition to Federalist policies. They also initiated the process
by which the rhetorical links between democracy and the
ideas of popular sovereignty and political equality were
forged. Morantz (1971) has shown that the republican press
began to use the term "democracy" in a favorable light as
early as 1794 in their glorification of popular sovereignty, and
criticism of the elitist politics of the Federalists.[35] This trend
toward the popularization of democracy proceeded by fits and
starts into the nineteenth century, eventually culminating in
the Democratic Party of "Old Hickory," Andrew Jackson.

VI

THE CHANGING political fortunes discussed above were, of
course, integrally related to broader socioeconomic changes

[35] One interesting indicator of the changing rhetorical value of these terms
is discussed by Morantz (1971), who examined the incidence of the words
"Democracy," "Democratic," and "Republican" in newspaper titles during
the period 1790–1850. From 1790 to 1820, 170 newspapers included one of
these keywords in their titles, of which sixteen, or nine percent, used "Democracy" or "Democratic." None of these papers appeared before 1800; only
three appeared before 1807.

From 1820 to 1850, on the other hand, 101, or sixty-three percent, were
"Democrat" or "Democratic" newspapers. This remarkable shift was, no
doubt, a reflection of the emergence of a self-styled Democratic party. But
the groundwork had been laid by the earlier Jeffersonian Republicans and
the Democratic-Republicans.

that were occurring at this time. In a relatively short span, the colonies moved from an unorganized "system" of diverse regional modes of production toward a mercantile economy integrated by the circulation of merchant capital.[36] The unevenly distributed economic growth that accompanied this economic transformation wrought tremendous changes in the social structure of the union, which in turn accelerated the decline of virtuous and deferential politics, and the concomitant rise of interests and factions (Pole 1966; Wood 1972; Pocock 1975). Naturally, it radically altered the patterns of political influence in the states, and in the nation as a whole.

Despite the significant political, social, and economic dislocations occasioned by this transformation, the new regime did not experience a "legitimation crisis" of cataclysmic proportions. Lienesch (1980) argues that such a crisis was forestalled by the deliberate manufacture of a constitutional tradition that protected the new regime from subversive criticism. According to Lienesch, this ersatz tradition was largely, but not exclusively, the work of the Federalists, who were faced with the difficult problem of establishing the moral authority of a regime founded on "realistic" principles that, to a significant extent, denied the morality of men. Their invention of a "tradition" capable of providing a sense of continuity between the Constitution and the Revolution, on the one hand, and the future progress of America, on the other, was an ideological solution to this incipient crisis.[37]

This chapter suggests that this appeal to constitutionalism

[36] Mayer and Fay (1977) and Williams (1966) describe this emergence of a production for exchange economy from a Marxist perspective. Their conclusions about this economic transition, the role of political institutions in promoting it, and the impact of international affairs on it are quite similar to those reached in North's (1966) more conventional account.

[37] Carey (1980) rightly points out that we may grant the importance of constitutionalism in this regard without conceding its deliberate manufacture. Lutz (1980) discusses the covenantal origins of constitutionalism, and Farry (1984) documents the different understandings of "compact," "covenant," and "constitution" that existed during the ratification period, and the bearing of these differences on the meaning of the "consent of the governed" in the debates on the Constitution.

was itself grounded in a republican tradition. Constitutions were evaluated in terms of their contribution to the maintenance and enhancement of republican politics, as we have seen. For that reason, the Federalists defended the Constitution because it promised to suspend the cycle of corruption and decline to which all previous republics had succumbed. The Constitution was predicated on the belief that a republic designed in accordance with realistic principles of human behavior might enjoy a life virtually without end. Past, present, and future were ostensibly merged in a *republican* continuity in which constitutionalism shared, and which served to legitimate the new Constitution by recalling its origins in the Revolution, and anticipating a future *sans* corruption (Shumer 1979).

At the same time, critics of the Constitution and the politics it inspired argued that this interruption of the cycle of political decay had been achieved at the cost of republicanism itself. They disputed the "republican" nature of this antidote to republican diseases, and claimed that the new Constitution, far from prolonging the life of the republic, actually terminated the political life of the body politic.

The fact that such significant and intense differences over the nature and ends of republican government were expressed *within* the confines of the republican tradition is a remarkable testimony to the strength of republicanism on the political thought of the Founding period. All important factions of this period in American politics claimed to be republican, in principle, if not in name; all used republican terminology to justify their own positions, and to criticize others'; and all appealed to Revolutionary republicansm as the inspirational exemplar. In short, republicanism, variously interpreted, defined the normative universe in which political discussion took place during the Founding period.

The capacity of this republican universe to permit—and, more importantly, to contain—the ideological differences that surfaced in the 1790s explains the comparative ease with which the new union survived the transition to a new socioeconomic order. It accounts for the relative ease with which a political *founding* was accomplished. In the next chapter we shall explore its durability as a *ruling* ideology, and in Chapter Four as a ruling ideology under pressure from a rival conception of politics.

CHAPTER THREE

Democratic Republicanism in the United States

I

WHILE THE FOUNDING of a polity is a significant event, its preservation is no less important, particularly where republican polities are concerned. That is because republicans understand their history in cyclical terms. Precisely because the corruption of virtue is an ever-present danger that threatens the life of all republics, the best that can be expected is that the onset of decay might be postponed, perhaps indefinitely, by a vigilant citizenry capable of remembering its virtuous beginning and continuously reenacting it (Shumer 1979).[1]

For republicans, time erodes; it does not fulfill (Hoye 1984). Hence, the principal political theme of republican philosophy involves the suspension of history by means of an appropriate constitutional balance. When that balance comes undone, there is a need to "return to first principles," i.e. to reconstitute the republican foundations that are firm enough to withstand, or at least forestall, corruption.[2] Republican history is, therefore, "degenerative," whereas liberal history

[1] Banner (1970, 25, n. 6) counts the Virginia and Kentucky Resolutions, Louisiana Purchase, Embargo, War of 1812, and the Hartford Convention among the instances of creative renewal in which the implications of the American republican ideology were addressed. For him, the Founding period, or as he calls it the Age of Revolution, lasted until 1815, since "the ideological strains of American politics were continuous from the pre-Revolutionary years until 1815."

[2] Uncertainty about whether or not an imbalance has in fact arisen is, of course, an important aspect of republican politics. Somkin's (1967) *Unquiet Eagle* is an exploration of republican uncertainty and citizens' reaction to it during the Jacksonian period.

tends toward the "progressive," emphasizing the developmental possibilities present in history.

This peculiarly republican understanding of history and its restricted possibilities has been subtly analyzed by Pocock (1975). He shows how deeply rooted this outlook was in early nineteenth-century America. Ross (1979) claims that the hold of republicanism persisted even longer, surfacing in the utopian thought of late nineteenth-century thinkers like Edward Bellamy. Indeed, she believes that this strain of American political thought was not finally displaced until the onset of the Progressive movement, which, not coincidentally, spawned an ardent brand of progressive historiography.

It is not surprising, therefore, that the fragility of republican politics was a dominant theme in American political discourse during the first years of the nineteenth century as Federalists and Republicans alike feared for the life of their young nation. For the Federalists, the chief danger was that of faction, and in the Republican majority they perceived the most dangerous of all factions. Their pessimism about the future of republican politics in America led them to increasingly strident denunciations of the incipient corruption of liberty embodied in the party of Jefferson.

The Jeffersonians, too, worried about the survival of the republic. Indeed, some of Jefferson's erstwhile supporters shared the Federalists' suspicions about the internal corruption of American politics by a misguided majoritarian faction. However, other "Jeffersonian Republicans" saw danger from another quarter. Foreign encroachment seemed to them the most immediate threat. The British in particular appeared eager to end the American experiment in republican government.

Finally, there was a more subtle corruption abroad in the land, which had to do with what Leo Marx (1964) has called "the machine in the garden." The pastoral ideal upon which Jefferson constructed his vision of the yeoman farmer, and which informed in a different way the Federalist image of a deferential social order, was fast becoming obsolete as commerce and manufacturing began to take root and flourish. This was a more pervasive, not to mention insidious, form of corruption, against which the Republic had few defenses.[3]

The emergence of self-styled political parties, as distinct from factions, was one aspect of this situation. This process was initiated in struggles over control of state Republican "parties," and it involved a significant reinterpretation of "republicanism" by the winners of these struggles. Republicanism came to refer to particular procedures for intraparty governance, and not to the aims or principles for which that party stood. By extension, it soon applied to matters of interparty contestation as well, as the "methods" of republican governance were transferred from party affairs to matters of state.

In effect, this reinterpretation of democratic republicanism involved greater emphasis on the "democratic" qualifier that identified the type of republicanism practiced in America. This heralded the emergence of democracy as a legitimate ideal in its own right, one that soon overtook its republican host. That part of our story will have to wait until the next chapter. For now, we must concern ourselves with the preservation of the republic in the immediate aftermath of its founding.

II

THE VICTORY of the Republican party in 1800 and its virtually unchallenged control of national government until the late 1820s signalled the end of significant contestation over the meaning of republican principles. The Federalists, to be sure, continued to insist on the authenticity of their republican credentials, and to castigate the democratic inclinations of their opponents, but to little avail (Morantz 1971). As the years

---

[3] The idea of Union was not yet entrenched and threats of secession were quite common, making it difficult for the idea of loyal or legitimate opposition to take hold (Kerber 1980). As we shall see in Chapter Five, the meaning of "Union" remained problematic for American republicans until the Civil War.

went by their ranks thinned, and after their ill-timed efforts to forge more friendly relations with Britain their credibility was essentially destroyed.

The beginning of this ignoble end was traced to the year 1800 by most thoughtful Federalists. The "revolution of 1800," as the Federalists came to call Jefferson's victory, was the point at which American politics once again began to degenerate, in their view. The corruption of politics had been interrupted briefly by the heroic efforts of the Revolutionary generation to free themselves from the decadence of English politics. Under the Articles the mischief of faction reappeared; once again, this predictable occurrence had been overcome by the extraordinary events surrounding the adoption of the Constitution. The events of 1800 and thereafter revealed how extraordinary and fragile this heroic accomplishment had been, and the Federalists believed that the timeless cycle of corruption and renewal had begun once again.

The idea of "revolution," in the sense of a re-turning in time, captured this meaning well, and so it was natural for the Federalists to use the only notion of historical change available to them to describe the significance of Jefferson's triumph.[4] That was because the election, as Fisher Ames knew, was "no little cabinet scene, where one minister comes into power and another goes out, but a great moral revolution proceeding from the vices and passions of men, shifting officers today, that measures, and principles, and systems, may be shifted to-morrow" (Banner 1970, 37). This "great moral revolution," left unchecked, represented the beginning of the end of the republic, for it signalled the triumph of unbridled democracy in the form of an untutored and immoderate ma-

---

[4] Pocock (1975) refers to this understanding of republican politics as the "Machiavellian moment," because it received its most penetrating analysis from Machiavelli. The sense of history as a timeless revolution involving the continuous unfolding of the cycle of founding and decay is the anxious background against which efforts to suspend time, i.e. establish a Machiavellian moment, unfold in republican politics.

joritarian faction, and the recrudescence of "absolutist democracy" as the degenerate form of democratic republicanism.

Undoubtedly, this pessimistic conclusion grew out of the
Federalists' keen disappointment over their loss of power and
influence in national politics. Nevertheless, the Federalists in
dissent were not an unprincipled lot. They were an embit-
tered opposition "*not* merely because they had lost office,
patronage, and power in the election of 1800, but because
America appeared to be developing a civilization which they
did not understand and of which they certainly did not ap-
prove" (Kerber 1980, 4). Consequently, their differences with
the Jeffersonians were as much cultural as political, though
they perceived the political recklessness of the Jeffersonians
as a major cause of the decline of civilization as they envisioned it.

The evidence of this was everywhere about them. To the
Federalists, the shift in the grounds and goals of scientific
inquiry from the timeless rationality of disciplines like math-
ematics toward natural history, the rejection of a classical curriculum, the revision of the judiciary system put in place by
the Federalists, and the subsequent impeachment of judges,
were all signs of this decline (Kerber, 1980). All demonstrated
the insensitivity of the Jeffersonian majority to the inevitability of social and political decay and their subsequent inability
to understand the fragility of the Revolutionary accomplishment.

True to their republican heritage, the Federalists interpreted such changes pessimistically. They could only portend
the destruction of the polity, since a well-founded republic,
once established, did not improve or progress. It simply persisted as a well-founded republic, or else became one of the
degenerate forms that philosophers since Aristotle were wont
to associate with political regimes. In the Federalists' view,
the Jeffersonians' failure to comprehend this singularly important truth, and their apparently perverse interest in fo-

menting rather than arresting, social and political change was sufficient evidence of their unworthiness to govern.

This was particularly apparent in the Jeffersonian attitude toward liberty, the cornerstone of republican politics. According to the Federalists, the Jeffersonians understood liberty only in a negative way. They associated it with the right to rebel against governors. They had no conception of "positive" liberty, construed as the right of self-government, with its implied duties and responsibilities, the most important of which had to do with deference on the part of citizens to wise leaders (Fischer 1965; Kerber 1980).[5] Consequently, the Jeffersonians were unfit to preserve the republic, for they had no conception of what that entailed, nor did they have the requisite virtue to do so.

Gouverneur Morris attributed this failure on the part of Jeffersonians to the fact that

> there is a moral tendency, and in some cases even a physical disposition among the people of this country to overturn the Government. . . . The habits of monarchic government are not yet worn away among our native citizens, and therefore the opposition to lawful authority is frequently considered as a generous effort of patriotic virtue. (Kerber 1980, 184)

However useful this disposition might have been during the Revolutionary years, it was manifestly inappropriate and destructive in the formative years of the Republic, the Federalists believed.

The susceptibility to violence and "mobbish" behavior, and the absence of deference to the virtue of wise men, were sure signs of corruption in the body politic, and the *New England Palladium* Federalists feared the worst: "If the people will not erect any barriers against their intemperance and giddiness, or will not respect and sustain them after they are erected,

---

[5] The distinction between positive and negative liberty is developed by Sir Isaiah Berlin (1958).

their power will soon be snatched out of their hands, and their own heads broken with it—as in *France*" (ibid., 193).

To a certain extent this tendency on the part of the people toward "mobbish" behavior was natural to all democratic republics, in the Federalists' view. However, it was greatly aggravated by the irresponsible rhetoric of the Jeffersonians, whose corruption of political discourse was the frequent target of Federalist invective. The Jeffersonians' successes in casting federalism in a monarchical light and in laying sole claim to the title of "republican" were especially important instances of this perfidy. The Federalists set out to rid American political discourse of this corruption.

The Federalists, declared Fessenden, "believe, with Mirabeau, that 'words are things.' If false, they give a wrong direction to the public mind, and of consequence to the physical powers of the community" (ibid., 195). Hence, the Charleston, South Carolina *Courier* claimed that it was necessary for the Federalist press to show that "the federalist prefers the federal constitution to all other forms of government; he values it for its republicanism. . . . It is to be lamented that there are republicans among us who are not federalists" (ibid., 196).

More often, of course, the Federalists simply refused to acknowledge their opponents as republicans. They were republican "pretenders," and Federalist satire was replete with scurrilous condemnations of Republican motives and actions. This satire, as Kerber (ibid., 11) notes, was primarily a way of reaching the "middling classes," who failed to respond to the more serious vocabulary lessons offered by the Federalist press on the true meaning of republicanism and federalism. Nevertheless, it was oriented toward the same end, namely, the reclamation of republican discourse.

Inevitably, the Federalist counteroffensive only *increased* the corruption of political discourse, much to the chagrin of Rufus King, who mourned that "words without meaning, or with wrong meaning have especially of late years done great harm. Liberty, Love of Country, Federalism, Republicanism,

Democracy, Jacobin, Glory, Philosophy and Honor are words in the mouth of everyone and used without precision by anyone; the abuse of words is as pernicious as the abuse of things" (ibid., 196–197).

In fact American government had degenerated into "pure unadulterated *logocracy*, or government of words," declared Washington Irving, who went on to explain:

> The whole nation does everything *viva voce*, or by word of mouth; and in their manner is one of the most military nations in existence. Every man who has what is here called the gift of gab, that is, a plentiful stock of verbosity, becomes a soldier outright; and is forever in a militant state. The country is entirely defended . . . by force of tongues. . . . This vast empire, therefore, may be compared to . . . a mighty windmill, and the orators, and the chatterers, and the slang-whangers [newspaper editors], are the breezes that put it into motion; unluckily, however, they are apt to blow in different ways, and their blasts counteracting each other—the mill is perplexed, the wheels stand still, the grist is unground, and the miller and his family starved. (ibid., 197)

III

THE GENERAL INCLINATION of the Federalists to interpret Republican domination as unmistakable evidence of internal corruption and social decay was strongly reinforced by their objections to Republican foreign policies that seemed to invite aggression from outsiders, the other great source of peril to a republic. The anticommercial thrust of embargo and non-continuation policies threatened to undermine the economic vitality of the young nation, and the provocation of a military confrontation with Great Britain courted invasion and Indian unrest. These policies of the Jeffersonians placed the republic in double jeopardy, and unnecessarily so, in the view of leading Federalists.

Both Jefferson and Madison attempted to use economic

coercion against the British in order to restrain the latter's interference with American trade and eliminate the impressment of American seamen into British naval service. However, the reliance on embargoes caused great economic hardship in New England, the only remaining Federalist stronghold, because of its dependence on trade—especially with Britain—as the principal source of livelihood for many of its inhabitants. While many Republicans were urging Madison to resort to even stronger measures, including a declaration of war, the Federalists and a small contingent of New England Republicans resisted those efforts and sought a political settlement that would be less ruinous, economically and militarily (Stagg 1983). They were convinced that such a settlement was possible, if only the Republican administration would pursue it sincerely (Banner 1970).

These efforts proved unsuccessful, and eventually Madison elected to invade Canada in order to bring greater pressure to bear on Britain. The Federalists resisted this move, although once war was declared, they gave grudging support to "Mr. Madison's War" so as not to appear traitorous. But as the war progressed, or rather failed to progress as Madison had intended, opposition to it among New Englanders continued to fester. The Federalists were quick to seize the advantage and accuse the administration of overly taxing New England's already depressed economy, while failing to provide an adequate defense against a British invasion. This claim was given credence by the ease with which the British occupied the District of Maine in 1814, which caused general alarm among the northeastern states, as the bulk of the regular army had been deployed farther south, and the Federalist governors had not mobilized their state militias to the same degree as other states (Stagg 1983).

According to the Federalists, this was merely another, more serious instance of the victimization of New England by national policies that worked to her disadvantage. Moreover, these sectional grievances were interpreted as a national problem: the national government had become an alien force, controlled by Republican interests in the South, in combination with western allies (Banner 1970). This alliance had undone the delicate balance of interests that Madison had once regarded as essential for the persistence of an extended republic, leaving the northeastern minority vulnerable to exploitation by the dominant majority.

For many Federalists this unbalanced situation reflected certain flaws in the Constitution that allowed southern interests to assume the dominant role in national policymaking. In particular, the infamous "three-fifths rule" for counting slaves in the apportionment of representatives seemed to guarantee a Congressional majority to the South, and by implication a dominant voice in the selection of the President. This was reinforced by the acquisition and settlement of western lands (especially those involved in Jefferson's Louisiana Purchase), and the subsequent admission of new states aligned with southern Republicans. Indeed, the Federalists' opposition to westward expansion revealed that whereas their predecessors of 1790 had defended the need for an extended republic, the Federalists of 1814 feared the consequences for New England should the republic become *too* extensive. Samuel Taggart, invoking an old Antifederalist argument, claimed that "in a territory so extensive as the United States, comprising within its limits, perhaps, nearly all the varieties of the human species, to be found in the civilized world, peoples whose sentiments, habits, manners, and prejudices, are very different, and whose local interests and attachments are various, it is not strange that the seed of division should exist" (ibid., 111).

Not surprisingly, this analysis was accompanied by demands for some sort of constitutional remedy for defects that permitted the Republican administration to pursue a course of action so deleterious to the economic and political interests of New England. Demands for another constitutional convention arose periodically from 1808 until 1814, coinciding roughly with the enactment of embargoes or the passage of wartime legislation, e.g. conscription measures. However, no meeting was acutally convened until December 15, 1814, in Hartford, Connecticut.

So it was that just twenty-seven years after the early Federalists had met in Philadelphia to consider modifications to the Articles of Confederation, a small number of Federalist delegates from Massachusetts, Connecticut, Rhode Island, Vermont, and New Hampshire met to consider "a radical reform in the national compact" (Stagg 1983, 471). The meeting began amidst widespread speculation that a recommendation for secession would be adopted, although Banner (1970) has recently shown that most delegates were more interested in the possibility of state interposition in matters involving the militia. Nevertheless, the report of the convention left no doubt that some members preferred secession, and that others had forsaken that position only because they believed it was unlikely to succeed if undertaken during wartime (Dwight 1970).

However, most of the report was devoted to a careful statement of the region's grievances and objections to Madison's prosecution of the war effort. Resolutions were also passed urging the elimination of the three-fifths rule and the apportionment of representatives according to the number of free persons residing in a state. Similarly, an amendment requiring a concurrence of two-thirds of the House and Senate for the admission of new states was proposed. (This would have given New England an effective veto over the admission of new states.) Finally, the convention suggested limiting Presidents to one term in office, and forbidding the consecutive election of two Presidents from the same state. These measures, along with the more specific remedies on embargoes, were transparent attempts to overthrow the hegemony of the Republicans and their leaders from the "Virginia Dynasty."

Still, as Banner (1970) notes, the decision by the Hartford Convention to remain in the union and to seek redress by means other than secession was strong testimony to the strength of the republican ethos among Federalists. For republicans, defection was treasonous; virtue demanded patriotism and loyalty. The only appropriate action for concerned republicans was the pursuit of solutions that might eventually reconstitute the republic on a firmer foundation.

The announcement of Jackson's victory in New Orleans almost immediately after the publication of the report of the Hartford Convention overshadowed this republican commitment, however, and the Republicans quickly condemned the "disloyal" Federalists for undermining a successful war effort. They were never a significant national political force thereafter.

IV

DESPITE THE BEST efforts of dissenting Federalists, the Jeffersonian interpretation of yeoman republicanism became the public philosophy of this period, and in so doing defined the universe of ideological discourse in early nineteenth-century America. Within that universe, however, internal disputes over the translation of opposition principles into administrative policy did occur. Except for a brief interlude during the War of 1812, the Republican administrations of the Virginia Dynasty found themselves opposed by a small but influential group of Old Republicans from their own party. Led by John Randolph, and supported by John Taylor of Caroline, this faction watched with horror and dismay as first Jefferson, and then Madison and Monroe, abandoned the "republican principles of '98" in the face of practical exigencies and popular pressures for policies long advocated by the Federalists.[6]

Jefferson, for example, felt compelled to retain Hamilton's system and its dreaded bank because they had assumed vital importance in the developing American economy: "We can pay his debts in 15 years: but we can never get rid of his financial system. It mortifies me to be strengthening principles which I deem radically vicious, but this vice is entailed

[6] The "principles of '98" were codified in the Kentucky and Virginia Resolutions of 1798, which were the Republicans' response to the Alien and Sedition Acts.

on us by the first error. . . . What is practicable must often control what is pure theory" (Hofstadter 1969, 159).

Jefferson's willingness to subordinate the "pure theory of republicanism" to practical considerations, and to adopt economic policies favored by the Federalists, earned him the contempt of Randolph, who referred to him as "that prince of projectors, St Thomas of Cantingbury" (Schlesinger 1945, 20). During Jefferson's second term, Randolph led a small group of ardent republicans, known as the *Tertium Quid*, in opposition to Jefferson's ill-fated proposal for a gunboat navy, his plans for a standing army, and his policy of embargo, all of which, Randolph believed, violated the republican spirit of minimalist government.[7]

The *Quid*'s shortlived and ineffectual Congressional challenge to the Jeffersonian administration was followed by Monroe's rump presidential candidacy of 1808. Randolph and others advanced Monroe's ambitions in defiance of Jefferson's attempt to install Madison as his successor. The bulk of Monroe's followers felt that he was a purer republican than Madison, whose earlier collaboration with Hamilton on the *Federalist Papers* rendered his philosophical inclinations suspect. Monroe, for his part, was seeking vindication against Jefferson and Madison for their rejection of the treaty he and Pinckney had concluded with Britain in 1806. Moreover, he continued to believe that such an accommodation was preferable to the strategy of economic coercion preferred by Madison or the militarist option preferred by the so-called "Invisibles" or "malcontents" in the Republican ranks (Stagg 1983).

Monroe's poor showing and the defeat of several Congressional *Quid* effectively stilled further electoral efforts to oppose Madison. However, the dissatisfaction over the apparent

[7] *Tertium Quid*, meaning a third something of ambiguous status, in this case a conservative faction within the dominant party of a two-party system. Risjord (1965) argues that the *Quid* and their postwar successors, the Richmond Junto, who comprised the Old Republicans, were the ideological progeny of the Antifederalist wing of the Republican party of the 1790s.

alliance between republican professions and federalist programs persisted, and as late as 1810 men like Tazewell and Taylor were urging Monroe to lead a third-party effort to restore the republican principles of 1798 to their proper place in American politics (Risjord 1965). Other "malcontents" engaged in considerable political manuevering to persuade John Armstrong, ambassador to France, to challenge Madison in 1812, but to no avail (Stagg 1983).

In Congress, however, Madison ran into increasing resistance from the *Quid* and New England Republicans. However, this internal opposition (as well as any remaining opposition on the part of the Federalists) soon fell victim to the surge of unity induced by the War of 1812 and the events immediately preceding it. Many Americans perceived British interference with American shipping as an affront to national honor, as well as an economic nuisance. Moreover, there was a growing conviction that the threat posed to the Republic by the British monarchy was in fact a threat to world republicanism itself (Brown 1964). With France returned to the absolutist fold, America represented the sole surviving democratic republic in the world, and many were convinced that it was her providential calling to preserve "the last hope of human liberty in the world" (Hofstadter 1969, 181). In the face of such a threat, the common interest in preserving the cause of republicanism seemed clear. Partisan and ideological differences were temporarily set aside, and the nation's commitment to republicanism was renewed.

V

IF THE WAR revitalized the idea of a common interest that transcended other differences of opinion, it also accelerated forces that would eventually render that notion implausible. The embargo crippled American agriculture, which was highly dependent on the exportation of cotton and tobacco. At the same time, the forced development of domestic manufactures and the production of war matériel further undermined the agrarian basis of the reigning republican ideology.

No one understood this more clearly than Jefferson, who lamented: "Our enemy has indeed the consolation of Satan on removing our first parents from Paradise: from a peaceable and agricultural nation, he makes us a military and manufacturing one" (Marx 1964, 144).

Of course this economic development furthered the decline of deferential politics, as well as the growth of a lumpenproletariat distrusted by Federalists and Republicans alike (Kerber 1980). This was a dependent class of citizens, concentrated in the city, and prone to "mobbish" behavior. Nevertheless, its existence was generally admitted only indirectly, in the form of fears about the absence of virtue among "the people."

These developments were not always perceived to be permanent. The Old Republicans, for their part, hoped to reverse this process once the war was over. By that time, however, a new generation of western and Middle Atlantic Republicans controlled the Congress, and the Old Republicans, under the leadership of the Richmond Junto, were defeated at every turn in their effort to restore the pure republicanism of an earlier age. A protective tariff was adopted, the Bank was rechartered, internal improvements by the federal government were begun, and federal interference in states' slavery policies was initiated. Factions, especially sectional ones, were everywhere in evidence, and by 1824 Nathaniel Macon was led to conclude that "the opinions of Jefferson and those who were with him are forgot" and that the Constitution of the Republic was in peril (Schlesinger 1945, 28).

No longer united by an external threat to the security of the Republic, and no longer joined in opposition to the Federalists, the Republican party began to divide over issues of economic development. The conjuncture of economic and sectional interests involved in such issues as the tariff and internal improvements produced a virulent factionalism qualitatively distinct from that of 1807, when the *Quid* most actively opposed Jefferson's administration. At that time Jefferson rather sanguinely remarked that

I had always expected that when the republicans should have put down all things under their feet, they would schismatize among themselves. I had always expected, too, that whatever names the parties might bear, the real division would be into moderate and ardent republicanism. In this division there is no great evil—not even if the minority obtain the ascendancy by the accession of federal votes to their candidate; because this gives us one shade only, instead of another, of republicanism. (Hofstadter 1969, 168)

But Jefferson had not anticipated that economic differences of interest would become so important as to overshadow perceptions of a "common good" on which the Republic was founded. Yet this is precisely what was beginning to occur in the second and third decades of the nineteenth century. The functional and sectional diversification of the American economy, and the increasing involvement of the government in promoting certain interests over others, made it increasingly difficult to perceive a substantive common interest capable of uniting party and republic. The consensus ideal of republican politics, which presumed a common good, was rapidly becoming irrelevant to American politics and society (Wallace 1968; Hofstadter 1969).

The rhetoric of republicanism reflected this erosion of consensus in a peculiar way. To be sure, politicians and newspapers continued to preach the virtues of republicanism and decry the evils of aristocracy and unrestrained democracy (Morantz 1971). This was particularly evident in state constitutional debates over the extension of suffrage and elimination of property requirements for voting, which briefly revived the old dispute between "aristocratic" and "democratic" republicans (neither label was self-applied).

Nevertheless, these appeals to "true" republicanism took on an increasingly hollow tone as references to specific ideas gave way to invocations of the "principles of '98" or the "ideas of the Revolution." Such ritualistic usages made the rhetoric of republicanism available to virtually all of the diverse and competing interests contained in the party by submerging substantive differences in the solidarity of the past. This was particularly evident in intraparty disputes that took place in states like New York, where a new breed of professional politician challenged an older generation of notables for control of the party. Issues and principles were often overshadowed by questions of organization in such states, and campaigns took on decidedly "nonideological" tones, as Wallace (1968) notes. Platforms contained almost no substantive planks on issues such as internal improvements or expansion of the franchise. Campaigns consisted largely of efforts to capitalize on the early achievements of the Republican party. Broadsides asked: "Republicans, will you abandon that party which has done so much for your country? Remember the dying words of the brave Lawrence and 'Don't give up the Ship!!' " (ibid., 470). Similarly, Republicans were exhorted to "remember that republicans saved the nation from anarchy; that republicans stood firm in the 'trying times' of '98. . . . O ye patriots of '76! Ye preservers of Democracy in '98; Ye defenders of our rights in '12, '13, '14; come forth . . ." (ibid., 470).

To a significant extent this empty rhetoric unified a party that was deeply divided on substantive issues. In the absence of an opposition, dissent remained within the Republican organization, placing a tremendous strain on intraparty discourse. The resort to nonideological interpretations of republicanism was one way in which members responded to this strain. The consensus represented by the hegemony of the Republicans was, therefore, only an apparent one, and it eventually began to crumble under the pressure of internal divisions in the ranks of the party.

VI

REPUBLICAN RHETORIC would eventually prove unable to overcome the very real differences of opinion and interest within the Republican party. When that happened the nation would witness the creation of a new party system during the Age of Jackson, as we shall see in the next chapter. Before that could happen, however, the natural antipathy of republicans toward parties had to be overcome. Parties, after all, were *partisan* organizations, the very idea of which seemed hostile toward the common good. For that reason, parties were viewed with suspicion by nearly all republicans, who saw in them evidence of the existence of factions, and hence corruption in the body politic.

Monroe's quest for unanimity and his persistent efforts to accommodate all interests, even those of the Federalists, within the Republican party, represented the culmination of this sentiment, as Hofstadter (1969) demonstrates. Nevertheless, as deeply rooted as it was, this republican hostility toward parties began to weaken during the third decade of the nineteenth century. Partly this reflected the emergence of a new generation of political leaders steeped in party affairs. Whereas Washington and his immediate successors had had no previous experience in party politics, which might have tempered their fear of faction, this new generation came to political maturity in the midst of competition between Federalists and Republicans, and among Republicans themselves. That competition was often extremely tense and acrimonious, but the republic did survive, contrary to the older republicans' expectations and dire predictions. Consequently, parties were somewhat less fearsome to this new generation of politicians, according to Wallace (1968) and Hofstadter (1969).

Many observers have remarked on the significance of this generational difference in experience with political parties in order to explain the persistence of parties into the nineteenth century and their subsequent regeneration in the "second party system" of the Jacksonian period. However, it was not just experience with parties that was significant in this respect; it was experience with a new and different kind of political party that was important. The parties of the so-called "first party system" were "interior" parties, as McCormick (1967), following Duverger, notes. That is, they were legislative factions dominated by personalities, with no substantial popular followings (for which reason some historians argue that they were not really parties at all, at least in the modern sense of that term). The rivalry between these parties, so obvious in the wrangling between Hamilton and Jefferson during the 1790s, was no doubt what Washington had in mind when excoriating the mischief of parties in his Farewell Address.

However, the nature and organization of parties was changing during the early years of the nineteenth cetury. The Republicans, and to a somewhat lesser extent the Federalists, were becoming popular organizations, insofar as they were developing mass bases.[8] Whereas the interior parties of the late eighteenth century seldom appealed to the masses for support, except in extraordinary cases such as the campaign for ratification, the mobilization of the electorate became an increasingly important aspect of party politics in the nineteenth century. Goodman (1967) and McCormick (1967) emphasize the significance of competitive presidential elections in this regard, but Williamson (1960) and Morantz (1971) describe similar effects originating from state constitutional debates over the extension of suffrage.

The transformation of interior, legislative factions into mass political organizations is perhaps most clearly visible in the internal struggles for control of state Republican parties during this period, for it is at that level that the battle between an older generation fearful of parties and a younger group of professional party politicians assumes human form. The initial groundwork for this transformation was laid by the Democratic-Republican Societies and, to a lesser extent, the Jeffer-

---

[8] Banner (1970, 132) explains that the Federalists, too, began to "modernize" their party after 1800. After briefly flirting with the idea of controlling the leveling influence of *democratic* republicanism via suffrage restrictions, they sought ways of channeling popular participation into "safe" areas, and that required a disciplined party organization with a mass constituency. The cultivation of a popular press with influence over public opinion, the resort to a caucus system, and the exploitation of their clerical ties were essential to this task, but in the process the Federalist party itself came to be at least partially democratized.

sonian Republicans, during the 1790s. As I showed in the preceding chapter, the Federalists attempted to discredit their opponents by labelling them democrats, hoping to capitalize on the unfavorable connotations of that term. However, their Republican opponents successfully countered that strategy by linking democracy to the ideas of popular sovereignty and political equality.

Still, this was largely a defensive measure on the part of the Republicans. They did not propose democracy as an alternative to republicanism. Rather, they minimized the damage to their position caused by the democratic label and then proceeded to launch a counter offensive of their own by denouncing the antirepublican sentiments of the Federalists.

After the conclusions of the War of 1812, however, some Republicans began to use democracy and its rhetoric as offensive weapons against the remnants of deferential politics in America. This was evident in several of the state constitutional debates mentioned previously. But the most significant appeals to democracy issued from intraparty feuds between professionals and notables. The case of New York is instructive in this regard, for it shows the way in which the idea of legitimate opposition, embodied in a party system, was grafted onto an otherwise hostile republican ideology.

In New York, the ideological justification of parties involved three distinct tasks. During the first phase, the new generation of professional politicians attempted to distinguish parties from factions, so as to exempt them from traditional republican proscriptions against the mischief of faction. This was accomplished in a most ingenious fashion, as Van Buren and the Albany Regency played upon public fears of faction while localizing their effect. Specifically, the Regency portrayed the supporters of DeWitt Clinton, an "old guard" notable steeped in the politics of an interior Republican party, as a faction antithetical to republican politics. At the same time, they succeeded in establishing their own republican credentials and their legitimate right to leadership of the New York Republicans.

During this phase of the struggle between the Clintonians and the Bucktails, as the former disdainfully called the Regency politicians, the identification of the Republican party with the republic itself was an important rhetorical resource.[9] Anything that threatened to corrupt the party also threatened ipso facto to destroy the Republic for which it stood. Insofar as Clinton was disposed to treat the party as an organization dedicated to his personal aggrandizement, the Bucktails argued, his faction was intrinsically antirepublican and therefore merited the full contempt reserved for enemies of the Republic.[10]

The Bucktails employed the rhetoric of democracy and egalitarianism as a means of rallying support for this position (Wallace 1968). The Bucktails claimed that "parties" centered around personalities like Clinton were not parties at all, but factions, and aristocratic ones at that. They were nothing more than political fiefdoms organized for the personal benefit of their leaders. According to the Albany *Argus*, they were "highly prejudicial to the interests of the people, and if successful [would] have a tendency to subvert our republican form of government" (ibid., 458).

The proper form of political organization in a republic, the Bucktails argued, was not that of personal faction but a true political party. Such a party was not the property of a man or

[9] Tammany Hall representatives to the 1817 session of the state assembly wore insignia, one of which was part of a deer's tail worn in the hat. This "Bucktail" was soon used to designate the opponents of DeWitt Clinton's canal policy, who had their headquarters at the Albany Regency (Mackenzie 1846, 50).

[10] Wilson (1984, 28) traces the identification of party and polity to Jefferson, who bequeathed it to Van Buren. Jefferson always expected party differences of the Whig and Tory sort to exist, because some trusted in the virtue of free citizens, while others did not. For this reason, Jefferson supposed that only one truly *popular* party could exist, and that it was the Republican party. In a democratic republic, therefore, the Republican party stood for the nation as a whole; in an essential sense it *was* the polity, by virtue of its confidence in the citizenry, over and against those who inclined toward an "aristocratic" republic dominated by notables.

family; it transcended any one of its members in being responsible to its membership as a whole. For the Bucktails, then, "the cardinal maxim with the great republican party [should be] . . . always to seek for, and when ascertained, always to follow the will of the majority" of its adherents (ibid., 458).

This found institutional expression in mechanisms of party discipline like the caucus doctrine, which required minority factions to submit to the will of a majority. Wallace emphasizes the moral, as opposed to the tactical, dimension of this mechanism:

> support of the caucus was also a matter of principle. Van Buren tied the basic republican ethos of majoritarianism securely to the caucus system: minority status was not a legitimate basis for fleeing the party standard; bolting was to be stigmatized as 'bad faith.' Were the Bucktails to violate their own conception of the behavior proper to the members of a true party, they would destroy their credentials as politicians of a new breed and relegate themselves to the status of a faction, indistinguishable from their Clintonian opponents. (ibid., 463)

Because of this the Bucktails' acquiescence in Clinton's gubernatorial nomination in 1817, in contrast to the Clintonians' "bad faith" bolt from the party in 1819, gained them an impregnable moral advantage. Their unwavering support of the majoritarian ethic, which was justified in terms of its ability to ensure party leaders' adherence to the will of the people, established them as the true party of the people, and from this blow the Clintonians never recovered.

VII

HAVING DISTINGUISHED their conception of a proper political party from the common understanding of "faction" the Bucktails were able to redirect some of the fear and suspicion that might otherwise have been aimed against them. This made it possible to undertake a second phase of the argument, in which a positive justification of parties was developed. In brief, this involved the construction of an argument to the effect that a proper political party was indispensable for the cultivation of civic virtue among the citizenry, and that it was therefore a bulwark of republican politics, rather than a threat to it, as were factions.

The previously mentioned instruments of party discipline were important in this connection, since they were the means by which individual members' interests and preferences were subordinated to those of the collectivity. Adherence to the decisions of the caucus represented a willingness to place common interests above personal satisfactions. It was to act in a virtuous manner, insofar as the exercise of virtue was, in traditional republican thinking, associated with the performance of duties that were essential to the preservation of the commonwealth. In this way, civic virtue came to be identified with party regularity.

Thus, the *Argus* claimed that "those who refuse to 'abide by the fairly expressed will of the majority' . . . forfeit all claims to the character of republicans and become recreant to the principles of that party" (ibid., 458–459). In order to ensure this responsiveness to its members, the Bucktails propounded a new code of political ethics, which dictated that "every man should sacrifice his own private opinions and feelings to the good of his party and the man who will not do it is unworthy to be supported by a party for any post of honor or profit" (ibid., 462).

The caucus was vital to the success of the Republican party, and by implication, the health of the American polity. "Whenever [the party] has been wise enough to employ the caucus or convention system, and to use in good faith the influence it is capable of imparting to the popular cause, [it] has been successful, and it has been defeated whenever that system has been laid aside or employed unfairly" (Van Buren 1867, 5–6). For that reason, Van Buren even opposed Andrew Jackson in 1824, preferring to support William Crawford, the caucus candidate. As the Albany *Argus* explained, Jackson's repudiation of "King Caucus" was a

> course . . . pleasant to all who strive for the destruction of the democratic party . . . They [Jackson's supporters] profess to be *republicans*, and yet they support *a man who is known to have been* ALWAYS A FEDERALIST—they profess to be the friends of the people, and yet, in Tennessee, as in New York, they have always resisted the equal and just rights of the people, and the extension of those privileges which are most valuable to them. It is the duty of every republican to expose these contradictions and inconsistencies of conduct and profession; and, as far as possible, counteract the purposes they are intended to answer, namely, THE PROSTRATION OF THE REPUBLICAN PARTY, *the subversion of the real interests of the people*, AND THE ELEVATION OF THE OLD ARISTOCRACY, *and the* disappointed, uneasy men of all parties. (Mackenzie 1846, 79)

The expectation that virtuous citizens would by their actions defer to considerations of the commonweal was hardly new to American politics. As Pole (1967) argues, "deferential politics" was pervasive during the Revolutionary period. But deference under the first party system meant deference to social notables who often became the leading personalities of interior parties, whereas deference under the second party system meant deference to the will of the majority of party members. This was the sense in which Van Buren and the Regency could maintain that party regularity and civic virtue were one and the same thing, against the Clintonian declamations against the "slavish" obedience of rank and file members.

In this way the glorification of intraparty democracy as a means of ridding republican America of the last vestiges of deferential politics eventually began to replace the rhetoric of republicanism in New York and other states. The practices that were said to define a true republican party, as opposed to those associated with personal factions, eventually became the very principles of the party itself, as Mordecai Noah explained: "Regular nominations . . . are not so much the engines as they are the principles of a party, because any system which tends to unite the people, to give them their rights, to promote harmony and unanimity, to effect reconciliation and submission to the will of the majority, and a relinquishment of private attachments, such a system we call a cardinal principle in the administration of a representative government" (Wallace 1968, 469). Thus, what began as an effort to democratize republicanism concluded in the elevation of democratic principles to a status equal to that of republicanism itself, as the former came to be perceived as essential to the latter.

VIII

ONCE VIRTUE and party regularity were made synonymous it was possible to argue that a truly Republican party was essential to the health of the republic. However, the Bucktails went even further, claiming that multiple parties were necessary. This pushed the argument concerning the legitimacy of parties into its third and decisive phase, in which the defense of "party" over and against "faction" became the defense of a party *system* as intrinsically republican.

This claim was defended on the grounds that parties were capable of transcending factions, particularly of the sectional variety. Partisan differences promised to ameliorate the truly dangerous divisions between personal factions, so rightly feared by the Founding Fathers. And they offered some hope for transcending the sectional differences in the nation that were growing ever more apparent. By substituting differences of principle for those of person and section, parties might bind the Republic together, even as they divided it along different, less dangerous, lines.

However, the defense was also based on the recognition that interparty competition was necessary in order to instill party discipline, and hence to inculcate virtue in the citizenry. The nonpartisan policy of the "era of good feeling" had led to disastrous policies of party amalgamation, the Bucktails argued. The quest for unanimity that characterized the administration of Jefferson, Madison, and Monroe failed to allow for the expression of legitimate differences of opinion and interest, even as it permitted the Federalists to infiltrate and corrupt the true friends of the Republic, i.e. the Republican party. It was far better, they argued, to acknowledge and express differences of principle than to ignore them in the interest of a false unity.

Increased competition between parties would also have the salutary effect of drawing a larger number of citizens into the political arena. Van Buren argued that party differences "rouse the sluggish to exertion, give increased energy to the most active intellect, excite a salutary vigilance over our public functionaries, and prevent the apathy which has proved the ruin of Republics" (ibid., 489).

Moreover, the public debate between parties would serve to refine the issues and enlarge the degree of acceptance of policies adopted in response to them, in much the same way that Madison had hoped that the election of wise representatives would. Thus, Governor Enos Throop argued that "organized parties watch and scan each other's doings, the public mind is instructed by ample discussions of public measures, and acts of violence are restrained by the convictions of the people, that the prevailing measures are the results of enlightened reason" (ibid., 48). Van Buren added that when "honest differences of opinion . . . are discussed and the principles of contending parties are supported with candor, fairness, and moderation, the very discord which is thus produced, may in a government like ours, be conducive to the public good" (ibid., 489).

All of this was given further credence by a conscious effort to reinterpret the short history of the republic in terms of party competition (Wilson 1984, 29). Van Buren's posthumously published *Inquiry into the Origin and Course of Political Parties in the United States* portrayed the history of the republic in terms of periods of partisan vitality, in which the health of the polity was assured, and periods of civic lethargy, in which the republic was in peril. In this story, even the Federalists, although branded disloyal, were seen as offering something useful to the republic by their participation in the spirited debate over the meaning of the public good and the best means of achieving it (Hofstadter 1969).

In one respect this argument was the most difficult to make, since it required the abandonment of the long-cherished equation of party and polity under the Republican label. Once the existence of other parties was conceded to be necessary for the instillation of party discipline, the legitimacy of opposition was established, and the Republican party could no longer claim to be the sole party of the republic. To be sure, it could still claim to be the best party, and Van Buren and his allies probably felt that that was more than sufficient to maintain their majoritarian status. Still, this marked a departure from the past in which Republicans and Federalists alike had branded each other disloyal and seditious.

On the other hand, the argument that balanced competition between the great divisions of the populace promoted the public good had precedent. Madison himself had made that argument in *Federalist 10*, as we saw in the last chapter. The extension of that argument to extraconstitutional arrangements, i.e. a party system, could draw upon that sentiment. It could also invoke the Antifederalist and Jeffersonian concern over the Federalists' inattention to the means by which civic virtue was to be inculcated in an extended republic governed by representative institutions. By presenting parties as organizations in which citizens learned to act virtuously, they became a necessary aspect of republican politics.

Thus, the Bucktails' rejection of the consensus ideal and the one party politics entailed by it required a sophisticated defense of a competitive party system (Hofstadter 1969; Wallace 1968). They recognized the value of sustained opposition as an extraconstitutional means of ensuring the existence of a citizenry both willing and able to hold government in check. Competitive parties would keep people informed about government and would actively engage them in the political affairs of the nation. Hence, competitive parties supplied the missing element of Federalist and Jeffersonian theories, namely, the means for ensuring a continuously vigilant citizenry.[11]

IX

PARTIES, THEN, represented an organizational solution to the mischief of faction, which the Federalists had failed to contain with their institutional remedies. Thus, the Regency politicians, and Van Buren in particular, embraced Machiavelli's insight into healthy conflict in a republic. As Shumer (1979) explains, conflict per se need not be a sign of corruption in the body politic. It may be genuinely political, in the classical sense, expressing legitimate differences of interest. Only when conflict turns into domination by factions does it become harmful. Hence, the idea of legitimate opposition, and its incarnation in a competitive party system, was potentially a way of preserving republican politics in an extensive and diversified nation.

The idea of a party *system* did not, of course, immediately displace the consensus ideal of Republican politics. The presidential election of 1828, for example, pitted the National Republicans and John Quincy Adams against the "Republican Supporters of General Jackson." The former represented a wing of the Republican party still strongly committed to the idea of a common national interest, to be realized through implementation of Henry Clay's American System. The latter, by contrast, consisted of a broad coalition of the new, professional politicians and the remnants of the Old Republican faction of the Republican party. Their candidate was an avowedly anticaucus, even antiparty, war hero who had more

[11] Madison's concern over this problem was mentioned in Chapter Two. Jefferson, too, was worried about the decline of vigilance, as his generational theory of revolutions and his system for ward elections suggest (Wills 1979). These "solutions" were never put into practice, however.

affinities with the Old Republicanism than with Van Buren and the Regency.

Nevertheless, the campaign of 1828 marked the decline of consensus politics, and the legitimation of the politics of contestation. A new *procedural* consensus was beginning to emerge, even as the older, *substantive* consensus was beginning to dissolve, and the uneasy relationship between the two informed virtually all political discussion for the next quarter of a century or more. In the next chapter, we shall examine the ways in which this tension between democratic means and republican ends was addressed by the various parties in the debate.

CHAPTER FOUR

Jacksonian Democracy

I

"To BALANCE a large state or society," wrote Hamilton, re-calling the widsom of Hume, "is a work of so great difficulty that no human genius, however comprehensive, is able, by the mere dint of reason and reflection, to effect it. The judg-ments of many unite in the work; EXPERIENCE must guide their labor; TIME must bring it to perfection; and FEELING of inconvenience must correct the mistakes which they inevita-bly fall into in their first trials and experiments" (Rossiter 1961, 526–527).

Balancing a large society is even more difficult when it .is undergoing a continual process of change. As societies grow and the interests included in them begin to multiply, the task of balancing becomes problematic, as does the republican politics that depends on that balance for its preservation. At such times, it is indeed reasonable to speak of political crises in the history of that society or state.

In the United States the crisis of republican politics oc-curred during the Age of Jackson, as the nation's citizens struggled to adapt their political institutions to the changed circumstances of the early nineteenth century. The most im-portant change in circumstance, of course, was the increasing heterogeneity of interests in the republic. When Tocqueville visited the United States in 1831 it was a vastly different na-tion from that observed by an earlier generation of French-men. The admission of Missouri in 1821 brought the number of states in the Union to twenty-four, and Arkansas and Mich-igan were added before the second volume of *Democracy in America* was published. The population of the nation was more than three times as large as it was in 1790, and its density was half again as great, despite the fact that the land area of the nation had more than doubled in size (*Statistical Abstract 1970*).

Moreover, the Union was becoming culturally and economically heterogeneous. The first wave of German immigration was just beginning to come ashore, soon to be followed by a massive wave of Irish Catholic immigrants. The Germans by and large joined the ranks of agricultural producers, while the Irish often provided the unskilled labor for a growing industrial sector of the economy (Kelley 1979). Commerce and manufacturing were thriving, and the nation was clearly in a stage preparatory to the "take-off" period of economic development (Rostow 1960).[1]

Coupled with this development was the emergence of a new form of political organization, the mass party. The Democracy of Jackson was the prototype for this way of organizing men and interests, and its remarkable success forced its would-be competitors to follow suit. As a result, a party *system* began to take shape, promising to crystallize public opinion and institutionalize political opposition (Hofstadter 1969). Yet this new vehicle for "aggregating interests"—the mass political party—also promised to alter the very foundations of republican politics in America. Henceforth, the conflict of organized interests replaced the ideal of consensual politics, raising once again the issue of corruption in the republic.

For many republicans, especially those of an older generation, the presence of partisan conflict on an extended scale and over a protracted period of time meant that the republic was succumbing to virulent factionalism. The fact that this occurred during a period of relative prosperity, or "luxury" as it was often called, and centered on issues of "public economy" only confirmed this suspicion. As William Leggett observed:

[1] Cf. Meyers's (1957) review of the modernization theses of Hammond, Redlich, Hacker, and Cochrane.

In common times the strife of parties is the mere struggle of ambitious leaders for power; now they are the deadly contests of the whole mass of the people whose primary interests are implicated in the event because the Government has usurped and exercised the power of legislating on their private affairs. The selfish feeling has been so strongly called into action by their abuse of authority as almost to overpower the social feeling which it should be the object of a good government to foster by every means in its power. (Blau 1954, 76)

This interpretation was thoroughly traditional. As we have seen, the sensitivity of republicans to corruption, and their advocacy of vigilance as a way of detecting and containing it, was a vital aspect of the republican tradition.[2] The apparent reduction of politics to a struggle over the spoils of office, and the corresponding diversion of public resources to partisan and personal uses was, after all, a characteristic feature of corrupt republics. History was replete with well-known examples of once-glorious polities ruined by this traditional disorder of republican states. For that reason, it was relatively easy to perceive the United States and its development in these terms, and to assimilate events to the timeless cycle of political degeneration that seemed to govern history.

However, there were those who rejected the inevitability of this cycle. For example, Professor George Tucker of the University of Virginia, writing in the *American Review*, rejected the necessity of political decline. Such a notion, he argued, was based on an incorrect analogy with laws governing animal life, whereas "governments may be more correctly compared with species than with individuals—while the lat-

---

[2] Some historians, e.g. Richard Hofstadter (1979), ascribe this sort of perspective to a "paranoid style of politics," particularly where it is accompanied by conspiratorial accounts of the factional usurpation of political power. Howe (1980) rightly objects to this characterization, noting that it unfairly reduces a complex social outlook to a simple psychological pathology, thereby denying the integrity of that *Weltanschauung*.

ter flourish for a time and then pass away, the former have the power of perpetual renovation" (Somkin 1967, 65). Hence, the fate of nations was subject to the wisdom of political action.

Tucker's argument was a generalized statement of a more commonly made claim to the effect that America's fate, at least, was unique. "The actual state and probable future prospects of our country, resemble those of no other land, and are without a parallel in past history," commented Gulian Verplanck in an address to students of Union College in 1836 (ibid., 68). By implication, the laws that governed the natural history of other republics need not apply to the United States; her future could not be inferred safely from their experiences.

The ideological origins of this sense of historical innocence are varied and complex; Lewis (1955) and Somkin (1967), among others, provide sensitive accounts of them. For our purposes, it is sufficient to observe that the brief for American "exceptionalism" placed the new nation outside of time, and so exempted the United States from the cycle of rise and decline, or foundation and decay. The providential bounty of the continent made the prospect of prosperity without foreseeable limits seem plausible; the mission of the country, indeed its "manifest destiny," was to enlarge its territory, multiply its population, develop its wealth, and serve as a beacon of republican liberty to all the world. Thus, expansion provided a spatial solution to the problem of republican temporality: it suspended time, and so eased the sense of foreboding uncertainty that, to borrow from Somkin, made the republican eagle unquiet during this period.[3]

To be sure, the possibility of progress conveyed by arguments concerning American exceptionalism did not *guarantee* the survival of the republic. Providence had blessed the for-

---

[3] There were those who dissented from this portrayal of a republic outside of time. Melville, for instance, frequently reminded Americans that "each age thinks its own eternal"—an error that blinded them to the fact that all men were "born with halters round their necks" (Somkin 1967, 88–89).

tunes of the republic, but it was the mission of virtuous citizens to exploit fully the unique opportunities open to them, as Machiavelli himself had argued. It is against this background that the "factionalism" of the period should be understood.

For the Jacksonians, the country's mission entailed an active policy of expansion, in which personal and public interests were jointly served. All obstacles to expansion had to be removed in order to fulfill the manifest destiny of the republic. Those who opposed expansion, and who resisted efforts to remove purported obstacles to "enlarging the area of freedom," were enemies of the republic. Their Whig opponents' support for an American System of privilege that shackled further development of the sort advocated by the Democrats displayed a willingness to subvert the prospects for establishing a republic outside of time so as to preserve a deferential structure of politics in which the Whig faction prevailed.

The Whigs for their part insisted that the fulfillment of the nation's mission, and therefore the maintenance of the republic, required a different course of action. They feared a majoritarian faction that seemed bent on destroying the democratic republic of the United States because of a misplaced (and entirely self-serving) overemphasis on the "democratic" modifier in that phrase. They stressed the "republican" noun, so to speak, and promoted an American System of internal improvements—both material and spiritual—that was calculated to "elevate" the masses by reinstilling a commitment to the common good. The inculcation of virtue was for them a way of making the democracy safe for the republic.

Thus, political discourse in the Age of Jackson centered on the relationship between the "democratic" and "republican" elements of democratic republicanism, and the appropriate means of reconciling them in practice so as to fulfill America's "mission" on earth.[4] The Democrats eventually triumphed by

[4] An interesting example of the fluid politics of this period may be found in publishers' treatment of Tocqueville's *Democracy in America*, which re-

virtue of their electoral prowess, or at least that is how most historians have interpreted the Age of Jackson. However, their success was greatly aided by the disintegration of the Whig party as its vision of an American commonwealth exploded under the pressure of sectional antagonisms. It was then left to Calhoun to propose a radical reconstitution of the republic that required the assent of "concurrent majorities" on decisions that affected the fate of the republic. The rejection of Calhoun's scheme left the nation with no balance point, and the same forces of expansion that promised to make the Union a republic outside of time began to generate tensions that inexorably pulled the nation back into the orbit of political and republican decay.

II

THE POPULAR REACTION against the politics of deference culminated in J. Q. Adams's crushing defeat in 1828. Adams's presidency represented the antithesis of the new "republican" philosophy of popular control. Conceived in the infamy of an alleged "corrupt bargain," it symbolized the perversion of republican government under the old style of politics in which personalities, rather than "the people," dominated government. Adams's impolitic message to Congress in support of Clay's American System, in which he urged representatives not to be "palsied by the will of our constituents" in considering matters of national importance, only confirmed the unpopularity of this way of governing.

In the end, however, Adams and his National Republicans were undone less by what he said or did than by the new techniques of popular mobilization they disdained. The supporters of Jackson used the rhetoric and methods of popular democracy to destroy the old style of personal politics, as we

corded, without comment, the coexistence of democracy and republicanism in the United States. By 1849 Tocqueville's masterpiece began to appear regularly under the title *The Republic of the United States of America and Its Political Institutions Reviewed and Examined* (Tocqueville 1948, 388). Barnes especially seemed to favor this title over *Democracy in America*.

saw in the last chapter. Their enormous success eventually
forced their opponents to adopt similar methods and appeals
in order to compete for voters' allegiance, thereby institution-
alizing a system of competitive mass parties (Hofstadter
1969). To be sure, this process was not completed until Van
Buren succeeded Jackson, for only then did electoral competition extend to the state and local levels (McCormick
1967). It took even longer for constituency-oriented patronage systems and legislative coalitions to form, which is why
Formisano (1974) describes this period in terms of "deferential participation," capturing the transitional nature of party
politics in the Jacksonian period. Indeed the two major parties seemed to reflect their ambiguity in their differing conceptions of "party" (Marshall 1969). The institutionalization
of party politics was, therefore, a considerably drawn-out
process.

However, the Jacksonian movement was not directed only
against political privilege. It was a reaction against another
kind of privilege as well, namely the "corrupt bargain" between commerce and government embodied in the American
System. The postwar collaboration between business and
government in the construction of internal improvements and
the establishment of credit had produced an extensive network of governmentally sanctioned economic privilege. Increasingly, farmers, laborers, and entrepreneuers found their
opportunities for advance blocked by an interlocking system
of exclusive monopolies, joint stock corporations, and commercial credit arrangements. Moreover, they found themselves periodically victimized by panics and recessions
brought on by speculation and monetary manipulation (Hofstadter 1948, 58).

Consequently, Jackson's pledge to eliminate privilege and
"extend the area of freedom" appealed to the "common
man's" economic aspirations, as well as his political sensitivi-
ties. The Jacksonian movement was, therefore, simultaneously a phase in the expansion of democracy and laissez-faire
capitalism (ibid., 56). It effectively unleashed the energies of

acquisitive individualism that had been increasingly frustrated by the contraints of mercantile policies and ushered in
an era of expansion and "manifest destiny."[5]

Nevertheless, the movement that wrought such fundamental changes in the nature of American politics and society was
profoundly *restorative* in cast (Kelley 1979; Meyers 1957).
The Jacksonians cherished the ideal of a chaste republican
order uncorrupted by the greed, extravagant materialism,
and inequality associated with industry and commerce (Meyers 1957, 12). And they justified their actions as necessary for
the restoration of their forefathers' republic and its sturdy
yeoman virtues.

To be sure, the Jacksonians amended Jefferson's notion of
the virtuous classes to include mechanics and laborers, as
well as planters and farmers. These people were the "bone
and sinew of the country," according to Jackson, because they
were involved in the actual production of goods and services.
The unvirtuous classes were those, e.g. bankers and speculators, who were not directly productive and were indeed
parasitic. Or, as William Leggett put it, "The one party is
composed, in a great measure, of the farmers, mechanics,
laborers, and other producers of the middling and lower
classes, according to the common gradation by the scale of
wealth, and the other of the consumers, the rich, the proud,
the privileged, of those who, if our Government were con-
verted into an aristocracy, would become our dukes, lords,
marquises, and baronets" (Blau 1954, 67).

Thus, the old association of virtue and freehold, by which

[5] Apparently, John L. O'Sullivan, editor of the *U.S. Magazine and Democratic Review* (which articulated the Jacksonian line) popularized the
phrase: "It is by right of our manifest destiny to overspread and to possess
the whole of the Continent which Providence has given us for the development of the great experiment of liberty and federative self-government en-
trusted to us" (Weinberg 1935, 145). Hence, a "manifest" destiny was added
to the "self-evident" truths of the Declaration, in a political rhetoric of ostensibly obvious considerations. The open texture of such claims, which permits various interpretations, may be a logical vice, but it is clearly a political
virtue!

those who owned land came to have a "stake" in the commonwealth, was substantially altered by the Jacksonians. Those who possessed forms of property other than land were brought into the fold of virtuous citizens, so long as they worked hard, saved, and invested their money in productive (as distinct from speculative) ventures. This dedication to accumulation served individuals' interests even as it contributed to the well-being of the commonwealth, and in this way the pursuits of private and public interests were not only reconciled, but fused into a dynamic moral force for expansion (Berthoff 1979).

Because of this, Tocqueville (1969) claimed that "individualism" was less pernicious in America than in Europe, where it was roundly criticized by communitarian thinkers of all persuasions (Lukes 1973). Though it might gain widespread acceptance among the public, individualism was not a philosophy *of* the public, as was republicanism. Individualism was an ideology of privatism, counseling a withdrawal from public affairs, contrary to republican injunctions concerning the need for an active and vigilant citizenry. Hence its emergence was generally considered a development highly uncongenial to republicanism.

However, the free enterprise advocated by the Jacksonians was not oriented exclusively toward the pursuit of self-interest. Rather, it emphasized the pursuit of self-interest *properly understood*. It was enlightened by considerations of the general interest, the satisfaction of which was both a condition for and consequence of the gratification of individual interests:

> The common man in the United States has understood the influence of the general prosperity on his own happiness, an idea so simple but nevertheless so little understood by the people. Moreover, he is accustomed to regard that prosperity as his own work. So he sees the public fortune as his own, and he works for the good of the state, not only

from duty or pride, but, I dare almost say, from greed.
(Tocqueville 1969, 237)

It was precisely for this reason that the Jacksonians condemned those who pursued a course of idleness and vice. The
life of luxury and ease, no matter how comfortable, was not
in anyone's self-interest *rightly understood*. It subtracted
from the general welfare by diverting resources from useful
ends and betrayed a moral turpitude inimical to the health of
the body politic (Berthoff 1979).

The capture of political institutions by men of this ilk, and
the concomitant perversion of the commonwealth by means
of a corrupt bargain, were evident in the power of banks and
speculators over yeoman citizens, according to the Jacksonians. A return to minimalist government was the Jacksonian
remedy for "extending the area of freedom." An energetic
federal government, acting on behalf of special interests, had
undermined the workings of "the voluntary principle" by
which society's "floating atoms will distribute and combine
themselves, as we see in the beautiful natural process of crystallization, into a far more perfect and harmonious result than
if government, with its 'fostering hand,' undertake to disturb,
under the plea of directing, the process (*U.S. Magazine* 1838,
7). Indeed, "legislation has been the fruitful parent of nine-
tenths of all the evil, moral and physical, by which mankind
has been afflicted since the creation of the world, and by
which human nature has been self-degraded, fettered, and
oppressed." Since "natural laws which will establish themselves and find their own level are the best laws," it was apparent that the best government is that which governs least
(ibid., 9).

If the return to minimalist government was the key to restoring the natural processes of social regulation, it was first
necessary to wrest control of the federal government from the
hands of those privileged interests it served. The Jacksonians
seized on the methods of popular democracy as a means to
achieve this goal. Free suffrage and majority rule were, for
them, vehicles by which the people might use the power of

numbers to offset the power of wealth in order to regain control of government so as to restrict its sphere of corrupting influence. The irresistible force of "the democracy" was to be turned against the politics of privilege, and the people themselves would renew the republican basis of American politics.

"The democracy" of course referred to common men, not the notables of the Old Republic. Therefore, it retained its connotations of class rule, though the class of virtuous commoners was defined in nearly universal terms, excluding only nonproducer classes. The Democracy was the organized expression of "the democracy;" it was the party that might serve as the governing agent of "the democracy" and its allies. The Democracy would restore virtuous men to their rightful place in the republic, and in so doing, restore virtue to the republic polity.

During the ten-year struggle against the banking system, the importance of the party took on special significance. The successive battles over the Bank charter, removal of deposits, and the independent treasury convinced many Democrats of the need for a permanent opposition to the monied interests. The party came to be seen as indispensable to republican politics: "We believe, then, in the principle of *democratic republicanism*, in its strongest and purest sense . . . [and] we consider the preservation of the present ascendancy of the democratic party as a great, if not vital, importance to the future destinies of this holy cause" (ibid., 2, 9–10).

The survival of the party as the instrument of the people's will was, therefore, inextricably linked to the success of the republican cause by the rhetoricians of the Democratic party, who used the imagery of the "Monster Bank" and the "Money Power" to great advantage in their efforts to mobilize the democracy. Democratic means of achieving republican ends began to acquire a legitimacy of their own and eventually came to rival those ends as the basic principles of the party of Jackson.

Nowhere is this process of displacement of ends by means more evident than in the evolution of their party label. The original "Republican Supporters of General Jackson" came to be known as "Democratic Republicans," and eventually just "Democrats" as the methods they advocated became identified with the cause of popular sovereignty against that of wealth and entrenched privilege.

The Democratic label, with its emphasis on procedural questions, was useful for another reason as well. It encompassed the aspirations of sectional factions within the party that agreed on their opposition to political and economic privilege, but disagreed on substantive matters like the tariff and internal improvements. Jackson's opposition to the tariff and internal improvements and his deflationary policies of hard money were not popular in the West, which desired expansionary and inflationary actions (Schlesinger 1945). Moreover, the South was growing increasingly defensive on the institution of slavery, now threatened by the admission of western "free states." Hence, support for popular sovereignty became the lowest common denominator for a Democratic party composed of interests seeking liberation from a variety of sectionally specific restraints on the "will of the people."

III

NOT ALL who shared the aspirations of the Jacksonians believed in the liberating potential of the Democracy and its methods. Some, including Orestes Brownson, felt that Democrats placed too much confidence in the efficacy of political reforms and were far too ready to conclude that "if we only once succeed in establishing democracy as a form of government . . . the end [liberty] will follow as a matter of course" (Brownson 1882–1887, 15:279). Such reasoning, Brownson argued, could only lead to the premature death of the democratic movement in the United States, for it seriously underestimated the difficulty of achieving liberty and justice in a fundamentally undemocratic society. Until that society was itself democratized, Brownson held out little hope for the successful operation of popular forms of government.[6]

[6] The undemocratic nature of society was a common theme of fiction during these years. The literature of this period emphasized the corruption of

Brownson's assessment of the undemocratic nature of American society was based on his perception of the impoverished condition of the laboring classes and the political implications thereof:

> No one can observe the signs of the times with much care, without perceiving that a crisis as to the relation of wealth and labor is approaching. . . . The old war between the King and the Barons is well-nigh ended, and so is that between the Barons and the Merchants and Manufacturers— landed capital and commercial capital. The business man has become the peer of my lord. And now commences the new struggle between the operative and his employer, between wealth and labor. Every day does this struggle extend further and wax stronger and fiercer; what or when the end will be God only knows. (Brownson 1840, 366)

This "new struggle between the operative and his employer" reflected the growing division of modern society into two classes, one of which owned the means of production, and the other of which performed the labor of production. The Old Republic had been founded on a one-class society in which ownership and labor were combined in the hands of a substantial body of yeoman farmers.[7] It was this unity of ownership and labor that constituted the special virtue of agrarianism and sustained the commonwealth by maintaining a condition of equality. With the emergence of industry and commercial agriculture, however, that unity had been de-

---

the democracy by existing social arrangements. Ziff suggests that both Cooper and Melville wrote as if the democratic character of the "common man" were natural, so that he was someone "on whom a [democratic] society could possibly be built; but he was not, however, its result, and indeed that society, as constituted, threatened rather than enhanced him" (1981, 129). For both, society corrupted the naturally democratic character of man, as revealed in the persons of the frontiersman and seaman, neither of whom was "in" society, or in time, for that matter.

[7] Since private property was an essential feature of the Old Republic it could not be classless. However, the republic could be a one-class society in which all, or nearly all, were "independent proprietors." On the distinction between class, one-class, and classless societies, see Macpherson (1977).

stroyed, and the egalitarian basis of the republic undone (ibid.).

The replacement of harmonious relations between citizens of roughly equal status and condition by conflictual relations between a dispossessed class of laborers and their wealthy overseers was particularly evident in the system of wage labor, which Brownson compared unfavorably with the southern system of slave labor: "One thing is certain; that of the amount actually produced by the operative, he retains a less proportion than it costs the master to feed, clothe and lodge his slave. Wages is a cunning device of the devil, for the benefit of tender consciences, who would retain all the advantages of the slave system, without the expense, trouble and odium of being slave-holders" (ibid., 370).

The existence of such gross material inequalities implied that proposals for moral and political reform were, by themselves, insufficiently radical: "What we contend is not, that free trade, universal suffrage, universal education, and religious culture, are not essential, indispensable means to the social regeneration we are in pursuit of; but that, if we stop with them, and leave the material order of society untouched, they will prove inadequate" (ibid., 476). The success of these other reforms depended, according to Brownson, on the prior elevation of the laboring classes to the status of independent proprietors, i.e. on the reunification of proprietary and labor functions. Only in this way could the fundamental equality of condition that characterized the early years of the republic be restored.[8]

Brownson was not certain how this reunification might be achieved, largely because he was never entirely clear about the origin of inequality. He did not believe that class inequalities were an inherent part of the accumulation process.

---

[8] The equality of condition was perhaps best described by Tocqueville, who saw in it the key to understanding American society in its totality. It was also the key to understanding the character of its citizens, insofar as "the chief passion which stirs men at such times is the love of this same equality" (Tocqueville 1969, 504).

Instead, he assumed that capitalism merely perpetuated an accidental maldistribution of wealth from some earlier time in human history. Thus, in the first part of his essay on "The Laboring Classes" he advocated the abolition of the priesthood, which he felt represented the original source of status and distinction. He came somewhat nearer the mark in the second part of that essay, wherein he proposed the elimination of hereditary property as the embodiment of an original maldistribution of wealth. Both recommendations earned him the scorn and vilification of the Whig *New York Review,* which regretted that Brownson could not be successively subjected to the treadmill, the penitentiary, the pillory, and the whipping-post (Schlesinger 1945, 302).

Because of the undemocratic organization of economic production, Brownson was convinced that the Jacksonians would fall in their attempt to restore an equality of opportunity by strictly political means. Indeed, Brownson thought it highly probable that the Jacksonian strategy would strengthen, rather than loosen, the bonds of privilege under which the common man chafed.

To begin with, the Democrats' exclusive preoccupation with popular sovereignty threatened to negate any possibility of limited government, their protestations to the contrary notwithstanding. To define democracy solely in terms of popular sovereignty implied that no restrictions on "the people" were legitimate. And if that were so, the area of individual freedom that the Jacksonians were so intent on extending would not exist apart from the sufferance of the majority (Brownson 1882–1887, vol. 15). Thus, even if "the people" succeeded in gaining control of government, it did not follow that liberty would be achieved. The Jacksonians' commitment to minimalist government was belied by their insistence on popular sovereignty and the political methods associated with it.

The Jacksonians also erred, according to Brownson, in their reliance on federal, as opposed to state, government as the instrument of their liberation. By investing the federal government, and the presidency in particular, with the power of the people, the Democrats had strengthened the very level of government most likely to favor business at the expense of farmers and laborers (ibid., 130). For it was the federal government that was charged with the responsibility for the general financial and currency operations of the country. In strengthening its powers, the Democrats only enhanced the possibilities for exploitation by the monied interests, should they gain control of the federal government.

That they would gain control of this newly energized government and use it for their own ends Brownson had no doubt: "To separate power from property, we hold to be impossible under our present system. Its interests will always predominate in the measures of government, though they may sometimes be defeated in elections" (Brownson 1840, 474–475). The Democrats were, therefore, deluding themselves in thinking that elections might control the direction of governmental action, for business capital enjoyed an immunity to elections by virtue of its structurally privileged position vis-à-vis government (Lindblom 1977).

Thus, the only real consequence of the new democratic methods was their legitimation of exploitation by monied interests. The new democracy enabled these privileged interests to "carry their measures into effect without suspicion, and make it believed that they were approved and carried into effect by the people themselves" (Brownson 1882–1887, 15:37). Brownson concluded that the Democrats' emphasis on democratic forms was hopelessly mistaken in its belief that political reform might be used to effect economic reform, i.e. that a democratic government would be both willing and able to eliminate the existing system of politico-economic privilege. The undemocratic nature of American society ensured the failure of democratic political reforms. Without a fundamental redistribution of wealth, democracy in America was impossible.

Brownson's despair over the prospects for social democracy led him to adopt an increasingly conservative politics as a way of minimizing the undemocratic results of the Jacksonian experiment with popular power. In the later years of what Schlesinger (1945) has called his "pilgrim's progress" from Fourierism to Catholicism, Brownson abandoned all hope for a peaceful redistribution of wealth and gave himself over to a shrill defense of the federal republican form of government which, he believed, was more likely to interact with the underlying socioeconomic order in such a way as to produce democratic "results," i.e. the achievement of justice and the elevation of the working class. Because the written Constitution corresponded to the unwritten, or providential constitution, it would produce the desired end—liberty (Brownson 1865).

Even this required restraint on the part of the people, however. If they were to upset the delicate correspondence between the written and the organic constitutions, liberty would be undone. Hence, Brownson ended his life a despairing conservative, echoing the arguments of Fisher Ames:

> The American genius is republican as opposed to monarchical, but it is not democratic. . . . The constitution is intended to be a contrivance for collecting the popular reason separated from popular passion, and enabling that which is not corrupt in the people to govern without subjection to that which is corrupt. The voice of the people, speaking through legal and constitutional forms is ordinarily the voice of reason . . . but the voice of the people outside [parties, newspapers,. etc.] is the voice of corrupt nature, of faction, of demagogues, disorderly passion, and selfish interests to which it is always fatal to listen. (Brownson 1882–1887, 16:90)

IV

IF THE JACKSONIANS built their constituency by appealing to the common man's *resentment* of political and economic privilege, their Whig opponents created a following by addressing his *hopes* for material advancement (Meyers 1957). The

Whigs offered the common man a share in an American System of inclusive, rather than exclusive, privilege. They envisioned a not-too-distant future of prosperity in which all men, laborers and financiers alike, would join the ranks of the privileged by virtue of hard work, industry, and skill, literally creating a nation of self-made men (Colton 1974).

The Whigs emphasized "internal improvements"—both spiritual and material—as a means of raising society to new and higher levels of development, thereby expanding the possibilities of political and economic freedom. Liberty was to be found in a more prosperous future. In that sense, the Whigs articulated a temporal solution to the problem of liberty in an increasingly industrial society, whereas the Jacksonians were content to reiterate Jefferson's spatial solution to the cycle of virtue and corruption (Wilson 1967).

Thus, the Whigs proposed an American System of development as an alternative to the manifest destiny of expansion. But development was not an automatic process. Even in America, which was uniquely blessed by an abundance of natural resources and a citizenry of hardy stock, there was need for informed guidance and direction of progress. For the Whigs, government was the primary agent of this progress. Government represented a strong and positive force to be used in calling forth a richer society from the unsettled possibilities of America (ibid.). In the economic realm this meant that government was responsible for providing the essential conditions for a sound economy, namely, a reliable currency, ample credit, and the impetus for internal improvements. And in the social realm, government was responsible for promoting virtue in its citizenry through education and exhortation.[9] Once the material and spiritual conditions for devel-

[9] The Whigs reversed the classical republican formula in arguing that "the State is for the aid of virtue, and not virtue for the State. Virtue is not means; it is the end." Hence, "it is a Republic that is necessary to virtue, and not virtue to a Republic" (*American Review* 1847, 242). The Whigs were of two minds as to which virtues ought to be most vigorously promoted (Wilson 1977). The "party of memory," represented by Webster, emphasized the

opment were assured, the natural energies of her people would carry America to her future of prosperity.

Given this corporate vision of development, it is not surprising that the Whigs rejected the Jacksonian and Brownsonian analyses of class conflict in America. According to men like Calvin Colton, there was no fundamental opposition between labor and capital in the process of development: "Every American laborer can stand up proudly and say, I AM THE AMERICAN CAPITALIST, which is not a metaphor but literal truth" (Schlesinger 1945, 271). In America, labor *was* capital, and whosoever was able to work, and find employment with fair pay, was rich to begin with and would become richer through thrift and industry, or so Colton argued in *The Junius Tracts*.

That laborers would always be assured of "employment with fair pay" Colton was certain. The relative scarcity of labor in America, and the ever-present frontier alternative, insured a continuing demand for workers, and at a rate of pay sufficiently generous to allow laborers to lay up one half to three quarters of their earnings as savings and vested capital. By combining their capital with others, laborers could form corporations, and through skillful investment they might eventually join the growing ranks of self-made men in an advancing America (Colton 1974).

The ease with which American labor was transformed into capital implied that classes per se did not exist in the Union. Any man might "start from an humble origin, and from small beginnings rise gradually in the world, as the reward of merit and industry" (Rozwenc 1963, 43). And the absence of hereditary privileges, e.g. entailment, ensured that "the wheel of

---

need for Union and a concomitant respect for the constitutional foundations thereof, especially in the face of efforts to "nullify" them. The "party of hope, of progress and of civilization," composed of men like Adams and Seward, looked forward to prosperity and emphasized more active virtues essential to improvement.

The distinction between these types of "parties" is from Emerson (1965), "Historic Notes of Life and Letters in New England."

fortune is in constant operation, and the poor in one generation furnish the rich of the next," as Edward Everett observed in 1838 (Schlesinger 1945, 270–271).

As the Whigs saw it, the primary threat to this vision of
harmony and upward-mobility was the imperial presidency of
Andrew Jackson.[10] The establishment of a strong executive
threatened the Constitutional order cherished by the "party
of memory," and the destructive manner in which its powers
were deployed against the American System threatened the
prosperous future envisioned by the "party of hope." Hence,
the Jacksonian presidency presented a double-edged threat
to the Whigs' corporate ideal, and they launched a vigorous
counteroffensive against the Democrats.

The Whig strategy followed the time-honored formula of
denouncing their opponents as impostors, and asserting their
own popular credentials. The Democrats, they argued, were
an unprincipled lot, among whom "all measures of a positive
kind, having in mind the substantial interests of the country,
are constantly avoided; because on such grounds, it is seen,
the harmony of the combination [party] would be constantly
endangered" (*American Review* 1845, 18). The Democratic
label, far from indicating any real concern for the people, was
nothing more than a convenient name for a party interested
in the spoils of office.

For that matter, the Democrats were not even a party so
much as a faction devoted to the personal aggrandizement of
Andrew Jackson.[11] And it was a monarchical faction at that,
for "a government, under the will of *One*, is doubtless a Mon-

[10] The imperial presidency of "King Andrew" inspired the choice of party
label for the Whigs. That appellation was calculated to establish the middle-
class background of the new party by calling to mind the British Whigs'
opposition to Tory supporters of the monarchy. By implication, the supporters of King Andrew were the descendants of the Tories. But by 1839, the
Whigs convened their nominating convention under the label "Democratic
Whig National Convention" (Van Deusen 1959).

[11] Ironically, this was precisely the strategy taken by Jackson's vice president, Martin Van Buren, during the struggle for control of the New York
Republican Party. Cf. Chapter Three.

archy whatever may be its Constitutional name" (Colton 1974, 7). Calling Jackson's one-man rule "democratic" did not make it so, though there were undoubtedly those who were taken in by this ruse.

The Whigs, by contrast, claimed to be bound by principles, not power or personality or spoils: "They recognize no authority of leaders that binds them to obsequiousness; it is not party, but *country* they go for; it is not MEN, but PRINCIPLES; and they adopt party organization, and sustain it, not as an *end*, but as a *means* to an end" (ibid., 10). The Whigs, therefore, were the "true" democrats, for it was they who had the interests of the people at heart and who defended the constitutional order against executive encroachment.

Unfortunately for the Whigs, the Democrats had successfully arrogated the immensely popular democratic label to their own use: The party of Jackson claimed "a name which it has most dishonestly filched, and to which alone it is indebted for more votes than it could have procured from any other cause whatever" (*American Review* 1845, 18). It was necessary, therefore, to reclaim the title of "Democrats" for Whigs' use. To allow the Loco Focos to retain the label would be "absolutely *suicidal.* . . . The world has pronounced in favor of *Democracy*, and is resolved to have it" (Colton 1974, 15).

Colton insisted that the Whig press refrain from calling their opponents "Democrats," since that implicitly conceded the legitimacy of common usage. He recommended that Whigs should, above all, retain the slogans of "Log Cabin" and "Hard Cider," for there was more democracy in them than there was in "Democracy" itself.[12] These slogans offered something of substance to the common man and would surely overcome the empty exhortations of the would-be Democrats (ibid., 2, 16).

The cynicism with which Colton recommended this strat-

---

[12] Not that the Whigs "recommend *drinking*. We only speak of 'Hard Cider' as a *symbol*" (Colton 1974, 16).

egy of symbolic manipulation has been documented by Schlesinger. In an anonymously published work entitled *A Voice From America to England,* Colton noted that any American party, regardless of whether its principles were radical or conservative, was well advised to use the rhetoric of democracy to sell its cause to the voters (Schlesinger 1945). This and the over-zealous appropriation and perfection of Democratic methods of electioneering have led many scholars to concur with Henry Adams, who observed that "of all the parties that have existed in the United States, the famous Whig party was the most feeble in ideas" (Howe 1980, 11).

V

OF COURSE there *were* Whigs of integrity; the ideas of men like Clay and Adams were significant and well within the confines of the Republican tradition. The work of Van Deusen (1959), Wilson (1967, 1977), and Howe (1980) has done much to restore the reputation of the Whigs, and certain aspects of it deserve comment here.

The Whigs' emphasis on improvement might seem inconsistent with the republican understanding of time and its corrosive effect on the body politic. Their explicit identification of improvement with progress suggested that time fulfills, at least when appropriate public policies are undertaken with that end in view. As such, the Whigs apparently entertained a broader range of historical possibilities than classical republicans, who saw only corruption and degeneration in the progress of time. For this reason, American historians commonly refer to the Whigs' ideological "optimism," often by way of contrast with the "pessimism" of many of their contemporaries.

At the same time, Howe (1980) has convincingly shown that the American Whigs owed much to the "Country" republicans of the Walpole era, and that they consciously affected the language and style of the "Commonwealthmen," down to the adoption of pen names from that period.[13] In-

---

[13] "Junius," for example, was the nom de plume used by the anonymous

deed, the American Whigs viewed themselves as the legitimate heirs of the republican tradition, engaged in mortal
combat with those who would corrupt and destroy it, an attitude that is abundantly clear in their moralistic denunciation of King Andrew and his spoilsmen. The legitimacy of this
view is given credence by the fact that Madison and Albert
Gallatin, two leaders of the "nationalistic" wing of the Jeffersonian Republicans, supported Clay's candidacy over that of
Jackson in 1832; and in 1824 Jefferson himself opposed Jackson's presidential candidacy (Howe 1980, 94).

Thus, on the one hand, the Whigs claimed to be the exponents of a political tradition that did not, indeed could not,
recognize the possibility of progress, and on the other, they
defended the American System as essential for the future
progress of the nation. It is not surprising that such apparently obvious contradictions have led to the condemnation of
the Whigs as inept defenders of the passing order of deference in American politics.

However, the Whigs themselves felt no inconsistency in
their position, perhaps because they had a different understanding of "progress" than contemporary observers, who are
wont to see in the Whigs' "optimism" the roots of liberal progressivism. To see this, it is necessary to recall that progress
was not the most common, nor even the most important, justification invoked by the Whigs on behalf of the American
System. Rather, they mounted a classically republican defense of "improvement" as a way of maintaining balance in
the republic, and so staving off the effects of corruption. The
American System was the Whigs' program for establishing a
"Machiavellian moment" in time, and it is in those terms that
their comments on progress should be interpreted.

This way of thinking is nicely illustrated by the Whigs' opposition to the aggressive land policies pursued by the Democrats in the name of America's "manifest destiny." The removal of Indians, "adventurist" policies toward Cuba, and

---

author of a set of commonwealth pamphlets that was widely circulated in the
colonies during the 1760s (Howe 1980, 92).

settlement in Oregon threatened to embroil the nation in dangerous wars with foreign adversaries of the republic. The war with Mexico only confirmed the Whigs' fears on this score; although the forces of the Union emerged victorious, the triumph over a "sister republic" hardly served the cause of liberty in a way that seemed consistent with the providential mission of America. Moreover, the prosecution of the war by Polk seemed to embody the Whigs' worst fears concerning "executive usurpation" of power, even as it spawned a new class of land speculators, war profiteers, political patrons, and ambitious generals, i.e. decidedly unvirtuous citizens, to the Whigs' way of thinking.

Thus, the Whigs saw no reason to adopt policies that "could only be attended with danger to ourselves, and which, besides necessarily injuring our great national interests, our commerce and agriculture, might break up our political institutions, and destroy for ever the home of freedom in the new world." For the sake of oppressed Europeans, no less than free Americans, "let us not endanger by a war policy the example which we give, or the home which we offer" (*American Review* 1852, 130).

The Whigs' stance on the tariff question was also colored by this view. Protectionism was calculated to lessen the vulnerability of the republic to the foreign policies of nations hostile to the cause of liberty. The Whigs

> believe that protection, feeble as it has been hitherto, is one chief element in the progress of our country; that but for this, we should have remained but little better than a colony of England, and should have resembled Canada or Australia, in our complete dependence upon our oppressing parent. But for protection, we should have been a nation without self-reliance and without enterprise. (*American Review* 1852, 126)

Here the improvement of natural resources and the development of commerce and manufacturing is applauded, but as a means of preserving the independence of the nation and sustaining the cause of liberty. Improvement, therefore, was neither an end in itself, as "progress" later came to be, nor did it extend to political affairs, which were the proper subject of republican philosophy. Instead, "modernization," to use Howe's (1980) term, was conceived as the appropriate strategy for *maintaining* the republic against its enemies, and this was thoroughly consistent with the commonwealth ideology of republican politics.[14]

The Whigs' greatest objection to the Jacksonian program was that it distracted the nation from the more important business of developing its already considerable bounty. As Horace Greeley put it,

> Opposed to the instinct of boundless acquisition stands that of Internal Improvement. A nation cannot simultaneously devote its energies to the absorption of others' territories and the improvement of its own. In a state of war, not law only is silent, but the pioneer's axe, the canal-digger's mattock, and the housebuilder's trowel also. (Howe 1980, 21)

Instead, men like Clay and John Quincy Adams preferred a program of improvement known as the American System as a way of binding the nation together. The development of a commercial infrastructure and the protection of indigenous manufactures from foreign competition

> shall secure to the Industry of our countrymen a just remuneration, and shall stimulate Mechanical and Manufacturing Enterprise, and thus provide a home consumption for the products of Agriculture, which may control and counteract the unsteady demands of foreign markets, and as shall promote that healthy interchange among ourselves of the fruits of our own skill and labor, which is so well

[14] Meek (1976) discusses the prevalence of the four stages theory of economic development during this period, as well as some of the more important efforts to assess the political implications of the commercialization of the Republic. The dialectic of commerce and virtue figures prominently in these efforts, as Pocock (1975) has stressed.

calculated to cement our Union, and maintain the spirit of national independence. (*American Review* 1851, 180)

Thus, the American System aimed at fostering national integration. A harmony of interests was to be established on a material basis, where commercial ties bound men together in a collective enterprise. Without such a system, economic development would not have this salutary effect, and the clash of economic (and therefore sectional) interests would eventually undermine the spirit of patriotism and the disposition toward the common good so necessary for the survival of republican politics.

Nor were the economic effects of an American System its only republican recommendation. As much as anything, the American System was a call to collective action. It symbolized a national objective to which less inclusive interests must defer, and so reminded citizens of their republican duties. This sacrifice of individual and partisan interests to the commonweal also received religious sanction in a way that reinforced republican mores. The improvement of nature's bounty and the discipline of self-control both assumed theological, and at times evangelical, overtones in Whig pronouncements during the Second Great Awakening. The corresponding Whig emphasis on education (both formal and rhetorical, i.e. in the realm of political discourse) was quite consistent with republican unease and frequent instructions on the need for vigilance and means of exercising it (Howe 1980).

The fusion of republican unease over corruption and a theological inclination toward moral instruction in Whig ideology is apparent in the sense of stewardship that informed their policies on improvement. The American System of politically fostered economic development achieved the status of a political imperative for Whigs. It was the surety of republican politics, and so it rightfully claimed the allegiance of all citizens. Each and every member of the community "owed" to past, present, and future generations that which was necessary to the survival of the commonwealth, and because the American System was necessary in that sense, it was not only expedient, but *right* for the republic. Those who opposed the American System were, therefore, unvirtuous; they were corrupt, and their control of the governing institutions of the nation deserved condemnation in most severe terms.

The Whig critique of the Jacksonians was redolent of a political eschatology reminiscent of classical republicanism, and indeed of classical utopianism in general, which depicts an ideal state of affairs from which no further progress was possible. Perfection, once achieved, needed no further fulfillment; indeed, any further changes could only be understood as deviations from perfection (Hansot 1974).

Modern utopianism, on the other hand, depicts stages of development in a dynamic process; improvement, rather than perfection, is the orienting theme of this outlook, which typically focuses upon the successive removal of social barriers to human fulfillment as the essence of historical progress. This is in marked contrast to classical utopianism, which avoids social criticism oriented toward the actualization of unrealized possibilities in favor of judgments that are aimed at teaching individuals to practice virtue and avoid unvirtuous actions (ibid.). This sort of judgment does not depend on the possibility of achieving perfection; it merely upholds an ideal of perfection for all to see and emulate to the best of their ability. Most individuals will fail to do so most of the time, but the ideal remains a constant reminder of what human beings ought to do.[15]

[15] It is interesting to compare an American "transcendentalist," Theodore Parker, on this point:

We have this characteristic of genius: we are dissatisfied with all that we have done. Somebody once said we were too vain to be proud. It is not wholly so; the national ideal is so far above us that any achievement seems little and low. . . . The political ideas of the nation are transcendent, not empirical. Human history could not justify the Declaration of Independence and its large statements of the new idea: the nation went behind human history and appealed to human nature. (Miller 1957, 358)

The "transcendental" criticism of society according to an ideal of "perfect" communitarianism is, of course, something that the so-called Transcendentalists and Whigs had in common.

Surely, it is this sort of understanding that informs the republican conception of citizenship and its obligations, with its constant exhortations to act virtuously, if only to forestall the inevitable corruption of time. Just as surely, it is this sort of perfectionism that allows us to understand the American Whigs' conception of material "progress" as a way of preserving the republic against the popular assault on deference and the concomitant rejection of a "tutorial" conception of political education and policymaking.

At the same time, the increasing stridency with which this criticism was made by the Whigs is an index of the waning strength of the idea of a commonwealth. Increasingly dangerous sectional divisions on the issue of slavery, and the exacerbation of class and ethnic differentials by an industrialization fueled by massive immigration made it difficult to speak of a Union, much less of an undivided American nation. Within such a context, the Whig platform was bound to be seen as a self-serving program for maintaining a structure of deference in which wealthy, Anglo-Saxon natives enjoyed a preponderance of power. Compared with the *democratic* republicanism of Jackson, the American System of "aristocratic" republicanism, embodied by men such as John Quincy Adams, had little popular appeal in an age committed to the proposition of *vox populi, vox Dei.*

VI

AMONG THOSE who clearly understood the implications of majoritarian democracy for a society that no longer shared an identifiable, substantive common interest was John C. Calhoun. The economic and sectional differentiation of American society meant that it was no longer reasonable to assume the existence of people whose will might be summarized and expressed by a single majority of their number. The majority no longer represented the people, but only the larger portion of them—a "numerical majority"—and majoritarian democracy, instead of being a true and perfect model of the people's government, was but the government of a part of the people

over another—the majority over the minority portion (Calhoun [1853] 1978, 24).

Given the nonidentity of the majority's and people's interests, it was apparent to Calhoun that the simple majoritarianism of the Jacksonian Democrats posed a serious threat to
minority interests. As the success of the Democrats demonstrated, national majorities could capture the legislative and
executive offices of the federal government, thereby reunit-
ing the very powers that the Framers had tried so desperately
to separate. Once in power, Calhoun was certain, such majorities would use the power of "the people" for their own
ends, and the unchecked power of the majority would reign
absolute.

Calhoun's fear of majoritarian tyranny was intimately associated with his abhorrence of party politics and the spoils system, which had proved so capable of mobilizing national majorities (Freehling 1965). Calhoun and other nullifiers saw the
triumph of the Democracy as evidence that the philosphers-
cum-statesmen of the early republic had been succeeded by
political brokers and spoilsmen who attained power through
"duplicity, cunning and subserviency to the masses" (Latner
1977). For them nullification was an antidote to the dema-
gogic corruption of politics that resulted in majoritarian tyranny.[16]

No doubt Calhoun's distaste for party politics was influenced by his belief that neither the Democrats nor the Whigs
adequately represented southern interests. The Whigs' economic policies and especially their advocacy of the tariff were
calculated to maintain the dominant position of northern
business capital vis-à-vis the landed capital of the cotton
South, according to Calhoun (Schlesinger 1945). The Democrats, on the other hand, harbored an ever-increasing num-

---

[16] Latner (1977) shows that Jackson, on the other hand, saw the *nullifiers*
as demagogues bent on corrupting politics in the interest of sectional, rather
than republican, considerations. Both Calhoun and Jackson remained within
the universe of republican discourse however, differing primarily in the factions they feared most.

ber of western abolitionists among their ranks, though they
did oppose the business interests of the northeast. The South
had minority factions in both parties, but Calhoun entertained few illusions about their ability to withstand the northern majorities enlarged by the pending admission of several
more "free states" into the Union.

Thus, the South was in an especially precarious position
vis-à-vis northern majorities. Its way of life, and the institution of slavery in particular, were vulnerable to majoritarian
encroachments no matter which party was successful. A Whig
majority was sure to implement policies that diverted southern wealth into northern hands, while a Democratic majority
threatened the very institution on which the southern economy depended.

Calhoun's masterful solution to the southern dilemma was
his theory of "concurrent majorities," which took interests, as
well as numbers, into account. Under this system, the concurrence of regional majorities would be necessary before
governmental action could occur. Calhoun proposed the
adoption of a plural executive, with each of the two great
interests, North and South, electing a federal executive officer. The joint approval of the two executives would be necessary in order to enact any legislation or engage in any executive action. This would ensure a veto for each interest,
protecting it from any untoward encroachment by the other.

Obviously, this sytem of concurrence was designed to protect the South. But the logic of Calhoun's argument, and indeed the very terms in which he couched it, applied to any
interest that enjoyed regional, but not national, majoritarian
support.[17] Thus, Calhoun appealed to all potentially threat-

[17] The coincidence of regional and socioeconomic interests during this period in American history would have made the implementation of Calhoun's
theory relatively unproblematic. However, the modern form of interest representation via group activity is evidence that nonregional versions of concurrent majoritarianism are conceivable. "Interest group liberalism" is perhaps the ultimate expression of veto politics, at least under "zero-sum"
conditions. (Thurow 1980).

ened interests by justifying his system in constitutional terms. Concurrent majoritarianism was essential to the preservation of limited government, according to Calhoun, for

> the necessary consequence of taking the sense of the community by the concurrent majority is, as has been explained, to give each interest or portion of the community a negative on the others. It is this mutual negative among its various conflicting interests which invests each with the power of protecting itself, and places the rights and safety of each where only they can be securely placed, under its own guardianship. Without this there can be no systematic, peaceful, or effective resistance to the natural tendency of each to come into conflict with others; and without this there can be no constitution. It is this negative power—the power of preventing or arresting the action of government, be it called by what term it may, veto, interposition, nullification, check or balance of power—which in fact forms the constitution. (Calhoun [1853] 1978, 28)

Thus, the power of the negative was the means by which Calhoun sought to protect minority interests. Those who accuse Calhoun of neglecting civil liberties even as he defends minorities against majorities (see, for example, Hofstadter 1948) miss the point of Calhoun's argument. Calhoun defended minority *interests* and not minority *rights*, and he did so in utilitarian, rather than Lockean, terms. Insofar as individuals' desire to better their condition was the mainspring of "progress, improvement, and civilization," it was necessary to ensure both liberty and security. For "liberty leaves each free to pursue the course he may deem best to promote his interest and happiness," while "security gives assurance to each that he shall not be deprived of the fruits of his exertions to better his condition" (Calhoun [1853] 1978, 40). Of the two, however, security was the more important, since it was essential to the *preservation* of the race, while liberty was only essential to its improvement (ibid., 40).

Calhoun rejected defenses of universal suffrage that derived its necessity from natural rights of liberty and equality. Natural rights, he argued, did not exist.[18] The "state of nature" from which they were derived, instead of being the natural state of man was, of all conceivable states, the one most repugnant to his feelings and most incompatible with his wants (ibid., 45). The problem of constitutionalism, then, was not to ensure nonexistent natural rights, but to secure a proper balance between the spheres of liberty and security, or freedom and power. Calhoun's scheme of concurrent majoritarianism was defended on the grounds that it established a better balance than that of numerical majoritarianism, i.e. that it was better calculated to preserve *and* improve the human condition.

The concurrent majority system was needed to remedy the weakness of the Constitution vis-à-vis numerical majorities, so that the sphere of liberty, in which men perfected their moral and intellectual faculties, might be maintained against the encroachments of power. Without it, no one, including the propertied interests of the north (as Calhoun frequently pointed out), was beyond the reach of a government animated by a national majority.

VII

WITH THE ARTICULATION of a theory of concurrent majoritarianism, the hegemony of republicanism in American politics was broken. Calhoun's attempt to provide a constitutional accommodation for diverse and competing interests undermined the traditional republican ideal of commonwealth politics. It also contradicted the Whig denial of class conflict in

---

[18] Calhoun's language echoes that of Bentham, who referred to the rhetoric of natural rights as "nonsense on stilts," though that fails to convey Bentham's concern for the pernicious effects of rhetorical "principles" of legislation (Rosenblum 1978).

Compare Calhoun's contempt for derivations of natural rights from a hypothetical state of nature: "These great and dangerous errors have their origin in the prevalent opinion that all men are born free and equal—than which nothing can be more unfounded and false" (Calhoun [1853] 1978, 44).

America and the Jacksonian attempt to ameliorate it, both of which paid obeisance to the virtuous foundation of republican politics.

In that respect Calhoun had much in common with the Federalists, and Madison especially. Madison's was a political community of contending interests that kept one another in check. However, the emergence of political parties that "aggregated interests," to use the language of political science, had made imbalance likely. Van Buren's *solution* to the problem of factionalism in the republic—a party system—therefore became Calhoun's *problem* as he looked for republican remedies for the diseases most incident to republican politics.

Calhoun's problem reveals the importance of Madison's antipathy toward parties in this theory of the extended, compound republic. Institutional safeguards made majoritarian tyranny difficult, but not impossible. Hence, Madison depended on a diversity of interests in order to "make it less probable that the majority of the whole will have a common motive to invade the rights of other citizens; or if such a common motive exists, it will be more difficult for all who feel it to discover their own strength and to act in unison with each other" (Rossiter 1961, 83). Such majorities of the moment as did form would dissipate their energy in trying to overcome the institutional obstacles of the compound republic.

Parties changed that calculation, as Calhoun's experience revealed. More or less enduring majorities became possible in a party system, and they showed every sign of brushing aside existing minority interests. Hence, a more positive "veto" was required to protect the latter. Calhoun found security in the system of concurrent majorities.

In order for that to work properly, however, a different kind of political community was required. That community was not one of *universitas*, based on an association of agents engaged in joint action oriented toward the achievement of some common *substantive* interest. It was instead a community of *societas*, bound together by authoritative *rules* or *procedures* for making collective decisions. However, if these rules were to be authoritative they had to be accepted as reasonable or their legitimacy presumed (Oakeshott 1975).

This presumption became increasingly untenable with the development of antagonistic sectional ideologies. The corrosive effect of these ideologies consummated the erosion of American republicanism, but at the same time they prevented any new consensus from emerging. Hence, they made it highly unlikely that any constitutional solutions, even such radical ones as proposed by Calhoun, would be capable of harnessing the disintegrating effect of socioeconomic development. At that point the appeal to reason was bound to give way to the resort to arms.

CHAPTER FIVE

Politics and Ideology in the Age of the Civil War

I

CALHOUN'S SUGGESTIONS for reconstituting the American republic did not appear until midcentury, although his involvement in the nullification controversy clearly presaged these later arguments. Until then, however, a tenuous balance of interests was made possible by the institutionalization of a party system. To be sure, the exact location of the balance point, and even the very meaning of "balance," shifted as the electoral fortunes of the major parties changed. Nevertheless, it is possible to understand the Age of Jackson in terms of competing interpretations of the American commonwealth and its historical possibilities. Indeed, the partisan debate over how best to establish a republic "outside of time," so to speak, is the ideological aspect of this process of political institutionalization.

The precariousness of this accomplishment is testimony to its political magnitude. It seems quite unlikely that such a balance would have been struck if "extending the area of freedom" had required the denunciation of slavery, a veritable bastion of deference and inequality, as undemocratic. The Whigs, too, were loath to raise the issue of slavery in national debate, and so slavery was organized out of political discourse via a conspiracy of silence on the peculiar institution of the South.

Madison, of course, had been quite clear on the need to

I borrow this title from Foner (1980), whose account of this period forms the basis for much of this chapter.

avoid the issue of slavery in order to preserve the Union. During the constitutional debates in Philadelphia he observed that "the real difference of interests lay, not between the large and small but between the Northern and Southern States" (Madison 1966, 295). The institution of slavery and its consequences formed a "line of discrimination" which, if allowed to surface, posed a great threat to the very possibility of the proposed Union (ibid., 295). The great silences of the Constitution allowed the Framers to finesse this issue and to persuade the South that its interests would be institutionally secured in the new regime. The Senate, in which *states* were represented, was an especially important safeguard for the South, since it commanded a majority of votes in the Senate until the middle of the nineteenth century.

The wisdom of Madison's insight was later manifested in the divisive debates over the admission of Missouri to the Union. The Senate at that time was evenly divided between eleven free and eleven slave states. The admission of Missouri threatened to upset the balance and, with it, the South's veto power over antislavery legislation. The Missouri Compromise temporarily resolved the dispute by admitting Missouri as a slave state, and creating a new, free state of Maine out of the northeastern counties of Massachusetts. It also established guidelines for the future admission of free and slave territories on terms agreeable to the South.

Nevertheless, the ease with which the issue of slavery split the Congressional Republicans at this time was not lost on Van Buren and the Regency politicians. Indeed, their defense of a competitive party system rested in large part on their belief that parties were essential if sectional conflicts were to be avoided: "We must always have party distinctions and the old ones are the best. If suppressed, geographical differences founded on local instincts or what is worse, prejudices between free and slave holding states will inevitably take their place" (Wallace 1968, 490). Precisely because parties transcended the interest of faction, they promised to contain political conflict within peaceful bounds.

Of course, this new solution presupposed that the parties themselves would represent intersectional coalitions of opinion and interest. Sectional parties, on the other hand, would not only fail to contain conflict, but would exacerbate it by mobilizing large sections of the populace against one another. Consequently, it was necessary for party leaders to suppress the one issue, slavery, that seemed capable of generating sectional parties. Throughout the 1830s, therefore, the Jacksonian Democrats and their Whig counterparts adamantly resisted abolitionist attempts to inject the issue into national politics. The Democrats especially avoided the issue of slavery, as the success of their struggle against the Money Power hinged on their ability to maintain an alliance with Southern sympathizers (Schlesinger 1945).

This policy of exclusion became increasingly difficult to maintain, however. The House did manage to pass the infamous Gag Rule in 1836, which silenced the reading of antislavery petitions in Congress. But the debate over slavery was no longer carried on solely by Congressmen, as it had once been.[1] It was also carried on in the mass media, and against that development the Gag Rule was ineffective. Indeed, it was this appeal to the masses by pro- and anti-slavery forces alike that differentiated mid-nineteenth century political discourse on slavery from earlier disputes. The same techniques of persuasion and mobilization that made parties possible also gave rise to other forms of mass political organization, as Foner (1980) observes. Abolitionists attempted to mobilize antislavery opinion and force reluctant politicians to halt the spread of slavery to the new territories, and even to eliminate it in the South itself. At the same time, proslavery forces tried to rally support to their endangered cause, and to use that support to persuade politicians to stand firm against the abolitionist appeals. In the course of this dialogue

[1] Commenting on the isolation of early Washington, D.C., Moore claims that "if there had been a civil war in 1819–1821 it would have been between the members of Congress, with the rest of the country looking on in amazement!" (1953, 175).

en masse distinct sectional ideologies began to emerge, and public opinion on the issue of slavery became polarized.[2]

Given this situation, it became increasingly difficult for party leaders to maintain their conspiracy of silence on slavery. It became impossible to do so when members of their own parties sought to use the issue of slavery as a means of establishing their own political constituencies and advancing their own ambitions and interests. As the parties began to disintegrate and realign along sectional lines, Van Buren's hopes for the Union were dashed, and the possibility of consensus shattered.

II

IN MANY WAYS the separation between North and South was complete well before the Civil War began. In his February 6, 1837, speech on "slavery as a positive good" Calhoun warned that

> those who imagine that the spirit [of abolitionism] now abroad in the North, will die away of itself, without shout or convulsion, have formed a very inadequate conception of its real character; it will continue to rise and spread, unless prompt and efficient measures to stay its progress be adopted. . . . It is easy to see the end. By the necessary course of events, if left to themselves, we must become, finally, two people[s]. (1980, 394)

By 1855, the *New York Tribune* declared that separation complete, saying "We are not one people, we are two peoples. We are a people for Freedom and a people for Slavery. Between the two, conflict is inevitable" (Foner 1980, 53).

The initial salvos in this war between sectional ideologies were fired by the abolitionists. Criticisms of the institution of slavery were not new to America, and indeed many southerners opposed its perpetuation. Cash (1941, 73) reports that

---

[2] The selections in Auer (1963) analyze the rhetorical dynamics of this process with specific reference to "debates" of the period.

four-fifths of the members of the 130 abolition societies established before 1827 lived in the South, and that the state of
Virginia itself had twice nearly abolished the "peculiar institution" of slavery.

But on January 1, 1831, William Lloyd Garrison's *The Liberator* was founded, signalling the rise of a new and more
radical opposition to slavery than had prevailed during the
first quarter of the nineteenth century.[3] This opposition was,
historians agree, based primarily on a moral repugnance toward slavery and was part of a more general orientation toward moral reform instigated by the religious revival associated with the Second Great Awakening (Foner 1980, 65). The
temperance movement, penal reforms, and the call for wom-
en's rights were all associated with this revival of religion.

For the most radical opponents of slavery, however, abolitionism became a religion in its own right:

> Itself an heir of the Revival, antislavery *was* a church, an
> appropriate one for men and women who had both a
> fiercely Protestant morality and a disdain for metaphysics.
> It expressed perfectly their abhorrence of the spiritual
> emptiness, moral cowardice, and denominational rivalries
> they found in their traditional churches. It gave them a
> means to withdraw from clerical domination and sectarian
> narrowness while permitting them to maintain a vision of
> Protestant unity—the solidarity of moral men and women
> brought together in godly works. (Walters 1977, 52–53)

In this way, the abolition movement transformed essentially
religious impulses and spiritual discontent into a construc-

[3] Before the 1830s, antislavery thought in America was dominated by the
colonization movement, which advocated the return of slaves to African colonies, e.g. Liberia. During the 1830s, however, American antislavery movements were strongly influenced by British abolitionists and their doctrine of
"immediatism"—a doctrine that demanded the immediate and complete
elimination of slavery in the Empire. The triumph of immediatism in 1833
in Britain had a profoundly radicalizing effect on American antislavery
thought (Davis 1962; 1966).

tive, acceptable role—that of moral exhortation as a prelude to redemption.[4]

The essence of their godly work consisted of the tireless and unceasing condemnation of slavery as a sin against God and man alike. Slavery, William Ellery Channing pointed out, denied the moral agency of the individual, for it prevented men from freely exercising their God-given ability to pursue a responsible course of action in the world:

> This is the essence of a moral being. He possesses, as a part of his nature, and the most essential part, a sense of Duty, which he is to reverence and follow, in opposition to all pleasure or pain, to all interfering human wills. The great purpose of all good education and discipline is, to make a man Master of Himself, to excite him to act from a principle in his own mind, to lead him to propose his own perfection as his supreme law and end. And is this highest purpose of man's nature to be reconciled with entire subjection to a foreign will, to an outward, overwhelming force, which is satisfied with nothing but complete submission? (Pease and Pease 1965, 116–117)

Hence, the institution of slavery denied the basic quality that separated men from beasts, and in so doing, contradicted the divine laws of the universe.[5]

Abolitionists took the declining economic position of the

[4] Walters (1977, 177–178) summarizes the debate over contention that the abolitionists seized on this role of moral reformation in order to compensate for their declining occupational status and concludes that there is a connection between the dislocations associated with industrialization and the reform impulse. However, he suggests that status change per se, and not a decline in status, may be the key factor in accounting for the timing and social origin of reform.

[5] For a discussion of the moral sense doctrine in abolitionist thought, see Walters (1977). He argues persuasively that the ascendance of "emotion" over "intellect" during this period in history enabled the abolitionists to harmonize their acceptance of the moral agency of slaves with their misgivings about racial differences in intellectual ability in a way that Jefferson, who endorsed the primacy of intellect, could not.

South *vis-à-vis* the North as evidence of divine justice: those who failed to abide by the laws of God were being punished for their transgressions. Thus, Garrison's review of Gamaliel Bailey's *The North and South: A Statistical View of the Condition of the Free and Slave States* led him to conclude that slavery was not only wrong, but comparatively unprofitable (Walters 1977, 124).[6] Yet the abolitionists worried that the North, by its complicity in the maintenance of slavery, might also share in the fate of the South as the latter depressed the economy as a whole. In that sense, abolitionists did not perceive slavery as a sectional problem, but a national one, insofar as it threatened to undermine the historic mission of America.

Therein lay the rationale for redirecting their proselytizing efforts from southern slaveholders, who showed little inclination toward repentance, to northerners, who not only shared in the sins of the South, but who also had it in their power to destroy slavery. The South acknowledged as much by its threats to secede if northerners retreated from their position of acquiescence in slavery.[7] Hence, the abolitionists assumed responsibility for agitating the conscience of a nation.

However, a significant split within the abolitionists soon developed over the question of whether or not to engage in political action in addition to moral agitation.[8] The Garriso-

[6] Fitzhugh, as we shall see, turned this argument around, claiming that the higher profitability of northern industry was evidence of its greater exploitation of labor.

[7] Freehling (1966) and Potter (1976) together provide a detailed account of the increasingly militant response of southerners to the "agitating" effects of the abolitionists on slaves.

[8] Pease and Pease (1965) present examples of the different varieties of abolitionism, while Walters (1977) analyzes the general contours of the movement as it unfolded after 1830. I focus on Garrison because of his unquestionable prominence as an abolitionist agitator in this period.

Elliott (1860) contains some of the more interesting treatises in defense of slavery, while Jenkins's (1960) work is the classic exposition of the different dimensions of the proslavery argument.

nians, on the one hand, initially disdained efforts to utilize parties as vehicles for gaining control of government. To a significant extent their attitude was based on Garrison's conviction that the Constitution was proslavery, and therefore a "Covenant with Death and an Agreement with Hell," as the masthead of *The Liberator* proclaimed in 1843. Garrison believed that the Constitution betrayed the principles of the Declaration of Independence, which were an expression of divine wisdom, and that it held no special claim to legitimacy. Consequently, his burning of the Constitution at the Fourth of July meeting of abolitionists in 1854 symbolized his rejection of it and his recommendation for northern secession.

But Garrison's disunionism, i.e. his opposition to the Union established by the Constitution, was not a rejection of the principle of unionism per se. As Walters (1977) has convincingly argued, Garrison and his supporters were firm nationalists who assumed that America's "manifest" destiny depended on a unified country.[9] Disunionism was, therefore, a strategic ploy designed to bring about the collapse of slavery by withdrawing northern support for it. Having eschewed violence and political action within the Slave Constitution as means to achieve that same end, they seized on disunionism as a way of unilaterally abolishing slavery and redeeming the nation and its future. They were willing to destroy the Union in order to preserve the nation.

[9] The most extreme "disunionists" were found in experimental communities, e.g. Noyes' Oneida commune, formed in isolation from the corrupting influences of northern society. Similarly, the Transcendentalists' critique of northern materialism and their Brooke Farm experiment in communal living expressed a confidence in the perfectability of individuals, which would render government and other coercive institutions superfluous.

Emerson is perhaps an exception to this tendency, for he conceded that government was a necessary evil where men are selfish and inclined to abuse others' persons and property. However, even he believed that the coercive powers of the state might be "transcended" by calling forth a new type of man and a community based on love: "To educate the wise man, the State exists; and with the appearance of the wise man, the State expires. The appearance of character makes the State unnecessary. The wise man is the State" (Emerson n.d., 378).

III

OTHER ABOLITIONISTS agreed that disunionism was an efficacious strategy against slavery, but they expressed confidence in the capacity of political action to achieve the same end, without destroying the Union (ibid.). Less radical than the Garrisonians, these abolitionists undertook the arduous task of translating moral indignation into practical political action by forcing the major parties to adapt their stance on slavery in response to third party challenges.

For the most part, the Democratic party successfully resisted these pressures until the 1850s, when it was no longer possible to assume a neutral, much less silent, position on slavery. As early as 1839, however, some members of the Democratic party were beginning to speak out on the issue of slavery. Thomas Morris of Ohio warned his Senate colleagues of the Southern Slave Power, an interest which he alleged was "more powerful and dangerous to the peace and prosperity of the country than Banks or any other interest, that has ever existed among us" (Foner 1970, 90–91). This Slave Power, Morris argued, had obtained governmental sanction for a system of economic privilege based on the exploitation of slave labor. In principle, therefore, the Slave Power was no different than the Money Power, except insofar as it had gained control of both the Senate and the presidency. Consequently, it too had to be destroyed by the power of the people, just as the Bank had been (ibid., 90–91).

Morris's breach of silence cost him reendorsement as Democratic leaders moved quickly to suppress discussion of slavery. Though "political antislavery," and especially the fear of the Slave Power, would become a standard part of the political rhetoric in the late 1840s, the Democratic party was not yet ready to jeopardize the alliance on which its electoral success rested.[10]

---

[10] "Political antislavery" was not based on moral objections to slavery, but on opposition to its extension to new territories. It was willing to tolerate slavery in the Deep South, but not in the West. Cf. section VI of this chapter.

The Whig party, on the other hand, was more vulnerable to infiltration by the abolitionists. As Benson (1961) and Formisano (1971) have shown, the abolitionist movement was strongest among those religious and ethnic groups that were the backbone of the Whig party in the north. Moreover, Calhoun's defection to the Democrats left the southern Whig party in the hands of the more moderate supporters of slavery, making the internal pressures for neutrality somewhat less intense. With hardline southern "neutralists" gone, and northern sympathizers under fire, the Whig party was especially susceptible to abolitionist pressures.

The Whigs also found themselves as the party in the middle on a rapidly polarizing issue. To successfully compete with the Democrats as a national party, some compromise on the slave question was essential. On the other hand, compromise weakened the Whigs at the local level, where the abolitionist Liberty party, formed in 1840, was gaining strength. When, in 1844, enough New York Whigs deserted Clay in favor of the Liberty candidate Birney to cost Clay the state and hence national election, the message was clear: "If compromise with the South on slavery questions meant losing the presidency in any case, they might as well protect and enhance their position in their own states by keeping pace with public opinion there" (Sundquist 1973, 47).

The Whigs' national fortunes became even more desperate in 1845 with the annexation of proslavery Texas and war with Mexico. On these issues antislavery Conscience Whigs of Massachusetts split with the compromise Cotton Whigs of the same state. The former had nothing to lose, as the latter dominated the state economically and politically. In the ensuing struggle the Conscience Whigs assumed progressively more radical positions, eventually opposing slavery not only in the territories but in the old South itself. They left the national party in 1848 when it nominated another slaveholder, Taylor, as its presidential candidate (ibid.).

At about the same time, the New York Democracy was torn by a longstanding struggle between the Barnburner and

Hunker factions. In 1846, David Wilmot, a Barnburner who had supported the annexation of Texas, introduced a Congressional Proviso to exclude slavery from all territory acquired in the war with Mexico. The Proviso reactivated this factional dispute, and in 1848 the Barnburners had temporarily left the party (Schlesinger 1945).

The Barnburners, the Conscience Whigs, and the Liberty party united to form the Free Soil party of 1848. The Free Soilers, behind Van Buren, did not carry any states, though they polled over 300,000 votes, taken from northern Democratic and Whig strongholds alike. But the sizeable number of abolitionists willing to support a third-party candidacy clearly spelled trouble for the Whig party, which moved ever closer to the abolitionist position in order to protect its local flanks. In 1850, the Whigs split over the issue of compromise, with many northerners following Seward in opposition to Clay. Not a single northern Whig in either house voted for the Kansas-Nebraska bill in 1854, sundering the few remaining ties with the southern Whigs. The destruction of the Whigs was complete, and the organization of political discourse decisively altered as one of two great intersectional "audiences" disintegrated.

IV

FACED WITH increasingly strident attacks by the abolitionists, as well as incipient rebellion among the slave ranks, the South abandoned its previous, highly qualified defenses of slavery in favor of comprehensive proslavery arguments. By 1837, Calhoun himself noted that

> agitation has produced one happy effect at least; it has compelled us at the South to look into the nature and character of this great institution, and to correct many false impressions that even we had entertained in relation to it. Many in the South once believed that it was a moral and political evil; that folly and delusion are gone; we see it now in its

true light, and regard it as the most safe and stable basis for free institutions in the world. (Foner 1980, 41)

At the same time, many southerners began to advance their own criticisms of the "Free Society" of the North, and to claim clear moral and practical advantages for the slave society of the South. Perhaps the most influential arguments were those advanced by George Fitzhugh in *Sociology for the South, or the Failure of Free Society* (1854) and *Cannibals All! or Slaves Without Masters* (1857). With this development a southern discourse was constituted, and the South became an audience for its own rhetoric, and not just the target of abolitionist reproaches.[11]

In these two widely read and circulated tracts, Fitzhugh enunciated a truly conservative political philosophy that directly contradicted the natural rights philosophies underlying the abolitionists' arguments against slavery, as well as the democratic ideology of popular sovereignty.[12] The cornerstone of Fitzhugh's philosophy was his claim that "*Labor makes values, and Wit exploits and accumulates them*" (Fitzhugh [1857] 1960, 5). Fitzhugh insisted that all human societies were necessarily founded on the domination of weaker individuals by stronger ones. Because men were unequal in their natural abilities, they were unequal in their liberties as well, for those with superior physical, moral and intellectual talents would invariably succeed in reducing those of lesser talent to servitude. No laws or institutions were capable of preventing this situation. In that sense, law but follows nature in making rulers of those who are wise and brave, and slaves of those endowed with ordinary talents (Fitzhugh 1854, 178–179).[13]

---

[11] As Fitzhugh's titles suggest, his tracts were as much an attack on the Free Society of the North, where workers were "slaves without masters," as they were a defense of southern slavery.

[12] I use "conservative" here to refer to ideologies that are oriented toward the conservation of an organic order of society.

[13] Or less elegantly, but more to the point, "some were born with saddles on their backs, and others booted and spurred to ride them—and the riding does them good" (Fitzhugh 1854, 179).

Hence, slaves were slaves by nature, and "all that law and government can do, is to regulate, modify and mitigate their slavery" (ibid., 178). Still, the fact that government could actually temper the severity of exploitation was an important, even decisive, consideration for Fitzhugh. If societies were coercive by degree, then their laws and institutions could be compared in terms of their ability to mitigate slavery. And on this score, Fitzhugh argued, the slave states of the South were far superior to the free states of the North, wherein the exploitation of the wage laborer far exceeded that of the southern slave.

The influence of Aristotle on southern defenses of slavery was pervasive, especially among those like Fitzhugh who rejected theories of racial inferiority. Such theories reduced slaves to subhuman status and rendered moot the moral obligation of the master to care for the slave. Fitzhugh, on the other hand, pointed to this moral relationship as one of the virtues of plantation slavery over wage slavery, where no such ties existed. For that reason, Fitzhugh complained that the socialists' claim that "wages is slavery" was a "gross libel on slavery," since the obligation to care for slaves did not cease on their inability to render services, as it did in the North (ibid., 251).

Fitzhugh had no trouble documenting the piteous plight of the so-called free laborer of the North, whose normal condition was one of "physical suffering, cankering, corroding care, and mental apprehension and pain" (ibid., 165). Forced to sell their labor in a market crowded with thousands of others in similar circumstances, the northern "slave class" fell prey to rapacious businessmen who, under the guise of impersonal market forces, practiced a degree of exploitation previously unknown to human history: "The men of property, those who own lands and money, are masters of the poor; masters with none of the feelings, interests or sympathies of masters; they employ [laborers] when they please, and for what they please, and may leave them to die in the highway, for it is the only home to which the poor in free countries are entitled" (ibid., 233).

In the South, on the other hand, where no pretense of free labor was made, the natural tendency for the stronger to exploit the weaker was mitigated by the mutual interest and affection of master and slave: "There is no rivalry, no competition to get employment among slaves, as among free laborers. Nor is there a war between master and slave. The master's interest prevents his reducing the slave's allowance or wages in infancy or sickness, for he might lose the slave by so doing. His feeling for his slave never permits him to stint him in old age. The slaves are all well fed, well clad, have plenty of fuel, and are happy" (ibid., 246). Hence, it was the southern plantation that was the "beau ideal" of communal reformers and socialists, for it formed the basis for a society that was both prosperous and civilized in its human relations (ibid., 245).

There was, however, a third element of southern society that did not share in the alleged benefits of plantation slavery. Poor whites, who owned no slaves, and who were unable to compete effectively against plantations in the cotton economy of the South, harbored deep resentment toward the Negro slave population. This resentment, Fitzhugh feared, might easily translate into opposition to the institution of slavery itself, undermining the very existence of southern society.[14] As a simple matter of expediency, the support of poor whites for slavery had to be secured: "Poor people can see things as well as rich people. We can't hide the facts [of their economic deprivation] from them. It is always better openly, honestly, and fearlessly to meet danger, than to fly from or avoid it . . . the path of safety is the path of duty!" (ibid., 148).

In order to ensure the unified support of southern whites for slavery, Fitzhugh advocated a thorough program of education and indoctrination in the merits of slavery as a civilized

---

[14] Cash (1941) explains the absence of resentment toward slaveholders on the part of the "white trash" in terms of racial solidarity, "ameliorating patronism," and the incomplete economic subjugation of poor whites. Fitzhugh apparently was not content with these defenses and sought a positive, material incentive for poor whites' support for slavery.

institution. Moreover, he strongly supported De Bow's plans for the industrial development of the South and the diversification of its economy. This would ensure ample and well-paying job opportunities for all whites, especially those who owned no slaves and consequently reaped no benefits from slavery.

This development of the South was to proceed under the auspices of government, rather than private capital. It was to be a controlled process, rather than a self-sustaining one, so as to avoid the emergence of a hostile and independent bourgeoisie and excessive concentrations of white workers of doubtful loyalty (Genovese 1967, 246). Consequently, government was to play a vigorous role in planning and promoting schemes of internal improvements, developing financial and marketing facilities, and fostering transportation (Woodward 1960, xviii). In the words of Fitzhugh, "The duty of government does not end with educating the people. As far as is practicable, it should open to them avenues of employment in which they may use what they have learned" (Fitzhugh 1854, 145).

Several commentators have overlooked the role of government in sponsoring this development of the South and have accused Fitzhugh of inconsistency in his preference for the civilized values of a plantation economy and his advocacy of commercial development (Hartz 1955, 181). Given his own analysis of the corrupting influence of industrialization on the morals of a free society, they argue, Fitzhugh ought to have seen that economic development was bound to erode the aristocratic society he so clearly preferred. But Fitzhugh's critique of wage slavery and its attendant consequences was *not* based on a rejection of industrialization per se, as these critics seem to suppose. Rather, it was based on his opposition to the *form* of industrialization practiced in the North. It was laissez-faire industrialization that was the object of his contempt.

As Fitzhugh saw it, the North's adherence to the ideal of a free industrial society was doubly flawed. Not only had the

North failed to eliminate slavery, which was, in any case, impossible, but it had also failed to control the extent and severity of exploitation. The South, by contrast, had accepted the inevitability of slavery and had erected institutions that softened the exploitation of the many by the few. Therein lay its superiority.

Fitzhugh traced the failures of the North to the abolitionists' misplaced confidence in the ability of men to shape their destinies as they willed. They had fallen prey to the same sentiments that gripped the authors of the Declaration of Independence, a document written at a time "when men's minds were heated and blinded by patriotic zeal and a false philosophy," and men became

> extremely presumptuous, and undertook to form governments on exact philosophical principles, just as men make clocks, watches or mills. They confounded the moral with the physical world, and this was not strange, because they had begun to doubt whether there was any other than a physical world. Society seemed to them a thing whose movement and action could be controlled with as much certainty as the motion of a spinning wheel, provided it was organized on proper principles. (Fitzhugh 1854, 175–176)

Fitzhugh was at a loss to explain such hubris, which was in his view clearly contradicted by the testimony of history regarding the primacy of organic constitutions over written ones. *Universal* liberty and equality were evidently impossible, given the constitution of human nature, and any attempts to realize such fictions were bound to turn out badly.

This is precisely what happened, according to Fitzhugh, as the North committed itself to a policy of laissez-faire in order to destroy privilege and achieve liberty and equality. The removal of government as a moderating influence on exploitative relationships, and the substitution of the principle of self-interest for a morality of affections and obligations, eliminated any constraints on exploitation. The effects of such a policy were both predictable and immediately discernible: the stronger few oppressed the weaker many to the point of extinction.

Thus, in the free society, "there is no equality, except in theory . . . and there is no liberty" (ibid., 233). In exchange for their " 'natural and inalienable right' to be taken care of and protected, to have guardians, trustees, husbands, or masters," the natural slaves of the North had received formal rights of equality and liberty that served only to license their unmitigated oppression at the hands of uncaring, unrestrained masters (Fitzhugh 1857, 69). Far better they should be enslaved, for their own advantage as well as that of society.

The resultant antagonism between labor and capital in free society threatened to destroy capital, as well as labor. The rights and liberties enjoyed by the master class of the North were in constant jeopardy from an uprising of desperate men. For that reason, no true civilization, nor any stable political institutions, were possible in the North. Consequently, Fitzhugh and others claimed a causal connection between slavery, which rested on the mutuality of interest of strong and weak, and the emergence of advanced societies: "To it [slavery] Greece and Rome, Egypt and Judea, and all other distinguished States of antiquity were indebted for their great prosperity and high civilization; a prosperity and a civilization which appear almost miraculous, when we look to their ignorance of the physical sciences" (1854, 241–242).

These ancient civilizations owed their political institutions to slavery, which made it possible for a privileged few to enjoy liberty and equality without fear of reprisal. The South's commitment to domestic slavery explained, therefore, "why it is that the political condition of the slave-holding States has been so much more stable and quiet than those of the North," and why it would prove vastly more favorable than that of other sections for the development of free and stable institutions (Calhoun 1980, 396).

Hence it was that the ideal of a Greek democracy—democracy for the privileged class of citizens—fascinated the mind of the South. Parrington describes the southern idea of a Greek democracy as an ideological compromise between democratic ideals common to all Americans and the realities of slavery. Southerners believed that democracy "is possible only in a society that recognizes inequality as a law of nature, but in which the virtuous and capable enter into a voluntary copartnership for the common good, accepting wardship of the incompetent in the interests of society" (Parrington 1954b, 74).

In our teminology, it represents yet another attempt to harmonize the passing ideology of republicanism with the ascendant ideology of democracy in a way that protected sectional interests. The South was after all the last remaining bastion of deference, wherein the virtues of the two races were ostensibly well-organized and republican politics still flourished.

V

WITH THE DISINTEGRATION of the Whigs and the closing of southern ranks, only the Democratic party remained as a forum for national, as opposed to sectional discourse. However, the foundation of silence upon which this forum rested was undone by Douglas' Kansas-Nebraska Bill in 1854, which effectively repealed the Missouri Compromise and installed the principle of popular sovereignty, or local control, as a means for deciding new states' policies on slavery. With the passage of the act, many northern Democrats, angered by the reopening of the issue for northern territories from which slavery had been excluded by the Missouri Compromise, left the party and joined with ex-Whigs and Free Soilers in the Northwest to form antislavery fusion parties. In the east, they joined with the American or Know-Nothing party to oppose Whig and Democratic parties alike. The combined opposition of Whigs, Republicans, Know-Nothings, and fusionists cost the Democrats dearly in the North, where they lost control of several governorships and legislatures.

At the same time, radical southerners also began to show

their dissatisfaction with Douglas' compromise, which had the practical effect of excluding slavery from much of the West, where antislavery sentiment was strong. This was unacceptable to the southern Fire Eaters, who had come to the conclusion that an extension of slavery, not only to the West, but to the Caribbean as well, was essential for the preservation of slavery in the South itself.[15] The extension of slavery would open possibilities for interregional slave trade, reviving the profitability of the southern economy. Moreover, it would create a geographical and political buffer zone between the South and the most rabidly abolitionist areas of the North, even as it restored the possibility of regaining southern control over the Senate (Genovese 1967).

Outflanked by those who demanded the abolition of slavery, on the one hand, and those who demanded its extension, on the other, the once monolithic Democratic party began to disintegrate under the same pressures that led to the Whigs' demise. In 1856, after the Democratic National Convention endorsed the Kansas-Nebraska Act and nominated a pro-southerner, James Buchanan, as its presidential candidate, northern antislave Democrats left the party in droves, agreeing with Hannibal Hamlin that "the old Democratic party is now the party of slavery" (Kelley 1979, 201). In 1860, southerners who opposed Douglas split from the party to back Breckinridge, and the destruction of the Democratic party was complete. A national discourse was no longer possible, and the tension between sectional discourses reached the point of breaking.

VI

A SECTIONAL PARTY opposed to slavery remained to be constructed. The experiment of the Free Soil party had demon-

[15] "Fire Eaters" and "Ultra-Southerners" were appellations used to describe the unyielding opposition to abolitionism of a group of southerners who called themselves "True Southrons." Takaki (1971) discusses their efforts to revive the African slave trade, which the preceding generation of southerners had joined the abolitionists in condemning.

strated the potency of an alliance between the abolitionists and another antislave segment of the population, the northern labor movement. However, the shortlived nature of that experiment also revealed the difficulties in preserving an alliance between those who opposed slavery on moral grounds, and those who opposed it for political and economic reasons.

The importance of labor was recognized by at least one abolitionist. Nathaniel P. Rogers, argued that northern labor was a constituency vital to the abolitionist cause:

> We have got to look to the working people of the North to sustain and carry on the Anti-Slavery Movement. The people who work and are disrespected here, and who disrespect labor themselves, and disrespect themselves because they labor—have got to abolish slavery. And in order to do this, they must be emancipated themselves first. (Foner 1980, 68–69)

But most abolitionists attributed the condition of northern labor to moral backsliding on its part rather than economic exploitation. Their conception of coercion was limited to face-to-face relations between individuals, e.g. those between masters and slaves. It did not include "structures" of coercion, e.g. market mechanisms, from which identifiable agents of coercion were absent (ibid.).[16] Consequently, the abolitionist critique of southern slavery was never extended to the "wage slavery" of the North. In a free society, economic inequalities were a natural consequence of individual differences in talent, ambition, diligence, and so on, and not a function of the social relations of production. Hence, Garrison heatedly criticized labor agitators for raising false issues and diverting attention from abolition:[17]

[16] Cf. Chapter One, and especially Ball (1978), on concepts of coercion in political theories.

[17] Davis (1975) reverses Garrison's argument, claiming that British abolitionists crystallized a set of middle-class values and orientations and succeeded in identifying them in the public mind with the interests of society at large. The general emphasis on moral reform, and the abolition of slavery

There is a prevalent opinion, that wealth and aristocracy are indissolubly allied; and the poor and vulgar are taught to consider the opulent as their natural enemies. Those who inculcate this pernicious doctrine are the worst enemies of the people. . . . It is a miserable characteristic of human nature to look with an envious eye upon those who are more fortunate in their pursuits, or more exalted in their station. (ibid., 62–63)

For their part, northern labor movements returned the hostility and suspicion of abolitionism in kind, eschewing its evangelical impetus as well as its conclusions regarding the "envious eye" of labor (Jentz 1977). But their opposition to abolitionism did not mean that northern labor was proslavery. On the contrary, the ideology of the labor movement was profoundly antislave, though for political and economic rather than moral reasons (Foner 1980).

The essence of northern labor's opposition to slavery was summed up in its commitment to "free labor," i.e. labor in control not only of the laboring self, as the abolitionists would have it, but also in command of its means of production. Without the latter, labor could not be truly free from coercion by unproductive, privileged classes. In that sense, the "free laborer" of the North was but the son of the "independent proprietor" of Jackson's age, and the grandson of Jefferson's "yeoman citizen." Each expressed the frustrated aspirations of a class of citizens whose material condition failed to correspond to its privileged position in the moral order of the republican universe.

In construing the position of labor in such broad terms, the free labor ideology of the North was "implicitly hostile to slavery . . . [for it] contradicted the central ideas and values of artisan radicalism—liberty, democracy, equality, independence" (Foner 1980, 61). However, this implicit hostility to slavery remained subordinated to northern labor's preoc-

---

in particular, therefore succeeded in diverting attention from the exploitation of labor.

cupation with its own condition, on the one hand, and its aversion to a mixture of the white and black labor forces, on the other. These two concerns found common cause in an opposition to the extension of slavery to the western territories.

Northern labor's commitment to the principle of free soil, or nonextension, rested on the belief that the ultimate solution to the plight of the wage laborer lay in the geographic and economic expansion made possible by the West. On the one hand, the frontier alternative supposedly ensured the scarcity of labor in the Northeast, driving up wages and alleviating the impoverishment of the work force. On the other hand, it allowed the most industrious laborers to escape from the wage system altogether by creating new opportunities for independent proprietorship in the West.

Foner (1970) has described the fundamentally middle-class orientation of this labor movement, which sought to expand the possibilities for upward mobility within a private enterprise arrangement. Lincoln summarized this ethos in a speech at New Haven, on March 6, 1860: "What is the true condition of the laborer? I take it that it is best to leave each man free to acquire property as fast as he can. Some will get wealthy. I don't believe in a law to prevent a man from getting rich; it would do more harm than good. So while we don't propose any war upon capital, we do wish to allow the humblest man an equal chance to get rich with anybody else. When one starts poor, as most do in the race of life, free society is such that he knows he can better his condition; he knows that there is no fixed condition of labor for his whole life" (Parrington 1954b, 147).

Thus, the public lands of the West were to be "the great regulator of the relations of Labor and Capital, the safety valve of our industrial and social engine," according to Horace Greeley (Foner 1970, 27). They were to be opened to homesteaders in order to extend the economy, alleviate the problems of the urban working class, and, as Owen Lovejoy Long put it, "greatly increase the number of those who belong to what is called the middle class" (ibid., 29). Free soil and free labor were, therefore, but two sides of the same coin.

If expansion was to solve the problems of northern labor, however, it was evident to most labor leaders that it must be coupled with opposition to the extension of slavery. This was not motivated by any "squeamish sensitiveness upon the subject of slavery, or morbid sympathy for the slave," as Wilmot explained in defense of his Proviso to exclude slavery from territories acquired in the war with Mexico. Rather, it was out of conviction that the territories ought to be reserved for the white laborer, who refused to associate with the servile labor of black men, which had a degrading effect on all labor (Foner 1980, 84).[18]

Racism was, therefore, an important element of the rhetoric of Free Soil. Although the racism of the Barnburners was less explicit than that of the Hunker faction of the New York Democracy, it contrasted sharply with the antislave sentiments of other conveners of the Free Soil Convention, e.g. Liberty party members. However, their organizational strength ensured the Barnburners a significant voice in the affairs of the Free Soil party of 1848. They succeeded in nominating their man, Van Buren, as the party's presidential standard bearer. More importantly, they blocked the attempt of Liberty party members to include a black suffrage plank in the party platform, and they consistently opposed extending the franchise to a "servile race."

In opposing the extension of slavery, while refraining from advocating social and political equality for blacks, the Free Soil party (at the behest of the Barnburners) marked a vital turning point in the development of the antislavery crusade. The Free Soil party represented antislavery in its least radical, but most popular, form, and it achieved a success never

[18] Foner (1980, 84) reports that Wilmot accepted the label "White Man's Proviso" as an accurate description of his measure, which equated white labor and free labor.

before won by antislavery forces in electoral politics (ibid.).
Although the Barnburners returned to the Democratic fold
in 1852, the groundwork had been laid for a successful sectional challenge to slavery.

VII

THE COMMITMENT to equal rights for blacks was never restored to the platform of political antislavery, for it was evident that such a stance would alienate northern labor, as well
as other segments of the population that shared its racial big-
otry.[19] Once again, the fundamental issues of race were organized out of political discourse, even in the North. Henceforth, a firm opposition to the extension of slavery (as distinct
from its complete abolition or the granting of equal rights)
formed the cornerstone of all fusion efforts in the North.

The most successful of these fusion efforts was, of course,
the Republican party. Formed on a local and statewide basis
in the Northwest during the aftermath of the Kansas-Nebraska Act, it had gained sufficient national support to offer
Frémont as a Republican party candidate for the presidency
in 1856.[20] Frémont carried eleven northern states to Buchanan's five and only a solidly Democratic South prevented
his election to the presidency.

Frémont would have been able to overcome even the solid
South had he been able to capture the support of conserva-

---

[19] Lincoln himself acknowledged the practical necessity of bowing to popular sentiment (which he admittedly shared) on the issue of equality: "We
well know that those of the great mass of whites will not [agree to equal
rights]. Whether this feeling accords with justice or sound judgment is not
the sole question, if, indeed, it is any part of it. A universal feeling, whether
well- or ill-founded, cannot be safely disregarded. We cannot then make
them equals" (Lincoln 1965, 51).

[20] For a detailed account of the formation of the Republican party, see
Foner (1970). Use of the "Republican" label sprang up "instinctively, with
obvious fitness," Horace Greeley said. It evoked the name of Jefferson,
whose Ordinance of 1787 had excluded slavery from the Northwest Territory,
and of the purifying rites of revolution that preceded it. Jefferson's personal
ambivalence on the matter of slavery was, apparently, ignored (Kelley 1979,
198, 199).

tive northern Whigs, who split their votes among Buchanan and the Know-Nothing Fillmore. However, many of the Whigs feared that the Republicans were too radical and sectional in orientation (Foner 1970). During the interim 1856–1860 moderate Republicans gained control of the party, even as events such as the Dred Scott decision forced conservatives into increasingly more radical opposition to the Slave Power, whose control seemingly extended to the Supreme Court itself. By 1860, the party was able to absorb the recalcitrant Whigs under the candidacy of Lincoln—"the second choice of everybody"—who himself had been a longtime Whig party loyalist (Foner 1970, 213).

In Lincoln, the Republicans had found a man who enjoyed little national prominence, and who therefore had few significant enemies in the North. Moreover, he showed no sign of exciting opposition, for his antislavery views were quite moderate. Though he had expressed his moral disgust with the institution of slavery, he opposed both the abolition of slavery in the South itself, and the extension of political equality in the North: "I will say here, while upon this subject, that I have no purpose, directly or indirectly, to interfere with the institution of slavery in the States where it exists. I believe I have no lawful right to do so, and I have no inclination to do so" (Lincoln 1965, 52).

Furthermore, I will say then that I am not, nor ever have been, in favor of bringing about in any way the social and political equality of the black and white races—that I am not nor ever have been in favor of making voters or jurors of Negroes, nor of qualifying them to hold office, nor to intermarry with white people; and I will say in addition to this that there is a physical difference between the white and black races which I believe will forever forbid the two races living together in terms of social and political equality. (ibid., 162)

The furthest Lincoln would go in speaking out on behalf of the slave was in granting the "natural rights enumerated in the Declaration of Independence, the right to life, liberty and the pursuit of happiness." In this regard, and in this regard only, the black man was the equal of the white: both were entitled to "eat the bread, without the leave of anybody else, which his own hand earns" (ibid., 53).

By his circumspect approach Lincoln avoided the "white backlash" of the vast majority of northerners, while also offering some consolation to abolitionists by his reverence for the Declaration of Independence. It was his opposition to the extension of slavery to the territories that won him widespread support, however:[21]

> The whole nation is interested that the best use shall be made of these Territories. We want them for homes of free white people. This they cannot be, to any considerable extent, if slavery shall be planted within them. Slave states are places for poor white people to remove from, not to remove to. New free states are the places for poor people to go to, and better their condition. For this use the nation needs these Territories. (Hofstadter 1948, 113)

"Here," as Hofstadter puts it, "was an argument that could strike a responsive chord in the nervous system of every Northern man, farmer or worker, abolitionist or racist: if a stop was not put somewhere upon the spread of slavery, the institution would become nation-wide" (ibid., 113). Self-interest and national interest found common ground in opposing the encroachment of the Slave Power and galvanized the Republican party and its diverse lot of supporters. With the Democratic party in disarray, Lincoln and the Republican party swept to victory. Four days after the election South Carolina voted to secede. Six other states quickly followed suit, and four more eventually joined the Confederacy after the attack on Fort Sumter. Once sectional parties replaced intersectional coalitions, the nation became truly a house divided.

[21] Even that opposition was qualified by Lincoln's willingness to acquiesce in the admission of slave states to the Union, in the event that such states "freely" chose to be so admitted.

VIII

GIVEN THE IDEOLOGICAL context in which they occurred, the Civil War and the events leading up to it assumed the form of an intense struggle between competing visions of the good society. Each side proposed a future for the Union modeled after its own image and likeness, and each side saw in the others' Slave Power or Black Republicanism a clear and present danger to those hopes for the future. The two visions were incompatible, and the conflict between them was irrepressible, as Seward noted.

As we have seen, this polarization of opinion, which was reflected in the disintegration of intersectional parties, was in large measure a product of the sectional agitators—northern and southern radicals who consciously strove to influence public opinion, and hence politicians, through speeches, newspapers, lectures, and postal campaigns (Foner 1980, 31).[22] As a result, political discourse became a mass phenom-

[22] In the second chapter of his book Foner contrasts his interpretation of the antebellum period with competing accounts, for which he provides basic references, which I shall not duplicate here. These rival accounts include those that emphasize the economic origins of the Civil War, as in the Beards' rather deterministic interpretation, or in more sophisticated versions, e.g. the classic *Time on the Cross* by Fogel and Engerman, or Genovese's *The Political Economy of Slavery*, as well as the innumerable responses these works have provoked.

A second type of interpretation construes the antebellum period as a crucial stage in the modernization process (Luraghi 1972). Variations on this theme include works that emphasize dislocations in social structures that attend rapid industrialization (cf. n. 4 of this chapter), and those that stress the fitful "nationalization" of American culture (Kelley 1969).

Then there are the so-called "new political historians," e.g. Benson (1961) and Formisano (1971), who downplay the significance of national political issues in favor of ethnocultural and religious differences in accounting for political cleavages and partisan change. Other studies that emphasize the religious angle, albeit in a very different way, include studies by Walters (1977, 1978), who sees antebellum politics as a period of "reformism." This contrasts with accounts by historians like Zinn (1970), who emphasize the "radical" nature of politics during this time.

Foner's efforts to synthesize these approaches by focusing on the way in

enon during this period, but in a peculiar way. It was not a single discourse addressed to a single, mass audience. Instead, there were multiple discourses aimed at differentiated audiences. These discourses enjoyed relative autonomy from one another. As it turned out, their relations with one another were conflictual, rather than consensual, for these were highly strategic discourses. They did not aim to persuade opponents, so much as to exhort followers to take action against opponents. The resulting ensemble of discourses tended to be highly unstable, and subject to swift and thoroughgoing change.

The contest between radicals of different persuasions touched off a process of ideological response and counter-response, the dynamics of which proved exceedingly difficult to contain. During the course of this debate, sectional ideologies became more and more sophisticated. As each came to focus on its lowest common denominator, with the widest possible base of support in its society, the political system proved incapable of preventing first the intrusion, then the triumph of sectional ideology as the organizing principle of political combat (ibid., 32).

In the end, the southern ideal of Greek democracy was defeated militarily. As we shall see in the next chapter, however, the northern ideal of a Free Society was also significantly undone by the economic forces unleashed by its successful war effort. Thus, both visions perished in the Civil War, and a later generation was forced to construct its own vision on the charred remains of its predecessors.

---

which underlying conflicts found expression in the ideologies of the age, which then reflected back upon people's understanding of these conflicts, is to my mind preferable, for the reasons set out in the Prologue.

CHAPTER SIX

The Triumph of Conservatism

I

WITH THE CONCLUSION of the Civil War, the nation set about the arduous task of Reconstruction, a project which, as Foner (1980) reminds us, applied to northern as well as southern society.[1] Both underwent a "reconstruction" of the relations between capital and labor, the South at the hands of a northern Congress, and the North as a result of advancing industrialization. In that respect, Reconstruction and the Gilded Age were but two aspects of the more general process by which the capitalist mode of production was reproduced in America on an extended scale.[2]

Significant discourses on the proper organization of society were occasioned by this process of reconstruction. Both southern and northern labor were, of course, parties to this dispute and made important contributions to it. By far the most innovative arguments, however, were advanced by the nation's farmers, though as we shall see their voices seldom found a willing ear in the established arenas of discourse, the political parties. Their arguments recalled the moral exaltation of producer classes that was so prevalent during the Jacksonian era. They decried the injustice of an emergent industrial order that made the producers of wealth captives of its

---

[1] See Curry (1974) for a summary and evaluation of recent reinterpretations of Reconstruction, most of which seem to be strongly conditioned by cognate understandings of the antebellum period.

[2] Moody (1973) reviews the contemporary scholarship on the transformation of the economy during the Gilded Age. Skowronek (1982) gives an exceptionally fine account of the correlative process of state-building in the same period, paying particular attention to the role of "courts and parties" in American political economy.

owners. And they advocated the use of the powers of the national government to rectify this situation.

One of the farmer's chief targets was the nation's money system. Indeed, the "money question" informed almost all of the political discussion of this period as citizens debated the proper role of money in society and the most felicitous organization of the exchange process. What made this discussion different from earlier ones, however, was the injection of *scientific* theories into this debate on social organization. Whereas previous discourses drew primarily or even exclusively on moral traditions to decide such matters, Americans during the Gilded Age began to entertain policy proposals that were ostensibly informed by knowledge about the laws of societal evolution.

Of course there was considerable disagreement about the true content of these laws and the policies that were alleged to follow from them (Fine 1956). Nevertheless, the introduction of "amoral" considerations undoubtedly undermined moral objections to the status quo, if only by presenting justifications for it that were literally incomprehensible within the traditional understandings of American politics. Moreover, the promise of progress contained in these scientific arguments softened the moral outrage at existing conditions that informed much of the Populists' rhetoric.

Thus, the reconstruction of American society was at the same time a reconstruction of its basic principles of self-understanding. The fluid politics of this period reflect this conceptual turmoil as the discourse of American politics was remade along scientific lines, and in the process the reigning ideology of democracy was radically transformed.

II

IN THE SOUTH, Reconstruction involved the establishment of a system of wage labor in a culture based primarily on slave labor. The influence of slavery was so great that alternative labor relations were almost inconceivable to the southern mind. Foner describes the inability of southerners to com-

prehend the possibility of a cotton economy organized around
a system of wage labor, rather than slavery:

> The confused early years of Reconstruction become more
> comprehensible when we consider the difficulty planters
> had in adjusting to their new status as employers, and
> freedmen in becoming free laborers. "The former relation
> has to be unlearnt by both parties," was how a South Car-
> olina planter put it. For many planters, the unlearning
> process was a painful one. The normal give and take of
> employer and employee was difficult to accept; "it seems
> humiliating," wrote one Georgian, "to be compelled to bar-
> gain and haggle with our servants about wages." One North
> Carolina farmer employed a freedman in the spring of
> 1865, promising to give him "whatever was right" when
> the crop was gathered. Another said he would pay wages
> "where I thought them earned, but this must be left to
> me." Behavior completely normal in the North, such as a
> freedman informing a Georgia farmer he was leaving be-
> cause "he thought he could do better," provoked cries of
> outrage and charges of ingratitude. (Foner 1980, 99)

To a significant extent, this inability to comprehend the
wage system imposed by the North was due to southerners'
experiences in maintaining and justifying slavery, which prevented them from seeing that labor might be induced to perform its appointed tasks by impersonal market forces, instead
of naked coercion. Planters' *beliefs* about plantation labor
practices partially constituted those selfsame practices. Their
inability to comprehend a system of wage labor was, therefore, responsible for their inability to act according to the
norms of a wage labor economy. In particular, planters were
convinced that blacks would refuse to work on plantations
unless compelled, and in that respect, they, no less than
northern abolitionists, significantly underestimated the fundamentally coercive nature of labor market forces.

That the critics of the "Free Society of the North" should
make this error may seem surprising until it is recalled that

southerners thought of black and white labor in distinctly different terms: "The free labor ideology, they insisted, ignored 'the characteristic indolence of the negro, which will ever be manifested and indulged in a condition of freedom' " (ibid., 103). Blacks were not susceptible to the same wage incentives as whites and therefore had to be compelled to labor, which compulsion did them good, according to men like Fitzhugh.

This longstanding prejudice was reinforced by the difficulty of reestablishing the cotton economy in the years immediately after the war, when the freedmen of the South demonstrated a preference for subsistence farming when access to land made that a viable alternative to plantation labor. However, the original insight of Fitzhugh and others was eventually restored by the depression of 1873, which probably returned more blacks to the plantation than virtually any of the policies, e.g. land restriction, that were designed to establish a free cotton economy (ibid.).[3]

By 1877, however, the ideology of free labor that informed the northern reconstruction of the southern system of labor was losing its force in the North itself. The rapid expansion of industrial capitalism in the postwar years (an expansion fueled in part by the northern war effort), and the attendant rise of an apparently permanent class of wage earners, rendered it increasingly difficult to maintain that wage labor was only a stopping point on the road to economic independence. Similarly, the increasing incidence of strikes and industrial violence made it difficult to affirm the fundamental harmony of capital and labor implicit in the free labor ideology.

The irony here is indeed striking. The North was eventually forced to accept the reality of conflict between labor and capital, a reality the South had understood all along (ibid., 127). That acceptance was not easily gained, however. Even among laborers, the free labor ideology remained strong until

[3] At the same time, poor whites, who before the war had been independent proprietors, became tenant farmers caught in the grip of the furnishing system of credit. They would form the backbone of the southern Populist movement (Goodwyn 1976).

late in the nineteenth century. Early attempts to organize labor, e.g. the National Labor Union and the Knights of Labor, were strongly imbued with the free labor ideology, which resisted

> an impersonal system that was transforming the worker from a skilled craftsman into an unskilled or semiskilled robot . . . an economic entity rather than an active and responsible individual who regarded his occupation as a means of fulfillment and who enjoyed an important and respected position in the community. (Grob 1969, 187–188)

Thus, the reform unionism engendered by the collision of free labor and industrial capital reflected the traditional Jacksonian concern for the status of producers and the virtue of the independent entrepreneuer.

By the last quarter of the century, however, it became evident that wage labor was destined to be the permanent condition of an ever-increasing number of individuals. The closing of the economic frontier, which actually preceded the closing of the geographic frontier announced by Turner in 1893, produced a new trade union ideology that animated subsequent organizing efforts. This trade union ideology was predicated on the acceptance of permanent wage labor status and consequently aimed at securing greater security and higher wages, rather than proprietorship. The transition from free labor to trade unionism represented, therefore, a decisive shift in the ideology of labor, transforming a resentment of capitalism into a tacit acceptance of the maturing economic order and labor's place within it (ibid.).

Against the immediate and material appeals of this trade union ideology, socialist labor organizers made little headway.[4] In part, this was due to serious disagreements on the left over the proper course of revolutionary action. Daniel De

---

[4] Kraditor (1981) provides a critical review of current explanations for the failure of radical labor parties to attract large memberships during this period of American history.

Leon, a one-time adherent of Edward Bellamy, who later abandoned "utopian socialism" in favor of a more "scientific" version of historical materialism, advocated the direct overthrow of capitalism. The proper vehicle for this action, De Leon assumed, was a class-conscious party of revolutionaries dedicated to the peaceful abolition of private ownership.

The essence of De Leon's approach lay in the subordination of existing trade unions to the Socialist Labor Party: "The party must dominate the trade union movement . . . it must dominate or be dominated," and in the latter case the failure of socialism would be assured (Foner 1964, 370). This policy of "boring from without," which rejected trade unionism as the primary vehicle of the labor movement, was opposed by other socialists, e.g. Morris Hillquit, who preferred to "bore from within" by working to assume control of the existing trade unions. Yet a third faction, headed by Debs and Berger, preferred to follow a course of independent political action and practiced a policy of noninterference in trade unions.[5]

The European flavor of socialist rhetoric reduced its appeal to American laborers accustomed to the ideology of free labor. Moreover, the traditional suspicion of positive government among "the democracy" made *political* action seem irrelevant, or even worse, counterproductive. Gompers, for his part, represented the vast majority of laborers who eschewed political action in favor of economic pressure in the form of collective bargaining. The Socialists' inability to agree on the proper stance toward unionism left Gompers with substantial maneuvering room, which he used to consolidate labor under the auspices of a nonsocialist ideology that was in any case

[5] Berger was known as "the American Bernstein" because of his support for "The Bernstein Doctrine in America," which appeared in the *Social Democratic Herald* of October, 1901 (Foner 1964, 371). Because the working class in America was not "ripe for socialism," the correct policy, according to Berger and his fellow travelers, was to struggle for reforms that might eventually produce a qualitative change in the organization of society. Hence their emphasis on the city-by-city victory of socialism under the auspices of good government reforms (ibid., 370).

much less of a departure from the older ideology of free labor.

Thus, labor's response to the emerging industrial order was essentially conservative in nature. Trade unionism triumphed over socialism as the successor to the ideology of free labor, and radical labor was tamed. Moreover, the political "neutrality" of organized labor was, as we shall see, a contributing factor in the defeat of agrarian radicals, whose efforts to forge a farmer-labor alliance were spurned by Gompers. This agrarian radicalism, which grew out of the soil of free labor and ultimately remained committed to capitalism, offered a systematic critique of the undemocratic aspects of the new industrial order. The Populists' experiences led them to reject economic action as insufficient, and to seek political remedies. Their inability to entice labor into a collective exploration of the proper organization of industrial society made it comparatively easy for established interests to ignore the radical voice of the agrarians. In effect, agricultural labor was excluded from the ongoing discourse on the relations between capital and labor in Reconstruction America.

III

WHILE WAGES LAY at the center of labor disputes in the Northeast, it was the "money question" that exercised farmers in the West and South. For it was the money question, in its various forms, e.g. the debates over resumption of greenbacks and the demonetization of silver, that dominated their politics during the last three decades of the nineteenth century. Much of its importance was, of course, due to the intrinsically divisive nature of pocketbook issues. Rather early on, however, the money question assumed an even greater importance, as a whole host of other problems, the resolution of which seemed to depend on the outcome of the money question, came to be associated with it. By the last decade of the century, the money question symbolized nothing less than the basic question of whether or not government was to respond "in a republican way to the requirements of the people as a whole, or only to certain special and self-interested segments" (Nugent 1967, 20).

This transfiguration of the money question is outlined by Nugent (1967; 1968), who traces its development as a political issue. The initial phase of discussion over the money question was marked by relative harmony, as the various parties to the dispute shared a set of common assumptions and ideas about money and its role in society. According to Nugent, virtually all participants in the debate adhered to the producer ethic, which held that labor was the sole source of value, and that money was a mark of civilization and progress because it facilitated production and exchange according to the classical laws of supply and demand. The key issue, then, boiled down to which monetary system best performed these functions. As such, the rhetoric of producerism underpinned all positions on the money question and acted as an integrating force in the political discussion over it (Nugent 1968, 18).

After 1873, however, the ravages of depression and the secular decline of commodity prices and wages divided parties to such an extent that, in the course of responding to one another's monetary policies, the common rhetoric was gradually destroyed:

> Under the conditions of social and economic distress that prevailed during the depression years of the seventies, the rhetorical terms and ideas that were formerly the common property of a number of groups became increasingly appropriated by particular groups to serve their several ends. Rhetoric proved too fragile to survive . . . and it became virtually indistinguishable from the ideological aims and wish-systems of separate groups. (ibid., 18)

The fragmentation of the rhetoric of harmony, and the emergence of competing social rhetorics, was initially played out in the series of skirmishes between "goldbugs" and "greenbackers." But the subsequent full-scale assault on finance capital was mounted by the Populists, and in particular, the People's party.

A modern system of fiat currency formed the cornerstone

of the new democratic order envisioned by the Populists. Radical agrarians rejected the bimetalism of the silverites just as emphatically as the monometalism of the goldbugs, preferring instead the adoption of a more flexible, "soft" currency unbacked by gold or silver. As such, they represented the last, and by far the most potent, expression of the greenback critique of nineteenth century finance capital in America (Goodwyn 1976).[6]

The greenback critique itself centered on the inadequate supply of currency engendered by hard money policies. Hard money meant tight money, which in turn led to high interest rates for farmers who depended on credit and the crop-lien system of financing. At the same time, tight money drove farm commodity prices down at harvest time, when the seasonal demands for credit to purchase crops boosted the value of money at a much faster rate than improved methods of production generated increases in commodity values.[7] Farmers were forced to buy dearly, and sell cheaply, and as a result many thousands were forced into tenancy, and many more thousands into bankruptcy. Those who survived lived in fear of the single crop failure that would absolutely impoverish them.[8]

[6] Goodwyn argues that those who view Populism as a profoundly reactionary movement, e.g. Hofstadter (1955) and Ferkiss (1957), as well as those who defend it as a truly radical response to industrialism, e.g. Pollack (1967) and Nugent (1963), have been mislead by Hicks' (1936) neglect of the Farmers' Alliance in favor of the People's party and its ill-fated venture into "free silverism." Goodwyn sees the Alliance's experiments with cooperative production and marketing as the embodiment of a new conception of democracy that represents the specific contribution of Populism, which is why I rely on his account.

[7] Because prices are a function of the ratio of commodity values to the value of money, prices may fall even though the value of commodities increases owing to improved methods of production. If the value of money increases at a faster rate than the value of commodities, prices will fall. This, of course, was typical of harvest time, when the demand on eastern financiers for credit to move the agricultural product was exceedingly high (Goodwyn 1976).

[8] Farmers were not the only victims of hard money policies. At various times during this period, businessmen and labor (both black and white) fell

Farmers who found it difficult to understand why a more abundant crop came to be worthless took little consolation from hard monetarist theories of overproduction. W. Scott Morgan of Arkansas complained:

To say that over-production is the cause of "hard times," is to say that the people are too industrious; that they could make a better living if they did not work so hard; that they have raised so much they are starving to death, and manufactured so many clothes that they are compelled to go naked. (Tindall 1966, 17)

The key problem, according to Nelson Dunning, editor of the *National Economist*, was this:

All economists agree that labor is the sole producer of wealth. If this proposition be true, might it not be proper to ask: Why does not the producer of this wealth possess it after production? What intervening cause steps in between producer and this wealth, and prevents his owning and enjoying what his brain and brawn have created? (ibid., 98)

The answer to this question, according to Dunning and other Populists, was to be found in a network of exchange relations that systematically stripped producers of their wealth. Under a properly functioning market arrangement, commodity prices were determined solely by the interaction of buyers and sellers of commodities. With the intervention of key middlemen, e.g. transporters and financiers, prices were no longer a function of supply and demand only. The middlemen, whose function was to facilitate exchange, were

---

victim to similar financial pressures and turned toward greenbacks for relief. The resiliency of entrenched notions about the intrinsic value of money, and the inability of greenbackers to transcend traditional party and sectional loyalties effectively defused these movements (Goodwyn 1976, 15).

Organized labor eventually dissociated itself from political action, as we have seen, and they offered little aid and comfort to the People's party, which they perceived as a party of independent proprietors rather than a labor party per se. Cf. Gompers' statement in Tindall (1966, 187).

able, by virtue of their monopolistic positions, to impose extraordinary surcharges on the producers of wealth. Consequently, these nonproducers were able to effectively "rob" producers who depended on them for marketing their goods.

Robbery was a key theme in Populist rhetoric, which was rooted in the notion that only producers create value. Nonproducers, e.g. banks and railroads, did not create value, but only made the realization of value possible. The ideal distributional system, according to this view, would facilitate exchange without imposing heavy duties on producers. Hence, the Populists frequently attacked distributional monopolies that violated the basic principle that "wealth belongs to him who creates it, and every dollar taken from industry without an equivalent is robbery. 'If any will not work, neither shall he eat.' The interests of rural and civic labor are the same; their enemies are identical" (ibid., 93).

The solution to the problem of "overproduction" lay, according to soft money advocates, in an expansion of the money supply. Fiat currency—greenbacks—could be used to stabilize prices and effect a more equitable distribution of the abundant product of America's farmers and laborers. Obviously, greenbackers were proposing inflation as a consciously redistributive policy. Just as obviously, goldbugs and other hard monetarists opposed this policy, which threatened to reverse the flow of value from debtor to creditor. At stake was the very nature of the national currency system, and by implication the relation between labor and capital.

In that sense, the greenback critique of finance capital was truly radical, and the hostile reception with which it met is not surprising. The successive failures of the National Labor Union (1871), the Greenback party (1876–1884), and the Union Labor party (1888) to force the issue onto the agenda of national politics demonstrated the tremendous resistance, among capitalists and laborers alike, to this sort of radical proposal. However, by the 1890s the greenback critique would prove irresistible, though not unconquerable.

IV

EVEN AS EARLY FORAYS into the political arena were being roundly defeated, agrarian radicals were beginning to experiment with alternative solutions to the problems of high interest rates and low commodity prices. Goodwyn (1976) provides a splendid account of the Texas Alliance's efforts to establish buying and selling cooperatives that would permit farmers to create favorable credit arrangements and withhold part of their produce in order to obtain a better price. Buoyed by small-scale successes, the Texas Alliance set out to spread the gospel of cooperation throughout the South and West via an elaborate lecture system, which provided an important educative and organizational vehicle. Cooperatives sprang up throughout the nation's agricultural region, and a new radicalism took shape.

The initial successes of farmer cooperatives proved hard to duplicate on a large scale, however. The Texas Alliance's attempt to establish a statewide cooperative exchange failed because of its inability to secure enough capital to sustain such a venture. Nevertheless, the cooperative experiments provided valuable lessons to agrarian radicals:

> The subsequent *experience* of these farmers, as they labored to make their co-ops functional in the face of implacable banker, railroad, and merchant opposition had a transforming political impact upon them. They learned to perceive the coercive elements of commercial exhange embedded in the structure of the emerging corporate system. This insight in itself did not insure political insurgency—the Alliance was not structurally geared for insurgent politics—but the experience did bring the farmers to a level of consciousness that facilitated the creation of a new democratic political institution, the People's Party. (Goodwyn 1981, 52)

This new consciousness achieved a revolutionary breakthrough when Charles Macune devised the so-called "subtreasury plan" to overcome the problems of capitalization that prevented the formation of large scale cooperatives. The subtreasury plan would mobilize the currency issuing power of the national government on behalf of the nation's producing classes:

> The federal government would underwrite the cooperatives by issuing greenbacks to provide credit for the farmer's crops, creating the basis of a more flexible national currency in the process; the necessary marketing and purchasing facilities would be achieved through government-owned warehouses, or "subtreasuries," and through federal subtreasury certificates paid to the farmer for his produce—credit which would remove furnishing merchants, commercial banks, and chattel mortgage companies from American agriculture. (Goodwyn 1976, 152)

The subtreasury plan became the centerpiece of the agrarian program for reform, galvanizing further organizational efforts in the South, West, and upper Midwest. The key question, of course, concerned the matter of how to put the plan into practice. Given the failure of past third-party efforts, Macune favored the development of a broad, nonpartisan movement capable of forcing one or both of the major parties to respond to popular pressures.

Others, e.g. William Lamb and L. L. Polk, were less optimistic about the possibility of breaking the hold of financial conservatives over the major parties. Heartened by the electoral success of Alliance candidates in Kansas, these men sensed the time was ripe for a new third party, a People's party, that would sweep to power on the basis of a new intersectional alignment of farmers and producers. It was this group that prevailed, and in 1892 the People's party incorporated the subtreasury plan into its Omaha Platform, nominated James C. Weaver as its presidential standard bearer, and set forth to do battle with the monied interests.

The Omaha Platform represented the culmination of a quarter century of radical opposition in American politics. Ignatius Donnelly's preamble denounced the robber barons of finance capital and their political stooges and announced the intention of the People's party "to restore the government of the Republic to the hands of 'the plain people,' with which class it originated." It pledged the People's party to marshall the power of government—"in other words, of the people"—to end oppression, injustice, and poverty in the land, and to "promote the general welfare, and secure the blessings of liberty for ourselves and our posterity" (Tindall 1966, 92).

Specifically, the platform demanded the repatriation of public lands owned by railroads and aliens, whose concentrated ownership prevented the vast majority of men from having access to the most important means of production.[9] The platform also demanded the nationalization of the railroads, which were vital to the marketing of agricultural produce. Finally, it demanded the implementation of the subtreasury plan, free coinage of silver, and expansion of the money supply, all as a way of stabilizing commodity prices and improving the market position of farmers.

As a package, these reforms constituted the Populists' response to the evils of a distribution system that frustrated the best efforts of a vital productive sector of the economy. At the same time Populists explicitly rejected socialism in favor of a more democratic capitalism:

> The dividing line between socialism and democracy is the right and recognition of private property: We favor a democracy and stand by the principle that governments are organized to perform for the whole people at cost, that service which the citizen and family cannot best perform for themselves. (Pollack 1967, 214)

[9] Others, too, were interested in the "land problem." Henry George's enormously popular *Progress and Poverty* (1879) focused on the concentration of land ownership and the illicit rents received therefrom. His single *ad valorem* tax on land would have forced landowners to utilize their land or rent to someone who would. George hoped this would lower rents, make land more accessible to lower income groups, and eliminate the subservient condition of farmers (Scott 1977).

Still, the Populists were willing to resort to state action in order to redress economic grievances. In contrast to the laissez-faire attitude prevailing in the rest of the nation, Populists like Governor Lorenzo Lewelling of Kansas asked,

> What is government if it does not make it possible for me to live? and provide for my family! . . . If the Government don't do that, what better is the Government to me than a state of barbarism and everywhere we slay, and slayer in turn is slain and so on the great theatre of life is one vast conspiracy all creatures from the worms to the man in turn rob their fellows. (Tindall 1966, 149)

No convincing answer to Lewelling's question came; only William Allen White's indignant query, "What's the matter with Kansas?" So the Populists continued to press their cause, using a tried-and-true rhetoric borrowed from the Jacksonians. But in a new context that rhetoric had a unique edge to it, as we shall see.

V

THE POPULISTS were not afraid to use government as a civilizing force, and as the Omaha Platform indicates, they would not have hesitated to nationalize the key industries of exchange. In that respect, Palmer (1972, 308) is right to note that the Populists, when they spoke of a return to the past, spoke of a return to the past *principles* of popular rule, but not past *policies* of minimalist government.

This innovative aspect of the Populists' contributions to political discourse has gone largely unappreciated, perhaps because they bear a superficial resemblance to the Jacksonians. Populist rhetoric was unoriginal, drawing its slogans and imagery from traditional sources (Hart 1978, 84). This is especially true of the Populist condemnations of monopolies, which echoed those of the Jacksonian Democrats. Indeed, the slogan of the Jacksonians, "Equal Rights for All, Special Privileges for None," became the masthead motto of Tom Watson's *People's Party Paper*. On the basis of such rhetorical similarities, Hofstadter (1955) and others have concluded that the Populists were the lineal descendants of the Jacksonian Democrats.

This conclusion is unwarranted, for it fails to account for the different circumstances in which these slogans were used. Because the meaning of rhetoric is always conditioned by the context in which it occurs and the uses to which it is put, the same slogan, e.g. "Equal Rights for All, Special Privileges for None," can mean quite different things in different settings. This is clearly the case when comparing Populist and Jacksonian antimonopoly rhetoric.

For one thing, the nature of monopoly had changed drastically in the intervening decades. The target of the Jacksonian rhetoric was the "Monster Bank," which was a *public* monopoly created and maintained by the national government. The Populists' targets, on the other hand, were *private* monopolies, not creations of the state (though they were certainly the beneficiaries of the state's policies). Consequently, the target of the respective antimonopolist rhetorics was quite different, indeed.

The political prescriptions of the Populists also differed from those of the Jacksonians. The Jacksonian rhetoric aimed to restore the lost innocence of an agrarian republic by eliminating the "corrupt bargain" of commerce and government.[10] State-supported monopolies, e.g. the National Bank, were to be destroyed by withdrawing government support for them, which would eliminate their monopolistic basis. Hence, Jacksonian antimonopoly rhetoric was consistently laissez-faire in tone, reflecting its underlying predilection for minimalist government.

Populist antimonopoly rhetoric, on the other hand, was animated by preference for an active, interventionist state, the power of which might be used to counterbalance that of monopolies. Since the new monopolies were not creations of the state, withdrawal of state support was no guarantee of their

[10] Cf. Chapter Four.

demise. A stronger response was needed in order to effectively combat their power and influence on the economy, and over politicians who dispensed favors to them in return for other considerations.

The same is true of the Populists' support for an independent treasury, which the Jacksonians also suggested. Jacksonians had proposed replacing the Bank with an independent Treasury that would act as the government's banker. Government funds would be held at various "subtreasuries" throughout the nation in order to facilitate government transactions. The intent of this plan was two-fold. It would make the Treasury independent of private banks, and it would restrict credit by removing public deposits from banks that had used those deposits to extend credit.

The impact of this scheme was dramatic, for it essentially confined the national government's monetary authority to control over coin and left control of the major part of the money supply—credit—in the hands of private banks (Hammond 1957, 543–544). In making the Treasury independent, the Democrats also made it ineffective as an instrument of monetary policy.

The Populists, by contrast, hoped to reverse this policy and undo the damage done by abandoning control over the money supply to the private sector. Their subtreasury plan represented an explicit attempt to establish the government as the preeminent actor in this area, and to abandon its spectator role of independence. Hence, their plan would have *expanded* credit and made it more readily available via government financing.

The Populists faced an extraordinarily difficult task in spreading this message. The lecture system was an effective means of organizing their natural constituency, but in trying to win the support of disgruntled Democrats and Republicans the Populists relied on the reform press. No less than 1,000 sympathetic newspapers sprang up in the West and South to spread the gospel of populism (Goodwyn 1976, 355). These papers trumpeted the theme of the "politics of the future," which presented the innovative ideas of the Omaha Platform in language that was traditional and reassuring.

Drawing heavily on religious imagery and construction, the reform press warned of the impending apocalypse of finance capitalism, the evil oppression of which could only excite "violent revolution accompanied by horrors and injustice at which humanity shudders" (Palmer 1972, 319). Against that possibility, the press offered the peaceful path of Populist reform, by which the People's party would deliver the nation from its trials and tribulations.

Beneath the religious imagery, however, lay the unmistakable economic message of populism. To ignore this, as Goodwyn (1976) argues, is to miss the real significance of populism. The Populists were neither more nor less religious than most of their contemporaries (nor, for that matter, were they any more conspiratorial or xenophobic). As the primary victims of the newly emerging economic order, they were outspoken critics of that order's undemocratic tendencies. In that sense populism was a reaction to the gross inequalities of the Gilded Age. But that reaction did not entail a rejection of industrialization per se, or even capitalist forms of industrialization. Rather, it objected to monopoly capitalism, and aimed to establish a new, more democratic order of capitalism in which the fruits of increased productivity were more widely shared and enjoyed.

In the end the People's party failed to convince enough Americans of the impending dangers to democracy. The greenback critique of finance capital fell on deaf ears, as the major parties were able to reactivate the lingering sectional loyalties of the Civil War and fend off the raiding efforts of the People's party. "Vote as you shoot, boys" proved stronger than the "politics of brotherly love" preached by the lecturers and reform press.

No better evidence of this defeat can be cited than the so-called success of populism, namely the Democrats' acceptance of the free silverism of Bryan. Yet this was the mere shadow of populism, as Goodwyn points out, the least dangerous, and most perverted, form of the greenback ideology. When that too was rejected, political discussion on the money question was stilled.

VI

THE POPULISTS' APPEAL to religious imagery was effectively countered by hard monetarists' efforts to marshall the scientific theory of evolutionism in support of their cause. This marked a radical departure from previous patterns of American thought, all of which had grounded their criticisms and defenses of politics in moral categories, e.g. virtue, or self-interest properly understood. However, the intellectual climate of the late nineteenth century was distinctly less hospitable to notions of individual rationality and moral agency, which were the hallmarks of the Scottish Enlightenment in America (Miller 1954). Instead, Americans were captivated by scientific theories of society, especially those based on the evolutionary theories of Darwin. Darwinism, in its various forms—social Darwinism, reform Darwinism, theistic evolutionism—held sway over the American mind, challenged only occasionally (and then only in intellectual circles) by idealist critiques of its materialist foundation (Royce), pragmatic defenses of mind (Peirce), and iconoclastic treatments of the crass materialism justified by it (Veblen).

Consequently, hard monetarists were able to make good use of Darwinist arguments, as William Graham Sumner, one of the more influential popularizers of social Darwinism, proved. Sumner's analysis of the money question was at once ingenious and sophisticated. He began by disputing the radicals' assertion that "hard times" had been brought on by a constricted supply of money. "Hard times," Sumner noted, were always relative, both across classes and in time. He argued that in fact, America in 1896 was generally prosperous, and that the radicals' assertion of "hard times" was peculiar to their own situation, which he alleged was due to overinvestment of capital and labor in agriculture. The lack of prosperity on the agrarian front was, therefore, not due to an

202 The Triumph of Conservatism

inadequate money supply, but was primarily the result of market forces. This would eventually be corrected by the laws of the market, operating to divert capital into other, more profitable, sectors of production (Sumner 1940, 2:44–46).

Sumner acknowledged that the problem was partially aggravated by the movement from a bimetallic to a monometallic monetary standard, which was both necessary and desirable for progress to continue:

> The movement of the great commercial nations towards a single gold currency is the most important event in the monetary history of our time and one which nothing can possibly arrest. It produces temporary distress, and the means of alleviating that distress are a proper subject of consideration; but the advantages which will be obtained for all time to come immeasurably surpass the present loss and inconveniences. (ibid., 66)

Sumner's comment on the appropriateness of considering "means of alleviating that distress" was almost certainly disingenuous, for he rejected both private philanthropy and public policies designed to alleviate the distress of poverty.[11] Both constituted unwarranted and ill-considered interferences in the natural process of evolution which, in Sumner's view, could only hinder the future progress of American civilization. Thus, Sumner rejected out of hand virtually all of

[11] Sumner's conclusion that social classes owe each other nothing save good will, mutual respect, and mutual guarantees of liberty and security, was not shared by another laissez-faire proponent, Andrew Carnegie, who felt that private philanthropy, at least, was justified: "This, then, is held to be the duty of the man of Wealth: First, to set an example of modest, unostentatious living . . . and after doing so to consider all surplus revenues which come to him simply as trust funds, which he is called upon to administer, and strictly bound to administer in the manner which, in his judgment, is best calculated to produce the most beneficial results for the community." In this, "we have the true antidote for the *temporary* unequal distribution of wealth, the reconciliation of the rich and the poor—a reign of harmony" (Boostin 1969, 527, 526; my emphasis).

the Populists' proposals for alleviating the "inconveniences" of poverty by governmental action and propounded instead a policy of minimalist government.

Sumner's defense of the minimalist state was grounded in a philosophy of social Darwinism. Following Spencer, Sumner argued that human development was subject to the same laws that governed evolution in the animal kingdom. In particular, it was subject to the law of the survival of the fittest, in which the fate of individuals and species were inextricably bound together in a struggle against nature. In this respect, men were no different than animals—all were locked in a deadly contest with nature, who yielded the fruits of survival grudgingly, and then only to those who most energetically and resolutely assailed her (ibid., 95). Only the fittest individuals survived this competition for nature's resources, and only the fittest societies, composed of the fittest members, managed to flourish in a hostile environment.

In this desperate struggle for survival, no individual or society was entitled to the life-giving rewards of nature, save by their industry and resourcefulness. Individuals and societies were rewarded in proportion to their effort. Those who toiled received, and those who were idle went unrewarded. In this way, nature promoted only those individuals and societies most capable of responding to the demands of competition for her favors.

Consequently, rights had no natural status whatsoever: "Before the tribunal of nature a man has no more right to life than a rattlesnake; he has no more right to liberty than any wild beast; his right to the pursuit of happiness is nothing but a license to maintain the struggle for existence, if he can find within himself the powers with which to do it" (Sumner 1940, 1:385).

But some rights did have a bearing on the outcome of the struggle for survival, for they represented adaptations that had proved particularly advantageous in the contest with nature. This was especially true of civil liberty, by which "each man is guaranteed the use of all his own powers exclusively for his own welfare" (Sumner 1974, 30). Societies that succeeded in developing such mores were able to transform the war of all against all into a concerted assault on nature:

> What civil liberty does is to turn the competition of man with man from violence and brute force into an industrial competition under which men vie with one another for the acquisition of material goods by industry, energy, skill, frugality, prudence, temperance, and other industrial virtues. (Sumner 1940, 2:96)

Thus, civil liberty was a selective adaptation par excellence because it channeled the individual pursuit of self-interest in a socially useful direction.

Sumner insisted that liberty does not guarantee an equal return to all; it merely guarantees that the fruits of individuals' labor, however unequal, will receive the same protection. Any attempt to alter this relationship was bound to have pernicious effects on individuals and societies, for it would encourage the survival of the unfit at the expense of those whose rewards attested to their fitness:

> Let it be understood that we cannot go outside of this alternative: liberty, inequality, survival of the fittest; not liberty, equality, survival of the unfittest. The former carries society forward and favors all its best members; the latter carries society downwards and favors all its worst members. (ibid., 95)

Consequently, Sumner resisted in principle all attempts to redress the disparities of wealth produced under capitalism. But he also defended a state policy of laissez-faire on prudential grounds. The complexity of natural and social phenomena, and humans' limited comprehension of them, prevented the formulation of clear and absolute rules or laws of political action. Hence, "When we go over to statecraft, we go over to art—to the domain, not of truth but expediency, not of scientific laws but of maxims" (ibid., 476). Maxims drawn from history and practical experiences in affairs of state provided the only possible guidelines for statecraft.

The first maxim of statecraft, according to Sumner, ought to flow from a recognition of the unscientific nature of its practice. Uncertainty ought to breed caution in affairs of state, especially those involving interference in social and economic affairs. Sumner roundly criticized "social doctors" who set out to cure society's ills:

> The amateur social doctors are like the amateur physicians—they always begin with the question of *remedies*, and they go at this without any diagnosis or any knowledge of the anatomy or physiology of society. They never have any doubt of the efficacy of their remedies. They never take account of any effects which may be apprehended from the remedy itself. It generally troubles them not a whit that their remedy implies a complete reconstruction of society, or even a reconstitution of human nature. Against all such social quackery the obvious injunction to the quacks is, to mind their own business. (Sumner 1974, 101)

Sumner's rejection of state-induced "reforms" stemmed from his belief that they all too often aggravated rather than mitigated humanity's struggle with nature. His favorite example was "The Forgotten Man" in schemes for social reform: "The type and formula of most schemes of philanthropy or humanitarianism is this: A and B put their heads together to decide what C shall be made to do for D." The Forgotten Man in this case, "C," is made to bear an unequal burden, and quite often without being allowed a voice in the matter (ibid., 107).

Well-intentioned schemers were not the only danger to social progress. A second maxim, according to Sumner, may be drawn from the observation that "history is only a tiresome repetition of one story. Persons and classes have sought to win possession of the power of the State in order to live luxuriously out of the earnings of others." Popular states were no better in this regard than monarchies or aristocracies; the source of the disease lay in the "vices and passions of human nature—cupidity, lust, vindictiveness, ambition, and vanity" (ibid., 27).

Consequently, Sumner argued, the only protection against the abuse of state power by classes lay in minimizing its power. All men, even those who expect to benefit by the use of state power, ought to consider the consequences to them should the state fall under the control of other groups and interests. And, he was certain, they would soon conclude that all had a common interest in restricting the state to providing liberty and securing order.

The problem of the class state was particularly acute in democratic republics like the United States, where the two main classes, the democracy and the plutocracy, stood opposed to one another, waiting to plunder each other via state action. Reformers who would use the power of the state to effect a redistribution of wealth, Sumner argued, "may find that instead of democratizing capitalism we have capitalized democracy—that is, have brought in plutocracy" (Sumner 1940, 1:102–103). In mobilizing the power of numbers against the power of wealth, these reformers were doubly mistaken. If they succeeded, they would have destroyed liberty in favor of equality, which according to Sumner, only protected the unfit numbers of society, leading in the long run to dissolution. On the other hand, the far more likely prospect was that capital would mobilize itself in order to resist political attempts to restrict its freedom and power.

Sumner had no doubts that capital would succeed in defending itself:

> Under a democracy . . . the contest between numbers and wealth is nothing but a contest between two sets of lawyers, one drawing Acts in behalf of the state, and the other devising means of defeating those Acts in behalf of their clients. The latter set is far better paid in consideration, in security and in money. (Sumner 1940, 2:230)

If any truly doubted the ability of capital to defend itself, Sumner pointed to its previous success: "The lobby is the army of the plutocracy" (Sumner 1974, 93).

Sumner was careful to distinguish plutocracy from the power of capital. The accumulation of capital he took as an index of material improvement, and a precondition for evolutionary progress. Concentrated wealth was likewise an indicator of an especially able competitor, one whose use of that wealth was bound to further the prosperity of society as a whole:

> The aggregation of large fortunes is not at all a thing to be regretted. On the contrary, it is a necessary condition of many forms of social advance. If we should set a limit to the accumulation of wealth, we should say to our most valuable producers, "We do not want you to do us the services which you best understand how to perform, beyond a certain point." It would be like killing off our generals in war. (ibid., 47–48)

Plutocracy, on the other hand, represented a corrupt and degenerate use of capital, insofar as it was used not industrially but politically, i.e. in an unproductive way. Sumner deplored this use of capital, but averred it was only natural that capital would seek to protect itself from political restrictions. In that sense plutocracy was only the natural result of an overly democratic zeal. Democracy and plutocracy bred one another, debilitating the body politic, and squandering its wealth. In the long run, both classes would suffer as they plunged their society into extinction.[12] It was better that political discourse on social organization be restricted to considerations of liberty only, and not equality, so that neither democratic capitalism nor capitalized democracy would put an end to America's progress.

[12] Similar sentiments were expressed in the literary works of Henry Adams, e.g. *Democracy* and *The Degradation of the Democratic Dogma*, albeit from a very different perspective than that of Sumner. Cf. Gill (1983) for a discussion of Adams' interpretation of American democracy.

The ideal form of government, then, was that dedicated to the preservation of liberty:

> A republic is . . . a form of self-government, and its first aim is not equality, but civil liberty. It keeps the people active in public functions and public duties; it requires their activity at stated periods when the power of the state has to be re-conferred on new agents. It breaks the continuity of power to guard against its abuse, and it abhors as much the irresponsible power of the many as of the one. It surrounds the individual with safeguards by its permanent constitutional provisions, and by no means leaves the individual or the state a prey to the determination of a numerical majority. In our system the guarantees to liberty and the practical machinery of self-government all come from the constitutional republic; the dangers chiefly from democracy. (Sumner 1940, 2:198–199)

Among other things, this sort of republican government required a high state of intelligence, political sense, and public virtue on the part of its citizenry. It required a commitment to elections as a means of transferring power. Above all, it required a popular instinct for liberty, without which institutional and constitutional safeguards were unimportant (ibid., 211).

In the case of America, at least, these requirements were ostensibly met, though Sumner believed that they would not persist unless the nation remained true to a scientifically vindicated policy of laissez-faire.

VII

NOT ALL SOCIAL Darwinists agreed with Sumner's conclusion that laissez-faire was the best policy in the face of evolutionary forces. Others, e.g. Lester Ward, claimed that laissez-faire was nothing short of suicidal, for it denied man the use of his most effective mechanism for adaptation, namely, the ability to comprehend and control natural processes. Men did not calmy submit to nature and her laws; rather, they used their knowledge of those laws to their own advantage in the struggle against nature. Indeed, it was this constant and conscious intervention in natural processes that was responsible for whatever prosperity was enjoyed by civilization (Ward 1967, 67).

The success of this intervention was immediately apparent in the realm of physical phenomena, where man "has made the winds, the waters, fire, steam, and electricity, do his bidding. All nature, both animate and inanimate, has been reduced to his service" (ibid., 50). None of this would have been possible if men had followed a policy of laissez-faire, and for this reason Ward dubbed Sumner's recommendation "suicidal."

What man had achieved by intervening in natural processes could also be achieved by intervening in social affairs, Ward argued. Only by assuming that social phenomena are, and will remain, opaque to man's powers of comprehension, i.e. by claiming that "man shall ultimately obtain dominion of the whole world except himself," could Sumner assert the rationality of laissez-faire. This, as Ward pointed out, was completely at odds with Sumner's own ambition to establish sociology on a scientific basis (ibid., 50). If the latter were possible, as both Sumner and Ward agreed it was, then the inescapable conclusion was that man ought to apply that knowledge to the practical affairs of society, just as knowledge of natural processes was applied to physical objects.[13] Should this happen, man would have extended his control over his environment to include social arrangements, as well as natu-

---

[13] Ward saw the failure of previous attempts to found a scientific sociology as a temporary setback only: "I regard society and social forces as constituting just as much a legitimate field for the exercise of human ingenuity as do the various material substances and physical forces. One field alone remains unsubdued . . . that of society itself, these unreclaimed forces are the social forces, of whose nature man seems to possess no knowledge, whose very existence he persistently ignores, and which he is consequently powerless to control" (Ward 1967, 50). Once controlled, however, the law of nature would be repealed and the law of mind enacted in its place, and man's destiny placed in his own hands.

ral conditions, and a qualitatively higher stage of evolution would be achieved (ibid., 12).

Thus, the proper course of action was intervention, not laissez-faire. Ward pointed out that Sumner tacitly conceded as much by admitting that government was necessary to insure liberty. Sumner had unwittingly shown that govermental intervention in social affairs was desirable. Consequently, whatever evils he attributed to government must, by the nature of the argument, be due to misgovernment, rather than government per se.

Once this was established, it was a relatively easy matter for Ward to demonstrate that the most pernicious kind of misgovernment was too little governance: "Modern society is suffering from the very opposite of paternalism,—from under-government, from the failure of government to keep pace with the change which civilization has wrought in substituting intellectual for physical qualities as the workers of injustice" (ibid., 183–184). Since the purpose of government is to insure liberty, its powers must be commensurate with that end. And since the greatest threat to liberty in the modern age is the power of concentrated wealth, and not brute force, government must be strengthened if it is to perform its proper function. Hence, "The true solution of the great social problem of this age is to be found in the ultimate establishment of a genuine people's government, with ample power to protect society against all forms of injustice, from whatever source, coupled with a warm and dutiful regard for the true interests of each and all, the poor as well as the rich" (ibid., 116).

Presumably, this implied an expanded role for political discourse oriented toward the discovery of proper areas of intervention. Though Ward thought that scientific knowledge might be brought to bear on these issues, he was skeptical that a general specification of the role of government could be made. The desirability of governmental action varied enormously from area to area, and the proper role of government was, therefore, specific to the policy area in question. However, Ward suggested that government ought to control vital natural resources (e.g. coal, oil, land), transporation systems, stock sales, and the various natural monopolies then operated by private concerns (ibid., 186–189). Indeed, the very range of activities Ward thought fit for governmental regulation has led one commentator to proclaim him "the philosophical architect of the welfare state" (ibid., xxxviii).

At no time did Ward advocate the total abolition of private property. That was impossible, practically speaking, given man's deep-seated "passion for proprietary acquisition" (ibid., 180). Moreover, it was undesirable, for the pursuit of wealth by individuals was a driving force of industrialization, and so was responsible for the many material benefits thereof. Thus, the real problem, as Ward saw it, was not wealth, or even its maldistribution, but the favored treatment business and wealth received at the hands of government.[14] The nation's "great system of jurisprudence relating to property and business," and its practices of granting franchises, subsidizing corporations, and permitting combinations were no longer necessary to promote economic development. Instead, "this system of artificial props, bolsterings, and scaffoldings has grown so perfect as to make exertion needless for the protected class and hopeless for the neglected mass" (ibid., 185–186).

Hence, it was necessary to redress this imbalance if civilization were to proceed. Interestingly, Ward did not think this should be done by reversing the state's probusiness policy. Rather, he felt the state ought to simply expand the number of interests protected:

> Nor should any one object to state protection of business interests. Even monopoly may be defended against aggressive competition on the ground of economy. The protection of the strong may not be too great, but there should be at

[14] "Even the amassing of colossal fortunes is not an evil in itself, since the very activity which it requires stimulates industry and benefits a large number" (Ward 1967, 181). Inheritance taxes would insure that fortunes did not lie idle.

the same time protection of the weak against the protected strong. (ibid., 191)

In this way the state would truly provide for all and show no partiality in its policy actions.

As a practical matter, the impartial state would be achieved when the people themselves decided to

> throw off all party allegiance, and demand of all candidates the strongest pledges of fidelity to their interests, and sustain none who do not honestly and earnestly fulfill these pledges. They need no revolutionary schemes of socialism, communism, or anarchy. The present machinery of government, especially in this country, is all they could wish. They have only to take possession of it and operate it in their own interest. (ibid., 116)

The chief obstacle to such a popular movement was the pervasive distrust of government by its citizens. This Ward attributed to a lingering, and increasingly irrational, fear of despotic government, which the advance of democracy had rendered exceedingly unlikely. However, those interests that benefited from a policy of laissez-faire, indeed whose interests required it, were "quick to see that the old odium that still lingers among the people can be made a bulwark of strength for their position."[15] Hence, they foreswore no opportunity to fan its flames back into existence, even after it "would naturally have smoldered and died out after its cause

[15] Ward denied that such interests received their rewards in proportion to their fitness or natural competitors. In other words, "class distinctions in society are wholly artificial, depend entirely on environing conditions, and are in no sense due to differences in native capacity. Differences in native capacity exist and are as great as they have ever been pictured, but they exist in all classes alike" (Ward 1967, 355). Therefore to defend the laws of political economy as natural and immutable was a rationalization at best, and disingenuous at worst. Ward suspected the latter, because business supported laissez-faire only where it suited its own interests and abandoned it when those interests were not served, as in the case of patents, protective tariffs, and so on.

ceased to exist" (ibid., 113). The rhetoric of "mobocracy" and the like were, of course, quite useful in this connection.

Therefore, proponents of the positive state were faced with the task of waging rhetorical warfare:

> It is the duty of all those who have the true reform of society at heart to point out in the most convincing manner that the people are no longer in any danger from governmental oppression, that their present danger lies in an entirely different direction, that what they really need is more government in its primary sense, greater protection of the exposed masses from the rapacity of the favored few and that, instead of distrusting and crippling government, they should greatly enlarge its power to grapple with these evils. (ibid., 113–114)

Ward was confident that popular opinion would progress to the point at which the myth of laissez-faire would be exploded, and a scientifically informed discourse on the principles of governance installed in its place. Such optimism, fueled in part by the "progressive" nature of evolution, and in part by the reasonably wide-spread appeal of reform organizations, was common at this time. There were those, however, who believed that true progress would be achieved only when the "welfare state" proposed by Ward was transformed into a truly socialist state or commonwealth.

VIII

REFORM DARWINISTS and Populists agreed that government ought to assume primary responsibility for insuring the democratic character of the new industral order. Consequently they advocated governmental intervention in the economy in order to curb the worst excesses of corporate capitalism. A judicious policy of regulation and, where necessary, nationalization would restore free enterprise by removing monopolistic barriers to competition. In this way, Reform Darwinists and Populists expressed their confidence in the ability of government to correct flaws in an otherwise sound economic system.

Not all critics of the existing order shared this confidence. American socialists, e.g. Henry Demerest Lloyd, were convinced that more radical action was required if the forces of democracy were to defeat the plutocrats. For Lloyd, the "excesses" of corporate capitalism were a structural feature of the free enterprise system, and not some aberration caused by a handful of corrupt robber barons. Hence, regulation was bound to fail, since it did not address the real cause of inequality:

> The possibility of regulation is a dream. As long as this control of the necessaries of life and this wealth remain private with individuals, it is they who will regulate, not we. The policy of regulation, disguise it as we may, is but moving to a compromise and equilibrium within the evil all complain of. (Lloyd 1894, 533)

Thus, the regulation of wealth was insufficient. Only its elimination would suffice, and that required the abolition of the institution of private property itself. The new industrial order would be truly democratic only "when that which is co-operatively produced is co-operatively enjoyed" (ibid., 521).

Fortunately, the socialists argued, American society had evolved to the point at which the abolition of private property was not only necessary, but possible. The vast productive potential of America had been realized within the confines of the old order of wealth. It was now possible to reorganize that order so as to produce not for wealth, but for commonwealth, thereby joining the "modern perfection of exchange and division of labor" with an "equal perfection of morals and sympathy" (ibid., 518).

Lloyd himself posed this as a matter of choice: either Americans would realize the superiority of socialism and reform their society voluntarily, or those reforms would be forced on them by the natural forces of evolution. The latter involved "the slow wreck and decay of superfluous and unwholesome men," and was the method of "brutes and brute civilizations" that experienced evolution as a violent and painful process. The former was the path of enlightened civilizations which, having recognized the inevitable, accepted it and rode the crest of civilization into the future (ibid., 518).

This evolutionary optimism was widely shared by American radicals, and it inspired the welfare statism of Lester Ward, as well as the utopian novels of Ignatius Donnelly, author of the Preamble to the Omaha Platform. However, the most optimistic case for the coming of socialism in America was made by Edward Bellamy in his extremely popular novel *Looking Backward* and its sequel, *Equality*.

For Bellamy, socialism represented the final achievement of democracy in America. The first gains had been registered by the Founding Fathers during the negative phase of the idea of democracy, wherein democracy was "conceived of solely as a substitute for royalty." During this period "the democratic idea remained a mere protest against a previous form of government, absolutely without any new positive or vital principal of its own" (Bellamy 1968, 19). The American republic was typical in this regard, for Bellamy was certain that "the signers of the immortal Declaration had no idea that democracy necessarily meant anything more than a device for getting along without kings. They conceived of it as a change in the forms of government only, and not at all in the principles and purposes of government" (ibid., 18).

Indeed, the Founders harbored some misgivings lest it "some time occur to the sovereign people that, being sovereign, it would be a good idea to use their sovereignty to improve their own condition" (ibid., 18). Hence, their resort to "ingenious clauses in paper Constitutions" to restrain the people, and insure a basic continuity in the function (if not the form) of government, which was to protect property.

The negative phase of democracy, then, represented the seizure by the people of the "outworks of the fortress of tyranny," namely, government. But the economic system, which was the "citadel" of tyranny and commanded "every part of the social structure" remained in the possession of private and irresponsible rulers (ibid., 22). Hence, there was no truly popular government, for "the people, indeed, nominally were sovereigns; but as these sovereigns were individually and as a class the economic serfs of the rich, and lived at their mercy, the so-called popular government became merely the stalking horse of the capitalists" (ibid., 21).

In order to complete the achievement of democracy, therefore, a second phase was necessary, which

> began with the awakening of the people to the perception that the deposing of kings, instead of being the main end and mission of democracy, was merely preliminary to its real programme, which was the use of the collective social machinery for the indefinite promotion of the welfare of the people at large. (ibid.,19)

With this recognition, the need to extend popular control to the economic realm was self-evident, and it would occur to the people that "they must either take the citadel or evacuate the outworks. They must either complete the work of establishing popular government which had been barely begun by their fathers, or abandon all that their fathers had accomplished" (ibid., 22–23).

This second, or positive, phase of democracy entailed a revolutionary change in people's ideas about government and its proper functions. It was necessary to disabuse citizens of the idea that the only legitimate function of government was to secure property for the few, and to acquaint them with the possibility of using government to "raise the material and moral welfare of the whole body of the sovereign people to the highest possible point at which the same degree of welfare could be secured to all—that is to say, an equal level" (ibid., 20).

Bellamy himself believed that this commitment to economic democracy and equality was logically bound up in the idea of democracy, since "all human beings are peers in rights and dignity" (ibid., 18). Nevertheless, he conceded the need for an extensive education of public opinion before the coming revolution. According to Bellamy, the corporations themselves would play an important role in this process of enlightenment, for they would provide important object lessons regarding the advantages of collectivism. His Doctor Leete, recounting the transformation of American society to an erstwhile time-traveller to the mid-twentieth century, recalled that

the change had been long foreseen. Public opinion had become fully ripe for it, and the whole mass of the people was behind it. . . . Fifty years before, the consolidation of the industries of the country under national control would have seemed a very daring experiment to the most sanguine. But by a series of object lessons, seen and studied by all men, the great corporations had taught the people an entirely new set of ideas on this subject. They had seen for many years syndicates handling revenues greater than those of states, and directing the labors of hundreds of thousands of men with an efficiency and economy unattainable in smaller operations. It had come to be recognized as an axiom that the larger the business the simpler the principles that can be applied to it; that, as the machine is truer than the hand, so the system, which in a great concern does the work of the master's eye in a small business, turns out more accurate results. Thus it came about that, thanks to the corporations themselves, when it was proposed that the nation should assume their functions, the suggestion implied nothing which seemed impracticable even to the timid. To be sure it was a step beyond any yet taken, a broader generalization, but the very fact that the nation would be the sole corporation in the field would, it was seen, relieve the undertaking of many difficulties with which the partial monopolies had contended. (Bellamy 1917, 42)

Thus, the epoch of trusts was to culminate in the Great Trust, in which the process of concentration was carried through to its logical conclusion, and the people of the United States assumed collective ownership of their productive enterprises. In so doing, American citizens would establish for the very first time in human history a truly democratic civilization.

Bellamy's confidence in the evolutionary progress of American society, and his vision of a democratic future, was warmly received by dissatisfied Americans, whose enthusiasm for *Looking Backward* matched an earlier generation's outrage at *Uncle Tom's Cabin*. Unfortunately for him, Bellamy's contribution to the discourse on the reconstruction of American society was appropriated by the "wrong" audience. As we shall see in the concluding section of this chapter, it was the corporations that learned from the people, and not vice-versa. And it was the corporations that successfully turned the power of government from an attack into a defense of "the citadel" of corporate capitalism.

IX

POLITICAL INTERVENTION in social affairs eventually became irresistible. Many political reform proposals initially made by nineteenth-century radicals were later enacted by the Progressives; the major parties' monopoly over political office, and their continued adherence to laissez-faire policy, was challenged by such electoral reforms as the direct election of Senators, the Australian ballot, and at-large, nonpartisan elections. This political "trust busting," in which political discourse was ostensibly democratized, was accompanied by increased regulation of industry and commerce, as the power of corporate America was nominally subordinated to that of the state.

However, the creation of a regulatory state proceeded haltingly. Newly established commissions and agencies frequently lacked either the legal authority or political capacity for accomplishing their appointed tasks, which were, after all, fairly modest (Skowronek, 1982). The resulting form of political intervention was, therefore, a mere shadow of the energetic government envisioned by the Populists and bore no resemblance whatsoever to the "Great Trust" imagined by Bellamy or the "commonwealth" of Henry Demerest Lloyd. Nor did it compare with European nations' responses to the dislocating effects of industrialization, confirming once again the "exceptionalism" of the American experience.

As a result, the reforms adopted during this era were generally quite limited and were in many cases welcomed by those at whom they were aimed. Indeed, Kolko (1963) argues that many of the so-called Progressive reforms were actually the creation of business and banking interests who turned to government regulation in order to protect themselves from economic and political adversity occasioned by the further evolution of capitalism. Both the timing and the form of government regulation were, therefore, decisively influenced by these interests, which succeeded in transforming laissez-faire into political capitalism. Accordingly, the Progressive Era represents "the triumph of conservatism," rather than the culmination of radicalism, or so Kolko claims.

The triumph of conservatism is clearly revealed in the way in which the money question was eventually resolved. The successive defeat of soft money programs and the silver movement represented a victory for hard money policies designed to insure "investor confidence" in American ventures. This was not an insignificant consideration, insofar as European investors placed two and a half billion dollars in the United States during 1880–1895, providing a very important source of venture capital for the burgeoning economy (ibid., 142). And, of course, the confidence of domestic capital, e.g. the House of Morgan, stimulated huge investments in such basic industries as steel and transportation.

Investor confidence was predicated on the inelasticity of hard money, which ensured the soundness of the dollar. However, this inelasticity made it exceedingly difficult to respond to seasonal and cyclical economic trends. Consequently, the "boom and bust" became a standard part of the economic landscape in America, as increased demands for money drove interest rates up, prices down, and investment opportunities away, until demand had slackened and the cycle could begin anew.

The inelasticity of a hard money supply was further aggravated by the relative decline of finance capital, which had once been relatively immune to boom and bust pressures by virtue of its control over a significant portion of money and credit. As Kolko notes, national banks' lending powers were much more stringently controlled than state banks', thereby encouraging a decentralization of control within the banking industry. This decentralization was compounded by the growing importance of self-financing in the industrial sector, which created even more centers of financial power.[16] Consequently, bankruptcy and failure became very real possibilities when the inevitable bust occurred, and the weakest competitors were eliminated.

Not surprisingly, those interests most threatened by this situation began to see the advantages of banking reform at a fairly early date. The American Bankers Association endorsed the "Baltimore Plan" for banking reform at its 1894 convention, and several other proposals were circulated during the late 1890s (ibid., 147). But opposition from small banks, which had not suffered a relative decline in influence, and conservative Republicans made the adoption of banking legislation unlikely.

The inability to generate cooperative action within the financial industry itself and the poor prospects of legislation eventually led to increased activity by the Treasury to provide some measure of central coordination to the banking system. At the behest of bankers, the Treasury began in 1903 to deposit monies as well as current revenues in banks, which allowed it to regulate the flow of money in the economy as a whole, and in strategic cities in particular (ibid., 151). Even

[16] Some firms, e.g. Standard Oil, became sufficiently large that they actually moved into the investment business, reversing the previous flow of finance capital to industry (Kolko 1963, 145).

this failed to prevent the panic of 1907, which forced both the New York and Chicago Clearing Houses to suspend payments on certificates (ibid., 155).

Thus, the need for sweeping reform became apparent to the entire banking community, though there was no general agreement on what form it should take. Different elements within the banking community offered different proposals, balancing the threat of panic against regulation in their particular interests. After much infighting and maneuvering, bankers and Progressives managed to unite behind the Federal Reserve Act of 1913, which organized the nation's banking system under the auspices of the federal government.

The Federal Reserve Act created a system of regional clearinghouses under the central direction of the Federal Reserve Board. It also provided a more flexible source of currency by allowing the regional banks to issue partially backed currency in return for commercial paper. Hence, the Act promised to ease the nation's economic problems by permitting centralized control over the money supply in different regions.

In fact, however, this centralized control was exercised by the banking community itself, and not the government. The Board itself enjoyed considerable autonomy and was composed primarily of appointees from the national financial community. Moreover, the regional banks themselves were owned by member banks and controlled by directors appointed from the regional banking community. Thus, discourse on the money question was radically constricted and was carried on within the banking community itself.

Because of its centrality, the New York Reserve Bank became the dominant actor in the Federal Reserve System, restoring the lost power of New York financiers. Carter Glass, one of the prime movers behind the Act, claimed that this was an intended consequence of it:

The proponents of the Federal Reserve Act had no idea of impairing the rightful prestige of New York as the financial metropolis of this hemisphere. They rather expected to confirm its distinction, and even hoped to assist powerfully in wresting the scepter from London and eventually making New York the financial center of the world . . . this has come to pass. And we may point to the amazing contrast between New York under the old system in 1907, shaken to its very foundations because of two bank failures, and New York at the present time, under the new system, serenely secure in its domestic banking operations and confidently financing the great enterprises of European nations at war. (Kolko 1963, 254)

This, then, is the irony of populism. The money question *was* eventually decided in favor of greater governmental regulation of banking and currency. The terms of that regulation were, however, exceedingly favorable to a financial community whose hard money policies had driven not only agrarian radicals, but the nation as a whole, to the brink of disaster. With this settlement, the money question, on which a generation had pinned their hopes for a more democratic nation, was removed from the arena of public discourse. It would not be discussed again until the Depression. At that time, the extent to which the moral underpinnings of the greenback critique had been eroded by "scientific" considerations and political calculations would become apparent.

CHAPTER SEVEN

Direct Democracy
and the Illusion of Fulfillment

I

THE EXCESSES of corporate capitalism did not disappear with the demise of the Populists. Indeed, they became so widespread and egregious that "muckrakers" soon found ample grist for their mill as they helped inaugurate that incredible period in American history known as the Progressive Era. During this time many of the Populists' specific proposals for augmenting popular control over parties and elected representatives were enthusiastically endorsed by the Progressives, who combined them with their own ideas about good government in a reform package that still governs many states and municipalities today.[1]

[1] The modesty of *economic* reforms has led some historians, e.g. Kolko (1963), to liken the Progressive era to a successful counterrevolution by business (especially big business). Others, e.g. Eric Goldman (1956), portray the Progressive reform as a largely middle-class, urban movement with a distinctive program of its own for addressing what Progressives understood to be the undesirable consequences of industrialization. Hofstadter (1955) concurs, emphasizing the "status revolution" by which union leaders, bosses, and corporate executives displaced middle-class professionals in the social hierarchy, engendering anxious efforts by the latter to reestablish their worth by "good deeds."

Still other interpretations attempt to situate progressivism in the process of modernization. For Hays (1980), this involved a gradual transition toward a more cosmopolitan society. Wiebe (1967) presents a similar view, although he stresses the discontinuous nature of modernization in America: around 1900 the older, traditional society collapsed and a new and distinctly modern one began to emerge. Ginger's *Age of Excess* (1965) portrays modernization in terms of the dynamics of capitalist accumulation, in which existing institutions' inability to solve the problem of overproduction led to greater exploitation of the working class and imperialist expansion.

This rationalization of politics was part of a larger process of modernization that was quite uneven. It occurred more rapidly in some contexts than others, and it penetrated more deeply into certain areas of life than others. Because it was so uneven, it would be a mistake to see the Progressive period as the culmination of modernization in the United States. Nevertheless, it is clear that by the first decade of the twentieth century the broad outlines of what Hays (1980, 244) calls the "new organizational society" were beginning to be visible in many areas of the country, particularly, but not exclusively, in the cities of the Northeast.

According to Hays, this new organizational society had three defining characteristics. First, more aspects of life and more living areas were becoming integrated as the means of transportation, communication, and commerce improved. Second, functional relations between those engaged in similar tasks, but at locations remote from each other in time and space, were fashioned. Third, and perhaps most important, large-scale technical systems for coordinating and controlling collective endeavors emerged, especially in economics, but also in politics and the military.

The regulatory state was one such system of control, and its program of regulation was much less objectionable, politically speaking, than the welfare state proposed by radicals, since it addressed the immediate and practical concerns of middle-class citizens and businessmen alike, without challenging the economic framework to which both were firmly attached. A judicious application of regulatory practices promised to facilitate the rationalization of the marketplace by political means, which would in turn curb the worst excesses of industrialization without compromising the prospects for continued growth—and private opportunity.

This conception of the regulatory state was justified on the grounds that a regulatory state would be an efficient and de-

---

Wiebe (1973) provides an excellent overview of the historical literature on the Progressive period.

pendable way of directing social processes, whereas other forms of intervention would not. These criteria—efficiency and dependability—were derived from ostensibly scientific analyses of organizational behavior and economic development that drew heavily upon an evolutionary understanding of American society and its possibilities. With the rise to prominence of these "scientific" analyses of social problems, political discourse became more "secular" than it had been prior to this time, as the providential mission of America was reinterpreted in light of the progressive tendencies that seemed inherent in evolutionary processes.

This was reflected in a realignment of the terms of political discourse. The traditional language of politics, which had been partially displaced by Darwinian categories of understanding in the late nineteenth century, suffered a further loss of currency as questions of efficiency and reliability replaced those of equity and justice on the political agenda. To be sure, political discussion was not entirely emptied of moral terms during the Progressive period; that would not be accomplished until after the New Deal. However, the grounds of discourse shifted so decisively that ethical considerations, when they were raised by men like Herbert Croly, often had a moralistic ring, the hollowness of which became apparent with the triumph of relativism in the philosophy of the period.

Thus, the rationalization of discourse and political economy proceeded together under the auspices of science. "Science" became the new source of authoritative knowledge of society and its development, and a "realistic" outlook and language pervaded popular investigations into politics. At times this realism led to critical conclusions regarding the quality of democracy in the new organizational society, but more often it provided grounds for hope that further progress would be forthcoming, and without too much human effort. This bred a sense of complacency that, because it was based on a "realistic" appraisal of American development, made it easy to dismiss dissenting opinions, especially when the latter were couched in moralistic terms that had become outmoded.

Where realistic analyses indicated that political action was necessary, however, there was a clear presumption in favor of measures grounded in science.[2] This implied an expanded role for competent individuals in politics, where competence was taken to be synonymous with intelligence or, even better, expertise. Reform movements that succeeded in demonstrating their contribution to the improvement of political competence were able to make their objections heard in the new discourse. By the same token, those who seemed "incompetent" to mainstream Americans were considered politically dangerous and in urgent need of an appropriate education. If they proved ineducable, stronger measures to control them were in order.

The ramifications for "democracy" of this stress on competence were enormous. Initially good government by experts seemed democratic, especially by contrast with the corruption of machine politics. It was, at least, *for* the people, while machine rule was neither by the people nor for them, but for the "vested interests" that stood in the way of good government. With the triumph of reform over the machines, this contrast was lost, and the positive meaning of good government became much more difficult to unravel, as the direction of progress became unclear and the search for an orienting point began.

Self-styled "Radical Progressives" like Herbert Croly, Walter Weyl, and Walter Lippmann formed the intellectual vanguard of this effort to uncover a national purpose for America. They envisioned a "new democracy" of enlightened citizens applying their skills in the construction of a "new republic"

[2] The new-found relevance of science to political affairs was due in part to a change in the conduct and meaning of science itself. Whereas science once referred to a body of codified knowledge, it was increasingly understood in the Progressive era to be a method of investigation or orientation toward reality (Wiebe 1967, 147). As such, it was no longer regarded as the study of divinely ordained laws of the universe or human behavior, but was instead the search for principles that, once applied to social life, would provide human beings with a measure of control over their collective destiny.

founded on principles of social justice. However, the "un-realism" of their hopes collided with the complacency of a culture that was content to operate under the assumption that the promise of American life was unproblematic. The moral objections of the radical Progressives had no force against this sentiment and its confidence in the science of progress.

II

WHILE THE MUCKRAKERS were exposing the corrupt prac-tices of businessmen and politicians in *fin de siècle* America, historians such as Charles and Mary Beard, Vernon L. Par-rington, and J. Allen Smith were questioning the democratic credentials of the political and economic order that made such practices possible.[3] This new breed of historians offered a "realistic" account of the development of the American po-litical economy, based on an ostensibly scientific analysis of class conflict and its dynamics. They concluded that the cause of democracy had been subverted by vested interests and urged a Progressive renewal of American society so as to im-prove the prospects for true deomocracy.

However, the case for strengthening the democracy in or-der to overcome the vested interests and realize a Progressive society was perhaps best expressed in the women's suffrage movement. The suffragettes equated the extension of suffrage with the expansion of democracy; it was to complete the proc-ess by which "coercive government" was replaced by the "consent of the governed" (Kraditor 1965). By adding the consent of women to that of honest men, the power of de-mocracy would be made irresistible. The hold of the vested interests on government would be broken, and politics made more democratic.

There were two principal arguments advanced in behalf of the extension of suffrage: the "argument from expediency"

---

[3] "Critical realism" was the phrase used by Parrington to describe this new awareness of the economic foundations of politics. Hofstadter (1968) sum-marizes the practice of Progressive historiography and contrasts it with both its antecedents and successors.

and the "argument from justice."[4] The former defended voting rights for women on prudential grounds by specifying the benefits to women and society that might stem from political participation by women. The latter justified the extension of suffrage by deriving it from the natural rights of all citizens, women included. Both ultimately drew upon a conception of democracy as "consent of the governed," but the practical meaning of this differed sharply according to the type of argument employed.

As many suffragettes noted, the argument from justice was little more than a restatement of the principles enunciated in the Declaration of Independence. That document spelled out the inalienable rights of all citizens in the republic, including their right to express or withhold their consent to be governed. On that basis, "liberty and equality," Elizabeth Cady Stanton averred, "are the birthright of every citizen of a republic," to which she added Charles Sumner's claim that "universal suffrage is the first proof and only basis of a genuine republic" (Buhle and Buhle 1978, 318).

Of course, the Declaration only spoke of the rights of men, and so it was necessary for women to claim rights equal to those of men. Stanton's famous "Solitude of Self" address before the United States Senate Committee on Woman Suffrage in 1892 contained a sophisticated defense of this claim, saying that gender differences were significant only for "the *incidental* relations of life, such as mother, wife, sister, daughter, which may involve some special duties and training." *Qua* citizen, however, women "must have the same right as all other members, according to the fundamental principles of our Government," since gender differences were irrelevant to *political* relations (ibid., 326; my emphasis).

In fact, Stanton's "Solitude of Self" presents a natural rights argument as radical as that proposed in *The Rights of Man*. According to her, individuals—men and women alike—were

---

[4] I owe this distinction to Kraditor (1965), whose fine account forms the basis of my discussion of the suffrage movement in the Progressive era.

personally responsible for their actions: they were arbiters of their own destiny. The solitude and solemnity of that responsibility demanded the consolation of "self-sovereignty" in all aspects of moral life, and that, she argued, was the strongest reason for extending equality to women, not only in politics, but in the trades and professions, and in social life in general (ibid., 326).

Stanton's (1894) *Suffrage a Natural Right* contains a very clear expression of this philosophy: "I have always taken the ground that suffrage is a natural right, the status of the citizen in a republic is the same as a king on his throne; the ballot is his sceptre of power, his crown of sovereignty" (ibid., 6). To restrict the franchise meant that women's natural rights were being violated, because their ability to protect themselves was compromised.

That this was contrary to nature Stanton did not doubt. "In the inauguration of government, when men made compacts for mutual protection and surrendered the rude weapons used when each one was a free lance, they did not surrender the natural right to protect themselves and their property by laws of their own making, they simply substituted the ballot for the bow and arrow" (ibid., 3). This, she shrewdly observed, was the underlying rationale for male suffrage, and "whenever and wherever the few were endowed with the right to make laws and choose their rulers, the many can claim the same origin for their rights also" (ibid., 6).

Thus, women were only demanding what was rightfully theirs, and that which men claimed for themselves, namely, the right to protect themselves as they saw fit. Husbands and fathers could not do this, for as George William Curtis said, "Men are not wise enough, nor generous enough, nor pure enough to legislate fairly for women" (ibid., 4). And "even if all men were wise, generous, and honorable, possessed of all the cardinal virtues, it would still be better for women to govern themselves, to exercise their own capacities and powers in assuming the responsibilities of citizenship" (ibid., 4).

Because self-government was a natural right, its denial was

unjust and immoral in a democratic society. As Stanton observed, women, "constituting, as we do one-half the people, bearing the burdens of one-half the national debt, equally responsible with man for the education, religion and morals of the rising generation," had all of the obligations of citizenship, but none of the rights, including those, e.g. the vote, that were necessary to protect their interests (Buhle and Buhle 1978, 306). "Common Sense" applied to women's suffrage justified the elimination of this insufferable state of affairs, as Mary Putnam-Jacobi (1915), invoking the memory of Paine, insisted.

III

THE ARGUMENT from expediency took many forms, depending on whether the benefits of political participation were alleged to accrue to women or society as a whole. The personal benefits to women were multiple. According to Kraditor (1965, 45) the vote would allegedly enlarge women's interests and intellect by placing upon them part of the responsibility of running the government, render them better mothers by enabling them to draw upon their personal experience when instructing children in citizenship, and make them better wives by establishing them on an equal footing with their husbands, thereby destroying a relationship that bred servility in one and tyranny in the other.

More to the point, suffrage would enable women to protect themselves via their influence on marriage and work laws, as well as legislation regarding crimes against women.[5] Not all women needed such protection, it was admitted, but

[5] The protective value of suffrage represents one of the points of convergence between the argument from justice and the argument from expediency. However, the latter regarded protection as a means for advancing very concrete interests via favorable legislation, whereas the former dealt with protection in much more abstract language, seldom dealing with interests, often dealing with rights.

The difference between the two conceptions of protection was most clearly revealed by the fact that not all women needed protection, according to the

there are other women among us—hard-working, patient, industrious—who require the suffrage . . . to enable them to better advance the interests of their own affairs. And there are poor and weak women among us, defenceless except so far as they may be touched by an occasional enthusiasm of philanthropy, who require the status of a definite representation—a medium through which they can make their wants known—which shall do for them, as the suffrage alone has been able to do for other masses of the poor and weak: give them means to defend themselves, enable them to take the initial step in rising out of otherwise easily-forgotten misery. (Putnam-Jacobi 1915, 220–221)

Those women who did not need such protection—"women among us of intelligence, of wealth, of leisure, of high character"—lacked only the opportunity to show their ability "to promote the welfare of the community in public affairs." Indeed, the well-being and progress of the nation depended on permitting them to do so since "*all* the intelligence in the State must be enlisted for its welfare" (ibid., 220). By denying women the right to vote, important skills and resources were being wasted; on these grounds alone the active involvement of women must be sought, it was argued.

Moreover, women had a special contribution to make in the area of social reform. Their support for Progressive causes, including welfare measures and urban reform, was touted as being necessary for overcoming the power of entrenched interests. Nowhere is this more obvious than in the campaign to clean up the cities, in which women's experience in the household was supposed to make them especially well-qualified to assist in "municipal housekeeping" (Kraditor 1965). Jane Addams (1960, 107), for example, wondered if the absence of a women's touch might not account for the dreariness of city life and asked, "If women have in any sense been

---

argument from expediency, for their interests were being met in other ways. Stanton, as we have seen, rejected this idea, claiming protection as a universal necessity under the argument from justice.

responsible for the gentler side of life which softens and blurs some of its harsher conditions, may they not have a duty to perform in our American cities?"

Addams was not content to play upon the image of the gentleness of women, however.[6] Her "Why Women Should Vote," which was published in 1910, was a masterpiece of political rhetoric, in which she derived the necessity of extending the suffrage from the traditional "duty" of women, i.e. "to keep her house clean and wholesome and to feed her children properly" (ibid., 104). This duty, of course, summarized women's place in society, according to those who opposed women's suffrage, and yet Addams was able to show that the successful performance of this duty in a modern society *required* women's involvement in politics.

Addams's argument was as simple as it was powerful: the impingement of city life on the domicile was pervasive and unavoidable, so that the "primary duties" of women could not be adequately discharged unless they joined more general movements oriented toward the amelioration of social ills. As she put it,

---

[6] In a marvelous satire Addams (1960, 107–113) imagines a society in which men were demanding the right to vote from already-enfranchised women. Might not women reply "first that men could find politics corrupting; second they would doubtless vote as their wives and mothers did; third that men's suffrage would only double the vote without changing results; fourth that men's suffrage would diminish respect for men; fifth that the best men would not vote?" (ibid., 112).

Moreover, could not women complain with considerable justification that men, who are so fond of fighting, even as little boys, would "forget that the real object of the State is to nurture and protect life, and out of sheer vainglory" devote huge sums of money to war, letting serious social problems go begging? (ibid., 108). Would men not fail to protect workers on the job because of their carelessness and indifference toward housekeeping duties? Would they not allow children to be exploited in the workplace, owing to the greed of men and their unfamiliarity with the tenderness and delicacy of children?

Each of these "arguments" is but the mirror image of those advanced by men opposed to extending the suffrage, who drew their inspiration from preconceived notions about women and their place in society.

A woman's simplest duty, one would say, is to keep her house clean and wholesome and to feed her children properly. Yet if she lives in a tenement house, as so many of my neighbors do, she cannot fulfill these simple obligations by her own efforts because she is utterly dependent upon the city administration for the conditions which render decent living possible. Her basement will not be dry, her stairways will not be fireproof, her house will not be provided with sufficient windows to give light and air, nor will it be equipped with sanitary plumbing, unless the Public Works Department sends inspectors who constantly insist that these elementary decencies be provided. Women who live in the country sweep their own dooryards and may either feed the refuse of the table to a flock of chickens or allow it innocently to decay in the open air and sunshine. In a crowded city quarter, however, if the street is not cleaned by the city authorities no amount of private sweeping will keep the tenement free from grime; if the garbage is not properly collected and destroyed a tenement-house mother may see her children sicken and die of diseases from which she alone is powerless to shield them, although her tenderness and devotion are unbounded. She cannot even secure untainted meat for her household, she cannot provide fresh fruit, unless the meat has been inspected by city officials, and the decayed fruit, which is so often placed upon sale in the tenement districts, has been destroyed in the interests of public health. In short, if woman would keep on with her old business of caring for her house and rearing her children she will have to have some conscience in regard to public affairs lying quite outside of her immediate household. The individual conscience and devotion are no longer effective. (Addams 1960, 104–105)

The force of this argument was undeniable in the new organizational society, and this and other arguments from expediency quickly gained popularity among the members of the suffrage movement. As Kraditor (1965) has shown, the use of the argument from justice declined accordingly. This shift in rhetorical strategy undoubtedly contributed to the eventual passage of the Nineteenth Amendment, but as we shall see in the next section, it also had a constricting effect on conceptions of democracy.

IV

THE INCREASED EMPHASIS on the argument from expediency and the corresponding decline of the argument from justice made it possible for many suffragettes to disavow the radical implications of their conception of democracy, and this enhanced the political prospects of the Nineteenth Amendment. The logic of the argument from justice was universally applicable; it covered *all* citizens, not just the women in the suffrage movement, which was predominantly a white, middle-class affair. The argument from justice implied that disenfranchisement by any means—poll taxes, literacy tests, or the more subtle devices of nonpartisan and at-large elections with short ballots, which cut against the ethnic constituency of the machines—was undemocratic. By arguing that all citizens had a right to participation in political decision-making, women who invoked the argument from justice were effectively urging the involvement of blacks, immigrants, and radical workers, in short, all citizens regardless of race, creed, or nationality. Despite vehement protestations to the contrary, the logical conclusion of the argument from natural rights was obvious to the antisuffrage clientele, and to many women in the movement as well.

The argument from justice was opposed by white supremacists, small employers, and reformers interested in breaking the hold of political machines on urban life, all of whom recognized the implications of the argument from justice, and all of whom supported formal or informal restrictions on suffrage. These restrictions were designed to minimize the influence of illiterate or otherwise "incompetent" citizens, while preserving, or in some cases restoring, the power of "right-thinking" Americans dedicated to the progress of the nation.

The combined strength of this opposition was a significant factor in prolonging the struggle for women's voting rights, which is described in Flexner (1974). The eclipse of the argument from justice by the argument from expediency made it possible to mute, if not silence, this opposition because it did not necessarily imply universal suffrage. In fact, the argument from expediency was sometimes used to defend the extension of suffrage to women as a way of reinforcing existing restrictions on blacks, immigrants, and other incompetents.

This was most obvious among southern groups that supported women's suffrage, where the inclusion of women was explicitly portrayed as a means of guaranteeing white supremacy. In 1906, Laura Clay argued that "if the women of the South were enfranchised, it would insure a permanent and enormous preponderance of the white race in politics, and preclude the necessity for any doubtful expedients to minimize the negro vote" (Kraditor 1965, 221).

To a certain extent, this position was a matter of political pragmatics. As Kate Gordon of Louisiana observed, "White supremacy is going to be maintained in the South by fair or foul means. The only ammunition I want is to strike at the unconstitutional points in any subterfuge that will not include white women in its protection" (ibid., 149).[7] Some women

---

[7] Belle Kearney, in an address to the National American Woman Suffrage Association convention in New Orleans, 1903, pursued this argument to a more extreme conclusion:

The civilization of the North is threatened by the influx of foreigners with their imported customs. . . . Someday the North will be compelled to look to the South for redemption from those evils on account of the purity of its Anglo-Saxon blood, the simplicity of its social and economic structure, the great advance of prohibitory law and the maintenance of the sanctity of its faith, which has been kept inviolate. Just as surely as the North will be forced to turn to the South for the nation's salvation, just so surely will the South be compelled to look to its Anglo-Saxon women as the medium through which to retain supremacy of the white race over the African. (Buhle and Buhle 1978, 349)

Her remarks were reportedly received enthusiastically.

disagreed with this strategy, but such concessions were necessary in order to gain support from southern Democrats, although as Flexner (1974, 311) reports, the latter ultimately opposed women's suffrage because they were afraid of the Negro woman's vote.

The effect of this strategy was to dissociate the suffrage movement in the South from the remnants of abolitionism, destroying a unity that had existed since the Grimké sisters and even before. A similar dissociation took place in northern urban areas, where the argument from expediency was used by some to defend women's suffrage as a bulwark against immigrants and workers. In testimony presented to the House Committee on the Judiciary, for example, no less a figure than Elizabeth Cady Stanton carefully distinguished the virtues of women, who were "peculiarly fitted to write, speak and vote intelligently on all these questions of such vital, far-reaching consequence to the welfare of society," and a foreign "multitude of coarse, ignorant" males, many of whom "cannot stand, because of their frequent potations," being guided to the ballot box, "for what purpose [they] neither know nor care, except to get the promised bribe" (Kraditor 1965, 109).

Stanton was obviously trying to prove the political competence of women, at least in comparison to many male voters, upon whom, in her opinion, restrictions were needed. The suffragettes also repeatedly emphasized the fact that native-born women outnumbered the combined population of foreign-born men and women, and so the former might counterbalance the latter, even if restrictions were not enforced. In that sense, the xenophobic practices that were common among Progressives during this period also infected the suffrage movement itself, although the eventual support of many immigrant organizations for women's suffrage ameliorated this tendency to some extent (Kraditor 1965).[8]

[8] Buhle (1983) recounts the story from the other side of the fence, so to speak, in her discussion of socialist organizations' stand on suffrage, which was marked by a tendency to subordinate considerations of sexual oppression to those of class exploitation. These groups' support for suffrage was based

The shift from arguments of justice to expediency, and the comparative success with which this met, is consistent with the rationalization of political discourse during the Progressive Era. This is obvious in the decline of moral arguments, e.g. those based on natural rights, but it is also apparent in the currency of pragmatic concerns about the contributions of women to society. The suffragettes' attempts to show the political competence of women, especially by way of contrast to the "incompetency" of immigrant males, were congruent with other efforts to rationalize politics by "improving" the avenues of elite recruitment and the efficiency of governing structures. Women, or at least those middle-class women most likely to vote, might raise the intellectual quotient of the electorate.

Thus, the argument from expediency made it possible for women to present the case for suffrage in an idiom that was well-understood in Progressive America. Competent women would improve politics and contribute to good government. Suffrage was no longer a question of right, it was a question of the most efficient utilization of social resources for the present and future, and on those grounds, the inclusion of women seemed eminently reasonable.

V

CERTAINLY THE MOST thoroughgoing effort to eliminate what Progressives considered political incompetence was the urban reform movement. This attempt to establish "direct democracy" in the cities explicitly aimed to reduce the influence of "unqualified" citizens in urban politics by attacking the machine, which the reformers regarded as the organized expression of incompetence and corruption in American politics. As Lincoln Steffens later recalled, "In those days educated citizens of cities said, and I think they believed—they

---

on the hope that it would strengthen labor's vote by drawing women workers into the electorate, but there was considerable unease over the effects of drawing "bourgeois" women in at the same time.

certainly acted upon the theory—that it was the ignorant foreign riff-raff of the big congested towns that made municipal politics so bad" (Hofstadter 1955, 177, n. 8).[9]

For that reason, urban reformers wanted to expand the influence of competent men (and occasionally women) in local affairs. The "gospel of efficiency," to use Roosevelt's phrase, justified these efforts to install "good government," which, because it was for the people and not the vested interests, was thought by the Progressives to be eminently democratic.[10]

The notion of democracy that underpinned this philosophy of urban reform was peculiar, as Haber (1964, 110) remarks. On the one hand, "direct democracy" implied a more intense popular involvement in politics than the machine, with its narrow, electoral conception of citizenship, permitted. Direct democracy meant that active, informed, and "civic-minded" people would participate in policy discussions and move American society forward. These New Citizens, as Hofstadter (1955) aptly characterizes them, were the mature "child[ren] of the new century" described so rhapsodically by William Allen White, children who would join with others in putting "something besides self-seeking into the ballot box" (White 1910, 253, 100).[11]

[9] Steffens's own inclination was to blame businessmen and politicians, as well as an apathetic public willing to tolerate their corrupt bargains. Hofstadter (1955) employs the notion of a "Yankee ethos of individual responsibility" to explore Steffens's (and by implication many other Progressives') outlook on politics and citizenship in an industrial society.

[10] Populist survivors who allied themselves with the Progressive cause did not share this favorable predisposition toward "competent" citizens because they believed that political questions always involved moral issues on which the people were imminently well-qualified to speak. They preferred to make government uncomplicated so that all could participate in public affairs. Then there would be no need to give undue emphasis to competence (Hofstadter, 1955).

[11] White believed that "democracy is, at base, altruism expressed in terms of self-government," and so "the widening faith of men in one another, in the combined wisdom of the numerical majority," meant that the nation would see a "growing abnegation of self to democracy" (ibid., 132, 63). A

On the other hand, this vigorous involvement was to be restricted to a sphere of politics from which administrative functions had been separated. Politics remained democratic, but administration was to be the province of specialists and experts. Hence, the real business of governing the city on a day-to-day basis was to be conducted at a distance from the people, in marked contrast to the intimate, albeit uneven, relations of *quid pro quo* so characteristic of machine politics.

The simultaneous intensification of political involvement and the restriction of its scope was supposed to make government more efficient by expanding the role of competence in politics. This also meant expanding the role of competent individuals, i.e. those well-versed in civic affairs and the scientific principles of management, in short, the sort of educated, middle-class individual of which the reform movement was largely composed. In that sense, the gospel of efficiency was ideally suited to those who embraced the principle of democracy, but feared "the democracy" of incompetent citizens. Hence, "The progressives who greeted efficiency with such enthusiasm were often those who proposed to let the people rule through a program in which the bulk of the people, most of the time, ruled hardly at all" (Haber 1964, xii).[12]

This program for efficient government involved two principal tasks. First, it required a more selective method for recruiting political leaders, and second, it necessitated a formal reorganization of governmental structures. The latter insured that civic-minded individuals would be able to perform

---

Progressive citizenry was forming in the United States and these "new citizens" would invigorate American politics and overthrow the principle of self-interest on which the machine was based.

[12] Wilson (1983, 143) argues that editorial changes in the composition and presentation of topical magazines, which were extremely popular during this period, promoted a "rhetoric of consumption" in which "the passivity of political spectatorship came to seem like active citizenship." Readers consumed the analyses of the muckrakers, who provided them with the "inside dope" on politics, which created an illusion of involvement in civic affairs. Thus, the magazines brought politics close to their readers, while keeping them far from politics, i.e. at a safe distance.

their appointed functions efficiently and economically, once they were in office, while the former increased the probability that competent persons would ascend to positions of power and influence in the first place. Both objectives could be realized by sweeping the machine from office, or so the Progressives believed.

The Progressive attack on the urban machine was the political version of trust busting, insofar as the machine monopolized city politics. By virtue of its electoral hegemony the machine controlled the city's work force, as well as the lucrative franchises and contracts that were let to private concerns, often in exchange for "honest graft." Not surprisingly, only those interests loyal to the machine received satisfaction in the form of public goods and services, and then only at an inflated cost—the machine behaved like the monopolist it was.

Under those circumstances, it was natural for the Progressives to emphasize the democratizing effects of reform schemes that were intended to cripple the machine by lessening its influence on elite recruitment and selection. The resort to direct primaries, in which well-educated people participated in disproportionate numbers, was only the most obvious example of this. Other reforms, more subtle in their operation, were also devised to remove politics, i.e. machine politics, from government. Secret ballots kept machine politicos from "instructing" voters, while nonpartisan elections removed an important cue to machine loyalists, many of whom were illiterate and relied upon party designations to register their choice. Short ballots made it more difficult to build multiethnic constituencies by reducing the number of offices that might be divided among them, and at-large elections undercut the advantage enjoyed by concentrated ethnic groups under a ward election system.

Such reforms made it difficult for machine politicians to operate and enhanced the likelihood that knowledgeable candidates would be selected to fill policy-making positions. The adoption of civil service requirements had a similar impact, destroying the patronage system by which machine loyalists received city jobs. Both sets of reforms had the practical effect of reducing the political power of a large group of voters who might have successfully resisted direct efforts to disenfranchise them, although that, too, was commonly suggested by Progressives interested in "good government."

Indeed, the imposition of a property qualification, a standard recommendation since the time of the Mugwumps, was often mentioned as a desirable restriction.[13] As Andrew White, the first president of Cornell University, wrote in 1890, "The work of a city being the creation and control of the city property, it should logically be managed as a piece of property by those who have created it, who have a title to it, or a real substantial part in it . . . [and not by] a crowd of illiterate peasants, freshly raked in from the Irish bogs, or Bohemian mines, or Italian robber nests" (Judd 1979, 93).

White's statement was only a slightly more colorful anticipation of similar expressions by Progressives, although some of them preferred a literacy test to property qualifications as a restriction on suffrage. Others, e.g. Elizabeth Cady Stanton, softened this even further by noting that a literacy test need not be restrictive, given the availability of public schools: "It is in the interest of the educated working-men, as it is of women, that this ignorant, worthless class of voters should be speedily diminished. With free schools and compulsory education, there is no excuse in this country for ignorance of the elements of learning" (Kraditor 1965, 111–112).

Complementing this newly rationalized process of political recruitment was the move toward commission and city-manager forms of government that were patterned upon the or-

[13] Attempts to restrict suffrage constituted one aspect of the xenophobia and antiradical tenor of the times, which also found expression in nativist efforts to restrict immigration or to "Americanize" aliens. In Higham's (1955) account nativists played only a small role in the early years of the Progressive movement, especially where urban reform was concerned. Only later, as war approached, did "100% Americanism" become a well-entrenched form of racism.

ganizational anatomy of the business corporation. Advocates of the commission plan argued that "a municipality is largely a business corporation," and that it should therefore seek "to apply business methods to public service" (Weinstein 1968, 96). According to this way of thinking, voters were the "stockholders" who would elect commissioners to serve on a "board of directors" charged with the responsibility of making significant policy decisions. These decisions would then be implemented by a corps of career bureaucrats who were the staff and line officers of the municipal corporation.

The council-manager form of government only refined this business model of government (Weinstein 1968). The manager (or in some cases the mayor in council-mayor governments) was to be the chief executive officer of the municipal corporation. As such, the manager would relay the policy decisions of city legislators to the administrators who were to implement them, and who would presumably be accountable to the manager for the discharge of their duties. A functionally organized bureaucracy of experts would serve the interests of the people, as expressed by their democratically elected leaders. Direct democracy became expert democracy under the business model of government.

It is not surprising that reformers interested in modernizing government looked toward the corporation for a model of effective organization.[14] The corporation was the paradigmatic technical system of organization. Although its impersonality and power were both resented and feared by those whose lives were adversely affected by its operation, the ease and efficiency with which the corporation accomplished its objec-

[14] Those in business were not shy about offering the corporation as a model to reformers. Charles Steinmetz felt that "all that is necessary is to extend methods of economic efficiency from the individual industrial corporation to the national organism as a whole" (Haber 1964, 110).

Steinmetz's views were not entirely representative of those in the private sector—he was a socialist, after all, but Gilbert (1972) analyzes other efforts by businessmen, e.g. "Razor" King Gillette, to transfer the technology of organization from the private to the public sector.

tives was a source of wonder and admiration to others. Moreover, the apparent harmony of interests that bound the diverse members of a corporation together—laborers, managers, and owners—captured the imagination of a generation of people that, as Hofstadter (1955) reminds us, had come of age during the industrial strife and social unrest of the 1890s.[15]

This apparent harmony of interests was based on the fact that corporations had a clearly defined objective—profitability—and a reward structure that ostensibly bestowed benefits on individuals in proportion to their contribution to the realization of this objective. This reward structure provided the material foundation upon which technical systems of control depended for their smooth operation; without such a structure of incentives it would have been considerably more difficult to coordinate the actions of the diverse interests represented in the corporate ranks.

Ironically, the machine was the closest political approximation of this. The machine had a definite goal—winning elections—and a patronage system of rewards that enabled it to function very much like a corporation. The replacement of the machine by "good government" failed to duplicate this accomplishment, despite the fact that "good government" was explicitly patterned on a business model of organiza-

[15] Weinstein (1968) describes the efforts of larger corporations to establish more cordial relations with labor in the interests of uninterrupted production. While small concerns of the sort represented by the National Association of Manufacturers adamantly opposed unionization, the leaders of the larger industrial enterprises were willing to accept conservative unions as the price of peace. Thus, the apparent harmony of corporate relations was not entirely a sham, though the visions of peace entertained by the men discussed by Gilbert (1972) were idyllic misrepresentations of the true state of industrial relations at this time.

Cf. Mitchell (1983) for a fascinating account of the way in which many large corporations adopted pension plans, life insurance schemes, stock ownership plans, unemployment funds, and many social service programs for their employees in order to create a public image of corporate responsibility.

tion.[16] The business model of government lacked the unified sense of purpose that characterized corporations and machines. It aimed at efficiency, but had no goal or objective according to which the efficiency of various actions might be assessed in a meaningful fashion.[17] "Politics" operated behind a façade of nonpartisanship that obscured deep divisions in the community over the proper course of political action (although the intensity of those divisions had been stifled by "direct democracy" measures to silence the voice of "political incompetents"). "Administration," too, was conducted behind a veil of bureaucratic neutrality and technical competence, which contributed to an appearance of harmonious interests where no such agreement existed.

Moreover, the separation of politics and administration created two distinct reward structures that were not well-articulated. The bureaucratic pathologies, e.g. goal displacement, with which we are so familiar today, grew out of the weakened accountability of civil servants no longer subject to the confining bonds of the patronage system. Consequently, the business model of good government seldom worked as well as its proponents hoped. Indeed, many political scientists now trace the functional fragmentation of city government by bureaucratic "machines" to this era.

To a significant extent this failure of reform may be attributed to the fact that reformers wrongly attributed efficiency to structural features of organization, rather than the context in which organizations operated. They failed to understand that the behavior or performance of corporations depended

[16] Katznelson (1981) and Shefter (1983) explain why machines were not radical in orientation or operation. The essays in Stave (1975) describe some of the few exceptions in which Socialist parties won control of cities, often implementing reforms that were fairly similar to those proposed by radical Progressives.

[17] Even (or especially) where the principles of scientific management were extensively used in public administration, "there was little talk of where efficient government was going and much rolling-up of sleeves and getting on with the business at hand" (Haber 1964, 111).

on the competitive environment in which they existed, more than their internal anatomy (which was itself shaped by the environment). In order to obtain the desired goal of efficiency it would have been necessary to make politics more competitive, without which the expected benefits could not be realized.

However, that would have required an orientation toward politics that recognized both the legitimacy and desirability of competition among interests. Such "disharmony" was inconsistent with the reformers' hope for progress toward a society in which class and ethnic differences had been transcended via the application of neutral, scientific principles of management.[18] The power of this image was so great that the "good government" crusade against the machine became little more than a struggle to replace a "bad" (because incompetent) monopoly with a "good" (because efficient) one. The triumph of "good government" was not the triumphal recognition of competition, but a denial of its necessary existence in politics—an ironic outcome for a movement steeped in the evolutionary theories of Reform Darwinism.[19]

VI

PROGRESSIVE REFORMS were not confined to the city. Indeed, the later phase of the Progressive movement was increasingly oriented toward national regulatory reform. In that sense, Teddy Roosevelt's New Nationalism and Woodrow Wilson's New Freedom marked a significant departure from the hard-line laissez-faire tradition of men like Sumner. The national government assumed responsibility for regulating important economic transactions, though the scope of this

[18] Alan Wolfe (1977) also makes this point.

[19] Oddly enough, it was the Progressive historians who undermined this view by reconstructing the economic basis of politics and analyzing the way in which class conflict had developed in America. Of course, they, too, hoped that a "critical realism" about the nature of political economy might lend itself to the creation of a Progressive society in which democracy reigned triumphant.

regulatory activity was fairly narrow. Moreover, this regulation was, with certain notable exceptions, e.g. the Federal
Reserve Act, ameliorative rather than anticipatory and was
directed toward particular actors, e.g. corporate monopolies,
rather than structural features of the national economy. The
presence of the regulatory state was therefore a mere shadow
of the incomplete state capitalism that Populists hoped to
achieve through the nationalization of key industries, e.g.
transportation and finance.

Radical Progressives were not content with mere regulation, however. Croly, for example, denounced the regulatory
approach of Wilson's New Freedom. For Wilson, regulation
was but a change in methods for insuring that competition
would remain the basic principle of social stabilization. Laissez-faire was no longer sufficient to ensure this. More active
means were required to both restore and promote competition. Thus, the difference between the new and old freedoms
was "plainly one of method rather than of purpose" (Croly,
1914, 16).

"True progressivism," on the other hand, had more radical
ambitions insofar as it aimed to provide "not merely a new
method, important as a new method may be, but a new faith,
upon the rock of which may be built a better structure of
individual and social life" (ibid., 25). The goal of true progressivism was to establish *The New Democracy*, to use the
title of Weyl's (1912) manifesto, in which the laissez-faire
ethos of "live and let live" was replaced by a new ethic of
"live and help live" and the fulfillment of everyone's needs,
not just those of a privileged few (ibid., 426).

Thus, progressivism was to move America to a new and
higher level of civilization. In comparison to this objective,
the method of regulation espoused by Wilson paled into in-
significance. Nothing short of a new interpretation of rights
was necessary, wherein the *social* rights of "life, leisure, a
share in our natural resources, and a dignified existence in
society" were to gain precedence over the narrow and exclusive claims of property (Weyl 1912, 161). In other words, *sub-*

stantive democracy was to replace the merely formal democracy of laissez-faire, as industry, society, and government were organized along more equitable lines. In the process, the plutocratic shackles upon moral and economic development were to be loosed, and truly human progress forged.

Behind this radical program, however, lay another, even larger objective of progressivism. Weyl's book *The New Democracy* was not only a blueprint for a new, more democratic society. It also identified the agent of such momentous change, namely "the new democracy" or class of commoners. Weyl, as well as Croly, used "democracy" in its original sense to refer to a particular class in society, and to societies in which that class held sway. "The democracy" was a class that stood opposed to "the plutocracy," whose greed had driven "the democracy" to the point of rebellion, making it an irresistible force of change.

Hence, it was "the democracy" that would bring "*The New Democracy*" into existence. Neither Weyl nor Croly believed "the plutocracy" was capable of withstanding the apparently inevitable "gathering of the forces of democracy" (ibid., 235–254). Moreover, they felt that the demands of "the democracy" were essentially justified, as the existing system of exploitation and corruption was neither necessary nor acceptable from a progressive point of view. Hence, the main question for Progressives concerned the direction in which the apparently inevitable change would move.

That question was not easily answered. The Progressives feared that "the democracy" might fail to become a force for *progressive* change unless it were appropriately educated for its historic mission. They were well aware of traditional arguments concerning the unprogressive orientations of "the democracy" and the danger of majoritarian tyranny (ibid). Indeed, it was precisely because they placed some credence in these arguments that Progressives attached so much importance to moral education as a way of making "the democracy" safe for America.

Nowhere is this more apparent than in Croly's (1914) chapter on "Social Education" in *Progressive Democracy*, in which he attempts to show how the instincts of "the democracy" might be directed in competent directions. Croly's proposals for carrying out this education are indeed fairly radical, involving a "socially educative distribution of work" that anticipated contemporary versions of workplace democracy (Croly 1914, 23). More striking, however, is the content of that education. Croly concludes, not surprisingly, that "the social education appropriate to the democracy must be, above all, a liberal education" (ibid., 412). The intellectual and moral emancipation provided by a liberal education to the privileged few must be extended to all in order to assure their loyalty and commitment to making the personal sacrifices necessary for achieving progressive democracy. Only in this way, and not through traditional arguments about self-denial and duty, could the assent of "the democracy" be secured and their energy "channelized" into building a better world for all.

Croly's denial of the efficacy of conservative ideologies of self-restraint was an explicit recognition of the abstract universality of a liberal ethos, which cannot, in principle, permanently deny privileges to anyone, let alone a majority. It was Croly's recognition that self-denial was not the only faith upon which society might be built that led him to see that liberalism could become the end for which "the democracy" struggled, rather than the object of its wrath. Enlightened liberalism, or progressivism, could provide a "new faith upon which rock a new society might be founded."

This would require dynamic leadership, to be sure, but Croly and other radical Progressives felt that Roosevelt embodied the qualities that were necessary to excite a "new nationalism" capable of sustaining such a monumental undertaking. Wilson's victory over Roosevelt in 1912 dashed that hope, but Croly and his fellows believed that Wilson might be "educated" on the need to reconstruct American society.[20]

[20] Noble (1958) describes the curious zigs and zags of the editorial policy

The emergence of men like Roosevelt and Wilson was timely, in their view, for the opportunity to engage in conscious nation-building was present for perhaps the first time in American history. The moment was at hand, the leadership assembled, and the popular imagination captured by the idea of progress. Only the possibility of war, or more precisely, American involvement in war, seemed to threaten the promise of American life.

VII

THE HISTORICAL significance of the new Progressive faith was discussed more explicitly in Croly's enormously influential book on *The Promise of American Life*, which was published in 1910. In distinctly modern terms Croly speculated on the possibility of recreating social life by a conscious dedication to cooperative, democratic living. A "comprehensive and formative" system of democracy, conceived as a "constructive social ideal," could be used to establish a "morally and socially desirable distribution of wealth," now that the contradictions of the old order were becoming apparent to all. He believed that "a more highly socialized democracy is the only practical substitute on the part of committed democrats for an excessively individualized democracy" that sanctioned a maldistribution of wealth that more and more people were finding intolerable (Croly 1910, 17, 23, 25).

Croly was not a latter-day Populist clothed in more respectable middle-class garb. In fact he scorned the "local malcontents" and "ignorant economic agitators" numbered among the supporters of Bryan, and he for one was willing to excuse the American people for "placing the Republicans in power, and in waiting until a safer substitute could be provided for the old order" (1914, 6).

Croly believed that the triumph of the conservatives over

---

of the *New Republic* as it strove to influence Wilson's policies. Forcey (1961) emphasizes Croly's obsession with the importance of leadership, and his inevitable frustration with the performance of Wilson, and even Roosevelt.

the Populists only postponed the day of reckoning, however. Emboldened by their success, the proponents of laissez-faire pushed their advantage to the limit and engaged in ever more indulgent abuses of power and privilege. In the end, "they succeeded far better than their enemies could have done by making public opinion understand the gravity of the existing evils and abuse" (ibid., 6). The conservatives provided a great object lesson that succeeded where Populist pedagogy had failed, and in so doing brought down upon their own heads the wave of regulation that was the legacy of the Progressive Era.

At the same time he did not think that democracy in America was something that would automatically emerge, according to some law of evolution. Rather it was something to be called forth and secured "by a combination of individual effort and proper political organization" (Croly 1910, 17). He assumed that "democracy must stand or fall on a platform of possible human perfectibility," and that as a result progressive action was necessary to realize the promise of American life (ibid., 400).

Noble's (1958) interpretation of Croly is quite telling in this regard. According to him Croly was no simple-minded utopian who believed that human beings were free to establish heaven on earth, once they chose to do so. Before that could happen, humans had to be freed from traditional orientations and patterns of interaction; the burden of history had to be lifted before men and women could truly make history by calling forth a Progressive society from the promise of American life. Industrialization was the liberating force that made social regeneration possible by dissolving the "steel chain of ideas" inherited from the past (Goldman 1956). The irrelevance of traditional institutions and practices to modern problems and possibilities would then be obvious to all—or could be made obvious via education—allowing human beings to assume conscious control over their destiny.

Croly realized that many people did not fully accept the idea that men were free to remake the institutions that had made them. Yet he insisted that "if human nature cannot be improved by institutions, democracy is at best a more than usually safe form of political organization" (ibid.). Americans had an obligation to move beyond such a negative conception of democracy as the absence of arbitrary restraint on individual initiative. The responsibility of striving to perfect the American system was the basis for a "higher American patriotism . . . [which] combines loyalty to tradition and precedent with the imaginative projection of an ideal national Promise," even if that meant sacrificing "traditional American ways of realizing" the vision of America as the "Land of Democracy" (Croly 1910, 3, 5).

Thus, the real substance of American liberalism was "an attitude of mind which seeks to bring understanding to bear upon action, which prevails in social life less through the functioning of liberal institutions than through the activity of an alert, aggressive, and disinterested public opinion" (Noble 1958, 37). The founding of the *New Republic* magazine in 1912 under the direction of Herbert Croly and with the assistance of Walter Weyl and Walter Lippmann was intended to cultivate the spirit of critical understanding of society and its possibilities, thereby stimulating reform.

When this did not succeed, i.e. when the Progressive spirit "flagged" in the face of vanishing opportunities to recreate society, the faith of radical Progressives such as Croly was sorely tested, and in some cases broken. Yet that faith was unreasonable, at least to the extent that it overestimated the capacity of education to inspire men and women to act virtuously. Croly accepted Montesquieu's proposition that "the principle of democracy is virtue," and for that reason he believed that "if a noble and civilized democracy is to subsist, the common citizen must be something of a saint and something of a hero," or at least be capable of the "sincere and enthusiastic imitation of heroes and saints" (Croly 1910, 454).

Instead the "common man" seemed content to accept progress as it came, without exerting an extraordinary effort to reconstruct all of society. This complacence was intensely disillusioning for the men at the *New Republic*. Walter Lippmann decided that the radical Progressives had placed too much stock in the willingness and ability of the American public to accept the challenge to rebuild the nation. He turned toward experts for the energy and commitment that he found lacking in the general citizenry for, as he put it, political reformers "must not assume that the mass has political genius, but that men, even if they had genius, would give only a little time and attention to public affairs" (Lippmann 1925, 27).

According to Lippmann, the enlightened public in which the Progressives had placed their trust was a "phantom," and a new agent of transformation had to be identified: "The lesson is, I think, a fairly clear one. In the absence of institutions and education by which the environment is so successfully reported that the realities of public life stand out sharply against self-centered opinion, the common interests very largely elude public opinion entirely, and can be managed only by a specialized class whose personal interests reach beyond locality" (Lippmann 1922, 310).

Lippmann insisted that "no reform, however sensational, is truly radical, which does not consciously provide a way of overcoming the subjectivism of human opinion based on the limitation of individual experience" (ibid., 397). Most citizens never escaped the parochialism of outlook that prevented them from viewing public affairs with disinterest; only those trained in the sciences had the inclination to take a global point of view. Hence, political decision-making ought to incorporate a greater reliance on "intelligence work" by experts whose "interests reach beyond locality."

After all, Lippmann argued, the purpose of modern government was not to burden a citizen with difficult issues and problems that were beyond his interest and comprehension, "but to push that burden away from him towards the responsible administrator" (ibid., 399). Truly virtuous citizens would, in fact, refuse the responsibility to decide these issues, reserving their opinion until after the effects of decisions on them were known, as this information was part of their experience and comprehension. Then they might pass judgment on elected officials, according to the use to which the latter had put the technical know-how made available by experts.

Thus, it was left to one of the most venerable spokesmen of radical Progressivism to express the ultimate version of expert democracy in the United States.

VIII

THUS THE RADICAL Progressives' challenge to liberalism to live up to its own ideals was relatively short-lived. Indeed, this brand of progressivism was less influential than the tamer Wilsonian variety, which basked in the reflected glow of this moral vision even as it put forth more modest proposals for improving democracy. Because this latter democratic vision was more restricted than that of radical Progressives, it is perhaps not surprising that Wilsonian Progressives celebrated the achievement of democracy, once their reforms had been adopted and implemented.

The moderation of this commitment was evident in Wilson's message to Congress on December 8, 1914, in which he announced that "our program of legislation with regard to the regulation of business is now complete. It has been put forth, as we intended as a whole, and leaves no conjecture as to what is to follow. The road at last lies clear and firm before business . . . the road to ungrudged, unclouded success" (Hofstadter 1948, 259–260).

There were those who felt that Wilson was all too prophetic in predicting success for business and who questioned the democratic achievements of the New Freedom. The International Workers of the World, for example, claimed that a truly "Industrial Democracy" could not be realized until "the worker on the job shall tell the boss when and where he shall work, how long, and for what wages and under what conditions" (Dubofsky 1969, 159).

With the outbreak of war, however, such radical interpretations of democracy were no longer countenanced, as they allegedly jeopardized the war effort. They were swiftly and surely suppressed, as indeed were many of the gains in political democracy, ironically in the name of a war "to make the world safe for democracy." Men like Parrington (1958, 411–413) observed with dismay the liberal retreat from democratic issues when confronted with evidence concerning the mediocrity of the masses. Similarly, in 1919 Wilson's old friend George L. Record took him severely to task for "ignoring the great issue which is slowly coming to the front, the question of economic democracy, abolition of privilege, and securing to men the full fruits of their labor or service" (Hofstadter 1948, 277).

The postwar ebb of whatever tinge of radicalism was implicit in Progressivism was accompanied by a thorough-going repression of the syndicalist and socialist left, complete with lynchings, shootings, jailings, and deportations. The voices of criticism, either by choice or force, were silent, and the achievement of democracy was accepted as accomplished fact.

Croly and his fellow radical Progressives were intensely frustrated by the xenophobic direction of American nationalism and the perversion of its reform impulse. Yet they found it exceptionally difficult to challenge the democratic complacency that marked the undemocratic and illiberal practices of the war and its aftermath. To a significant extent this difficulty reflected a congenital weakness of Progressive thought, which harbored a relativistic outlook that fatally compromised radical Progressives' efforts to articulate a moral critique of American society. As a result, the power of their message declined in proportion to the degree to which radical Progressives were "out of step" with the prevailing attitudes of their times, while their own philosophy prevented them from reasserting the intellectual leadership in the moral life of society they had once enjoyed.

These weaknesses flowed from the same source that made Progressivism so powerful in the early years of the twentieth century, namely, its historical sensibility, which distinguished Progressivism from more traditional political orientations (Ross 1979). As we saw in Chapter Four, the possibility of establishing a republic outside of time was widely entertained during the Jacksonian era. That hope was exploded by the closing of the frontier and the onset of modernization during the Gilded Age, but the social Darwinism so prevalent during this period reduced history to a category of natural "evolution." As such it denied the possibility, or at least desirability, of resisting the disintegration of the republic as it moved into the modern, industrial era. Only "Reform Darwinism" challenged the historical resignation implicit in laissez-faire by holding out hope for controlled evolution.

The Progressives quickly seized this opening and made the possibility of intervention in social, economic, and political affairs the cornerstone of this philosophy. This appreciation of historical opportunities for Progressive action complemented the confidence in "scientific management" that was so widespread during the early years of the movement. Croly's call for action dovetailed neatly with newly discovered strategies for achieving desired ends, but what he and Weyl and others like them failed to anticipate was the extent to which the apparently successful application of these techniques might create the illusion that the task of reconstruction was essentially accomplished, and that the promise of American life had been attained. The historical *pursuit* of progress, to which Croly was committed, ended for others once the world had been made safe for democracy.

Hence, during the waning years of the Progressive movement Croly could only insist that true progress had not yet been realized, and that further progress was both possible and necessary. However, he was unable to describe the truly Progressive society in terms that were both concrete and morally compelling. His commitment to an historical understanding of the origin and possibilities of human society had no defense against historicist inclinations that led very quickly into the morass of moral relativism. Such a framework would not permit the inclusion of transcendental elements out of which a compelling vision of the object of the pursuit of progress might be constructed, and so it ultimately rested on a faith in the progressive direction of American history (Noble 1958).

The "facts" of complacency seemed to undermine this faith. The impassioned call for "a rendezvous with destiny," to borrow from Franklin Delano Roosevelt, via Goldman (1956), was therefore reduced to an unending exhortation to progress. Without a measure of progress, however, that exhortation was bound to seem rather empty, unless those who heard it shared Croly's faith in the direction of history. And if they shared that faith, a response of complacency was just as reasonable, and far less taxing, than reform. Moreover, the unparalleled prosperity of the twenties made the ascetic orientation of the reformer seem quite superfluous, and the ensuing hedonism of the period laid the foundation for democratic consumerism, the new democracy of the New Deal.

CHAPTER EIGHT

Democratic Consumerism

I

THE RELATIONSHIP between capitalism and democracy is an uneasy one. When times are good, economically speaking, the tension between the two is relaxed, but with the onset of "hard times" the confrontation between "the democracy" and "the plutocracy" can become quite intense, and may even usher in a fundamental alteration of the basic relationship between the two.

The confrontation of the late nineteenth century produced such a change, though not until the twentieth century had dawned and the restless spirit of progressivism made its presence felt. The Progressives eschewed the old policy of laissez-faire in favor of a modest policy of political regulation of private industry. In effect, the power of the democracy was pitted against the power of unscrupulous capitalists, though not against capitalism per se. Thus, regulated capitalism came to be identified with democratic capitalism in the Progressive mind, and that identification exerted a powerful influence on American politics for nearly thirty years.

However, the occurrence of the Great Depression rendered that identification problematic. The value of stock answers apparently declines in proportion to that of stock issues during hard times. As a result, the hegemony of Progressive democracy was broken, and no less than four competing conceptions of democracy emerged during the thirties. Three of these interpretations—those of the New Dealers, the Socialists, and the so-called Depression Demagogues—repudiated the value of regulation for resolving conflicts between democracy and capitalism in favor of more fundamental restrictions on capitalism. Only the Republicans and their allies in the American Liberty League resisted further efforts to democratize capitalism because they believed that such efforts would produce a net loss in those rights and privileges traditionally associated with American democracy.

The special significance of this dispute stems from the fact that the eventual "winner," the New Deal conception of democratic consumerism, succeeded in spite of the fact that it made no special *moral* claims for itself. It advanced no ideal of society to which the United States might return, or toward which it might move. Instead, it offered the secular "ideal" of continuous and widespread consumption as the basic desideratum of social life.

Given the circumstances, this was no mean promise. Its popularity is quite understandable. Still, the triumph of this conception of democracy over conceptions that appealed to traditional American sources of legitimacy, e.g. religious and liberal notions of justice and freedom, is remarkable. It becomes even more noteworthy when its easy victory over the visionary ideals of social democracy are taken into account. For it then becomes apparent that this rise of a conception of democracy that looks neither to the past nor to the future signified the relative decline of all ethical conceptions of democracy, regardless of their specific moral content. Henceforth, the meaning and legitimacy of democracy in America was linked to economic performance and the abundance of consumer goods, rather than moral achievement (Wolin 1981b).

The reasons for this dramatic shift in the legitimating grounds of democracy are numerous and complex. They include the ineffective performance of the spokesmen for other conceptions of democracy, which in turn must be explained with reference to situational and historical factors that made it impossible to mount a sustained opposition to the democratic consumerism of the New Deal. The conjuncture of a discredited right, a disorganized left, and an unorganized radical fringe left the field open for a politically astute adminis-

tration to forge a winning coalition on the basis of an ostensibly common social interest in consumption. With
meaningful, i.e. substantive, conceptions of democracy in disrepute or disarray, it became possible for an amoral and
wholly procedural conception of democracy to hold sway.
Once in place it demonstrated a truly remarkable staying
power, as both a system and a public philosophy of "interest
group liberalism" grew up around and in support of it (Lowi
1969).

This "demoralization" of democracy was made possible by
the rationalization of discourse that began in the late nineteenth century and continued in the Progressive era. As the
grounds of political debate shifted toward more scientific terrain, considerations of efficiency and dependability became
leading indicators of political performance, and democratic
governments were judged according to their technical success
in stabilizing the economy. Naturally, this alteration of the
terms of discourse occurred slowly and unevenly, but the extent to which it had taken place before the New Deal is evident in the subordination of the latent moral content of the
more radical versions of progressivism to its "realistic" elements after World War I.

The illusion of fulfillment that war spawned by this realism
was shattered by the Depression. The failure of the regulatory state was an indisputable "fact" that contradicted the
promise of American life. In order to restore that promise,
new political methods seemed necessary to resolve the tension between democracy and capitalism—at least on a provisional basis. Because this provisional resolution was peculiarly amoral, however, the course of American political
discourse was decisively altered by virtue of the fact that future liberal democrats found it exceptionally difficult to challenge.

Thus, the New Deal was the beginning of the end of ideology in American politics—and also the origin of a thoroughly rationalized political discourse in which liberal democratic principles of argumentation were seriously compro-

mised. That part of our story must wait, though, until we understand the way in which consumer democracy emerged victorious from the Depression.

II

THE APPARENT FAILURE of regulation to curb the "excesses" of capitalism became apparent in October 1929. In the aftermath of the crash new and more radical policies gained popularity. Against this rising tide of sympathy for more drastic intervention the American right called upon well-established traditions to reinforce its claim that radical action was not required, and, further, that it would subvert the very foundations of American liberty.

In this cause a much attenuated version of Wilson's "Progressive" democracy was defended by the American right during the 1930s. The Republican party, and especially the American Liberty League, fought a spirited rear-guard action against all further attempts to democratize capitalism by means of political intervention in the economic realm. Recognizing the popularity of their opponents' attack on unfettered capitalism, they sought refuge in the traditional American defense against popular causes, namely, the idea of constitutional democracy.

Yet the Republicans, and Hoover especially, were not dyed-in-the-wool advocates of laissez-faire. On more than one occasion Hoover observed that just as concentrated political power was dangerous to liberty, so too was concentrated economic power: "We can no more have economic power without checks and balances than we can have political power without checks and balances. Either one leads to tyranny" (Hoover 1972, 67). Consequently, he was not an opponent of regulation so long as it did not become "government in or dictating to business" à la the New Deal. The latter was un-American, while the former was an explicit feature of the American System of Regulation that had evolved during the first three decades of the twentieth century.

In this respect Hoover followed the example of Wilson and

his New Freedom. The American System of Regulation relied on competition where possible, but did not shrink from governmental regulation where necessary. Monopolies, banks and "other functions of trust," overaccumulations of hereditary wealth, and of course organized labor were legitimate targets of regulation, so long as it was minimal, duly promulgated in law, and left to states and localities wherever possible. Ultimately, however, "the fundamental regulation of the nation is the Ten Commandments and the Sermon on the Mount" (ibid., 69). Again, the moral, and in this case religious, foundations of social life were emphasized, in contradistinction to the New Deal's conception of the consumer society, which we shall soon meet.

That left considerable room for voluntary cooperation and self government by the people outside the government. The greatest threat to this vast system of cooperation, in the eyes of the American right, was posed by Roosevelt's explicit attempt to incite class warfare. It was this perception of Roosevelt's willingness to sow the seeds of class discord in order to reap a rich electoral harvest that led many on the right to voice antimajoritarian sentiments. These sentiments were hardly new on the American scene, nor were they couched in particularly original terms. Instead, they assumed the form of a defense of constitutional democracy over and against the democratic despotism of majority rule. The fact that the despot in this case was a popular majority in favor of the New Deal did not excuse its actions. If anything it made the right even more apprehensive concerning the prospects for the "American way of life."[1]

In some instances this apprehension was rooted in frankly elitist conceptions about the common man and his political sensibilities, or lack thereof (Wolfskill 1962). More often it rested upon a deep suspicion of Roosevelt and his "Brain Trust," and their alleged skill at manipulating popular opin-

---

[1] The "American way of life" apparently derives from Landon's 1936 campaign slogan, "Save the American Way of Life" (Safire 1968).

ion. This was especially apparent in a book called *Democratic Despotism*, written in 1936 by a charter member of the Liberty League, Raoul Desvernine. While the entire book pays backhanded tribute to Roosevelt's wily ways, it devotes a whole chapter to "The Technique of the Revolution" as perpetrated by the New Dealers. There we find the New Dealers accused of intentional misuse of democratic methods to achieve undemocratic, i.e. illiberal, ends. Did they need a mass base of support? Then they captured the Democratic party, only to repudiate its platform of traditional American ideals. Did they need to change the way people thought about the proper role of government? Then they resorted to propaganda and incited class warfare. Did they need to augment the powers of the executive? Then they fabricated "emergencies" intended to stretch the constitutional powers of the presidency to the limit, and beyond.

Here we come to the heart of the matter, the unconstitutional and even anticonstitutional attitude of the New Dealers, as perceived by the right. Roosevelt and his Brain Trust exhibited their disdain for such matters by tampering with the guardians of the Constitution, the Supreme Court. Even more serious, however, was their stated belief "that law emanates solely from the will of the majority of the people, and can, therefore, be modifed at any time to meet majority wishes" (Desvernine 1936, 176–177). This struck at the very function of the Court and was far more serious than any tampering with its form.

No more pernicious doctrine could be imagined by the members of the Liberty League. For them the American political system was

> predicated on the doctrine that there are some immutable laws of nature and certain other divinely sanctioned rights, which the Constitution and our tradition recognized as being above and beyond the power of the majority, or of any other group of individuals or officials of the Government. There are, also, other rights, which because of man's

historic experience, that are specifically protected by the Constitution, and which can only be modified under the prescribed method set forth in the Constitution; and, consequently the majority is not free to modify them as it pleases, but only in the manner prescribed by the Constitution. That is why our system has been characterized as a government *of laws, not of men.* (ibid., 177)

This was constitutional democracy, which established absolute limits on majoritarian power and created regular procedures for expressing the will of the majority within those limits over which it properly held sway. By failing to recognize, or at least respect, the primacy of fundamental over ordinary law, the New Dealers stood poised to destroy the very bulwark of liberal freedoms, and the very soul of Americanism (ibid.).

The key problem that confronts all constitutional democrats is that of establishing acceptable limits on majoritarian action without compromising popular sovereignty. By the very nature of their argument constitutional democrats must make a distinction between majorities of the moment, whose actions may be legitimately hampered, and more or less permanent majorities, whose actions cannot be denied without relinquishing claim to the title of democrat. The issue, then, is to decide which majorities may be obstructed. From this point of view, constitutional democrats differ only in the manner in which they distinguish ordinary from extraordinary majorities.

The Republicans and members of the American Liberty League were no exception to this rule. By inclination and for reasons of expediency, they could not stand absolutely and unconditionally against the intervention of a popular government in the affairs of the economy. Though they despaired of the consequences of such action, they could not deny its legitimacy without first showing that such action was not performed by the appropriate majority. The problem of the right, then, was to show that the New Deal majority and its actions were not duly constituted and were in fact contrary to both the spirit and the law of the American Constitution. In this way, and in this way only, could the legitimacy of the New Deal be denied without abandoning the position that true and constitutional majorities were entitled to rule their societies.

Thus, the Republicans tried to show that the New Deal violated the fundamental spirit of the American constitution, which was intended to preserve and promote *individual* liberty. Toward that end they warned of the danger to the "American System of Liberty" posed by the "regimentation" of life under the New Deal. They attacked the proposals of Roosevelt, who threatened, according to Hoover, to alter the whole foundation of national life (Hoover 1972, 85). That foundation consisted of true liberalism, as distinct from the ostensibly liberal promises of the New Deal. The spirit of the former was to create free men, while the latter led only to regimentation: "It is a false liberalism that interprets itself into dictation by government. Every step in that direction crushes the very roots of liberalism. It is the road not to liberty but to less liberty" (Hoover 1972, 72).

True liberalism did not strive to spread bureaucracy, but to set bounds to it. True liberalism sought a legitimate freedom first in the confident belief that without freedom the pursuit of other blessings was in vain. Liberalism was a force proceeding from the deep realization that economic freedom could not be sacrificed if political freedom was to be preserved (ibid.).

Liberal democracy, then, was constitutional democracy, and it was incumbent on the right to insist on this identity. For that reason, Hoover's concern over the New Deal's usurpation of the liberal label was well-founded, though he was unsuccessful in stopping it (Beer 1978). By 1936 he was forced to concede that "today, however, the term Liberal is claimed by every sect that would limit human freedom and stagnate the human soul—whether they be Fascists, Socialists, Communists, Epics, or New Dealers" (ibid., 72). The advantages to be so gained were apparent, and the effectiveness of these claims obvious. Consequently, Hoover was reduced to arguing that the label mattered little, so long as the basic principles of laissez-faire were advocated. The only "true liberals" were, therefore, the Republicans and members of the Liberty League.[2]

In the mid-1930s these arguments on behalf of the Constitution were put forth by a party of memory that was no longer in power. As such they found little support among a public whose immediate memories were of misery, and whose imagination was captured by a party of hope under the tutelage of a consummate politician. The election of 1936, in which Landon received only eight electoral votes on the strength of thirty-six percent of the popular vote, virtually destroyed the Liberty League, which in only two years' time had assimilated 124,856 members and seriously entertained the possibility of helping unseat Roosevelt. It dealt the Republican party a blow from which it took over a generation to recover. With their defeat the voice of classical liberal democracy was effectively stilled for almost thirty years, and when it was once again raised it was a much more temperate, some would say temporizing, liberalism that informed it.

III

EVEN AS THE American right was raising the traditional defense of what their opponents called plutocracy, "the democracy" was being wooed by those who played on another American tradition that we earlier referred to as the greenback critique of American capitalism. Indeed, several monetarist proposals for achieving "financial democracy" surfaced

[2] Cf. Rotunda (1968) and Beer (1965) on the capture of the "liberal" label by the New Deal Democrats. Beer (1978) suggests that this capture resulted in the adoption by the right of the little-used label of "conservative," and he traces the contrapuntal development of "liberalism" and "conservatism" in American politics since the New Deal. Interestingly, he concludes that we are now in a period of "equilibrium without purpose," since neither side enjoys a decisive advantage.

during the thirties, and in the course of their emergence the traditional debate between the plutocracy and the democracy was reconstituted. Once again the poor accused the rich of robbing them of their just desserts through a corrupt monetary system, while the rich attributed economic problems to "hard times."

In retrospect it is not difficult to understand why neopopulist proposals for creating a financial democracy generated considerable enthusiasm and support. By late 1935 Roosevelt's popularity had slipped to its lowest point since his election, and many of his one-time supporters were growing impatient with the slowness of the New Dealers' trial-and-error method of experimentation, and its downright cautious approach to economic policy-making. Disenchantment with the New Deal was greatest among the followers of the neopopulist "Depression Demagogues" and other fascistic groups, e.g. William Dudley Pelley's nativist Silver Shirts, Holt Gewiner's Klannish Black Shirts, not to mention a veritable clothing store of other Blue, Khaki, Gray, Brown, and White Shirt movements and fringe groups (Bennett 1969). These popular movements gave some credibility to the Liberty League's fears concerning unvarnished majoritarian tyranny, though they greatly overestimated the seriousness of this threat.

The most prominent challenges came from the South and West, both of which were areas of vital importance to Roosevelt's reelection. In the West two challenges to the New Deal emerged, both from California. Upton Sinclair's plan to End Poverty in California (EPIC) helped him wrest the Democratic gubernatorial nomination from George Creel, the voice of the West Coast New Deal. On the strength of the Twelve Principles of EPIC, Sinclair captured thirty-seven percent of the popular vote cast for governor in the California election of 1934.[3]

[3] EPIC promised to end unemployment and poverty by creating a parallel socialist economy out of the unutilized or underutilized productive capacity of California's farms and industries. This economy would compete with, and

Of greater national consequence, however, was the Old Age Revolving Pension plan of Francis E. Townsend, which was designed to ease the burden of the elderly even as it "primed the pump" of the depressed national economy. The Townsend Plan was simple, even simplistic, in its conception of what was necessary to return America to prosperity. If the problem in America was due to the absence of sufficient demand, then the obvious solution lay in giving consumers the wherewithal to translate their needs and desires into effective economic demand. This could be accomplished by guaranteeing a $200 per month pension to persons aged sixty and over, about eight to ten million of whom were expected to participate in the plan. This would inject some two billion dollars into the economy per month, and when the expected tenfold circulation of each of these dollars was taken into account, a powerful stimulus for economic improvement was likely, the Townsendites believed.

Other groups, too, promoted remedies that served their particular interests as a device for restoring health to the economy as a whole. The Nonpartisan League, with William Lemke at its helm, revived the special claims of the ultimate producer class, the farmers. And, of course, there was the fabulous Kingfish, Huey Long, who championed the cause of that broadest of all classes of disadvantaged citizens, the honest poor.

It was Long who posed the most serious, albeit short-lived, threat to Roosevelt and the New Deal, for it was he who seemed capable of leading the solid South out of the Democratic camp, and who showed surprising strength in the industrial North as well.[4] The basis of this popularity lay in the Kingfish's neopopulism, which revived many of the old Pop-

---

eventually overwhelm, the state's private sector. EPIC was perhaps most notable for its assertion that "autocracy in industry cannot exist alongside democracy in politics."

[4] A secret poll commissioned by Jim Farley in 1936 revealed that Long might draw as many as four million votes as a third-party presidential contender (Bennett 1969, 122). The results of that poll are reproduced in Brinkley (1982).

ulist arguments and programs, not to mention language and imagery. Indeed, the very slogan of Long's Share Our Wealth Clubs—"Every Man a King"—was borrowed from that old silverite, William Jennings Bryan (Bennett 1969, 124).[5]

The essence of the Share Our Wealth program consisted of a promise "to limit poverty by providing that every deserving family shall share in the wealth of America for not less than one-third of the average wealth, thereby to possess not less than $5,000 free of debt" (Long 1934, 1). This was to be financed by a confiscatory tax on fortunes in excess of fifty million dollars.

Long's plan was not socialistic by any means. It did not argue for the abolition of private property, or even for its redistribution on an ambitious scale. It certainly did not argue for a division of the national wealth equally among all citizens. Rather, it simply took from the very richest and gave to the very poorest, leaving everyone else unaffected.[6]

The extent to which Share Our Wealth remained wedded

---

[5] Williams (1960) claims that while Long was influenced by Winn Parish traditions of populism and socialism, he was no populist, and in fact hit on the idea of Share Our Wealth while meditating on the Freedmen's Bureau of the Reconstruction South. Brinkley (1982, 163–164) documents the similarity of style and substance between earlier populist rhetoric and Long's public statements and discusses the political advantages that may have led him to refrain from explicitly acknowledging his debt to populism.

[6] In fact, Long promised much more than to Share Our Wealth. In his prophetic *My First Days in the White House*, he proposed to spend ten billion dollars to eliminate dust storms via an elaborate system of water projects, create a popularly elected central bank, nationalize the railroads, send every child to college, eliminate crime, and inaugurate a fledgling national health care program. The extravagance of these promises no doubt lies behind characterizations of Long as a demagogue. But as Long himself put it after making similarly "exaggerated" promises to Louisianans, "I would describe a demagogue as a politician who don't keep his promises. On that basis, I'm the first man to have power in Louisiana who ain't a demagogue because I kept every promise I ever made!" (Bennett 1969, 122). Much of what Long promised, and his critics said could not be done, eventually came to pass, through no doing of Long, who was fatally wounded by an assassin in 1935.

to capitalism is most clearly revealed by the fact that the promise of $5,000 was not, at least initially, a promise of a guaranteed income. It was originally proposed as a one-time subsidy, based on an inventory of the nation's actual and potential wealth. This subsidy would readmit the poor to the ranks of American consumers, from which they had fallen, and to which they were unable to return by their own efforts. This solution reflected Long's belief that the Depression was a result of underconsumption, rather than overproduction. The swelling ranks of the poor constituted a class of nonconsumers, while the concentration of wealth in the hands of the few created a situation in which those who could consume owned far more wealth than they and their children could ever hope to spend (ibid.). Thus, goods went unsold, not because they were not needed, but because those who could afford them did not need them, while those who did need them could not afford them.

Long seemed unconcerned about how this situation had arisen. For the most part he was content to blame it on corrupt men, the great barons of finance who believed it was necessary for them to own everything, whose pleasure consisted in "the starvation of the masses, and in their possessing things they cannot use, and their children cannot use, but who bask in the splendor of sunlight, casting darkness and despair and impressing it on everyone else" (ibid., 10).

Since the problem was one of greed, the solution to underconsumption was straightforward—simply expropriate excess wealth and restore the downtrodden to financial solvency. To be sure, it might be necessary to do this on a regular basis—"ever[y] so often," as Long put it—particularly if the greedy persisted in obviously successful efforts to amass a disproportionate share of wealth. Nevertheless, that meant only that Americans would be enjoined to follow the Scriptural injunction to forgive debts every seven years or so, and to scatter property every fifty years (ibid., 9).

The possibility that such crises of overaccumulation and underconsumption might be an intrinsic feature of capitalism was apparently never considered by Long. Consequently, he proposed no "long-term" solution to them, although he did endorse the Reverend Charles E. Coughlin's proposal for a popularly elected central bank. Thus, it was left to Coughlin to supply the necessary analysis of the dynamic tendencies of capitalism that lay beneath all the monetarist solutions discussed above.[7]

For Coughlin, as well as Long, Lemke, and Townsend, the Depression presented Americans with a grim paradox: poverty in the midst of plenty. None of them, least of all Coughlin, disputed the enormous productive capacity of modern capitalism. Spurred on by tremendous scientific and technological advances generated by World War I, modern capitalism had effectively solved the production problem. For the first time in history it was within men's grasp to enjoy surcease from the burden of labor, and for all men to join the leisure class: "My friends, do not forget that there is plenty for all—plenty of food, of shelter, of clothing; plenty of medicine for the sick; plenty of profits; plenty of leisure for you and me to expend upon learning, upon entertainment, upon cultivating both the mind and the soul" (Coughlin 1934, 85).

However, modern capitalism prevented all from enjoying the well-deserved fruits of their labor, even as it made their labor more productive and less necessary, for it was predicated upon production for profit. It was therefore incapable of solving the "distribution problem," i.e. the problem of allocating a just share of the social product to labor. Moreover, modern capitalism was prone to periodic crises of underconsumption and overproduction, as the distribution problem went unsolved by market forces.

The principal cause of this, in Coughlin's view, lay in the

[7] The redistribution of wealth, either directly or indirectly via inflationary schemes, was the common goal of the so-called Depression Demagogues. Indeed, that is probably why they were considered demagogues in the first place. Popular control over the nation's *money and credit* was therefore an essential feature of their plans, whereas the New Deal, which did not seek to redistribute wealth, relied on *fiscal* policy to combat the Depression.

private control of the basic media of exchange—money and credit. In this regard, Coughlin and Long did not differ in their analyses of the relationship between the money question and the Depression paradox of poverty in the midst of plenty. Precisely because the media of exchange were owned by the few, a rational and just distribution of the social product was impossible, at least so long as production for profit was the basic imperative of the nation's economy.

Coughlin had a somewhat more sophisticated understanding of this problem than did Long. Though he castigated the greed of "money changers" and "plutocrats" as did Long and even FDR, Coughlin perceived that a production for profit economy required an extensive system of money and credit arrangements. Necessarily, this gave rise to the privileged class of money changers who dominated both labor and capital. Hence, the real conflict in society was not between labor and capital, but between society and finance capital: "The social question today is no longer a question between employers and employees. Employers, employees and unemployed are now all in the same boat—all helpless in the power of high finance which produces nothing but which consumes and controls the wealth which belongs to you and me" (ibid., 101). Thus, it was necessary for manufacturers and laborers both "to strike together for independence from Wall Street," since "nine tenths of the difficulties between labor and capital have sprung from the lustful loins of modern financialism" (ibid., 132).

By locating the source of the distribution problem in Wall Street, and more generally within the international banking community, Coughlin succeeded in deflecting attention from instances of exploitation that took place on the local levels, e.g. sweatshop operations, foreclosures, and denial of credit. It was at this level, in the context of daily life, that people experienced the Depression and the distribution problem in all their immediacy and concreteness. Their grievances arose out of confrontations between workers and their employers, merchants and consumers, bankers and homeowners and farmers, and the deeply felt sense of injury that accompanied these interactions was precisely what made Long's and Coughlin's message so appealing.

At the same time, it was difficult for those who still clung to traditional values to comprehend these experiences. "Modernization" was then not complete; many rural areas, particularly in the South, were only beginning to experience the events that had shaped the outlook of urban Progressives two decades earlier. The reaction of people in these areas to the enormous social, political, and economic changes that were occurring was decidedly hostile, as the old values were reasserted in a desperate effort to resist a process that many secretly feared was irresistible (Brinkley 1982).

The experiences of exploitation clashed with many of the values that were being reasserted at this time, for the latter drew their strength and coherence from a communitarian ethos that presumed a fundamental harmony of social interests. The apparent contradiction was resolved by seeking the causes of conflict outside the community, which Coughlin and Long made easy by their attacks on financial institutions. Oftentimes their denunciations were quite graphic and personal, facilitating the process of scapegoating (ibid.).

The ensuing attack was not entirely misdirected, even though the underlying problem was poorly conceived. Roosevelt himself had experimented with monetarist reforms by revising the gold standard, but with little success. This did not deter Coughlin, for whom the task was clear. It was necessary to declare independence and to establish a "financial democracy" (1935, 168; 1934, 98). This could be done, he argued, without resorting to the socialist alternative, which he thought as oppressive as capitalism. In both, control over the distribution of wealth was centralized. Whether wealth was controlled by financiers or commissars made no difference as far as Coughlin was concerned. In either case there was no financial democracy and hence no social justice (Coughlin 1934, 72).

The true solution, the Christian solution, lay in the middle road between capitalism and socialism. It lay in "state capitalism," which retained private ownership on a broad scale, while nationalizing the key media of exchange (ibid., 77, 80). In this respect, Coughlin's program was eminently Populist. The National Union for Social Justice stood for public ownership of essential industries, and "because our most necessary public necessity is money, the National Union for Social Justice upholds the principle that it should be owned, coined, regulated and controlled by the people of this democratic country" (Coughlin 1935, 159–160). Toward that end, Coughlin proposed a national bank with exclusive powers to create money and generate credit, to be controlled by a popularly elected board of directors. In this way the failure of the Federal Reserve Act to vest control over the currency in the people rather than banks would be rectified and "financial democracy" made possible.

Coughlin ceaselessly promoted his reform proposals, exploiting the new electronic medium, the radio, to great advantage, rivaling even FDR in his mastery of this technique. Nevertheless, Coughlin knew that for his program to be enacted his listeners would have to be welded into an effective organization for political action—not a political party, but "a Union to be reckoned with by every Senator, by every Congressman and by every President whom we elect to legislate and to execute the laws of this country for the welfare of the majority of the people in this country" (ibid., 22).

When it became apparent that this strategy would not work, Coughlin joined forces with Townsend and Gerald L. K. Smith, Long's successor in the Share Our Wealth movement, to form the Union party. Coughlin's handpicked candidate, William Lemke, managed to poll only two percent of the popular vote in the presidential election of 1936, dashing this strategy as well. After this ill-fated venture into partisan politics, Coughlin became disillusioned with the prospects for the adoption of his policy program without prior reform of the basic governing institutions of the United States. Hence, he broadened the scope of his attack to include major constitutional reforms, which he hoped would eventuate in a government more responsive to the people, or at any rate to his policies and proposals (Bennett 1969; Brinkley 1982).

It was also at this point that Coughlin's anti-Semitism became most apparent, partly because he accepted the popular identification of Jews and moneylenders. The moneylenders were the chief obstacle, in Coughlin's eyes, for they had corrupted democracy by infiltrating both parties: "As for modern democracy it degenerated into a system whereby, at least in this country, two political parties, under the leadership of the bankers and the banker-controlled industrialists, so manipulated conventions and elections and so controlled, either directly or indirectly, the majesty of the state that there was too little democracy and too much plutocracy" (Coughlin 1935, 98). Consequently, "representation has proven to be misrepresentation" since the "invisible government" of high finance effectively controlled popularly elected governments (Coughlin 1938, 102).

Thus, in order to reform modern capitalism, i.e. to create state capitalism, it was first necessary to reform representative democracy. Here Coughlin proposed the corporate state—corporate state capitalism—founded on explicit functional representation. Members of the House were to be selected from functional, rather than geographical constituencies. They would also select the President, while senators from each state would represent the interests of capital and labor, respectively (ibid., 95–97).

Such a radical departure required justification, and Coughlin supplied a popular one. He disputed the democratic credentials of the old system of misrepresentation by parties, claiming that "in its final analysis, democracy means that the majority of citizens can select that type of government which will function best for the common good with the understanding that the citizens always hold the constitutional right to change the system of government when deliberate choice of the majority decides to do so" (ibid., 93–94).

Here, in baldest form, was the idea most feared by the
American right, namely, the idea that the people had the
sovereign power to remake even fundamental law as they saw
fit. Thus, the traditional rivalry between popular sovereignty
and constitutional democracy was reconstituted during the
Depression years, but with this difference: the traditional
sources of legitimacy and moral authority that underpinned
earlier notions of community had been seriously undermined.
The community itself had been transformed under the pressure of capitalist development, and many of the traditional
bases of rhetorical appeal lost their power to command allegiance and motivate action. As a result, the persuasiveness of
these old rhetorical arguments had greatly declined, and they
fared badly against a new rhetoric more in tune with the
emerging community of consumers.

Indeed, it was the success of the New Deal in shaping this
community of consumers via a new rhetoric of democracy that
rendered the old clash between "the democracy" and "the
plutocracy" obsolete. New Deal democracy fashioned a new
and compelling class compromise out of an ostensibly univer-.
sal interest in uninterrupted consumption. The bonds of social organization were given a material interpretation, and
this, in turn, had profound implications for the meaning and
purpose of democracy.

IV

INITIALLY THE DEMOCRATIC party shared the Republican
commitment to "true liberalism" buttressed by the regulatory state. Their 1932 platform did not promise new and dramatic measures to cope with the nation's economic problems.
Instead, it reflected the conventional wisdom about the
proper way to cure economic recessions, namely by cutting
public expenditures. Hoover was condemned as a profligate
spender, and the party made "a covenant with the people" to
accomplish "a saving of not less than twenty-five per cent in
the cost of federal government" so as to establish a sound
currency and restore economic prosperity (Merrill 1964, 76).

Despite their nominal acceptance of the conventional wisdom concerning the proper role of a democratic government vis-à-vis the economy, the Democrats, or at least their leader, Franklin Delano Roosevelt, did not concede the authority of economic orthodoxy without question or qualification. Roosevelt refused to accept the purely theoretical arguments of laissez-faire economists. He even went so far as to argue that "we must lay hold of the fact that economic laws are not made by nature. They are made by human beings" (Leuchtenburg 1963, 344). Consequently, Roosevelt and the New Deal Democrats refused to be constrained by traditional policy considerations in their policy-making efforts.

At the same time New Deal Democrats also rejected the orthodoxies of the socialist left concerning the causes of the Depression and its remedies. Their skepticism was truly catholic and was applied to dogmas on the left as well as right when it came down to making practical decisions on economic matters. The New Dealers eschewed programmatic action in favor of an experimental approach to problem-solving. No less a New Dealer than Roosevelt himself summed up this attitude by saying that "the country needs and, unless I mistake its temper, the country demands bold, persistent experimentation. It is common sense to take a method and try it. If it fails, admit it frankly, and try another. But above all, try something" (Hofstadter 1948, 315).

The flexibility of this attitude toward policy-making, which defied tradition even as it disdained utopian schemes for the future, lent an air of serendipity to Roosevelt's administration. Even the name "New Deal" was an unanticipated find for Roosevelt, who attached no special significance to it as he concluded his 1932 acceptance speech to the national Democratic convention by saying "I pledge you, I pledge myself, to a new deal for the American people" (Leuchtenburg 1963, 8). Only an alert cartoonist, who picked up on it and used it to refer to Roosevelt's "program," saved it from oblivion and transformed it into one of the most effective slogans in all of American politics.

It was precisely this atheoretical aspect of the New Deal that led Dewey, the philosopher of experimentation par excellence, to repudiate Roosevelt's program. For Dewey, the experimental method did not just involve doing a little of this and a little of that in hope that things might improve. Just as in the physical sciences, it implied a coherent body of ideas, a theory that gives direction to the effort (Dewey 1963, 62).

That the New Deal lacked such a theory was evident in its own inconsistencies and indecision, as well as in the genuine confusion of its libertarian opponents, who did not know if it represented fascism, sovietism, or communism, but were sure it stood for some kind of collectivism (Desvernine 1936). Even Raymond Moley admitted the ideological incoherence of the New Deal; he later commented that "to look upon these policies as the result of a unified plan was to believe that the accumulation of stuffed snakes, baseball pictures, school flags, old tennis shoes, carpenter's tools, geometry books and chemistry sets in a boy's bedroom could have been put there by an interior decorator" (Leuchtenburg 1963, 33).

But the New Deal did have *political* unity. As Hofstadter observes, "The New Deal will never be understood by anyone who looks for a single thread of policy, a far-reaching, far-seeing plan. It was a series of improvisations, many adopted very suddenly, many contradictory. Such unity as it had was in political strategy, not economics" (1948, 331–332). That strategy was, to a certain extent, opportunistic. New Deal experimentation always proceeded with reference to the interests of groups that were vital elements of Roosevelt's constituency, and always within the context of what Skocpol (1980) refers to as "existing political constraints."

Seen from this perspective, the famous shift to the left inaugurated by the "second New Deal" in 1935 represents Roosevelt's reaction to a changing political situation rather than an ideological conversion on his part. Faced with growing opposition from both the right and left over the lack of successful experimentation, Roosevelt lost no time in staking out a more politically advantageous position once the Supreme

Court gave him room to maneuver by declaring the National Industrial Recovery Act unconstitutional.

However, the political strategy of the New Deal was not simply or only opportunistic. There was a certain rationale to New Deal experimentation that went well beyond its policy eclecticism to include considerations about the policy-making process itself. Especially important in this regard was the question of how decisions on experimental policies were to be made, and in what sense these decisions might be described as "democratic." New Deal experimentation, as Tugwell (1935) noted, was "democratic experimentation" insofar as it was oriented toward a popularly directed and controlled system of policy-making, i.e. one that was constrained neither by the inordinate influence of big business nor by some preconceived "plan." Seen in this light, the greatest experiment of the New Deal lay in its creation of an entirely new mode of policy-making, and not in its trial-and-error policies per se. If the latter lacked unity or coherence in Dewey's sense, that was because the new mode of democratic experimentation, precisely because it was democratic, did not produce such outcomes.

To see this it is necessary to explore further the New Dealers' assumptions about the nature of the problems they faced and the range of solutions open to them. The ultimate goal of the New Deal was to reestablish an equilibrium between consumption and production, and by implication, between capital and labor. Whether the Depression was attributed to overproduction or underconsumption it was self-evidently characterized by an imbalance between demand and supply. How to restore balance to the economy and maintain it became the major question of the day, with the different parties to the dispute disagreeing over the proper role of government in coming to grips with this problem.

For the New Dealers it was apparent that the market could no longer correct this imbalance without causing considerable social and economic distress, not to mention political discomfort. The concentration of industry and the growing presence of monopoly capital were responsible for this, as they accentuated both the peaks and the troughs of the cycle of boom and bust (ibid.). Moreover, the New Dealers frankly admitted the impossibility, and in some cases undesirability, of trying to reverse this tendency toward concentration. Neither trust-busting, which was designed to restore competition, nor regulation, which aimed to simulate its effects, were any longer viable. Instead, it was necessary to resort to "enlightened administration" in order to achieve the desired equilibrium between production and consumption (Merrill 1964).

Thus, government had to assume responsibilities previously left to the market. That much, at least, was clear. But this hardly distinguished the New Dealers from their neopopulist adversaries, who, as we saw in the preceding section, were more than willing to have government assume control over vital industries, e.g. banking. That was as far as men such as Coughlin were prepared to go, however, and in fact much of their criticism of the New Deal was based on their opposition to other forms of governmental intervention. They opposed the "regimentation" and bureaucratization of social life by the NRA and Public Works Administration, preferring to rely on simple monetary reforms to correct the nation's economic problems.

What was unique, however, was the New Dealers' conception of how this "enlightened administration" was to be both effective and democratic at the same time. For this a method of democratic experimentation was needed. The logic of their solution was established as follows. If the market could no longer achieve the desired result at an acceptable cost, and if government could not and should not attempt to correct the market weaknesses responsible for this situation, then it seemed only natural that government would have to create new, countervailing centers of power that might effectively contend with big business (Galbraith 1952). In effect, competition between interests, which was the natural mechanism for producing the desired equilibrium, would be reconstituted in a new, public arena where they might meet on a more or less equal footing. This could be done by incorporating previously excluded groups, e.g. farmers and laborers, into the policy-making process itself, where their political resources would better enable them to offset the economic resources available to big business.

Thus, when it became evident that competition could no longer be sustained in the economic realm, even with significant involvement of the regulatory state, the New Dealers simply created a new arena of power. This arena was infused with new and hard-won responsibilities, to be sure. However, its primary advantage consisted of the fact that it recreated the possibility of collective decision-making based on competition rather than domination. Since many different kinds of resources were politically relevant, the effective monopoly of business might be broken by shifting power from an arena where only one maldistributed resource, ownership, had currency, to another, where several currencies were redeemable. A complex system of "interest group liberalism" thus emerged, one that produced policies that were the result of negotiation rather than planning, and which reflected a multiplicity of opposing interests rather than a single dominant interest, e.g. big business.[8]

In such a policy-making system, the role of government was radically transformed. From a coercive instrument of regulation it turned into an arbiter of disputes between interests. Indeed, even this may be too strong, for Tugwell argued that government would act only as the "senior and controlling

[8] "Interest group liberalism" is Lowi's (1969) description of this system of governmentally instituted and sustained countervailing power. Lowi argues that the distinguishing feature of this system is its preoccupation with distributive, rather than redistributive, policies, since compromise is more easily achieved on "non zero-sum" issues. This insight is confirmed by Beer (1978), himself a New Dealer, who argues that the New Deal never intended to redistribute wealth, though it did aim at redistributing power. The latter may imply the former, but the converse need not be true, so long as enough "new" resources for distribution exist. Thurow (1980) argues that this is no longer the case, and that politics and political decision-making processes are likely to become much more conflictual in a zero-sum society.

partner" in the negotiations, representing the general interest of all in establishing a "concert of interests" (1935, 20).

The "concert of interests" to be orchestrated by government required a willingness to compromise on the part of the interests involved if a peaceful resolution of their differences was to be forthcoming. Without this, the functional representation implicit in "interest group liberalism" would exacerbate social tensions rather than alleviate them. Consequently, some common ground had to be discovered so that the chief divisions of interest, which were undeniably class related, might be transcended. Since workers and owners were both consumers, and both had a common vested interest in uninterrupted consumption, which guaranteed profits as well as wages, it seemed a natural choice.

Thus we find Ickes proclaiming that "it is as consumers that we all have a common interest, regardless of what productive work we may be engaged in" (Ickes 1934, 142). The United States was not faced, as some believed, with a choice between laissez-faire, in which owners oppressed workers, and socialism, in which the opposite occurred. Instead, workers and owners could work out their differences within a corporatist state so as to best serve their common interest in continued and widespread consumption.[9]

This abstract conception of unity was given a material underpinning by greatly expanding the range of goods and services provided by the newly invigorated political system. National, or in some cases nationally subsidized, programs for agricultural support, unemployment compensation, old-age insurance, and categorical assistance for the deserving poor were established as the consumption of public goods increased, especially by groups that had not previously been the recipients of governmental largesse. These entitlement programs provided the macroeconomic leverage needed to

[9] New Deal corporatism was societal corporatism, whereas the Demagogues proposed state corporatism as a solution to the Depression. Cf. Schmitter (1974) on this distinction.

implement Keynesian policies for stabilization, and at the same time they satisfied "consumer preferences" to which the market, which recognized only effective demand, was not otherwise responsive. In time other political interests would demand entrance to the political arena and access to public goods, generating an imperative of growth sufficient to meet these new demands. However, the New Deal is remarkable for inaugurating a qualitatively distinct phase in the commodification of politics, to use Westbrook's (1983) phrase, and justifying it in terms of democratic consumerism.[10]

The essence, then, of the New Deal was "Equal privileges for all, special rights for none," instead of the time-honored "Equal rights for all, special privileges for none." Hence, it was with some perplexity that New Dealers responded to charges that they were interested in "regimenting" social life. To them, the real danger to the American way of life was the threat posed by a "private industrial regimentation" of life that prevented the bulk of Americans from enjoying the liberating effects of bounteous production (Tugwell 1935, 195–196). Such a system invited both economic collapse and political attack, whereas a system of interest group liberalism allowed the greatest safety and latitude for continued economic growth and vitality. The "greatest good of the greatest number" would thereby be served, and a nation of democratic consumers created.

This, then was the ideal of the New Deal: a cybernetic

[10] Whereas most commentators emphasize the expanded supply of goods and services made available to political "consumers" during the New Deal, Westbrook (1983) details the transformation of the electoral process by political advertising, and the corresponding identification of citizen and consumer.

This complemented the effects of mass advertising on other social practices relevant to the role of citizens. Wilson (1983) discusses the twentieth-century commodification of information sources, which began around the turn of the century with the promulgation of a "rhetoric of consumption" in mass magazines. The dissemination of consumerism in these and other mass publications was fueled by the emergence of advertising and advertising strategies in *fin de siècle* America (Lears, 1983).

system of consumption, in which the people, *qua* consumers, exercised and enjoyed their sovereignty through a system of interest group liberalism. It was an ideal that was neither utopian nor apologetic. It simply promised to make life more comfortable and secure—not inconsiderable promises at the time. Compared with its laissez-faire opposition, the New Deal was an obvious choice. However, there was a strong relativity to this notion of democratic consumerism, a belief that it was ever in a state of becoming (Wolfskill 1969, 59). Eventually, the loss of this sense of immanence would prove its downfall, for it had no moral grounds for sustaining it through "hard times."

V

IN RETROSPECT the most conspicuous failure of the thirties was the inability of the left to capitalize on the Depression, the very occurrence of which seemed to vindicate arguments concerning the crisis tendencies inherent in an economic system predicated on the private ownership of the means of production. The collapse of the nation's economy ought to have made it easier perhaps than at any other time in American history to promote the cause of social democracy as the necessary completion of political democracy. The ineffectiveness of the socialists in advancing an ideal of democracy that anticipated a classless society is therefore all the more surprising, given the apparently auspicious opportunity presented them by the Great Depression.

The reasons for this failure are not widely agreed upon, though Sombart (1976) suggests that the working class audience to which the socialist message was addressed was not very radical, even in the depths of "hard times." Whatever potential for radical action existed was quickly channeled into trade union activities, including the formation of the Congress of Industrial Organizations, which accepted the basic structure of economic relations and aimed only at solidifying organized labor's position in them.

The relative ease with which labor was assimilated cannot

be explained without reference to the role of the left, however. The parties of the left failed to exploit whatever radical sentiments existed in the working class and, more importantly, to incite further radicalization. In that respect the left in general, and the Socialists in particular, simply failed to use the great object lesson of the Depression to educate the working class and overcome "trade union consciousness."

The failure of the left to organize a counter-hegemony opposed to the New Deal largely reflects the disorganization of the left itself. To a certain extent this was a result of the intense repression of "un-American" ideas that followed the First World War. In the face of arrest and deportation the left was forced underground and was only beginning to resurface when the Crash occurred. Hence, before organizing the working class under its auspices, the American left had to organize itself.

The most likely organization around which a united front might have formed was the Socialist party of America. Unfortunately for the left, the party was singularly unable to overcome divisions within its own ranks, let alone serve as an umbrella organization in opposition to the New Deal.[11] The principal factions within the Socialist party—the evolutionary socialists, the revolutionary socialists, and a Progressive centrist faction under the leadership of Norman Thomas—could not agree on the utility of political democracy for bring-

[11] The history of the Socialist party is told in a series of factional disputes and purges, beginning with its formation in 1901 out of Debs' Social Democracy and a splinter faction from the Socialist Labor party. Typically, these two groups wrangled for over nine months before settling on the Socialist Party of America as the name for their organization (Kipnis 1952). The party was racked by internal dissension between syndicalists and evolutionary socialists, and in 1919, not one but two communist parties formed out of those leftists who were purged by the Old Guard evolutionary socialists (Howe and Coser 1957). Eventually, the Old Guard itself left the party after losing control to more militant factions. By 1937 the left in America was hopelessly splintered among the Socialist Labor party, the Socialist Workers party, the Socialist party, the Social Democratic Federation, and the Communist party, to mention the most prominent organizations.

ing about social democracy. Their dispute produced some of
the period's most innovative thinking about democracy, but
the mass appeal of those thoughts was never really tested, as
the debate was carried out almost exclusively within the party
itself. Though it was eventually resolved against the evolutionary socialists, their departure from the party effectively
destroyed whatever chance the party had to bring its message
of social democracy to the working class, since the Old Guard
was the primary link to existing unions and labor organizations.

The intraparty struggle over the nature of democracy and
its relation to socialism was triggered by the adoption in 1934
of a new Declaration of Principles at the national Socialist
party convention in Detroit. The dispute between the Old
Guard and the Progressive-militant alliance over the 1934
Declaration was fueled by a number of important differences
over party control, the proper stance toward trade unions, on
the one hand, and farmers, on the other, and the party's attitude toward the Communist Party of America (CPA) and the
Stalinist regime. However, these differences were themselves underpinned by more fundamental differences of opinion over the proper relationship between socialism and democracy, and it was this line of cleavage that was activated in
Detroit.

On the surface, the floor debate and the ensuing exchanges
in the party press centered on the party's antiwar policy. In
particular, the Declaration announced that the party and its
members

> will loyally support, in the tragic event of war, any of their
> comrades who for anti-war activities not in contravention
> of Socialist principles, or for refusal to perform war service,
> come into conflict with public opinion or the law. More-
> over, recognizing the suicidal nature of modern combat and
> the incalculable strain of wars' consequences which rest
> most heavily upon the working class, they will refuse col-
> lectively to sanction or support any international war: they

will, on the contrary, by agitation and opposition do their best not to be broken up by the war, but to break up the war. They will meet war and the detailed plans for war already mapped out by the war-making arms of the government, by massed war resistance, organized so far as practicable in a general strike of labor unions and professional groups in a united effort to make the waging of war a practical impossibility and to convert the capitalist war crisis into a victory for Socialism. (Warren 1974, 193)

To the Old Guard, such a commitment would completely undermine party discipline by obliging the party to support individual acts of terrorism. Such "anarcho-syndicalist" tactics were bound to bring the Socialists into disrepute among workers, who would associate them with the Communists, and would moreover invite yet another round of violence and repression precisely when it was most necessary for the Socialist voice to be heard. Hence, the Old Guard insisted that the fight against imperialist wars "must be made in the open, above ground. Socialists refuse to give the capitalist class an excuse to drive us underground, even though contemplated conspiratorial activities may feed the hunger" of imaginative and irresponsible "playboy revolutionaries" among militants (Panken 1934, 3; Oneal 1934, 8).

The Old Guard considered this party commitment unnecessary, given the existence of peaceful, legal, and above all efficacious avenues of resistance. They emphatically rejected the underlying premise of the entire Declaration, which was summed up in its concluding paragraph:

The Socialist Party proclaims anew its faith in economic and political democracy. It unhesitatingly applies itself to the task of replacing the bogus democracy of capitalist parliamentarism by a genuine workers' democracy. Capitalism is doomed. If it can be superseded by a majority vote, the Socialist Party will rejoice. If the crisis comes through the denial of majority rights after the electorate has given us a mandate we shall not hesitate to crush by our labor soli-

darity the reckless forces of reaction and to consolidate the
Socialist state. If the capitalist system should collapse in a
general chaos and confusion, which cannot permit of orderly procedure, the Socialist Party, whether or not in such
a case it is a majority, will not shrink from the responsibility of organizing and maintaining a government under the
rule of the producing masses. True democracy is a worthy
means to progress; but true democracy must be created by
the workers of the world. (Warren 1974, 194)

While bourgeois democracy was conceded by all Socialists
to be a form of class rule, the Old Guard was not prepared
to dismiss it as bogus. For them, the elements of democracy,
e.g. free speech and free press, represented past political victories of the working class over the bourgeoisie. They were
not granted so much as seized and were therefore far from
being bogus.

More importantly, these democratic rights were essential
for the continuing progress of the socialist movement. As
Panken put it, "Our appeal must be made to the working
class. To that end we need free speech, free press and free
assemblage. That is only possible if we defend and maintain
the results of what we have won by our struggle on the economic and political fields. . . . Socialism to progress needs
freedom" (Panken 1934, 6).

Aside from the strategic importance of democratic instru-
mentalities in the class struggle, the Old Guard raised another important consideration. Oneal pointed out that "to
make the sweeping statement that democracy is 'bogus' is to
do the very thing that reaction itself is doing all over the
world" (Oneal 1934, 8). It was in the interest of capitalists to
discredit democracy so as to gain further control over the
dissident working class in times of crisis. By denouncing democracy as bogus the Socialists would find themselves in collaboration with the forces of reaction—"a form of united front
that few of us ever anticipated" (ibid., 8).

It should be emphasized that the Old Guard was emphatically not endorsing the achievement and maintenance of bourgeois democratic institutions as the end for which Socialists strove. Bourgeois democracy was conceded by all Socialists to be an instrument of class domination and therefore antithetical to their common goal of establishing true democracy.[12] However, by defending bourgeois democracy, the Old Guard was committing itself to a parliamentary strategy that depended for its success on the ability of the working class to use democracy as a means for transcending capitalism. This is where the militant response found its mark.

The militants, and Progressives for that matter, argued that bourgeois democracy could never be the midwife of socialism. As Thomas put it, "It is not enough, however, to say that capitalist democracy is limited in extent. There is something wrong with its quality" (Thomas 1934b, 12). Because of its class basis, capitalism was fundamentally incompatible with true democracy, which was classless. For that reason, the militants, while far from denying the very real gains made by workers in their struggle against the bourgeoisie, felt justified in calling it "bogus" (ibid., 12).

Nevertheless, the left wing was sensitive to the need to distinguish their criticisms of democracy from those of the fascists. The notion of the dictatorship of the proletariat was, of course, available to them as a characterization of the relationship between socialism and democracy. However, the odium that attached to that phrase by virtue of its use in justifying Stalin's regime suggested to many of them, Thomas included, the need to formulate an alternative conception of democracy (Thomas 1934a).

---

[12] True democracy was social democracy, i.e. democracy in which freedom and equality were extended to the economic realm of society. For all Socialists true democracy was possible only in a classless society, since economic freedom and equality were preconditions for effective political freedom and equality. On this unanimity, compare "The Program of the New York Militant Socialists" in *The World Tomorrow* (June 14, 1934) with a statement to which the Old Guard subscribed, and which was published under the title "Socialism and Democracy" in *The New Leader* (Saturday, June 23, 1934, p. 3).

One of the more explicit statements of this problem was provided by Andrew Biemiller in 1934. Biemiller argued that the transition from bourgeois to true democracy could only be brought about through an intermediate state of "proletarian democracy" (Biemiller 1934). Like bourgeois democracy, proletarian democracy was a form of class rule, exercised against one class on behalf of another. The chief difference, of course, was that the proletariat represented the general interest of all in emancipation, while the bourgeoisie stood for the interests of the few over those of the many. Hence the qualitative superiority of proletarian to bourgeois democracy.

Obviously, Biemiller had simply "Americanized" the concept of the dictatorship of the proletariat by asserting its democratic credentials. It was "democratic" to the extent that it was the dictatorship of a class whose historic mission involved the liberation of all classes. Biemiller was careful to insist that the authenticity of this proletarian democracy depended on its exercise by a class rather than a vanguard party. The dictatorship of the proletariat as practiced in the Soviet Union was not, according to him, truly democratic, and it was for that reason that he and Thomas preferred to speak of proletarian democracy rather than dictatorship.

Aside from the tactical advantages of this move, which dissociated the left-wing Socialists from the CPA and Stalin's regime, this shift in terminology had important theoretical repercussions. It was left to Devere Allen, the author of the Declaration, to elaborate on them. In an extremely important article entitled "The Conquest of Democracy," Allen (1935) succeeded in shifting the debate from a discussion over strategy and tactics to one concerning the very nature of democracy itself. Before this article appeared the debate centered on the question of whether or not bourgeois democratic methods were capable of producing social democratic ends. Even Biemiller's argument operated within this instrumentalist framework as he sought to uncover the conditions under which bourgeois democracy might be transformed into proletarian democracy, and thence into true, i.e. classless, democracy.[13]

Allen dissolved this problem by arguing for the inseparability of democratic "means" and "ends" in socialism. The socialist goal of a workers' democracy, he argued, was less a state or condition than a political practice that represented a more generalized form of the practices by which socialism was to be won (ibid., 10–11). Hence, the question of the relationship between socialism and democracy was not reducible to that of identifying the best or most appropriate set of strategies and tactics for moving from one state or condition, bourgeois democracy, to another, true democracy. Rather, it necessarily entailed the discovery of a practical unity of means and ends that was itself constitutive of "true democracy." Consequently, Allen concluded, those who argued for evolutionary socialism à la the Old Guard, as well as those who advocated the formation of a vanguard party, e.g. the CPA, were equally mistaken. Neither had arrived at a practical unity of means and ends that defined true socialism.

Bourgeois democratic institutions, by virtue of their class limitations, provided insufficient democracy for the incubation and development of workers' democracy. By the same token, "a workers' rule achieved by undemocratic methods among the revolutionary workers themselves will never be anything more than a workers' government, which is by no means a workers' democracy, and which may conceivably become at last the most tyrannical and reactionary instrument imaginable" (ibid., 11). Socialism, therefore, required a cooperative exploration by workers and farmers into democratic practices, both as a way of preparing the working classes for their mission and as a way of realizing it. Hence, true democracy was practical democracy, because it was practice, and because it was efficacious in bringing about more democracy.

[13] His answer was that this transformation could take place only if workers realistically approached existing democratic institutions, recognizing their limitations and keeping "extra-legal options" open for revolutionary action (Biemiller 1934).

Allen's point found no mass audience, however. The Old
Guard, having lost control of the party apparatus as well as
its program, departed to the Social Democratic Federation
and the American Labor Party. As a consequence, the Socialists lost any chance of speaking with one voice, and in the
cacophony of the wider struggle to interpret democracy their
multiple opinions were overwhelmed. Thus, a conception of
democracy that invoked a morality of the "present as future"
went down to ignominious defeat.

VI

THE DEFEAT of social democracy culminated a thorough-
going transformation of American discourses on democracy.
No longer would competing interpretations be rooted in
moral traditions recalling an age of innocence long since past,
nor would they anticipate movement toward the Just Society.
From the New Deal on, American conceptions of democracy
came to be associated with a particular kind of government,
one whose primary responsibility was to serve the material
interests of a consumer community. To use the language of
Habermas (1975), value came to replace meaning as the foundation of democratic authority, and from this substitution
flow many of the most important "problems" of contemporary
democracy and attendant discourses.

We shall explore the ramifications of this transformation
more fully in the next chapter. However, it should be apparent even now that the legitimacy of a government rooted in
material rather than moral considerations is problematic. It is
contingent on economic performance, for the class compromise effected by democratic consumerism depends on a continuous and ever-expanding supply of consumer goods. When
liberal democratic regimes prove unable to guarantee this,
their democratic credentials may be questioned by the community of consumers to which they are ostensibly dedicated.

In this respect legitimation crises threaten to become
chronic problems for liberal democracies insofar as they lack
the ability to control or direct private economies in "democratic directions" (ibid.). Moreover, they have no defense for

their authority, having explicitly rejected moralistic considerations. They are therefore vulnerable to failures of performance, having no recourse to ethical "excuses" for their inability to satisfy the demands of certain classes within the community of consumers.[14]

At the same time, however, liberal democracy has been rendered immune to moral criticisms. Precisely because its democratic claims are *not* founded on explicit ethical considerations, liberal democracy is less vulnerable to substantive objections, which in any case have little appeal in a community bound together by material, rather than moral, considerations. The nonideological appearance is, of course, a function of the universality of the class of consumers, whereas other ideologies give preference to the particular interests of classes in a particular mode of production, e.g. "the democracy" or "the plutocracy." The nonideological appearance of liberal democracy is, therefore, highly resistant to fundamental criticism, as it reduces political questions to technical considerations concerning economic "finetuning" or "midcourse corrections."

Thus, the real significance of the New Deal contest over the meaning of democracy lies in the way in which it has affected the organization of subsequent discourses on democracy. By shifting the grounds of democracy from ethical to technical considerations, the range of acceptable questions on social organization and collective action has been reduced considerably. Criticisms bearing on the organization of production and political decision-making have been subordinated to questions concerning administrative technique precisely because the reigning conception of democracy established the tone for contemporary political discussion. The consequences of this "systematic distortion" will be the subject of the next chapter.

---

[14] This highlights the importance of the demise of ideologies of self-denial that were used to justify economic hardship for the many. Cf. the preceding chapter's discussion on the Progressives.

CHAPTER NINE

The Eclipse of Liberal Democracy

I

IN THIS CHAPTER we shall continue to trace the eclipse of moral discourse on democracy that began during the New Deal. As we have seen the New Deal decisively altered the organization of American political discourse by silencing partisan interpretations of democracy. With the emergence of an ostensibly common interest in continuous *consumption*, conflict between classes (defined in terms of their relation to the means of *production*) was rhetorically transcended. Since all Americans were consumers, they formed a universal "class," and the image of America as a class-divided society began to dissipate.

This had a curious effect on conceptions of democracy, which had previously been construed as a class concept in the traditional sense. Indeed, it was this reference to the class structure of society that supported conflicting interpretations of democracy in the first place. Because democracy referred to rule by a particular class, it became a rallying cry for that class, on the one hand, and a term of opprobrium for opponents of that class, on the other.

But as the image of a class-divided society waned, democracy lost all reference to divisions in society and came instead to embody the common interest of all in consumption—especially of "public" goods.[1] Thus, a concept that once explic-

---

[1] "The strongest evidence for the quiet revolution in the public philosophy that has taken place over the past half-century is in the changed terms of public discourse. The state of the nation becomes meaningful only when we are able to talk about it as 'rates' of various kinds—rates of 'inflation,' 'interest,' 'productivity,' 'money supply,' 'capital formation,' and, last but not least,

itly referred to a particular kind of social order, and which was used to justify that order, on the one hand, and criticize it, on the other, lost its political edge. It was no longer a potent weapon of class criticism, but at the same time it was no longer part of the arsenal of class defense, either.

Consequently, the sporadic dialogue on American democracy came more and more to resemble a monologue on the performance of consumer democracy. The structure of society was no longer in question, only its leaders' ability to satisfy the "general will" of American consumers of public goods. As a result, discourse was reoriented toward questions about the politics of distribution, and away from redistributional issues.

This transformation of politics was significantly extended by the Great Society, which expanded the bounds of democratic consumption and the sphere of distributive politics. The number of interests included in the system of interest group liberalism was increased with the help of new techniques for identifying and incorporating unorganized interest "groups." At the same time, the Great Society proved remarkably adept at resisting efforts to interrupt the ongoing monologue on democratic consumerism.

The Students for a Democratic Society, for example, challenged the passivity of politics practiced during this era and warned of the disproportionate influence it allowed powerful interests to accumulate. Women, too, objected to the emptiness of consumption, and to the oppression of women that was so much a part of this American "ideal." And blacks raised their voices to claim the rightful share of the benefits that had been denied them, and to demand more control over the decisions that went into the definition of American democratic ideals.

The demand for more participation in political discourse was shared by these members of the "counterculture." They

'unemployment.' " Of reduced "importance are the main notions through which the society once understood its identity, notions such as 'democracy,' 'republic,' 'the Constitution,' and 'the nation' whose meaning was essentially political" (Wolin 1981b, 27).

sought to establish new conceptions of democracy, based on newly relevant divisions in American society—power, sex, and race.[2] None of these divisions, out of which partisan discourse springs, was ever well-articulated with the "old" class cleavages of American discourse, though all eventually moved in that direction after first rejecting class analyses as irrelevant to their concerns. Instead, liberation movements proceeded to construct independent conversations with the dominant, monologic culture.

These movements did not succeed in creating a new dialogue on democracy. After the success of their initial engagement with "the system," their grievances were acknowledged, or in some cases, repressed. Either way, silence returned to American politics, but as we shall see, only after that silence revealed itself for what it truly was—silence, not consensus.

II

THE SMASHING VICTORY of democratic consumerism over its moralistic rivals culminated in the "end of ideology" in the late fifties. In the West the "exhaustion of political ideals" rooted in fundamentally ethical conceptions of political life created a moral vacuum in political discourse (Bell 1962, 404). At the same time it provided an opening for a more scientific approach to social reform, or so hoped the heralds of the end

[2] The accounts I present here and in the next chapter are quite one-sided. I make no attempt to convey a sense of the whole range of political expression in the 1960s. The Old Left, as well as the extreme right, are not represented here, and others are similarly neglected. This is deliberate. My impression of the hegemonic influence of democratic consumerism led me to concentrate on countercultural interpretations that accepted the irrelevance of class-based versions of democracy, even as they explored new ways of advancing partisan interpretations of democracy. This seemed a useful way of demonstrating the imperviousness of democratic consumerism to traditional, moral criticism, while revealing its partial vulnerability to complaints about the overly narrow scope of consumer democracy. This point may become clearer as the story progresses, but a disclaimer of impartiality seems appropriate here.

of ideology, e.g. Daniel Bell. With passion exhausted, reason might assume its proper place in political discourse and the organization of society.

By "reason" these heralds meant a hard-headed "professionalization of reform," as Daniel Moynihan put it. This type of reform promised to create "a society that can put an end to the 'animal miseries' and stupid controversies that afflict most peoples" by bringing knowledge to bear on social problems (Gettleman and Mermelstein 1967, 474). No longer would policy-making be the preserve of shrill rhetoricians and rigid ideologues. With the end of ideology, more rational, scientific approaches to problems of poverty, unemployment, and discrimination might come to fruition.

This "technocratic takeover" of policy-making was a hallmark of the Great Society (Beer 1978). In effect, the democratic experimentation of the New Deal gave way to a more analytic approach to problem-solving, one that no longer drew its inspiration and energy from popular pressures but instead from the accumulated wisdom of the behavioral revolution in the social sciences. The Great Society was not the good society, therefore, but a well-regulated one in which the benefits of democratic consumption were systematically extended to newly identified consumers, e.g. blacks and other minorities, as well as to the poor.[3]

Whereas the New Deal community of consumers was built upon already organized groups, e.g. farmers, labor unions, and business organizations, the Great Society, informed by social science, incorporated heretofore unorganized groups of consumers, mainly the poor and minorities who had not shared in the affluence of American society. The further de-

---

[3] The term *Great Society* apparently came to Lyndon Johnson by way of presidential speechwriter Richard Goodwin, who borrowed it from Barbara Ward, who presumably was familiar with Graham Wallas' *The Great Society*, and perhaps with the medieval Great Society of Wat Tyler (Gettleman and Mermelstein 1967, 13–15). The radical connotations of the term were understandably "lost in the translation" to the rhetoric of consensus practiced by Johnson.

mocratization of consumption was, in other words, carried out from above, without benefit of substantial grass roots involvement, except where that involvement was itself induced from above in the form of "maximum feasible participation." Where there was grass roots participation, it usually consisted of opposition to the Great Society's policy of "cooptation," which left fundamental grievances unresolved.

On the surface, then, the Great Society represented a more inclusive, and hence more "democratic" community of consumers. The breadth of this consensus was manifested in the landslide election of Lyndon Johnson in 1964. Johnson, the great "consensuscrat," laid to rest the old cleavage between liberals and conservatives as the latter came to accept the principle of governmental intervention, though they objected to the "liberal" presumption that the federal government was the only or most appropriate interventionist.[4]

Beer (ibid.) refers to this change in conservative thought as the rise of "mesoconservatism." Whereas the "paleoconservatism" of Hoover and even Goldwater was essentially laissez-faire in orientation, the "mesoconservatism" of people like Ronald Reagan was not. Mesoconservatives often entertained highly ambitious schemes of government intervention, particularly on moral issues. Their main dispute with the Great Society centered on its *federal* architecture, which mesoconservatives rejected in favor of state and local initiatives.[5] The ascendance of mesoconservatism therefore marks the end of all ideologies except the reigning public philosophy of interest group liberalism, now modified to include subnational government interests and arenas of power.

The amorality of this "nonideological" ideology of consumerism did not pass unnoticed. Paul Goodman, for example,

[4] "Consensuscrat" is Russell Baker's description of Johnson's politics (Gettleman and Mermelstein 1967).

[5] Wolin (1981b) confirms Beer's insight into the "mesoconservatism" of Reagan, whose conformity to the "new public philosophy" of science and economics clearly reveals his break with the older, more traditional conservatism of Goldwater and his "liberal" predecessors.

observed that "by the middle of the Administration of Eisenhower, it was impossible for a public spokesman to say 'the American Way of Life' with a straight face" (Gettleman and Mermelstein 1967, 518). Nevertheless, this moral cynicism was concealed behind moralistic terminology. Kennedy's Posture of Sacrifice, Goldwater's Moral Order, and Johnson's Great Society all betrayed a yearning for a moral cause beyond consumerism, though all were conceived in the corruption of discourse that signified the end of ideology.

By the late sixties and early seventies this corruption of discourse was obvious to all as the "end of ideology" assumed the form of a general "crisis of authority" (Lowi 1969). In the absence of any convincing moral justifications for the uses of public power, people began to question authority when the performance of authorities failed to measure up to their expectations or the ambitious promises of political leaders. Out of this came the "crisis of democracy," which is now widely recognized as a moral problem.

III

NOT ALL GROUPS in American society welcomed the end of ideology and the professionalization of reform as heartily as did the architects of the Great Society. As we saw in the preceding section, conservatives opposed the massive intervention of the federal government in hitherto private affairs. At the same time, the so-called New Left criticized the Great Society for its distinctly liberal ambitions, which stopped far short of radical solutions to deep-seated social problems.[6]

Among all the groups and organizations that constituted the amorphous movement known as the New Left, the Students for a Democratic Society (SDS) was distinguished by its commitment to a fairly well-articulated ideal of democracy, which formed the basis for its critique of American society, as well as its program for radical action. Although the

---

[6] Because of the alleged irrelevance of class-based interpretations of American society, a "New Left" was needed in place of the "old left."

SDS is perhaps best remembered for its role in opposing U.S. involvement in Vietnam, its more enduring contribution to American politics is undoubtedly the notion of participatory democracy, as described in their Port Huron Statement, adopted in 1962.

"Participatory democracy" was introduced to American political discourse by the SDS with the explicit intention of putting an end to the "theoretic chaos" brought about by the end of ideology. The SDS conceded the accuracy of Bell's phrase as a description of American politics at that time, but it denied Bell's further inference that the end of ideology signaled the supercession of idealistic (utopian) ways of thinking by more rational accounts of human society and its latent possibilities.

The SDS saw that the end of ideology carried within itself a certain aimlessness or lack of direction that no amount of professionalism could replace. The end of ideology presumed the existence of a "generation plagued by program without vision." Implicit in the professionalization of reform was a devaluation and corruption of the activity of "making values explicit," which was "an initial task in establishing alternatives"; that meant significant political change was becoming increasingly less likely (Goldwin 1971, 4). In the absence of alternatives, the status quo, with all its undemocratic features, e.g. racial discrimination and the threat of a nuclear holocaust, reigned supreme.

Thus, the end of ideology was synonymous with "the pervading feeling that there simply are no alternatives, that our times have witnessed the exhaustion not only of utopias, but of any new departures as well" (ibid., 3). Nevertheless, all was not lost. For the same forces responsible for destroying "vision" had also generated deeply felt anxieties and collective self-doubts about the accomplishments of American democracy, or so the SDS believed:

> Some would have us believe that Americans feel contentment amidst prosperity—but might it not better be called

a glaze above deeply felt anxieties about their role in the new world? And if these anxieties produce a developed indifference to human affairs, do they not as well produce a yearning to believe there *is* an alternative to the present, that something *can* be done to change circumstances in the school, the workplaces, the bureaucracies, the government? (ibid., 3)

Under such circumstances, the SDS remained convinced that

the search for truly democratic alternatives to the present, and a commitment to social experimentation with them, is a worthy and fulfilling human enterprise, one which moves us and, we hope, others today. On such a basis we offer this document of our convictions and analysis: as an effort in understanding and changing the conditions of humanity in the late twentieth century, an effort rooted in the ancient, still unfulfilled conception of man attaining determining influence over his circumstances of life. (ibid., 3–4).

The SDS insisted, against all evidence known to mainstream social science, on the capacity of men for reason, freedom, and love.[7] They attributed the frustration of these capacities to the undemocratic organization of American society, especially its failure to provide meaningful opportunities for political participation, the medium in which these capacities would unfold. Consequently, the SDS sought the establishment "of a democracy of individual participation, governed by two central aims: that the individual share in those social decisions determining the quality and direction of his life; that society be organized to encourage independence in men and provide the media for their common participation" (ibid., 7).

This was their ideal of participatory democracy, which be-

[7] I use *man* and *men* here because that is the language of the Port Huron Statement. As we shall see, the SDS was not especially sympathetic to women's liberation, which led many women to defect.

came the rallying cry of the New Left.[8] In a participatory democracy, politics would be quintessentially discursive in nature. The governing principles of participatory democracy were

> that decision-making of basic social consequence be carried on by public groupings;
>
> that politics be seen positively, as the art of collectively creating an acceptable pattern of social relations;
>
> that politics has the function of bringing people out of isolation and into community, thus being a necessary, though not sufficient, means of finding meaning in personal life;
>
> that the political order should serve to clarify problems in a way instrumental to their solution; it should provide outlets for the expression of personal grievance and aspiration; opposing views should be organized so as to illuminate choices and facilitate the attainment of goals; channels should be commonly available to relate men to knowledge and to power so that private problems—from bad recreation facilities to personal alienation—are formulated as general issues. (ibid., 7)

Moreover, the realm of politics was construed to include the "economic sphere," as well as the sphere of governance per se. The SDS argued "that work should involve incentives worthier than money or survival. It should be educative, not stultifying; creative, not mechanical; self-directed, not manipulated, encouraging independence, a respect for others, a sense of dignity and a willingness to accept social responsibility, since it is this experience that has crucial influence on habits, perceptions, and individual ethics" (ibid., 7).

---

[8] A democracy without a public is presumably akin to a republic without virtue, or a monarchy without royalty. A constitutive element is missing, and this absence is clearly reflected in the phrase "participatory democracy," in which the adjective, being redundant, seems rather anomalous. But the anomaly is real, not apparent, given the SDS' analysis of the causes and consequences of apathy.

In addition the Port Huron Statement argued "that the economic experience is so personally decisive that the individual must share in its full determination; that the economy itself is of such social importance that its major resources and means of production should be open to democratic participation and subject to democratic social regulation" (ibid., 7).

Although the SDS eventually became even more critical of corporate capitalism and its imperialist tendencies, it is evident that from the very beginning participatory democracy provided a vantage point from which the existing economic sphere might be criticized. Coupled with its obvious utility for criticizing American governance, this made the idea of participatory democracy a powerful tool for condemning the complacency of American politics. Against this vision, the accomplishments of the Great Society paled: "America is without community, impulse, without the inner momentum necessary for an age when societies cannot successfully perpetuate themselves by their military weapons, when democracy must be viable because of the quality of life, not its quantity of rockets" (ibid., 12).

IV

THE SDS HOPED that by stating a vision, by answering the question, "What is the perimeter of human possibility in this epoch?" apathy might be overcome (ibid., 13). And they saw an important role for militant students in this defiant attempt "to seek the unattainable . . . so [as] to avoid the unimaginable" fate of complicity in the status quo (ibid., 15). By restoring a vision of participatory democracy, students might serve as the catalyst for social change, fulfilling their role in bringing about a democratic society.

Initially, the SDS pursued a strategy of reform in order to realize its goal of participatory democracy. This was based on an analysis presented in *America and the New Era*, often dubbed the "Son of Port Huron," which discerned an impending crisis in the prevailing "structure of quiescence," which was faced with the civil rights movement and other radical challenges. This "beginning of a breakdown in the American consensus provides the possibility for genuinely critical and independent participation of intellectuals and students in national life" (Sale 1973, 91). Consequently, the SDS began to explore new forms of insurgent politics that might successfully challenge the nation to pursue participatory democracy.[9]

The SDS and other New Left organizations began to experiment with community action projects as a means of transforming American society. Todd Gitlin, an SDS organizer, recalled the original motivation for this action in the following way:

> At first, as SDS people and others moved into poor communities in 1964, the main ideas were these: In a system that satisfies many needs for most Americans, the poor are still demonstrably in need—and know it. They are also less tied to the dominant values, just as—and partly because— they are less central to the economy that creates and expresses these values. They have a certain permanence necessary for a sustained movement. Though a minority they are a substantial minority. They exhibit a potential for movement—for understanding their situation, breaking loose, and committing themselves to a radical alternative. (1967, 13)

In the minds of many members of the New Left, poor people's "potential for movement" marked them as the most likely agent of revolution, replacing the working class as the liberator of humanity. And it was the job of the community organizer to help transform this potential into actuality—to realize it in a practical way.

[9] This section follows Sale's (1973) account of the evolution of SDS from a catalyst for reform to a resistance movement and eventually toward a "vanguard of the revolution." His account, as well as Young's (1977), rightly emphasizes the connection between ideological and praxeological changes in the Movement, especially as those unfolded in the context of the political struggle with the System.

Community unions were the SDS organizers' primary means for accomplishing this task. Ostensibly these unions were functioning participatory democracies organized around issues of local concern. Typically, these issues had little to do with class conflict between workers and owners. Instead:

> The underclass has its most abrasive contacts with the ruling elites less at the point of production than outside it. Bad housing, meager and degrading "welfare," destructive urban renewal, vicious police, hostile and irrelevant schools, inadequate community facilities (hospitals, nurseries, trafficlights, parks, etc.) are the general rule and are felt as a pattern of victimization above and beyond each of these separate issues. The job of the organizer is to find those people most aroused by felt grievances; to organize, with them, action on those issues; to amplify the feeling that these are common, caused problems, not individual faults, accidents or exceptions; to build through tangibly successful action a confidence in the weight of collective action, and to discover and teach through failures the limits of present capabilities and the work that lies ahead. (ibid., 13)

By concentrating on concrete grievances SDS organizers hoped to overcome the political apathy so prevalent in the "underclass." At the same time, however, the SDS expected community unions "to embody and symbolize and prove the possibility of a democratic society," even in the midst of an undemocratic nation (ibid., 14). As Staughton Lynd put it, it was "the building of a brotherly way of life even in the jaws of the Leviathan" (ibid., 14).

Thus, the SDS viewed community unions as an experiment in democratic movement building, much as the Populists saw producer cooperatives as a mobilizing force in American politics. The unions' local successes and strategies might serve as an example of what could be achieved by collective action, once the spell of apathy was broken. In this way, the culture of poverty might furnish a culture of resistance to the oppressive structure of American society (ibid.).

If this culture of resistance among those whom Marcuse (1964, 257) described as "without hope" was to be effective on a national scale, however, isolated models of participatory democracy embodied in community unions were not enough. Somehow, networks connecting these "counter-institutions" had to be constructed, and alliances with radical caucuses within the welfare professions forged.[10] Only then might the power of "the System" be confronted with the systematic power of "the Movement."

This posed a genuine dilemma for advocates of participatory democracy. On the one hand, the vision of democracy they held necessarily implied forms of social organizations that were not dominated by elites. On the other hand, the political imperatives of counterorganization, particularly in a culture of poverty, seemed to require a division of labor in which organizers enjoyed a privileged position of power and information. The contradiction was clear, as it generally is when a vanguard assumes responsibility for mobilizing its clientele.

Nor was this only a theoretical dilemma. As Gitlin (1967,

[10] Gitlin had some remarkably insightful, and at the same time naive, things to say about the radical "potential" of the professions:

Once these allies are drawn to the movement, they can become functioning radicals with a fresh orientation toward the society as well as toward the meanings and potentials of their professions. Contact with a poor people's movement, more than a merely theoretical grasp of the need to change the relation of professionals to "clients," can prove decisive: First, the professionals can get to know the poor as people. . . . Second, they can learn to make their skills accountable to constituencies with collective needs. . . . Third, radical organizers gain access to raise questions about the structure of the profession and its radical requirements. Fourth, as allies are exposed to blatant attempts to repress the movement, they become more open to radical interpretations of the political process. Fifth, they can develop methods of work, within the movement and on its borders, which sustain their political radicalism and give it roots. . . . Otherwise, without serious contact, angry "clients" and organized professionals—the two greatest forces for a potent radicalism—are likely to end up facing off as antagonists, hopelessly divided over questions of control and priorities. (1967, 18)

13) candidly admitted, open conflict between community organizers and community residents over matters of strategy
and tactics were fairly common. For some, this was a sign of
success: It meant that residents had learned their lessons
well, and were ready and willing to assume control of their
own destinies. At the same time, the parochial concerns of
these groups threatened to undermine the movement's network and alliances, which were crucial if participatory democracy were to succeed at a national level.

As Greg Calvert put this problem, participatory democracy
was useful as a visionary ideal, but inadequate "as a style of
work for a serious radical organization" (Sale 1973, 393). According to him, the major organizational problem of SDS
grew out of the fact that it recruited on the basis of participatory rhetoric and then attempted to do its political work as
if the rhetoric were sufficient to create the nonrepressive society of equals. In the operation of local chapters this usually
meant the avoidance of an elected leadership (in the name of
antielitism), the reliance on long, formless mass meetings (in
the name of individual participation), and the absence of careful strategic thinking (in the name of spontaneity). The real
results of this mode of operation were the following: elitist
manipulation by individuals or cliques, which operated freely
because there was no defined leadership responsibility; the
disillusionment of large numbers of new recruits who found
it impossible to participate in the manipulated mass meetings
and who were given no opportunity to develop politically
through other structural forms of participation; and the frustration of serious activists because neither serious organizational forms nor long-range programs were developed (Calvert 1967, 8).

To combat these tendencies new organizational forms were
required, forms that encouraged genuine participation among
the membership. Work-study groups and collectively accountable steering committees were needed, so that the
would-be educators of poor people would themselves be
schooled in the liberating medium of political participation

(ibid., 8). These new forms would make "serious" community action easier to undertake and focus.

At the same time, the members of the SDS were increasingly preoccupied with the war in Vietnam and draft-resistance, which brought them into direct conflict with the "coercive and antidemocratic" power of the government. The stance of the organization quickly changed "from protest to resistance," based on the "hope that struggle and confrontation with the existing system of humanity will create freedom in the midst of a life-destroying society" (Sale 1973, 316).

This shift in stance had important ideological implications. It presented a departure from the "liberal consciousness" of reforming other people's lives, and a movement toward a "radical consciousness" built upon "the perception of *oneself* as unfree, as oppressed," as Greg Calvert put it (ibid., 318). Resistance was predicated on the personal experience of "unfreedom," and it required a broader and more active opposition to the forces of domination than did earlier experiments with community organizing, which in any event were passing from the control of the SDS.

The concrete experience of personal oppression would subsequently become the cornerstone of women's liberation movements, but the largely middle-class, male membership of the SDS gave a more conventional interpretation to the origin of radical consciousness. By the spring of 1967, SDS theoreticians had refined the concept of a "new working class" made up of individuals with "technical, clerical, and professional jobs that require educational backgrounds," as well as those who performed this educative function. The members of this new class, mostly students, were "becoming the most structurally relevant and necessary components of the productive processes of modern American capitalism." Because of "their structural, technical role in maintaining, developing and rationalizing American capitalism," students enjoyed a strategic advantage that, if they chose to exploit it, gave them the powerful leverage that was needed for effective resistance (ibid., 338–340).

Although this understanding was never as powerful as the more concrete experience with conscription, it did make the "personal oppression" of students readily comprehensible in terms of traditional leftist analyses, while holding out hope for the eventual success of resistance. Those hopes dimmed considerably as the System failed to respond to students' demands to end the war. The student movement was apparently not broad enough to exert the necessary political pressure, particularly in the face of "counterrevolutionary" measures undertaken in the name of law and order.

Faced with the need for an adequate analysis of the strength of counterrevolutionary forces in a society that was supposed to be on the verge of a new era, the national leadership turned increasingly toward neo-Marxist theories of domination and revolution. Competition with the Progressive Labor party for the affection of groups, especially among the "old" working class, necessary for broadening the movement's political base reinforced this tendency, as did the infiltration of the SDS by members of the PLP, most of whom espoused such theories (ibid.).

At this point in its development, the SDS was faced with a critical choice, according to Gitlin. Either the New Left must take itself seriously "as a specifically post-scarcity and visionary force with revolutionary democratic vision; *or* it buys clarity on the cheap, taking refuge from the distinctiveness of metropolitan conditions in mirror-models of the underdeveloped socialism of Russia and the Third World." The former option required the New Left to comprehend its unprecedented identity as a social force and use "its reality as a strength from which to encounter anti-colonial and working class energy and to devise common approaches," while the latter walked the beaten trails of the Old Left, seeking "a historically prepackaged version in which students or déclassé intellectuals are strictly appendages to really 'real' social forces or are either the vanguard or tail of the really real" (ibid., 505).

The SDS, or at least its leadership, chose the second option, transforming a "resistance movement" into a revolution-

ary vanguard that would culminate in the urban guerrilla warfare of the Weathermen. The imperatives of revolution
seemed to dictate this response to the repressive actions of
the System, but participatory democracy was one of the cas-
ualties of this abandonment of the "new working class" theme
in favor of the more radical neo-Marxist analyses of American
imperialism (Young, 1977). In fact, the SDS national office
became increasingly concerned with its steering functions,
which reflected the ideological shift from resistance to revolution. By 1969, the national office was exercising a much
tighter discipline over regional offices on programmatic matters, and grass-roots expressions of dissatisfaction were beginning to emerge. A parody of *New Left Notes*, which had as
its masthead motto "Let the People Decide," appeared in the
Northeast under the title *New Laugh Notes*, with a motto of
"Let the *Right* People Decide," and personal attacks on the
more militant members of the national office, e.g. Bernardine
Dohrn, were also circulated (Sale 1973, 522).

The creation of a cadre style of organization designed to
function as the vanguard of the revolution culminated in the
Weathermen, whose "Days of Rage" campaign represented
the cadre in action. The isolation of the Weathermen from
the rest of a movement grown quite heterogeneous was only
the most extreme instance of the "distance problem" that
characterized the relations between the national office and
rank-and-file members of the SDS, many of whom simply did
not understand the increasing militancy of their leaders
(ibid.). This problem was exacerbated by the leaders' insistence on subordinating certain issues, e.g. the oppression of
women, to "correct line" analyses of the class antagonisms of
imperialism. The resulting disunity seriously compromised
political effectiveness as disgruntled members went elsewhere in search of participatory democracy.

V

AS EARLY AS 1964 women in the movement began to speak
out on the oppression of women in American society and in
the movement to change that society, as well. In that year,

Ruby Doris Smith Robinson, one of the founding members of the Student Nonviolent Coordinating Committee (SNCC), presented a paper on "The Position of Women in SNCC," only to be met by Stokely Carmichael's retort that "the only position for women in SNCC is prone" (Yates 1975, 7). Women in the SDS met with more vulgar renditions of this same theme when they tried to initiate a discussion of the "women's issue" at a conference in 1965. And in 1966, when women demanded inclusion of a plank on women's liberation, they were pelted with tomatoes and thrown out of an SDS convention (Hole and Levine 1971, 112).

The Women's Liberation Workshop of the SDS responded by adopting a manifesto in which they demanded that their SDS brothers "recognize that they must deal with their own problems of male chauvinism in their personal, social and political relationships."[11] And they called upon their fellow women "to demand full participation in all aspects of movement work, from licking stamps to assuming leadership positions" (Yates 1975, 7–8). The latter was in response to the relegation of women members to what Marge Piercy called the "shitwork" of organization, while the more glamorous roles, e.g. theorizing and leading, were reserved for men (Morgan 1970, 476). It was also a response to the perceived exploitation of women in sexual matters. This point of contestation was especially pronounced in the late sixties.

However, the male leadership of the SDS and other movement organizations, e.g. the National Conference for a New Politics and the 1969 Mobilization for Peace, insisted on stifling discussion of such "trivial" issues in order not to divert attention from the larger objectives of civil rights and peace. New Left discourse was limited to "political" matters, and "whole areas of women's lives were declared off-limits to discussion" because they involved "personal" matters (Redstockings 1978, 145).

[11] The term *male chauvinism* apparently entered American political discourse via this manifesto (Yates 1975, 95).

The persistent refusal of the male leadership of New Left organizations to consider women's interests seriously and the unreconstructed chauvinism with which these interests were dismissed convinced many women of the need for an independent women's movement.[12] If there was no place for women in the discourse of the New Left, then it was essential for radical women to initiate their own discourse, addressed to a more receptive audience—other women.

The decision by these women to separate themselves from the established organizations of the left was, therefore, an attempt to expand the limits of political discussion in America. Frustrated in their efforts to engage the left in discussion of the oppressed condition of women, they set out to establish new forums for discourse, and to attract new participants with first-hand knowledge of oppression. The proliferation of women's organizations during this period attests to the vitality of this new discourse, even as it reflects the diversity of opinion among women themselves about "what women want."[13]

One of the more influential of the early women's organi-

[12] In 1967, a call for the liberation of women as an oppressed group was approved over the strenuous objections and disruptive tactics of male members of the National Council. *New Left Notes* later trivialized this statement by reprinting it alongside of a cartoon of a girl wearing earrings, a polkadot minidress, and matching, visible panties, holding a sign that said, "We Want Our Rights and We Want Them Now" (Evans 1978, 192). As late as 1969 one SDS chapter published a pamphlet proclaiming that "the system is like a woman; you have to fuck it to make it change" (Sale 1973, 526).

[13] Hole and Levine (1971) present a detailed analysis of this *Rebirth of Feminism*, while Yates (1975) summarizes the principal ideological differences of the main currents of American feminism. In what follows, I present *one* version of feminism that is particularly relevant to the subject of this book. I cannot do justice to this diversity here.

Evans (1978) provides an excellent account of the relation between women's liberation, the New Left, and the civil rights movement. She illustrates the way in which exposure to the civil rights movement and the New Left simultaneously politicized many women, while denying them access to meaningful leadership roles in the attack on the System. The idea of the separate women's movement was born out of this frustration and given credence by the success of Black Power advocates of a "separatist" strategy.

zations was the Redstockings, founded in 1969 by Ellen Willis
and Shulamith Firestone as a group within the New York
Radical Women.[14] The Redstockings were radical feminists
who insisted that the exploitation of women by men reflected
a class distinction more fundamental than that identified by
Marx as the engine of modern history. In so doing the Redstockings gave women's liberation an identity of its own. This
is undoubtedly what made Firestone's book on *The Dialectic
of Sex* such a vital force in the women's movement. The essence of this radical feminist argument is also presented in
the Redstockings' Manifesto, one of the more widely read
statements of the ideas of the women's movement and their
relationship to democracy. In simple, resolute language the
Manifesto describes the oppression of women, analyzes its
causes, and proposes a method by which women can reach a
liberated—and liberating—understanding of their situation.

The central argument of the Redstockings' Manifesto is that
women are an oppressed class. As such, their oppression is
total—*all* facets of *every* woman's life bear its marks. The experience of oppression, while felt by individuals, is not personal and idiosyncratic, but political and systematic. Hence,
the liberation of women was necessarily a collective enterprise to be carried out *by* women *for* women. The "sisterhood" of women expressed this solidarity among women, and
the slogan "Sisterhood Is Powerful" summarized the political
potential of class action based on it (Yates 1975, 102).

But consciousness of their sisterhood was precisely what
most women did not have. They had been kept from seeing
their personal suffering as a political condition because of
their physical and psychological isolation from one another.
According to the Manifesto, "This creates the illusion that a
woman's relationship with her man is a matter of interplay
between two unique personalities and can be worked out in-

[14] *Redstockings* was coined by Firestone. It was "intended to represent a
synthesis of two traditions: that of the earlier feminist theoreticians and writers who were insultingly called "Bluestockings" in the nineteenth century,
and the militant political tradition of radicals—the red of revolution" (Redstockings 1978, 55).

dividually. In reality, every such relationship is a *class* relationship, and the conflicts between individual men and
women are *political* conflicts that can only be solved collectively" (Morgan 1970, 598).

This did not mean that women were responsible for their
oppression, or had in some way consented to it. The Redstockings rejected "brainwashing" theories of sexual oppression, which implicated women in their own exploitation by
portraying them as unusually susceptible to psychological manipulation. Rather, the Redstockings argued that the oppression of women was the direct result of continuous, daily pressure from men, whose control of political, economic, and
cultural institutions was ultimately guaranteed by physical
force (ibid., 599).

Thus, the Redstockings articulated a pro-woman line of
thought that placed the responsibility for sexual oppression
squarely on the shoulders of men (Hole and Levine 1971,
139ff.). Such arguments lie at the heart of radical feminism,
which refuses to follow feminist radicals in reducing sexual
oppression to the more general exploitation of labor.[15] Instead, radical feminists like the Redstockings insisted that
"male supremacy is the oldest, most basic form of domination. All other forms of exploitation and oppression (racism,
capitalism, imperialism, etc.) are extensions of male supremacy: men dominate women, a few men dominate the rest"
(Morgan 1970, 599).

Because existing theories of oppression, e.g. Marxism, did
not take this into account, they were singularly unfit for wom-
en's liberation. Consequently, new and more appropriate

[15] The difference between the noun *feminism* and the adjective *feminist* is
highly significant in this rhetorical context. Feminist radicals are radicals
first, and feminists second, whereas radical feminists identify *sexual* oppression as the poisonous root to be removed. (*Radical*, of course, is from the
Latin rootword *radix*, which means *root*.) Ironically, it was Marx himself who
resurrected the political significance of *radical*. In his "Contribution to the
Critique of Hegel's *Philosophy of Right*," he wrote that "to be radical is to
grasp matters at the root. But for man the root is man himself" (O'Malley
1970, 137). No doubt radical feminists would concur, but for a different reason!

theories were needed. The Redstockings and other radical feminists sought to ground their understanding of women's oppression in the actual experience of oppression: "We regard our personal experience, and our feelings about that experience, as the basis for an analysis of our common situation. We cannot rely on existing ideologies as they are all products of male supremacist culture. We question every generalization and accept none that are not confirmed by our experience" (ibid., 600).

Experience was the source of understanding, and understanding, or the "naming of what's really going on," was the basis of radical action, wrote Katie Sarachild (Redstockings 1978, 148). Hence, consciousness–raising seemed to be an ideal revolutionary method, for the analysis of concrete experiences of oppression could provide "an ongoing and continuing source of theory and ideas for action" (ibid., 147).

In that sense, consciousness–raising "wasn't seen as merely a stage in feminist development which would then lead to another phase, an action phase, but as an essential part of the overall feminist strategy" (ibid., 147). Consciousness-raising was simultaneously a method for arriving at the "truth" of women's situation and a technique for mobilization. Moreover, in its most developed form consciousness raising was a *reflexive* process. According to Barbara Susan:

> It is our hope that consciousness raising in groups of women who are not the same will help us to understand each other and help us all in building a movement which answers to the needs of more than just the most privileged woman. Our analysis is an expanding one, it changes as more and more women enter the movement and contribute their knowledge and experience thereby widening and correcting our understanding of oppression. (Yates 1975, 106)

For that reason women's groups in general, and the Redstockings in particular, expended a great deal of energy in developing techniques for consciousness-raising. A "Program for Feminist Consciousness-Raising" was developed by Sarachild, in which a step-by-step procedure for examining concrete experiences, drawing generalizations from them, overcoming "resistances" to the truth of these generalizations, and taking action upon them was detailed (Redstockings 1978, 202–203). A curriculum of topics for discussion was also suggested (Hole and Levine 1971, 138–139).

At the same time the Redstockings were careful to develop a set of "Protective Rules for Consciousness-Raising." According to Ware:

> These rules are read by the group before each session. Basically, they require each sister to bear testimony and, while doing so, to stick to specifics. Another strict rule is that the group hear every woman's particular testimony before moving on to generalization from the specific experiences. Judgment and comment on a sister's experiences are not allowed and, when a sister has a particular attitude to urge, she must state her reason for insisting on forcing the group or the person testifying to speak to her question. (1970, 44)

In effect these rules were principles for democratic discourse, reflecting the Redstockings' commitment to achieving internal democracy. They were *protective* rules designed "to ensure that every woman in our movement has an equal chance to participate, assume responsibility, and develop her political potential" (Morgan 1970, 600).

Because the rules had a political objective, they were not designed to guarantee the therapeutic efficacy of consciousness-raising. Precisely because consciousness-raising was oriented toward discovering the truth of Carol Hanish's proposition that "the personal is political," it was not seen as a kind of therapy. Therapy implied the reconciliation of a woman to her fate, whereas liberation implied a redefinition of that fate itself. By revealing personal experiences of sexual oppression as concrete manifestations of male domination, consciousness-raising made such a redefinition possible, though not by any means inevitable: "With greater understanding, one discovers new necessity for action—and new possibilities for it" (Redstockings 1978, 148).

In time, the historical experiences of women, too, became an object of consciousness-raising. As women's personal experiences began to include feminist efforts to change history, the importance of extending their analysis to include the past, as well as the present, oppression of women became evident (ibid., 37). For history, or more precisely, feminist history, was a rich source of inspiration and solidarity, linking women of all ages to one another in their struggle against male supremacy.[16] More importantly, true history recorded the victories of women in this struggle. It recognized the political ground won by women at great cost, *and secured it* by insuring that it would not have to be won again. History of, by, and for women was the surety of whatever progress had been made, preserving whatever truths had been discovered as a matter of public record (ibid., 42).

It was the strategic importance of history that led women like Shulamith Firestone to unearth the "real" history of the suffragette movement and to chronicle the development of the women's liberation movement. For the loss of women's history, both past and recent, was perceived as a critical weakness, one that threatened to halt the momentum of the movement by allowing its identity and ideas to be defined and interpreted by others, most of whom were unsympathetic to the cause. Indeed, Sarachild, "the mother of consciousness-raising" in the women's movement, saw this revisionism and the fight against it as one of the most important issues confronting the movement in the seventies, and she urged "raising consciousness of the need for going to the original sources for really knowing anything, understanding and clarification" (ibid., 42). Hence, the possession of history was a vital weapon in the battle against revisionism.

In that sense feminist historiography recapitulated the fun-

---

[16] Sarachild (Redstockings 1978, 13–43) provides an illuminating account of radical feminists' ambivalence toward history, which had been used by the left as well as right to discredit the women's movement. With the realization that "the purpose of history is to illuminate our experience, not to deny it" and that "the present must rule the use of the past," a truly feminist historiography was launched.

damental insight of consciousness-raising. Truth and understanding of the sort that inspires action must be discovered
in the original, lived experiences of oppressed women, and
not in abstract formulations. Otherwise, the validity of the
proposition that "the personal is political" remains in doubt.
Nevertheless, there is a very real danger that reflection of
the sort implied by consciousness-raising will lead to inaction.
Although it was originally proposed as a corrective to the
"mindless activism" of some women's groups, the consciousness-raising practiced by the Redstockings became counterproductive. In defending their claim that "the personal is political" against the refusal of the New Left to consider the oppression of women as a political problem, "the group turned
completely inward, and in the name of 'politics' in fact focused almost exclusively on 'the personal' " (Hole and Levine
1971, 140). As the political became personal, so to speak, the
group brought about its own demise. As one observer noted,
"When you stop looking out, and turn exclusively inward, at
some point you begin to feed on each other. If you don't
direct your anger externally—politically—you turn it against
yourself" (ibid., 141), and self-destruction is the result.

Thus, the Redstockings found themselves in a position not
too dissimilar from that of the SDS. Both groups attempted
to enhance the possibility of democratic change by launching
independent discussions as a counterpoint to what they perceived as a closed political dialogue. But this type of endeavor
invites rhetorical extremism, which becomes self-defeating as
soon as it succeeds in interjecting itself into the dialogue it
challenges. The spoken and written word then assume a life
of their own, and though the discourse on democracy may be
altered by them, it is often accompanied by the silencing of
at least some discussants.

VI

THE DECLARATION of independence by women who had once
been active in New Left politics was not the first defection
from that cause. That occurred during the mid sixties, when
militant young blacks severed ties with white radicals in order

to build a Black Power movement. As was true in the case of women, the main issues involved in this split centered on black demands for self-determination within the Movement itself. It is true that whites accepted the legitimacy of black liberation, whereas they failed to accord the same treatment to women's liberation. But white radicals' refusal to subordinate completely the specific demands of blacks to those of a broader movement did not necessarily mean that black liberation was viewed as an autonomous cause. Subordination aside, many possible relations between the New Left and black organizations were conceivable, and not all of them were democratic.

This point was made as early as 1962 by the black historian Harold Cruse. In a contribution to *Studies on the Left* Cruse warned against the "revolutionary paternalism" that historically characterized the attitude of white radicals toward "Negro" movements. The existence of powerful black nationalist sentiments within the burgeoning civil rights movement meant that black organizations would not accept this attitude: "There is no longer room for the 'revolutionary paternalism' that has been the hallmark of organizations such as the Communist Party. This is what the 'New Left' must clearly understand in its future relations with Negro movements that are indigenous to the Negro community" (Weinstein and Eakins 1970, 368–369).

However, this warning about the potentially conflicting goals of black and white radicals seemed unnecessary during the early sixties. White students, many of whom were members of the SDS, joined with black students, many of whom were active in the SNCC, in unified opposition to segregation in the South. The cooperation of whites and blacks in sit-ins, freedom rides, marches, and voter registration drives seemed to belie any serious division of interests.

In part this was made possible by the rhetoric of nonviolence practiced by the SNCC.[17] The outlook of the early

---

[17] Among all the early civil rights groups, the SNCC provides the most

SNCC was similar to that of the Southern Christian Leadership Conference and other groups advocating nonviolent direct action as an alternative to the National Association for the Advancement of Colored People's (NAACP) "legal" strategy for combating racial discrimination. This is evident in the "Statement of Purpose" adopted by the SNCC at its founding in 1960:

> We affirm the philosophical or religious ideal of nonviolence as the foundation of our purpose, the pre-supposition of our faith, and the manner of our action. Nonviolence as it grows from Judaic-Christian traditions seeks a social order of justice permeated by love. Integration of human endeavor represents the crucial first step towards such a society.
>
> Through nonviolence, courage displaces fear; love transforms hate. Acceptance dissipates prejudice; hope ends despair. Peace dominates war; faith reconciles doubt. Mutual regard cancels enmity. Justice for all overthrows injustice. The redemptive community supersedes systems of gross social immorality.
>
> Love is the central motif of nonviolence. Love is the force by which God binds man to Himself and man to man. Such love goes to the extreme; it remains loving and forgiving even in the midst of hostility. It matches the capacity of evil to inflict suffering with an even more enduring capacity to absorb evil, all the while persisting in love.
>
> By appealing to conscience and standing on the moral nature of human existence, nonviolence nurtures the atmosphere in which reconciliation and justice become actual possibilities. (Marty 1969, 175)

This last paragraph is particularly important, for it reveals the fundamental presupposition of nonviolence as a strategy for

---

interesting passage from the rhetoric of nonviolence to that of Black Power. For that reason I shall limit my discussion of black organizations to a discussion of the SNCC.

changing society. Nonviolence assumes that there is an underlying morality to which appeals might be made on behalf of oppressed groups. The entire rhetoric of nonviolent direct action is aimed at the activation of this universal morality, so that the ideals present therein—reconciliation and justice—may be realized. Hence, this rhetoric presumes that an interracial dialogue is possible because of the moral nature of *all* human existence (ibid.).

On this basis the SNCC and other civil rights organizations of the early sixties built their strategy for overcoming racial discrimination. Racial conflict was defined primarily as a *southern* problem, identified with specific grievances involving the denial of civil rights to blacks. Nonviolent direct action was a way of calling attention to this undemocratic aspect of American society. By appealing to the conscience of white Americans, particularly those in the North, the civil rights movement hoped to encourage sympathetic whites to intervene on blacks' behalf, ending "second class citizenship" in the South.

In that sense, nonviolence was a rhetoric designed to challenge white Americans to live up to their democratic ideals. It did not question the validity of those ideals, only their inadequate realization. Whether this reflected the shared entrapment of American blacks and whites in a liberal society or whether it reflected a realistic assessment of what could be reasonably expected or practically wrested from white America is not the issue (Merriman and Parent 1981). The important point is that an appeal to conscience of this sort could not in the end be rejected without seriously endangering Americans' perception of their society as democratic. Precisely because the rhetoric of nonviolence accepted the prevailing conception of democracy, its legitimacy could not be denied.

The rhetoric of nonviolence proved quite effective in recruiting liberal sympathizers. At the same time, radical white students found in nonviolent direct action a "legitimate" way of articulating their criticism of undemocratic features of

American society. However, the very success of nonviolent direct action in attracting white activists to black causes inevitably heightened black fears about the declining autonomy of black liberation. By late 1963, black members of the SNCC began to express doubts about the role of whites in their organization, and in 1964 racial tensions ran high in a SNCC training camp for white volunteers to the Freedom Summer campaign in Mississippi (Matusow 1971).

Nevertheless, the SNCC stopped short of closing their membership to whites in 1964. For whites were quite useful in other ways:

> SNCC was tired of reporting the truth about Mississippi to the press and having it read by the inside of the wastebasket. If they were ever to expose Mississippi racism to America it would only be through using whites. The Mississippi Summer Project was a calculated political act. Put a thousand white kids into the state and the press would watch everything and print it. . . . And who could tell? Maybe one of them white boys would get himself killed and really make some publicity. A few said it. Most thought it. It happened. (Lester 1969, 21)

The press, of course, covered the events in Mississippi extensively, but that did not save the Freedom Summer project from becoming an intensely disillusioning experience for the SNCC. In spite of their success in forming the Mississippi Freedom Democratic party (FDP), the SNCC failed to gain a hearing in the national Democratic party, which refused to certify the credentials of the FDP at the 1964 presidential convention. Liberal white allies refused to back the FDP, and "Freedom Summer, which began with SNCC fighting for entrance into the American political system, ended with the radical conviction that that system was beyond redemption" (Matusow 1971, 143–144).

Once the possibility of redemption was dismissed, however, the whole rhetoric of nonviolence became irrelevant. Based as it was on the redemptive power of an appeal to conscience, it had no place in a party or society with no con-science. This realization, brought home by the debacle in At-lantic City, plunged the SNCC into ideological and organi-zational disarray as it struggled to find a new basis for action.

The SNCC found such a basis in the black nationalism of the northern ghettos, where few blacks had ever believed that gaining civil rights would materially improve the situa-tion of blacks in America (ibid., 147). For these blacks, the problem was not *de jure* segregation, but *de facto* discrimi-nation, and the virulence of the "backlash" in the North was testimony to white Americans' unwillingness to treat *this* as a legitimate topic for political discourse.

To combat this racism, an entirely new rhetoric of Black Power was needed. But first it was necessary to discredit the rhetoric of nonviolence, which still had a powerful hold on blacks, even though the SNCC felt it was no longer adequate for achieving self-determination for blacks in *American* (not just southern) society. This in fact was the primary purpose of *Black Power: The Politics of Liberation in America*, by Stokely Carmichael and Charles Hamilton (1967).

In this powerful treatise Carmichael and Hamilton mince few words in describing how counterproductive the rhetoric of nonviolence had been. In a critique that Dr. Martin Luther King reluctantly conceded was essentially correct, Carmi-chael and Hamilton charged that "each time the black people in those cities saw Dr. Martin Luther King get slapped they became angry. When they saw little girls bombed to death *in a church* and civil rights workers ambushed and murdered, they were angrier; and when nothing happened, they were steaming mad. We had nothing to offer that they could see, except to go out and be beaten again. We helped to build their frustration (1967, 50)."

But the language of love and suffering did not permit any other response to the violence of white racism. Since the power of this discourse with white America rested on a moral appeal to a conscience the existence of which was presumed from the start, there really was nothing left to do "except to go out and be beaten again." Not even self-defense was permitted, for that would have rendered the injustice of white racism less glaring.

The irrelevance of this "language of yesterday" was apparent to Carmichael and Hamilton. But they did not conclude that because *this* dialogue on race was inadequate that all dialogues on race were doomed to failure. As Burgess (1969) observes, this latter conclusion was the idiom of Black Muslims, whose discourse was directed entirely toward black America. The SNCC and other Black Power advocates refused to terminate the dialogue with white America, though they did insist on making it much more radical than that carried on by the civil rights movement. That is to say, the SNCC insisted that the terms of racial discourse in America be fully democratic. Discussion was not to be confined to those issues that the majority was willing to entertain, nor were blacks to perform in ways dictated by whites as "legitimate." Instead, blacks would raise the issues important to them, and in terms that were relevant to their experience. *Self*-determination, in the broadest possible sense, was the new principle of discourse.

There was, of course, no guarantee that the ensuing discourse would result in agreement or that it would be free of conflict. However, the SNCC insisted that the very possibility of a multiracial democracy depended on a discourse of self-determination. A radicalization of discourse was, therefore, a necessary, though perhaps insufficient, condition for democratic progress (Lester 1969).

The decisive turn in the rhetorical policy of the SNCC occurred in 1966, when the SNCC banned whites from holding positions of leadership in the organization. In a position paper entitled "Who is the Real Villain—Uncle Tom or Simon Legree?" the SNCC argued that the presence of whites in the organization had an intimidating effect on the black people they were trying to organize (Wagstaff 1969). This, as well as whites' inability to escape completely from the influence of demeaning stereotypes of blacks, threatened to reproduce the pattern of "revolutionary paternalism" about which Cruse had warned. Consequently, the potential of indigenous liberation movements for achieving complete self-determination was being stifled.

This did not mean that white sympathizers had no role to play in the liberation of blacks. Their job was to go where the problem of racism was most pronounced—white America. Rather than organizing blacks, which implied that something about blacks had to be changed before the problem was eliminated, "White people should go into White communities where the Whites have created power for the express [purpose] of denying Blacks dignity and self-determination" (ibid., 113). Only when white people changed themselves would black liberation be achieved fully.

Thus, the real villain was Simon Legree. Both inside and outside the black movement, Simon Legree made his presence felt and his domination known. As a matter of self-defense, then, it was necessary to challenge that power *in* the movement, so as to challenge it *by* the movement. A closed movement was essential for liberation.

To most whites (and many blacks) this move seemed perverse and contradictory. How, after all, could an integrated society be created from two separate societies, one black and the other white? But this was precisely the point of Black Power advocates. This question was only puzzling to those who failed to see that the United States was *already* a divided society. Black Power did not mean that a more or less unified nation was going to be divided by blacks in order to create a more harmonious, multiracial society. Rather, it meant that an already divided society could only become a democratic community if blacks were autonomous, and not dependent. And since autonomy meant self-determination, it entailed the power of blacks to define themselves and their role in society—Black Power (Burgess 1969).

Thus, the basic premise of the rhetoric of Black Power was this: American culture was fundamentally, though not unalterably, racist. The unity presumed by the rhetoric of nonviolence did not really exist. It was something that had to be created out of a fundamentally divided society. And it was toward this creative act that the rhetoric of Black Power was directed. It was the language upon which a new black community might be founded, and a new, democratic dialogue with white America initiated.

The term *Black Power* itself was a potent symbol for mobilizing this new black community, and a prefiguration of its role in democratic discourse.[18] As Hamilton put it, "Black Power is concerned with organizing the rage of Black people and with putting new, hard questions and demands to White America" (Wagstaff 1969, 126). In so doing, the rhetoric of Black Power simultaneously acknowledged the legitimate rage of blacks (something that the rhetoric of nonviolence could hardly recognize, given its commitment to the language of love and suffering) and identified a progressive outlet for it—"putting demands" to white America.

Black *demands* for self-determination were something to which whites were not accustomed, particularly when the putting of those demands was no longer voluntarily restricted to nonviolent actions. Whites wanted to know "if Black Power was antiwhite and if it meant killing white folks," thereby missing the political import of this black demand for self-determination (Lester 1969, 98–100). They failed to see that between nonviolence and violence lies a class of self-defensive actions that is inextricably linked to self-determination.

The political rhetoric of white America was riddled with such false antinomies and the hysterical implications of them (Carmichael and Hamilton 1967). This was most apparent in whites' characterization of Black Power as black racism, or

[18] Stokely Carmichael is usually credited with the invention of the term *Black Power* while completing James Meredith's March Against Fear in Mississippi. But as James Baldwin observes, "He [Carmichael] didn't coin it. He simply dug it up again from where it's been lying since the first slaves hit the gangplank. I have never known a Negro in all my life who was not obsessed with Black Power" (Wagstaff 1969, 120).

Ku Klux Klan racism in reverse. Black Power advocates strongly resisted this interpretation:

> There is no analogy—by any stretch of definition or imagination—between the advocates of Black Power and white racists. Racism is not merely exclusion on the basis of race but exclusion for the purpose of subjugating or maintaining subjugation. The goal of the racists is to keep black people on the bottom, arbitrarily and dictatorially, as they have done in this country for over three hundred years. The goal of black self-determination and black self-identity—Black Power—is full participation in the decisionmaking processes affecting the lives of black people, and recognition of the virtues in themselves as black people. (ibid., 47)

Only those who were completely oblivious to the realities of power in the United States could equate Black Power with the systematic oppression of one race by another that was the historical legacy of white racism. Black racism was literally an impossibility in America; to hold otherwise was to propagate a "deliberate and absurd lie" (ibid., 47).

Still, Black Power advocates were never completely successful in removing the stigma of "black racism" from their movement. As a result, their radical message never found a large audience, particularly as the SNCC moved toward independent political action and the Black Panther party. And their message *was* radical. Whereas the civil rights movement had never questioned the fairness of the rules that constituted liberal democracy in the United States, proponents of Black Power did. They did not seek civil rights, but rather a new set of rules that recognized the substantive justice of racial autonomy.

This movement from considerations about the fair application of rules to questions about the fairness of the rules themselves was a radical move on the part of the SNCC and other black organizations. However, it was a move strongly resisted by white America, and not only for racist reasons. For once the fairness of the rules themselves becomes an issue, then

other substantive objections, including those of economic inequality, might suddenly emerge. Some of this was in fact
already present in the ideology of Black Power, which aspired
to a society based on "free people, not free enterprise" (ibid.,
41). The materialist, as well as racist, inclinations of the white
middle class were rejected by the achievements of Black
Power in favor of other, more "civilized" values.

At this point, however, the rhetoric of black liberation had
come almost full circle. Having moved away from white radicals and their analysis of American society in order to achieve
independence, it now began to return to radical analyses of
capitalism, and especially its imperialist tendencies. Not surprisingly, black radicals preferred to ally themselves with
Third World revolutionaries, rather than white leftists. But
the problems of building an international movement proved
even more insurmountable than those of building a national
one, and the voice of black radicalism rather rapidly disappeared from American political discourse.

VII

FOR A BRIEF MOMENT during the sixties the counterculture
of opposition seemed capable of overcoming the passivity of
a citizenry mesmerized by the end of ideology. The demands
of blacks, women, and, to a lesser extent, the poor for a
greater role in political discourse challenged the dominant
conception of interest-group liberalism and its preference for
administration by professionals. The System was forced to defend itself, and to justify its claim to be democratic against
strong moral challenges to the contrary. Lacking a moral basis
of its own, the System did so by improving the flow of public
goods to new groups in politics. The Great Society was proclaimed, the sphere of interest group liberalism was expanded, new "consumer" groups recognized, and responsiveness—the true measure of democratic consumerism's
performance—increased.

Nevertheless, the role of opposition quickly proved unable
to contain the diverse interests assembled under it. The con-

fluence of liberation movements, so imposing in its potential, was never actually realized as the main currents flowed their separate ways, each too powerful to lose its identity in a mingling of waters. Each secured important concessions from the System, but all failed to achieve their ultimate objective of a participatory democracy in which basic issues of social organization were addressed in a relatively unconstrained discourse of citizens.

The outcome of this turbulent decade is, therefore, difficult to describe. The dominant culture and its values eventually triumphed, but only after their vulnerability to moral challenges was revealed. Democratic consumerism was preserved, but its fate was inextricably linked to continuous improvements in providing public goods, i.e. policies. Lacking any convincing moral basis of its own, democratic consumerism could only respond with "more" democracy when confronted by moralistic condemnations of its performance. This logic was clearly unveiled by the rhetoric of the sixties, from which the dissidents of the seventies evidently learned well, as we shall see.

This immediately raises the question of limits and the capacity of the System to meet new demands for more democracy. The insatiability of democratic consumers may well exceed dominant institutions' ability to respond to such challenges. For that reason, it seems entirely appropriate to speak of the crisis of democratic consumerism that was precipitated by the challenge of participatory democracy, since crises occur when "the old is dying, but the new cannot yet be born."

CHAPTER TEN

The Functionalization of Discourse

I

THE COMPARATIVE EASE with which countercultural objections were absorbed into American political discourse is evident in the ephemeral life of "the Movement."[1] The virtual disappearance of hippies, yippies, Redstockings, Black Panthers, and so on—in short, of "radical" groups—is remarkable and seems to confirm the truth of Marcuse's observation that as critical interpretations "become part and parcel of the established culture. . . . they seem to lose their edge and to merge with the old and familiar. This familiarity with the truth illuminates the extent to which society has become indifferent and insusceptible to the impact of critical thought" (Shapiro 1972, 285).

The "insusceptibility" of the dominant culture to critical interpretations did not stem from an outright denial of their validity. That would have necessitated a sustained defense of "the System" and its accomplishments, as well as a denial of its "imperialistic," "sexist," or "racist" shortcomings (or at least a disclaimer concerning the seriousness of these problems). In short, it would have meant an engagement with the counterculture and its sense of injustice. Such engagements are always risky, since they involve a commitment to reasoned discourse in which only the force of the stronger argument comes into play. As a result, there are no guarantees

---

[1] This seems less true of the women's movement, which has made important, if not always politically visible, gains during the seventies. However, the failure of the Equal Rights Amendment, one of the least radical projects of women, suggests the growing resistance of the "silent majority" to dissident challenges in this area as well.

that hegemonic values will be confirmed in such engagements; it is always possible that their "unreasonableness" will be demonstrated. That is why counterculture movements seek engagements, whereas dominant cultures generally avoid them.

Thus, the insusceptibility to criticism arose from another quarter; it was not the result of a denial of the validity of criticism, so much as it was a reflection of their absorption. Critical interpretations "became part and parcel of the established culture" as Marcuse observed, and in the process radical and sometimes unanswerable objections were transformed into more moderate interpretations to which the established culture responded in its own terms. By the very act of responding to these criticisms, suitably modified and interpreted according to dominant values, the established culture derived strength and moral satisfaction from being "open to criticism." In this way its reasonableness was reconfirmed, and without risk, since the grounds of confirmation were those of the "Establishment" itself.

This may explain why the Movement was unable to establish a mass following. Even if it did not respond to radical demands for a restructuring of power in society, the System did address some of the more concrete needs of groups that had not shared in the benefits of a more affluent life style. In so doing, the System affirmed the political claims of the modern citizen on state and society, absorbed moral criticisms based on the frustration of those claims, and made violent means of redress seem unnecessary—and also illegitimate.

The erection of the Great Society was the means by which this was accomplished. During the Johnson administration in particular, consumer democracy was greatly enlarged under the auspices of a War on Poverty and a host of related social welfare programs (Grønbjerg 1977). The number of entitlement programs expanded rapidly, as did the size of the population served by them and the amount of money spent on them. The magnitude of this expansion of the welfare state dwarfed the accomplishments of the New Deal, as ever more groups came to receive publically provided or subsidized goods and services. The number of consumer democrats multiplied as more and more citizens were given a "stake in the system," and progress toward greater equality was apparently made via the recognition of the previously unacknowledged claims of new groups.

These accomplishments of the System made protest seem unreasonable. The affluent society delivered the goods to most of its members, most of the time. The costs of affluence, including waste, destruction, and the increasing subordination of individual needs to systemic requirements appeared either small by comparison to the benefits of affluence, or regrettable, but necessary, costs of doing business.

This kind of "cost-benefit" analysis of consumer democracy was made palatable by the widely held conviction that the U.S. had entered an era of "post-scarcity" politics in which the benefits to be enjoyed would grow exponentially, while the costs to be borne would decline rapidly as more efficient and less destructive technologies were discovered. The scientific discoveries and technical innovations of the postwar years made possible dramatic increases in productivity and improvements in the standard of living. The unprecedented growth rates of the period made the Great Society conceivable, politically speaking, since they made it possible to finance the War on Poverty without any (immediate) increases in redistributive taxation. Nor was there any obvious reason to suspect that this trend would not continue, thereby solving the difficult conflicts that plagued politics in the "age of scarcity." Only much latter would doubts emerge concerning the capacity of the System for ameliorative action, at least when it was simultaneously conducting an overseas war.

This confidence in the continuation of growth and affluence infected the counterculture, as well as the Establishment. The visions of the "Free Society" that were posed as alternatives to the Great Society were no less indebted to post-scarcity assumptions than the plans of the "professional reformers" who were the architects of the American welfare state. Countercultural critiques were predicated on the belief that "surplus repression" could be eliminated without compromising the material progress that flowed from the increasingly effective application of knowledge to the extraction of wealth from natural resources. The Free Society was nothing more than a civilized version of the Great Society—and nothing less than a fully universal conception of democratic consumerism.

To a significant extent this understanding reduced social criticism to a discussion of the "distribution problem," i.e. the best or most equitable way of sharing the benefits of affluence in society. Only in rare cases did people question the extent to which the social and technological conditions that made affluence possible were consistent with democratic principles. And even those who did wonder about this did not always confront the possibility that these conditions had an objective existence of their own, drastically limiting the choice of alternative life styles to those that were compatible with the political and technological imperatives of affluence. Consequently, the choice of life styles and even broad-scale social forms seemed almost unlimited, when in fact the range of choices was radically constrained by an instrumental orientation that Marcuse dubbed "one-dimensional."

This point was never fully grasped by most radical critics of the Great Society, and as a result the force of their objections was easily blunted by the expansion of consumer democracy. By their acceptance of affluence as an accomplished fact these critics forfeited any chance of launching a more fundamental criticism of the sort assayed by Marcuse, whose own analysis of the sociotechnical "apparatus" that made affluence possible was quite influential, even if it was not well-developed, or "adequately theorized," to use the current parlance. As a result, the conceptions of the democratic society that were conceived as alternatives to the Great Society were, with few exceptions, quite unimaginative extrapolations of the affluent society according to which "the millenium is the technological promised land; it is an age in which technology has solved all the problems technology created, a time when

clumsy postcrisis politics has been replaced by precrisis behavioral engineering" (Thompson 1971, 154).

At the same time, much of the democratic thinking of this
period seriously overestimated the ease with which a more
democratic society might be achieved. The inevitable frustration of such naive hopes by the "insusceptibility to criticism"
of the Establishment and the corresponding disintegration of
the Movement left many of its members genuinely perplexed
as to what had gone wrong. The anguish that accompanied
this perplexity was real, but not entirely unexpected. As
Lasch observed, the New Left acted "out of an ideal of personal heroism rather than from an analysis of the sources of
tension in American society and the possibilities for change,"
and so it was bound to vacillate "between existential despair
and absurdly inflated estimates of its own potential" (Clecak
1973, 235). Of course the latter tendency only fed the former,
and the defeat of the Movement gave rise to the disconsola-
tion and personal withdrawal so characteristic of Movement
radicals' subsequent lives.

II

EVENTUALLY, PARTICIPANTS in the Movement came to realize that the System's capacity for absorbing criticism without responding to its terms was even greater than they had
suspected:

> The experiences of the SDS ought to be sobering for our
> poetic "community of the faithful" which began as a New
> Left and which ended in dogmatic posturing and programs
> which could not be implemented without an apocalyptic
> revolutionary movement. We have not achieved one single
> radical reform which transferred power from the corporate
> elite to the people. The military posture of the Black
> Panther Party has produced many martyrs but not armed
> self-defense of the black community; the experiences of the
> 1960s, with all their pain and struggle, have not left one
> mass-based organization which has the power to resist
> either repression or co-optation; some of our friends are

dead—too many; some of our friends are underground in a
noble but spurious attempt to make classical terrorism the
catalytic force for the creation of a viable revolutionary
movement. We who tried most desperately to turn Amer-
ica-the-Obscene into America-the-Beautiful failed misera-
bly and our brothers and sisters are dying as a result of that
failure. (Calvert and Neiman 1971, x)

However, the Movement's ultimate stagnation was not simply the result of the insusceptibility of the dominant culture
to criticism. It was also due in part to the Movement's failure
to take that insusceptibility into account. The theoreticians of
the Movement did not adequately analyze the System and its
staying power, and thus they unwittingly reinforced the dominant culture's defensive capabilities by misdirecting Movement strategies and tactics. To be sure, even "correct" actions
might well have failed to redefine prevailing cultural norms,
given their apparent insusceptibility to criticism. Still, there
is no doubt that theoretical inadequacies did contribute to the
practical failure of the Movement to achieve its objectives
during the sixties and early seventies.

This is now conceded by many members of the New Left—
witness the confessional statement by Calvert and Neiman
(1971), as well as the analysis of the "critical interruption" of
the Movement's progress by Breines and others (1970). It is
confirmed by sympathetic historians of the New Left, e.g.
Nigel Young (1977), and by more orthodox efforts to situate
the demise of the New Left within the broader trajectory of
radical failures in the U.S. (Cantor 1978; Clecak 1973). Essentially, these interpretations concur with Bouchier's conclusion that a "persistent streak of utopianism" vitiated whatever valid insights and creative suggestions the New Left had
to offer (1979, 77). Lacking the theoretical sophistication to
understand the implications of their utopianism, the members of the New Left were led to engage in a string of politically disastrous adventures that isolated them from potential
allies.[2]

_____

[2] Clecak (1973) cites the Weatherman faction of the SDS as the extreme

Young (1977) describes these misadventures as a "surge of millennial activism" in response to the frustration of Movement efforts to bring about an alternative society. Like syndicalism before it, the New Left "failed to develop an adequate strategy in relation to power in America—the 'shell of the old society' within which these new structures were supposed to emerge" (ibid., 332). The inevitable defeats that followed from this failure drove the Movement toward vanguard operations in the Leninist tradition, so as to avoid the ineffective strategies and tactics associated with the "infantile disorder" that characterized the early years of the Movement.

This occurred despite the familiarity of many New Left intellectual leaders with the critical theorists of the Frankfurt School, e.g. Adorno and Marcuse. According to them, the deracination of political life in the modern age must be one of the fundamental themes of contemporary social theory, especially of the Marxist or "critical" varieties, where this development is explicitly linked to the evolution of commodity production. Lukács' (1971) critical reformulation of Max Weber's dialectic of *Zweckrationalität*, and his analyses of reification and commodity fetishism are still the outstanding examples of this in the Marxist tradition. However, it was the critical theorists of the Frankfurt school who applied this notion in a systematic and comprehensive way to the analysis of contemporary mass culture, processes of socialization, and the deformation of personality. In so doing, the members of the Frankfurt school attempted to complement Marx's political economy with a cultural analysis that avoided the economic determinism of vulgar Marxists, and at the same time provided a foundation for criticizing the undemocratic tendencies of advanced capitalist societies (Jay 1973).

The increased attention paid by critical theorists to so-called superstructural phenomena was not, however, a retreat from either the principles of historical materialism or the be-

---

example of ill-advised efforts to "break on through to the other side" of the revolution by means of guerrilla warfare, which succeeded only in inviting repressive measures, even as it destroyed the credibility of Movement pronunciations in favor of participatory democracy.

lief in the extraordinary importance of economic relationships in shaping societies. Instead, as Horkheimer (1972, 24) forcefully argued, this move reflected a concern that social theory in general, and vulgar Marxism in particular, gave too *little* emphasis to the influence of economic relationships by restricting attention to the economic realm. In effect this underestimated the effect of economic relations, the ramifications of which extended to *all* spheres of society in the epoch of advanced captialism. Consequently, it was necessary for critical theorists to expose the pervasiveness of domination so as to further the enlightenment project.

That is, the broadening of social theory to include the *totality* of social relationships was necessary in order to comprehend both the objective possibilities for, and subjective conditions of, an emancipated society. For critical theory to be a material force, it had to provide an adequate analysis of the extent of domination, and the dynamic tendencies that might, once grasped, lead men and women to eliminate historically unnecessary forms of domination.

The concept of totality referred to the same range of phenomena that students and other radicals tried to capture under the rubric of *the System*. However, in most of their analyses the System went largely unanalyzed. It was taken for granted in discussions that were primarily concerned with rejecting the System in favor of a "free society," variously understood. The immorality of the System seemed obvious, and the choice of freedom so natural that it did not seem necessary to inquire too deeply into the processes by which the System was produced and maintained.[3] As a result most of the intellectual leaders of the Movement never fully grasped the pervasive influence of "instrumental" modes of thought and action in the dominant culture—and even within

[3] Even where the immorality of the System was not obvious, it could be made so, thereby making the choice clear. The underlying logic of this orientation was consistent with that which informed nonviolent approaches to civil rights: an appeal to reason and morality was all that was needed to deflect the dominant culture from its worst tendencies. Cf. Chapter Nine.

the counterculture itself. The free society of alternative life styles was, after all, conceived in an affluent society in which problems of scarcity seemed remote, and precisely for this reason the New Left was impatient with the System's failure to respond to the unmet needs of people—at home and abroad. The presence of poverty amidst plenty symbolized the irrationality of a System that claimed democratic status, while it failed to provide benefits to those in need.

Of course, this analysis of the situation deflected attention from the conditions underlying affluence, even as it made the extension of consumer democracy a credible response by the System. However, a more radical critique of the affluent society was possible, one focused less on the exclusive features of the affluent society that on certain inclusive aspects of it. Such objections could not be refuted by the System's efforts to become less exclusive, and so represented a stronger test of the insusceptibility of the Establishment top criticism.

III

THE THEORETICAL shortcomings of countercultural analyses of contemporary society are especially apparent in books like Charles Reich's *The Greening of America*, which quickly became one of the sacred texts of the Movement, despite the fact that people like Marcuse ridiculed it as "the Establishment version of the great rebellion" (Kātz 1982, 189).

Reich's work bears a superficial resemblance to Marcuse's analyses, at least insofar as it deals with the unreasonable aspects of an affluent society thoroughly imbued with technocratic values. For Reich:

The great question of these times is how to live in and with a technological society; what mind and what way of life can preserve man's humanity and his very existence against the domination of the forces he has created. This question is at the root of the American crisis, beneath all the immediate issues of lawlessness, poverty, meaninglessness, and war. It is this question to which America's new generation is beginning to discover an answer, an answer based on a renewal of life that carries the hope of restoring us to our sources and ourselves. (1970, 16)

That answer, of course, was the development of a new outlook—"Consciousness III." Consciousness III did not involve a repudiation of technology or economic growth; indeed, it presupposed "the present state of technology, and could not have arisen without it" (ibid., 18). Therefore, Consciousness III was not equivalent to the "romantic" criticisms of the affluent society made by, say, Theodore Roszak in *The Making of a Counterculture* (1969) or *Where the Wasteland Ends* (1973). Instead, Consciousness III

seeks to transcend science and technology, to restore them to their proper place as tools of man rather than as the determinants of man's existence. It is by no means anti-technological, it does not want to break machines, but it does not want machines to run men. It makes the wholly rational assertion that machines should do the bidding of man, of man who knows and respects his own nature and the natural order of which he is a part. (Reich 1970, 382–383)

According to Reich it was necessary to restore science and technology to their proper place because they had assumed a domineering role in the Corporate State of the later part of the twentieth century.[4] Consciousness III arose out of the unnecessary betrayal of human life by the Corporate State and the technocratic values embedded in it. It was the "product of two interacting forces: the promise of life that is made to young Americans by all of our affluence, technology, liberation and ideals, and the threat to that promise posed by

[4] The Corporate State was Reich's version of "the System": it referred to a political economy in which private and public power were organized so as to pursue a single (*sic*) value—"the value of technology-organization-efficiency-growth-progress" (Reich 1970, 94–95).

everything from neon ugliness and boring jobs to the Vietnam War and the shadow of nuclear holocaust" (ibid., 234).

In the Corporate State machines did not do the bidding of humans; humans did the bidding of machines insofar as their lives were organized around the technological imperatives of mass production and consumption. The irrationality of the Corporate State consisted of this reversal of the proper relationship between humans and machines, and the corresponding alienation of men and women from a world of their own making. It was necessary to repudiate the Corporate State in all its irrationality, and to choose the rationality of a society in which science and technology were put in their "proper place" for true liberation to be realized.

Reich and other critics of the technocratic society agreed that such a choice was in fact conceivable; the material conditions for "the greening of America" had already developed. The undeniable advance of science and technology had so enhanced the nation's ability to produce necessary goods and services that the age of scarcity had all but ended, and with it the necessity of sublimating individual needs and wants to social imperatives. The repression engendered by these imperatives, e.g. deferred gratification and the work ethic, which once sustained collective life, was now superfluous and could be eliminated without substantially reducing the standard of living enjoyed by the majority of Americans. As a result, the sphere of freedom could expand, while the sphere of necessity contracted by virtue of the increased productivity made possible by technological advances.

This revolution in needs and motivation was essential, "for culture controls the economic and political machine, and not vice versa" (ibid., 329). A change in values was, therefore, a necessary prelude to successful revolution of any sort. It transcended even the class struggle, for in the Corporate State "we are all the proletariat, and there is no longer any ruling class except the machine itself" (ibid., 334). Hence, it was now in the interest of everyone to regain control of his or her

destiny by refusing to accept the values implicit in (and necessary for) the Corporate State.

A "revolution by consciousness can be accomplished when
enough individuals change that part of their lives" having to
do with the acceptance of technocratic values (ibid., 343).
That is because "the Corporate State runs by means of a willing producer, who desires status, and a willing consumer,
who desires what the State makes him want." But if a revolution by consciousness takes place, the ideological underpinnings of the Corporate State vanish, and new possibilities
emerge. Then the Corporate State "can no longer sell people
things to satisfy any but *real* needs, which means that the
consumer has regained power over what is produced. And it
can no longer get anyone to work except for *real* satisfactions,
which means that the status system is at an end, and people
within organizations regain power over the organizations and
structures of society" (ibid., 329; my emphases).

Thus, the replacement of the Corporate State by one subject to human control begins "the moment the individual
frees himself from automatic acceptance of the imperatives of
society and the false consciousness which society imposes."
That permits the individual "to build his own philosophy and
values, his own life style, and his own culture from a new
beginning" (ibid., 241). Hence, Consciousness III and the
revolution it entails are "epitomized in the concept of 'choosing a life style'; the idea that an individual need not accept
the pattern that society has formed for him, but may make
his own choice" (ibid., 395).

Moreover, this choice in favor of a society in which science
and technology were put in their proper place was already
being made by a substantial number of people who effectively
joined the counterculture by selecting alternative life styles.
Jean-François Revel, a latter-day French observer of American culture, observed that, in contrast to Europe, the "revolution" had already begun in the U.S.: American youth "is
actually *creating* a revolution in place of, and prior to, visu-
alizing a revolution" according to preconceived notions (1971,

235). The revolutionary transformation of the technocratic society was preceeding apace "without Marx or Jesus" in the
United States.[5]

Because they proceeded without Marx or Jesus, young
American revolutionaries went forth without the wisdom of
either. Reich's reduction of revolution to the act of "choosing
a lifestyle" only aggravated the problem by ignoring the man-
ifold constraints that governed personal choices in this era, as
in any other. As Marx knew, "men make their own history,
but they do not make it under circumstances chosen by themselves, but under circumstances directly found, given and
transmitted from the past. The tradition of all the dead generations weighs like a nightmare on the brain of the living"
(Marx and Engels 1972, 437). Only by neglecting the "weight
of tradition" could Reich conclude that the destruction of the
Corporate State might be accomplished "without violence,
without seizure of political power, without overthrow of any
existing group of people"—in short, without altering anything
but minds (Reich 1970, 327).

Of course, Reich assumed that by altering their minds
American revolutionaries would also alter the conduct of their
lives, since beliefs constituted, in part, the web of relations
in which they found themselves enmeshed. However, Reich
never seriously entertained the possibility that American so-

[5] Revel explained the difference this way: "Revolution is not a settling of
accounts with the past, but with the future. American revolutionaries sense
this; and that it is the reason for American originality in comparison to Europe" (1971, 235). In Europe would-be revolutionaries were preoccupied
with their relation to earlier revolutionary movements, especially those of
Marxist persuasion, whereas their American counterparts broke with the past
in the name of the future.

This orientation toward the future was not peculiar to the counterculture
movement of the 1960s. R.W.B. Lewis (1955) traces the proclivity of nineteenth-century Americans to situate themselves always at the beginning of
history, having no history of their own that might constrain them. This "innocence of Adam" (whose *history* began after expulsion from the Garden of
Eden) has its analogue in the various "city on a hill" interpretations of American colonization.

ciety had become so thoroughly "one-dimensional" in orientation that a revolution by consciousness was no longer a genuine possibility. The idea of a "totalitarian democracy" in which the toleration of alternative life styles and opinions might become a repressive force, rather than a liberating practice, apparently did not occur to him. It was left to Herbert Marcuse to consider that frightening prospect.

IV

HERBERT MARCUSE, the chief "guru" of the counterculture during the 1960s, joined Reich in condemning technocratic modes of thought and action.[6] Both Marcuse and Reich did, of course, condemn the inegalitarian aspects of the affluent society, and so were critical of its exclusive features. However, their denunciations of the totalitarian, i.e. inclusive, aspects of the affluent society were far more compelling and consequential, insofar as they could not be answered by a simple extension of consumer democracy, which, if anything, strengthened their case vis-à-vis the domination of technology and technological values.

Marcuse's analysis of the System as an apparently seamless web of domination in which all are caught was presented in *One-Dimensional Man*, published in 1964. His analysis of totalitarianism in the U.S.S.R. appeared in *Soviet Marxism*, which was published in 1958. Taken together these two books outline the pervasive influence of "technological reason" in the modern industrial world, i.e. a world in which collective decision-making is reduced to a consideration of policies designed to promote an administrative system, the necessity (and desirability) of which was taken for granted.

Marcuse did not join the "romantic" critics of industrial society, as did many of his contemporaries. He embraced the

---

[6] Young (1977) reviews Marcuse's intellectual influence on the Movement in comparison with that of other intellectuals, e.g. C. Wright Mills, Norman O. Brown, and Charles Reich, as well as "indigenous" theorists within the Movement itself.

potential for liberation that was bound up with technological progress and the growth of scientific knowledge. At the same time he decried the way in which the application of that knowledge resulted in the identification of liberation with material abundance, and the concomitant subordination of human needs to those of a system oriented exclusively toward the provision of consumer goods.[7]

This was *not* an intrinsic feature of scientific rationality, and so the repudiation of the narrow applications of science in the affluent society did not entail a rejection of science per se. As Leiss (1974) shows, Marcuse conceded that modern science is instrumental in a certain sense, but that did not mean that it was necessarily bound to technology as an instrument of political domination. That depended on the social setting in which science operated. In a context different from that of advanced capitalism, scientific rationality could become a force for the nonrepressive mastery of nature, i.e. a mastery that did not require domination over human beings as a precondition for pacifying nature in the struggle for existence.

In that case, "the new science would be guided by goals of peace, happiness, and the beautification of the environment in an ongoing process of rational discourse and interaction among scientists and nonscientists. The progress of its specific internal rationality would be affected only insofar as these new goals would produce different priorities in the allocations of resources for research and experimentation" (ibid., 208–209). Science would then serve human needs, rather than powerful interests.

That was in marked contrast to the present science "whose tasks and problems are determined in a social setting of conflicts, wars, and perpetual ideological mobilization" (ibid., 208). In that context the very discoveries that made the affluent society possible made totalitarian forms of social organi-

---

[7] Kātz (1982, 168) reports that Irving Kristol felt obliged to point out to the readers of his review of *One-Dimensional Man* in *Fortune* magazine that Marcuse's portrayal of the material of life in the affluent society was meant to be *critical!*

zations necessary, insofar as they entailed the subordination of individuals' needs to system imperatives. The smooth functioning of the system required appropriate patterns of thought and action on the part of individuals, particularly in the economic realm. Where appropriate patterns of work, consumption, and, to a lesser extent, politics were absent, the system did not function well, and a growth rate sufficient to sustain the affluent society would not materialize. Thus, the same technological advances that improved our standard of living also (and at the same time) instituted new, more effective, and more pleasant forms of social control.

The inculcation of functional patterns of thought and action in the affluent society did not require force or coercion; they had become "second nature" to individuals in the affluent society. Marcuse believed that "certain cultural needs can 'sink down' into the biology of man . . . [and take] root in the organic structure of man, in his 'nature,' or rather 'second nature' " (1969, 20, n. 1).

Marcuse rested his hopes for an alternative society on the possibility that the need for freedom and creative expression of individuality had put down deep roots in the "second nature" of men and women and so would ultimately lead them to seek gratification in new, more congenial forms of social life. But he feared that such needs might be overwhelmed by other, less authentic "needs" generated by the System, needs that had already begun to imprison people in a totalitarian society:

> The so-called consumer economy and the politics of corporate capitalism have created a second nature of man which ties him libidinally and aggressively to the commodity form. The need for possessing, consuming, handling, and constantly renewing the gadgets, devices, instruments, engines, offered to and imposed upon people, for using these wares even at the danger of one's own destruction, has become a "biological" need in the sense just defined. The second nature of man thus militates against any change

that would disrupt and perhaps even abolish this dependence of man on a market ever more densely filled with
merchandise—abolish his existence as a consumer consum-
ing himself in buying and selling. The needs generated by
this system are thus eminently stabilizing, conservative
needs: the counter-revolution anchored in the instinctual
structure. (ibid., 20–21)

In the one-dimensional society, then, the fulfillment of
needs is no longer the primary issue: "What is now at stake
are the needs themselves. At this stage, the question is no
longer: how can the individual satisfy his own needs without
hurting others, but rather: how can he satisfy his needs without hurting himself, without reproducing, through his aspirations and satisfactions, his dependence on an exploitative
apparatus which, in satisfying his needs, perpetuates his servitude?" (ibid., 14).

For Marcuse, this was a historical question, both in the
sense of being momentous, and in terms of the possibility of
responding positively:

Is such a change in the "nature" of man conceivable? I
believe so, because technical progress has reached a stage
in which reality no longer need be defined by the debilitating competition for social survival and advancement.
. . . The growth of the productive forces suggests possibilities of human liberty very different from, and beyond
those envisaged at the earlier stage. Moreover, these real
possibilities suggest that the gap which separates a free society from the existing societies would be wider and deeper
precisely to the degree to which the repressive power and
productivity of the latter shape man and his environment
in their image and interest. (ibid., 14–15)

Against the tendency to deny the possibilities for liberation
that were present in technological development, it was necessary to utter the Great Refusal to the reality principle that
governed the affluent society and made criticism of it seem

unreasonable. It was necessary to insist on the "truth of imagination": "The truth of imagination relates not only to the past
but also to the future: the forms of freedom and happiness
which it invokes claim to deliver the historical *reality*. In its
refusal to accept as final the limitations imposed upon freedom and happiness by the reality principle, in its refusal to
forget what *can be*, lies the critical function of phantasy"
(Marcuse 1955, 135).[8]

The Great Refusal was not simply an idealistic negation of
the affluent society, however. Although Marcuse shared other
critical theorists' disillusionment with the revolutionary potential of the working class, especially in light of European
experiences with fascism, he did not despair completely. He
searched for an alternative agent of liberation, and thought
he had found one in the "substratum of the outcasts and outsiders, the exploited and persecuted of other races and other
colors, the unemployed and unemployable" who remained
outside the System and so escaped its deadening influence
(Marcuse 1964, 256). It was because of those without hope
that hope for a movement capable of uttering the Great Refusal was reasonable.

An Essay on Liberation (1969) was an exploration of the
forces that may eventually lead to the Great Refusal.[9] The
Essay is Marcuse's analysis of the "new sensibility" toward
liberation that he thought the counterculture represented.
Marcuse was especially impressed by experimental uses of
language by the counterculture, for that represented an effort
to undo the "functionalization of language" by which one-dimensional patterns of thought and action were perpetuated.
The emergence of a new language was, therefore, evidence
that a *critical* dimension was being restored to the closed

[8] In this connection, Marcuse quotes André Breton, *Les Manifestes Du
Surrealisme*: "To reduce imagination to slavery—even if one's so-called happiness is at stake—means to violate all that one finds in one's inmost self of
ultimate justice. Imagination alone tells me what *can be*" (1955, 135).

[9] Kätz (1982, 184) notes that Marcuse's working title for this essay was
"Beyond One-Dimensional Man."

universe of discourse associated with instrumental modes of interaction: "It has been said that the degree to which a revolution is developing *qualitatively* different social conditions and relationships may perhaps be indicated by the development of a different language: the rupture with the continuum of domination must also be a rupture with the vocabulary of domination" (Marcuse 1969, 40).

In this connection Marcuse pointed to the methodical reversal of meaning by subcultures of Establishment terms like *grass, trip,* and so on, and the invention of new terms, e.g. *flower power,* all of which assumed connotations opposed to mainstream understandings and values. As suggestive as this tendency was, however, it was less significant than the construction of an idiom of Black Power by Hamilton, Carmichael, and others: "A far more subversive universe of discourse announces itself in the language of black militants. Here is systematic linguistic rebellion, which smashes the ideological context in which words are employed and defined, and places them into the opposite context—negation of the established one" (ibid., 41–42).[10]

In comparison with these developments in the black community, even the more visible activities of the student movement seemed less threatening to the dominant culture. After all, the student movement, although it was "revolutionary in its theory, in its instincts, and its ultimate goals," was "not a revolutionary force, perhaps not even an avant-garde so long as there are no masses capable and willing to follow." It was simply "the ferment of hope in the overpowering and stifling capitalist metropoles" (ibid., 65).

In some respects, the *Essay on Liberation* is the hopeful counterweight to the more despairing conclusions of *One-Dimensional Man.* However, even in *One-Dimensional Man* Marcuse argued that "democratic totalitarianism" was not im-

---

[10] Marcuse himself did this by popularizing such apparently contradictory notions as "repressive tolerance" and "democratic totalitarianism" to illustrate the ideological underpinnings of cherished notions in the affluent society.

pregnable: "[this book] will vacillate throughout between two contradictory hypotheses: (1) that advanced industrial society is capable of containing qualitative change for the foreseeable future; and (2) that forces and tendencies exist which may break this containment and explode the society. I do not think that a clear answer can be given. Both tendencies are there, side by side—and even the one in the other" (1964, xv).

The contradictory nature of the affluent society meant that one-dimensionality was not yet an accomplished fact. Thus, Marcuse did not advance the thesis of one-dimensionality in its strongest form, his critics claims to the contrary notwithstanding.[11] The very existence of the counterculture was testimony to the fact that liberation was conceivable, even if the odds against its realization were very long. Still, it was necessary to insist on this possibility, for to do otherwise was to concede the inescapability of "democratic totalitarianism," i.e. to reinforce one-dimensional patterns of thought and action by accepting them as unavoidable.

That is why Marcuse always contended that it was the duty of intellectuals to recall and preserve real historical possibilities that, according to the logic of the reality principle, have become utopian:

> The relegation of real possibilities to the no-man's land of utopia is itself an essential element of the ideology of the performance principle. If the construction of a non-repressive instinctual development is oriented, not on the sub-historical past, but on the historical present and mature civilization, the very notion of utopia loses its meaning. The negation of the performance principle emerges not against but *with* the progress of conscious rationality; it presupposes the highest maturity of civilization. (Marcuse 1955, 136)

[11] Hence, critical theory was not impossible, and Marcuse's critique of one-dimensional society was not necessarily inconsistent with his portrayal of it as a "society without opposition" characterized by a "paralysis of criticism," as some have argued.

The "historic break in the continuum of domination" implied by this negation certainly did not imply a total escape from domination of all sorts: "All the technological progress, the conquest of nature, the rationalization of man and society have not eliminated the necessity of alienated labor, the necessity of working mechanically, unpleasurably, in a manner that does not represent individual self-realization" (ibid., 203).

The "realm of necessity" is ultimately inescapable, even after the "historic break." However, its scope may be reduced, and more importantly, its domination of the "realm of freedom" may be reversed: No matter how justly and rationally the material production may be organized, it can never be a realm of freedom and gratification; but it can release time and energy for the free play of human faculties outside the realm of alienated labor. The more complete the alienation of labor, the greater the potential of freedom: total automation would be the optimum (ibid., 142).

That is because "it is the sphere outside labor which defines freedom and fulfillment, and it is the definition of the human existence in terms of this sphere which constitutes the negation of the performance principle." For that reason, a "historical turn in the direction of progress is rendered possible only on the basis of the achievements of the performance principle and of its potentialities, [and] it transforms the human existence in its entirety, including the work world and the struggle with nature" (ibid., 142).

In this way, "the expanding realm of freedom becomes truly a realm of play—of the free play of individual faculties. Thus liberated, they will generate new forms of realization and of discovering the world, which in turn will reshape the realm of necessity and the struggle for existence" (ibid., 204). In the truly rational society, then, a

> liberated consciousness would promote the development of a science and technology free to discover and realize the possibilities of things and men in the protection and gratification of life, playing with the potentialities of form and

matter for the attainment of this goal. Technique would then tend to become art, and art would tend to form reality: the opposition between imagination and reason, higher and lower faculties, poetic and scientific thought, would be invalidated. (Marcuse 1969, 32)

V

THE CONTRAST between repressive and unrepressive civilizations is the leitmotif of Marcuse's writings. However, that contrast is never made in concrete terms. Instead Marcuse merely sketches the broad outlines of a liberated society founded on a mastery of nature that is informed by human needs, rather than the imperatives of power. The form of the good society remains undetermined, as indeed it must if critical theory is to preserve the permanent possibility of criticism and revolution.

Nevertheless, we can perhaps catch a glimpse of the liberated society in the literature of this period, particularly where that literature incorporates technological improvements as the basis for liberation. Science fiction is one such genre, and the work of Ursula K. LeGuin is especially well suited for the task at hand, for it represents a kind of "future history" based on an understanding of already existing trends in modern society. The contrast between liberated and repressive civilizations is the principal theme of her enormously popular book, *The Dispossessed*, which sold millions of copies during the 1970s.[12] Although she does not refer to Marcuse in her work, LeGuin's characterization of the difference between the anarchist planet of Anarres and the "archist" world of Urras expresses concretely many of the themes raised in *Eros and Civilization*. As such, *The Dispossessed* provides a remarkable statement of the "possible worlds" latent in modern industrial society, worlds separated, as we shall see, only by revolutionary action.

---

[12] *The Dispossessed* won critical, as well as popular, acclaim, garnering both a Hugo Award and a Nebula Award in 1974.

One of the possible worlds that might emerge from contemporary civilization is, of course, a mere perpetuation of the status quo, and that is precisely what civilization on Urras represents. Two superpowers, A-Io and Thu, vie with one another for world domination in proxy wars conducted on "neutral" terrain in underdeveloped countries. A-Io is a "propertarian" society, ridden with economic inequality, while Thu is a socialist society in which the dreams of revolutionaries have been replaced by the realities of totalitarian state power. Consequently, both A-Io and Thu are "archist" societies in which order is maintained by the authorities, i.e. those who possess economic and political power, and who use that power to preserve their privileged position in society.

It is to A-Io that Shevak, a physicist from Annares, travels. Shevak has nearly perfected his General Temporal Theory, which would, among other things, completely revolutionize interstellar travel. The potential for domination on a galactic scale is not lost upon the powers that be in A-Io, who connive with one another to steal Shevak's theory and use it to their advantage.

Shevak's eagerness to share his ideas with his fellows makes this an easy strategy to pursue. For Shevak, the General Temporal Theory is a way of overcoming the distance between sentient beings separated in space and time. It is a means of bringing such beings closer together, not in the spirit of imperialism, but in the hope of solidarity. By revealing the essential unity of being, the General Temporal Theory promises to enlighten and liberate those who see only differences between themselves and others, and who respond with violence and repression to those whose values are alien to their own way of life. It is truly a critical theory, and Shevak's efforts to share it with others recapitulate the dilemmas that all would-be liberators must confront. Indeed, his adventures are the means by which the educator, Shevak, is educated in the art of revolution.

Shevak is aware, of course, that the power of his theory may be used to oppress, rather than liberate. Nevertheless, he secretly believes that the inhabitants of A-Io, or more precisely, their rulers, are not beyond redemption. Seduced by the unrepressed and opulent life style of the ruling class of A-Io, he naively persists in hoping that some sort of bargain may be struck with them, so that the benefits made possible by his General Temporal Theory might be enjoyed by all, rather than restricted to the privileged few. Eventually, his experiences in the underground revolution waged by the impoverished masses against the propertarian elite leads Shevak to abandon his delusion, to offer his "critical" theory to a more enlightened alien race, after which he returns home to Annares.

Annares is the other possible world or alternative life style contained in present industrial societies, for its inhabitants are the descendants of expatriates from Urras. They are the offspring of a previous generation of underground revolutionaries who, in exchange for their freedom, agreed to cease their war against the propertarians and quit the planet Urras. The Odonians, as the settlers of Annares are known, therefore represent the past accomplishments as well as the future possibilities that were present in the underground movement that was ruthlessly suppressed during Shevak's visit to Urras.

Indeed it was his concern over the need to sustain the revolutionary accomplishment of the founders of Annares that led Shevak to Urras in the first place. He did not go only as a missionary from Annares to Urras; he went in order *to return* to Annares. By returning, he reenacted the settlement of Annares, and so Shevak stumbled upon a way of renewing the revolutionary fervor of that first band of colonists who set out to make a brave new world founded on anarchistic principles.

A refounding of the revolutionary spirit was necessary, Shevak felt, because the ultimate example of an unrepressed society, the anarchist civilization of Annares, was in danger of succumbing to a new, more insidious form of repression, namely, conformity. The original settlement had not disintegrated into chaos, as the propertarian exponents of law and order predicted. The struggle to eke out a collective existence in an inhospitable environment insured against that. The plenitude enjoyed by the ruling class in A-Io was unknown on Annares, even though the level of technological development on the two planets was roughly the same. By the same token, the impoverishment of the masses of A-Io was also unknown, except when natural disasters forced that on everyone equally.[13]

LeGuin describes in great detail the orderly manner in which the Odonians conducted their individual and collective affairs without resort to laws and other instruments of coercion. Nonauthoritarian patterns of sexual gratification, childrearing, education, and employment characterize their society, in which the "surplus repression" of propertarianism is systematically eliminated. By comparison with their brethren on Urras, the inhabitants of Annares enjoy virtually unlimited freedom in the conduct of their daily lives and the satisfaction of their felt needs. Indeed, were it not for the scarcity of game and water on the planet Annares, any individual was free "to do one thing today and another tomorrow, to hunt in the morning, fish in the afternoon, rear cattle in the evening, criticize after dinner, just as I have a mind, without ever becoming hunter, fisherman, shepherd or critic!" as Marx hoped (Marx and Engels 1972, 124).

Free as it was, Odonian society was not without order. Though its inhabitants rejected orders and those who gave them, they did manage to organize collective endeavors and to support an elaborate division of labor. These activities were sustained by an ethic of functionalism, according to which all individuals understood themselves in terms of their contribution to the smooth functioning of the social organism. In this context the identity of individuals was shaped in the exercise of a freedom *to share* their talents with others, rather than by some relentless search for freedom *from* the demands of collective life on the members of society.

[13] This is an interesting example of the type of situation envisioned by Marcuse, in which the standard of living in a liberated society falls below that enjoyed during its repressive stages of development, precisely because of the resort to a less exploitative deployment of technological expertise.

As Shevak realized, however, an ethic of functionalism may easily become a potent weapon against nonconformity. When that happens, anarchy is transformed from a condition of liberation to one in which the tyranny of the majority reigns supreme via a kind of repressive tolerance. No power or oppressive force is as irresistible as the weight of the "free society" against an individual deviant, especially when deviance is viewed not simply as an aberration, but as "dysfunctional" to the collectivity.

Yet that is what Shevak had become. Even though he continued to do his share of manual labor and menial tasks and to practice Odonian customs, his persistent efforts to share his physics with other worlds threatened to destroy the isolation that made functional conformity so inescapable. His physics made it likely, even probable, that other mores, including those of A-Io, would become known to Odonians, many of whom feared the corrupting influence of that which their forbearers had struggled so hard to avoid.

That, of course, was precisely Shevak's "function" in Odonian civilization, namely, to reintroduce the revolutionary spirit that struggled against all forms of oppression and domination, including the repressive tendencies of the pressure to conform. Shevak's function, as he knew, was to be dysfunctional for a revolutionary society that had become complacent by virtue of its past accomplishments, and so had lost sight of its future possibilities. Odonian society was no longer revolutionary in Shevak's time, and his efforts to reinstill the spirit of permanent revolution composed the events portrayed in *The Dispossessed*.[14]

VI

LeGuin's science fiction contains few of the ordinary trappings of this literary genre; her future societies are not

---

[14] The title itself conveys this message: LeGuin's story is about those who spurn property and possession and must continually dispossess themselves of social practices that embody surplus repression, of whatever sort.

technological marvels, so much as they are political alternatives. Urras and Annares represent civilizations that we might become, depending on the choices we make under the circumstances that condition our life on earth. Those choices will determine the course of our future, and books like *The Dispossessed* try to anticipate that course in order to help us understand the consequences of the choices that now confront us.

The best science fiction, then, has a certain didactic quality to it. It aims to increase our capacity for looking into the future so as to understand the present a little better. Naturally, this assumes that our capacity for facing the future is capable of expansion—which implies that it may also contract, in the absence of the appropriate stimulation. It is ironic, then, that science fiction seems to be most popular in a culture that in some ways appears incapable of orienting itself toward the future, at least in its everyday life.

That, at least, was the judgment of Alvin Toffler in his enormously popular *Future Shock* (1971), a book that emphasized the impermanence of life in an affluent society, in contradistinction to the stability implied by some analyses of technological "reification."[15] "Future shock" was the temporal equivalent of culture shock. It was a condition of bewilderment, frustration, and disorientation induced by rapid and pervasive changes in social life. Future shock, as Toffler described it, was "the distress, both physical and psychological, that arises from an overload of the human organism's physical adaptive systems and its decision-making processes. Put more simply, future shock is the human response to overstimulation" (1971, 326).

This overstimulation was the inevitable result of the increasing transience, novelty, and diversity of human relations to things, places, people, organizations, and ideas. The entire

[15] Of course these two lines of argument need not be inconsistent, and indeed it may be that Toffler failed to appreciate the extent to which many changes take place within a broader context of social relations that is relatively permanent.

fabric of super-industrial society was subject to rapid change brought on by the "accelerative thrust" of technological and scientific innovations that literally transform the world in which men and women live. The continuous transformation of society meant, therefore, that human beings were constantly faced with new and increasingly more complex environments that demanded personal and social adaptation as the price of survival. Those who failed to adapt experienced future shock, and when an entire culture experiences future shock, it faced a generalized crisis of adaptation (ibid.).

The successful resolution of this crisis of adaptation by a culture depended on its response to it, particularly in the area of politics, since the state in modern societies has assumed responsibility for steering or guiding the system. Of course, a successful response required much more then normal or even extraordinary action by politicians. It required a new kind of political technology altogether, since the existing mode of governance was itself part of the *generalized* crisis of adaptation to future shock.

Toffler was quite explicit on this point. "Simply put, the political technology of the industrial age [representative government] is no longer appropriate for the new civilization taking form around us." Representative government had become obsolete because it is "structurally incapable of making competent decisions about the world we inhabit." Predicated as it was on the existence of a relatively high degree of social homogeneity, this technology for manufacturing collective decisions could not operate effectively in the highly diversified society made possible by technological development. Consequently, "it should hardly surprise us if the result of this mismatch between our decisional technology and the decisonal environment is a cacophanous confusion, countless self-canceling decisions, noise, fury, and gross ineptitude" (Toffler 1978a, xiii–xv).

Moreover, "if we add to the pressures generated by diversity those that arise from the *acceleration* of change, we drastically scale up the intensity of the decisional crisis . . . [what we then witness] is crushing decisional overload—in short, *political* future shock." The situation could only be overcome by either further centralization of power, in the hope of outrunning the acceleration of complexity, or by the decentralization of power, which may reduce the decision load on the "center" by sharing it with more people (ibid., xvi–xvii; my emphasis).

For Toffler the first "solution" led to "ever-greater centralization, technocracy, and totalitarianism," while the second leads toward "a new, more advanced level of democracy." It was a myth, he argued, that "centralism of totalitarian decision-making is 'efficient' while democracy only 'muddles through.' " Rather, democracy, by "increasing channels for feedback, and especially negative feedback, between citizens and government decision-makers decreases the risk of error. It also meant that errors, once made, can be more quickly and cheaply corrected . . . Democracy, in this sense, is not just theoretically 'nice'—it is highly 'efficient' " (ibid., xviii).

That also explained the superiority of democratic political technologies over those that depended upon "experts" for guidance. The latter were less efficient, and more prone to error in determining the shape of the future, than were democracies, because they made inadequate provision for corrective feedback mechanisms. This did not mean that democracy and technology were antagonistic, however:

> We certainly need experts and specialists; they are indispensable, in fact. But in anticipatory democracy, goals are not set by elites or experts alone. . . . where futures activity exists, we need to open it to all sectors of society, making a special effort to involve women, the poor, working people, minority groups, young and old—and to involve them at all levels of leadership as well. (Toffler 1978b, 362)

The need to include all sectors of society in futures activity was justified by Toffler on both theoretical and practical grounds. With respect to the former, the logic of cybernetic collective decision-making augured in favor of maximum feasible participation, as it were. A multiplication of opportunities for participation meant that feedback would be increased, and increased feedback enhanced the likelihood that errors would be detected, and once detected, corrected.

Moreover, "as the number of social components grows and change makes the whole system less stable, it becomes less and less possible to ignore the demands of political minorities. . . . in the new, fast-paced cybernetic society, [these minorities] can, by sabotage, strike, or a thousand other means, disrupt the entire system." Consequently, "the best way to deal with angry or recalcitrant minorities is to open the system further, bringing them into it as full partners, permitting them to participate in social goal-setting." Incorporation was a way of "wiring them into the system, making them a part of the guidance machinery of the society" by which stabilization was assured (Toffler 1971, 476–477, 477, 479).

By itself, though, more democracy was not enough. Democracy must also be future-oriented: "Participation without future consciousness is not democracy at all; it is a mockery of democracy. In leaving the long-range issues to others by default, citizens groups wind up participating—if at all—in the making of purely implementary decisions, squabbling over how to carry out the long-range designs of others" (Toffler 1978a, xviii). Indeed, "a democracy that doesn't anticipate the future cannot survive. A society that is good at anticipating but allows the future to be captured by elites is no longer a democracy. As we move into the future, anticipatory democracies will be the only surviving kind" (Toffler 1978b, 365). Hence, democracy must be *anticipatory*: it must fuse citizen feedback with future consciousness: "Anticipatory democracy is a process—a way of reaching decisions that determine our future. . . . the term 'anticipatory' stresses the need for greater attention to the long range future. The term 'democracy' stresses the need for vastly increased popular participation and feedback" (ibid., 361–362).

Anticipatory democracy is, therefore, not so much about politics as it is about "metapolitics," or the process of making democratic political decisions for the future. It is "a continuing plebiscite on the future" (Toffler 1971, 478). That plebiscite would actually be carried on in "social future assemblies" in which participants would make reasonably informed choices among alternative futures, based on information supplied by a technical staff. "In this way, each assembly might arrive, in the end, not merely in vaguely expressed disjointed hopes, but at coherent statements of priorities for tomorrow—posed in terms that could be compared with the goal statements of other groups" (ibid., 481).

Toffler believed that this process of social assessment "would brace and cleanse a population weary to death of technical discussions of how to get someplace it is not sure it wants to go." Moreover "by focusing public attention for once on long-range goals rather than immediate programs alone, by asking people to choose a preferable future from among a range of alternative possibilities, these assemblies could dramatize the possibilities for humanizing the future." In effect this would allow humans to "assume conscious control of evolution itself . . . shaping tomorrow . . . [by] design[ing] the future" (ibid., 484–485).

Thus, the ultimate objective of social futurism was the subjection of the process of social evolution itself to conscious human guidance via political cybernetics, "for this is the supreme instant, the turning point in history at which man either vanquishes the processes of change or vanishes, at which, from being the unconscious puppet of evolution he becomes either its victim or its master" (ibid., 485–486).

VII

THE SENSE of urgency with respect to the future was something that Marcuse and Reich shared with Toffler, despite the obvious differences in their analyses of the affluent society. All three sensed certain unrealized possibilities in American society during the time at which they wrote, and they were anxious to see those possibilities acted upon "before it was too late," i.e. before they were foreclosed by other, less human possibilities. Liberation seemed to hang in the balance for them, and indeed for many of their contemporaries.

Nevertheless, in their dissatisfaction with the status quo, and especially in their suggestions for moving toward an alternative society, Reich, Marcuse, and Toffler all took certain aspects of the affluent society for granted. Despite their criticisms of it, all seemed reasonably confident that problems of scarcity had more or less been solved by technological advances, and that the social conflicts peculiar to societies in which scarcity reigned had been rendered moot. Conflicting values remained of course, but they involved a historically different set of choices than those of earlier, less advanced societies.

By the mid seventies, however, that confidence seemed misplaced, as the U.S. economy ceased to grow as rapidly as it had during the sixties and inflation sapped its vitality. The recrudescence of scarcity shifted attention from the future and its prospects back to the present and its problems as remedies for "stagflation" were sought to no avail. In the process the importance of sustained economic growth, not only for futuristically inclined theorists, but also for the legitimacy of existing institutions, became apparent. Ironically, this made contemporary American society more vulnerable—or susceptible, as Marcuse would have it—to change than this group of theorists had perhaps thought possible, but at the same time it undercut their hopes for a future that represented a stage of development beyond scarcity.

Ironically, Marcuse's own analysis pointed toward this unsuspected possibility. Marcuse argued that the "performance principle" reigned supreme in affluent societies such as the United States. The actions of individuals in the areas of work, leisure, and politics were consistently subordinated to the requirements of the System itself. Only behavior that was functional for the operation of the System was rewarded, and so long as the System was able to provide the necessary rewards, appropriate patterns of thought and action were reproduced and even reinforced. The System was therefore self-sustaining: system imperatives became more or less completely internalized by individuals whose "second nature" performed essential stabilizing functions.

But the System itself was subject to the very same performance principle that governed citizens in the affluent society. Unless the System performed sufficiently well to produce those goods and services that served as rewards for appropriate actions, the stability of the System was in jeopardy. Without rewards individuals might not act according to System imperatives. Existing patterns of activity in the workplace, marketplace, and political arena might crumble, making it even more difficult for the System to perform in the appointed ways, thereby compounding the difficulty of reestablishing equilibrium. A crisis might then emerge as the System and its failures were subjected to the "performance principle" and alternative "systems" considered.

The vulnerability of the System to such critical evaluations was clearly revealed during the seventies as stagflation impaired its ability to sustain the increasing level of affluence to which people had become accustomed. Elected politicians in particular came under heavy fire for promising, and then failing, to provide the necessary leadership for solving economic problems. Elections became plebiscites on economic performance, and various "misery indices" appeared and quickly became rough-and-ready measures for evaluating performance and deciding elections.[16]

However, it was not just politicians who were held accountable for the System's relatively poor performance. The successive failure of politicians from either major political party to implement effective policies eventually raised questions about the regime itself. The failure of governors was ultimately linked to purported flaws in the structure of governance, and a "crisis of democracy" emerged in the U.S., and elsewhere. This will be the subject of the next chapter.

[16] The relationship between economic performance and support for congressional candidates is considered by Hibbing and Alford (1981), who also review past research in this area. Hibbs (1982) examines the impact of macroeconomic considerations, e.g. inflation and unemployment, on presidential popularity.

CHAPTER ELEVEN

The Crisis of Liberal Democracy

I

THE REEMERGENCE of scarcity as a political issue clearly revealed the extent to which the legitimacy of liberal democratic regimes was related to their economic performance. In the words of Oakeshott, "Governments have become inclined to commend themselves to their subjects merely in terms of their power and incidental achievements, and their subjects have become inclined to look only for this recommendation" when evaluating them (1975, 192). Economic growth was one of the most salient of these "incidental achievements" of liberal democratic regimes (or any regime, for that matter). Ironically, this was especially true in affluent societies, where economic growth became a political imperative of the first order.[1]

Growth was essential if affluence was to be extended, both to groups previously excluded from the benefits of affluence, and to consumers interested in improving their standard of living. In the absence of growth, neither of these objectives could be accomplished without engaging in highly conflictual policies of income redistribution. Then, too, high rates of real growth made industrial conflict easier to resolve. Wage increases could be demanded and granted, without reducing profit margins, so long as they could be offset by increased productivity and sales. That made class conflict seem less rel-

[1] Connolly (1981) discusses the "imperative of growth" in relation to the "social infrastructure of consumption" that characterizes what I have called consumer democracy. Hence I shall confine myself to a general overview of the problem, since my main purpose is not to show that there is an imperative of growth, but rather to assess its consequences for democratic ideologies.

evant to discussions about democracy and reaffirmed the plausibility of a common interest in continuous consumption as a foundation for political decision-making.

In the U.S., economic growth was particularly important after the commencement of the War on Poverty and the expansion of social welfare spending during the Johnson administration. Entitlement programs multiplied and an increasing number of people joined the ranks of consumer democrats, if not under their own purchasing power, then by virtue of government transfer payments (Huntington 1975). Those who were prevented from falling below the poverty level, as well as those who were raised above it, by "safety net" programs were "proof" that the System was oriented toward the establishment of a more humane order, and not just an improvement in the aggregate standard of living.[2]

Naturally, the welfare state was expensive to maintain. It required relatively high rates of sustained economic growth in order to provide the necessary revenues for increased spending on social welfare. As Connolly observes,

> The welfare state cannot accumulate the revenues it needs
> to redress the adverse effects of private enterprise unless
> the private system provides it with a large tax dividend;

[2] See Levitan and Taggart (1976) for a defense of the ameliorative accomplishments of the welfare state. Thurow (1980) offers a more cautious interpretation, claiming that government merely succeeded in preventing the gap between rich and poor from growing wider, without actually reducing it.

Piven and Cloward (1971) claim that the expansion of the welfare state during this period was simply a device for controlling potentially radical groups by offering them a very small stake in the system. They later argue that the contraction of the welfare state under the Reagan administration must be understood in terms of the need to reduce "unproductive" social spending and to create more economic insecurity so as to increase profit margins and spur investment (Piven and Cloward 1982). Lower taxes and cheaper wage bills would, of course, accomplish the first of these objectives, but not the second, unless attractive investment opportunities present themselves (Mandel 1976).

Cf. Gilder (1981) for a conservative critique of the welfare state, although even he does not suggest its complete dismantling.

and the tax dividend depends on the success of economic expansion in the private sector. The welfare state is thus deeply dependent on the system it seeks to regulate; it must subsidize and nourish the private economy even while it strives to tame and regulate it. (1981, 11)

In the absence of growth, revenues must come from monies that would otherwise have been allocated to defense, or from tax increases. Alternatively, the activities of the welfare state have to be restricted, or else deficit spending results. Over the long run this generates inflationary pressures that cause economic stagnation and perhaps even reduced growth rates, further compounding the problem.[3]

Thus growth was essential if the sort of criticism that was raised by counterculture movements against the System during the 1960s was to be met without engendering opposition from taxpaying members of the dominant culture. Growth enabled consumer democracy to defeat rival, moralistic interpretations of democracy by appealing to the general interest of all classes in preserving a system that "delivered the goods" to a very substantial and increasing portion of the population.

However, affluence did not *simply* co-opt dissent, although that may have been an important ingredient in its success. By itself affluence is not a sufficient basis for establishing the legitimacy of a social order. That has always required a *moral* tradition from which arguments in favor of liberal democratic regimes might be drawn. As Nelson (1980) observes, neither democracy in general, nor particular versions of democracy are self-justifying. Their validity depends on the prior acceptance of an independent account of what is morally right or just, and a demonstration that democratic institutions, variously defined, are necessary for the realization of such ethical ends.

Charles Taylor has tried to characterize the moral substra-

[3] Of course, this is precisely what happened, once growth slowed during the seventies.

tum upon which liberal democratic regimes like that in the
United States depend in terms of a peculiarly modern orientation. As summarized by Taylor, this modern outlook identifies the good life in terms of institutions that permit individuals to pursue their own interests in reasonable ways and
with some measure of success. In practice this means that all
individuals enjoy certain rights to participate in the process
of collective decision-making, and to make certain claims on
the product of their labor. The modern subject is, therefore,
"an equal rights–bearer." Having this status "is part of what
sustains one's identity"; without it "identity must either
flounder or the predicament is experienced as intolerable"
(Taylor 1981, 114–115).

The denial of this status in practice has, therefore, consistently generated moral critiques of social institutions and
practices that are judged to be dehumanizing, i.e. that deny
the status of equal rights–bearers to particular groups in society. Usually, however, the affirmation of this status in societies experiencing economic growth and universal suffrage
has amounted to a prima facie case for the legitimacy of existing institutions and practices. After all, the achievement of
sustained growth was more than a material accomplishment;
it was a moral one as well, at least insofar as it was accompanied by the extension of at least some of its benefits to
those who had not previously enjoyed the fruits of membership in society. To the extent that "disadvantaged" people
shared in the proceeds of economic growth, their status as
modern subjects enjoying equal rights was affirmed. At the
same time, the social arrangements that seemed to make the
extension of equality possible were vindicated and deemed
worthy of allegiance.[4]

---

[4] Even widely enjoyed affluence may not guarantee the legitimacy of the
regime in power. Growth is and always has been subject to a related criticism. A society in which this growth reigns "is in trouble if it stands self-
convicted, in the eyes of its members, of pure materialism, that is of aiming
purely at material enrichment" (Taylor 1981, 117). This is particularly true
when the achievement of "material enrichment" depends on forms of social

Of course the strength of this vindication of the status quo depended on the extent to which disadvantaged groups actually shared in the benefits of growth and prosperity. On that score, the extension of the welfare state during the Great Society and its aftermath seemed to represent significant progress, although in retrospect both the size of those gains and their permanence have been questioned.[5] As growth slowed, however, pressing questions of equity could no longer be resolved without entering the contentious area of redistributive policies. The costs of incorporating new groups into society and extending to them the status of equal rights–bearers had to be taken from the share of already incorporated groups via increased taxation. Otherwise a fiscal crisis could not be averted (O'Connor 1973).

The trade-off between legitimacy and fiscal solvency gradually became evident during the 1970s. To extend the welfare state, and so incorporate more groups as equal rights–bearers, was exceedingly costly in fiscal terms, and in the absence of growth this could only be accomplished over the resistance of taxpayers. On the other hand, the failure of government to incorporate new groups represented a standing challenge to the legitimacy of existing arrangements, insofar as it denied those groups their proper status in modern society. The gradual contraction of the welfare state under the Reagan administration suggests the way in which this tension was eventually resolved in the U.S. (Piven and Cloward 1982).

---

organization that seem purely instrumental and exploitative of human beings and natural resources. Then the critique of materialism and the institutions that sustain it finds special force and attraction.

[5] Connolly (1979; 1981) argues that the recognition of the legitimate claims or entitlements of disadvantaged groups upon the system seems to devalue the accomplishments of workers motivated by the achievement ethic. This is most obvious in the redistribution of income under zero-sum conditions, but it is implicit in any welfare program of entitlements in which deserts are not linked to contributions, but to status (e.g. citizenship). Connolly presents this as an obstacle to be recognized and overcome by those interested in welfare reform, but Orwin (1983) defends the creed of earned entitlements on liberal philosophical grounds.

Not surprisingly the contradictory imperatives of state action—growth and legitimacy—eventually led to a "crisis situation" in which the capacity of liberal democratic regimes to satisfy *either* consideration was questioned by those on the right as well as those on the left. A new contest over the meaning of democracy was in the offing as the basic tension between liberal and democratic principles reemerged.

II

ONE SUGGESTION for resolving the tension between liberalism and democracy came from the so-called neoconservatives, who essentially proposed to make democracy safe for liberalism by further reducing the radical content of democratic ideals. According to the Trilateral Commission's report on *The Crisis of Democracy*, Western industrial nations in general are afflicted by a "democratic distemper" which threatens to undermine, and perhaps even destroy, their governability (Crozier 1975). Countercultures everywhere have inspired a democratic surge of expectations for more participation and greater equality among the citizens of these nations. The magnitude of this surge in demands is so large that no regime could possibly satisfy it. The frustration engendered by the inability of Western regimes to meet these expectations has led to a withdrawal of legitimacy that has further undermined these regimes' ability to respond to their citizens and govern effectively. Only by putting democracy into more realistic perspective, reducing its utopian content, and limiting its applicability, can the situation be reversed, and governability be restored to Western nations. Citizens, in other words, must become more "realistic" about liberal democratic regimes' capacity to satisfy their demands.[6]

[6] The emphasis on realism is consistent with most of what passes for democratic theory today. Sartori insists that the deontology of democracy, i.e. its utopian content, must be taken seriously only when it is used to criticize nondemocratic regimes. When it is deployed against regimes that are approximately democratic, however, this utopian content ought to be minimized, lest it begin to work against the very regimes it has called into exist-

The situation seems especially severe in the United States, where "the strength of democracy poses a problem for the governability of democracy in a way which is not the case elsewhere" (Huntington 1975, 115). Because political authority is weak in the U.S., at least by comparison with Western Europe and Japan, it is particularly vulnerable "during a creedal passion period of intense commitment to democratic and egalitarian ideals."[7] Unless some way of moderating these commitments to democracy and equality is found, "the danger of overloading the political system with demands which extend its functions and undermine its authority" would still remain (ibid., 114).

In other words, the "suicide of democracy" in the U.S. was a distinct possibility. As excessive demands for "more" democracy overwhelmed the System, its legitimacy was eroded, and demands for an alternative society arose. In this way democratic regimes might be toppled by the unrealistic demands of "the democracy," who might very well choose the efficiency of an authoritarian regime over the "muddling through" of democracy. Hence, democratic "suicide is more likely to be the product of overindulgence than of any other cause. A value which is normally good in itself is not neces-

---

ence (Sartori [1962] 1973, 65). Hence, he urges the adoption of a scientific concept of democracy.

However, C. B. Macpherson (1984) argues that realism does not necessarily exhaust the meaning of science, as Sartori and other theorists of democratic elitism aver (Bachrach 1967). At its best, science is also visionary, if not utopian: witness the work of Galileo, Copernicus, Newton, Einstein, and other scientific "revolutionaries" (Kuhn 1962). To the extent that democratic theory can envision "realistic" possibilities for making societies more democratic than they now are, it need not settle for the decidedly unvisionary and apologetic role advocated by Sartori.

[7] Huntington later provided a general overview of American history in terms of these periods of "creedal passion" that set off "political earthquakes" with profound repercussions for political institutions and practices. While conceding the value of certain reforms engendered during these periods, he worried that "given the perversity of reform, moral extremism in pursuit of liberal democracy could generate a strong tide toward authoritarian efficiency," i.e. the death of democracy by suicide (1981, 232).

sarily optimized when it is maximized. . . . There are also potentially desirable limits to the indefinite extension of democracy. Democracy will have a longer life if it has a more balanced existence" (ibid., 115). Only if the inclusion of previously excluded groups in the benefits of consumer democracy was accompanied by greater self-restraint on the part of all groups could the problem be eased.

A similar sort of argument was presented by Daniel Bell (1976). In *The Cultural Contradictions of Capitalism* Bell argues that the union of economic and political liberalism implicit in liberal democracy is highly unstable. The pressures toward mass consumption inherent in capitalism have radically transformed the acquisitive impulse that lies at the heart of economic liberalism. Whereas this impulse had once been tempered by a religious asceticism and directed toward highly functional forms of economic activity, it has become an immoderate, hedonistic impulse toward self-gratification. Consumption has replaced production as the cultural pastime par excellence, thereby undermining the motivational foundation of capitalism itself. In this way, culture contradicts capitalism and threatens to destroy its dynamic qualities.

Moreover, Bell argues, this corruption of spirit has proved contagious, for self-aggrandizement has become the leading principle of politics, as well as economics. Gone is the tradition of *civitas*—"that spontaneous willingness to obey the law, to respect the rights of others, to forego the temptations of private enrichment at the expense of the public weal" (Bell 1976, 245). Interest group liberalism has taken its place as the new "public philosophy," though in truth it is a profoundly antipublic philosophy, insofar as it sacrifices all public concerns to private interests. Hence, the satisfaction of private interests becomes the normal mode of liberal democratic politics, just as it becomes the typical form of economic behavior.

The most pernicious effects of this corruption of politics are evident in the chronic susceptibility of liberal democracies to fiscal crises and inflation. As the state comes to be seen as a primary supplier of private wants, as well as public goods, expectations concerning entitlements abound, and demands for governmental redress increase without end. Indeed, liberal democratic governments quickly become "overloaded" as demands are no longer restrained by considerations of the public weal, and as citizens' willingness to pay for these entitlements via taxes is exceeded.

From such crises of governance come crises of legitimacy, for liberal democracies lack any convincing moral justification for *not* responding to these heightened demands. Democratic procedures formally guarantee virtually unlimited access to government. They depend, therefore, on restraint on the part of citizens as the primary means for avoiding "overload" situations. When citizens are no longer restrained by cultural dispositions toward the common weal, liberal democracies are left defenseless, and their subsequent inability to respond to all demands necessarily engenders frustration and even anomie.

The similarities between this argument and that of the Trilateral Commission are apparent. But the conclusions Bell draws are rather different from those of Crozier and his colleagues. For Bell the roots of the crisis are to be found in the eclipse of political liberalism by economic liberalism (ibid., 27). The latter is incapable of supplying a moral foundation for democratic decision-making. Since politics is now only one more arena of contestation over who gets what, when, and how, no outcome has any special merit or preferred status. In particular, decisions "in the public interest" cannot claim superiority over those of any other interests, because there is no identifiable public interest under economic liberalism. Hence, there is no restraint on the part of citizens who press their demands on government far past the point at which it can ensure the survival of the community.[8]

Consequently, the crisis of liberal democracy is, for Bell, ultimately a crisis of morality, on which the fate of the com-

---

[8] This eclipse was documented in Chapter Nine, wherein the ascendance of a "classless" ideology of consumption was discussed.

munity depends. The restoration of the public interest to a preferred place in politics depends on the reinvigoration of political liberalism, which accepts the tension between public and private spheres without completely subordinating one to the other. In short, a new philosophy of the public household is needed if the harmony between liberalism and democracy is to be reestablished, and the legitimacy of liberal democratic regimes maintained.[9]

III

IF LIBERAL democracies are incapable of fulfilling the aspirations of their citizens, then trimming those aspirations may be one way of easing the situation, as Bell and, in a different way, the Trilateral Commission recommend. However, it is at least conceivable that the capacity of liberal democracies to respond to these aspirations might be enhanced, if present limits on this capacity may be relaxed.

This point is well-made by Peter Steinfels (1979), who concedes the existence of a crisis of democracy, while wondering if that crisis is not a sign of too little democracy, rather than an excess of it, as Crozier and colleagues would have it. In Steinfels' view, the origin of the crisis, and any solution to it, must be sought in those factors that prevent liberal democratic regimes from becoming more democratic. Consequently, the ideal of democracy still has a critical role to play, and that entails bringing the real world of democracy into closer conformity with the ideal world of democracy.

This way of putting it suggests that the crisis of democracy is actually a crisis of liberal democracy, for it is the liberalism implicit in the Trilateral Commission's Report that ultimately establishes the limits of what Western regimes may and may not "realistically" do. It is liberalism, in other words, that circumscribes these regimes' capacity to provide more opportunities for participation and greater equality—"more democ-

[9] For a similar analysis and recommendation, see Lowi (1969). Lowi presents his "juridical democracy" as the corrective to an overly self-indulgent liberalism.

racy"—in response to citizens' demands for them. Hence, the crisis of democracy must stem from the tension between liberalism and democracy, and any resolution of that crisis will depend on the resolution of this ideological tension.

That is the case that C. B. Macpherson makes. Macpherson, too, sees the predominance of the acquisitive side of liberalism—what he calls possessive individualism—as the cause of liberal democracies' inability to meet the democratic aspirations of their citizens. For it is possessive individualism, with its narrow conception of human needs and aspirations, and its excessively narrow-minded commitment to market economies as the proper mechanism for meeting those needs, that renders liberal democracies' achievements suspect both at home and abroad.

Indeed, it was Macpherson who sounded an early alarm about the growing contradiction between liberalism and democracy in the West. In a remarkable little book entitled *The Real World of Democracy* (1965), Macpherson made the rather startling claim that the contest between East and West would ultimately be waged on moral, rather than economic or military grounds. The contest, he said, was between competing conceptions of democracy, each claiming to offer the prospects for the full development of its citizenry's human potential. The regimes that best made good on this claim would enjoy, if not a hegemonic position, at least a moral advantage vis-à-vis regimes embodying alternative conceptions of democracy.

Macpherson's most troubling argument, however, centered on the likelihood that liberal democracies might be eclipsed by other democracies in this moral contest, unless significant improvements in the area of equality were made. For nonliberal democracies were succeeding in their efforts to reduce economic inequalities, and would, he argued, eventually turn toward the more tractable problem of insuring political liberty. Hence, the West was in danger of being overtaken by nations that advanced, and achieved, broader democratic claims than those associated with liberal democracy.

Moreover, Western liberal democracies seemed quite unprepared to meet these challenges in the real world of democracy, not least because they failed to take nonliberal regimes' claims to democratic status seriously. Nonliberal regimes based their democratic claims on rule by the people, or more precisely, by the general will of the people. Since these regimes were founded on either one-class or classless societies, i.e. societies in which there were ostensibly no *fundamental* divisions of interest, political actions could be justified plausibly by reference to the general will of "the people."

Liberal regimes also failed to see that their own democratic claims had been cast in a rather dubious light by changes in liberal society itself. The barriers to the full and free development of everyone's human potential had become more, not less, pronounced in late capitalism. The purely formal nature of liberal democracy had grown increasingly apparent, and had rendered the moral position of liberal democracy that much weaker, as the challenge of participatory democrats in the sixties made clear.

Thus, the credibility of nonliberal democracies seemed to be waxing, even as that of liberal democracies appeared to be waning. Unless liberal democracy could be reconstituted in more convincing terms, Macpherson feared that the posthumous-sounding title of his later work, *The Life and Times of Liberal Democracy* (1977), would prove all too prophetic in announcing the demise of liberal democracy.

Macpherson is not resigned to this outcome, however. He believes that liberal democracies could be made more democratic, in an economic sense, and that this would be entirely consistent with traditional liberal concerns for the dignity and worth of the individual. Much of his recent work has been devoted to showing what sort of changes are necessary if liberal democracy is to become more democratic, how those changes might come about, and why they are consistent with the ethical tenets of liberalism.[10]

The essence of this argument consists of Macpherson's ef-

[10] For critical evaluations of Macpherson's contribution see Seaman (1982), Lukes (1979), and Dunn (1974).

forts to construct a nonmarket theory of liberal democracy. His theory is derived from the ethical liberalism of thinkers like John Stuart Mill and revolves around an ontological "concept of man as essentially an exerter and enjoyer of his own powers" (Macpherson 1973, 32). Possessive individualism reduces humans to utility maximizers, when they ought to be considered power maximizers in the broadest possible sense: as exerters, enjoyers, and developers of their individual human capacities (ibid., 36).

Consequently, the democratic achievements of societies are to be measured according to the extent to which their members enjoy an equal right to develop their powers in *all* relevant spheres of life, including politics and economics. Thus, democratic societies are those in which the opportunities for development are not foreclosed in an inequitable and arbitrary manner. This in turn implies the absence of proprietary claims on the means of production, and the presence of expanded opportunities for participation in the workplace and politics, and of course the elimination of racism and sexism. Only in this way can the equal right to self-development be secured, and the future of liberal democracy preserved (Macpherson 1973; 1977).

The primary obstacle to this reformation of liberal democracy is, according to Macpherson, the widespread assumption that liberal democracy necessarily entails a commitment to market economies and their attendant inequalities. So long as the "liberal" in liberal democracy is understood primarily in utilitarian terms, no significant progress in overcoming inequality is possible, and no revitalization of liberal democracy can occur. Recognizing this, Macpherson has tried to show that no such commitment is *logically* entailed in liberal democracy, and that other aspects of liberalism are readily available for recasting liberal democracy in morally advantageous terms.

Thus, *The Life and Times of Liberal Democracy* shows in detailed fashion that the connection between liberal democracy and market economies is historically contingent, and not logically necessary. Indeed, the very terms "liberal" (when liberal is taken to mean possessive individualism) and "democracy" refer to potentially contradictory ideas that happened to find common cause in bourgeois struggles against aristocratic and monarchical regimes. During the course of the nineteenth century, and especially in the twentieth century, however, the tensions between these contradictory elements became ever more apparent, as the contrast between economic inequality and formal political equality sharpened.

Liberal democratic thinkers have been singularly unable to reconcile these tensions, and indeed the most recent of them have reverted to predemocratic liberalism in order to justify the workings of the market economy (Macpherson 1973, 179). In so doing, however, the moral force of liberal democracy has been undermined, leaving it exceedingly vulnerable to challenges from nonliberal democracies that explicitly eschew the inequalities bred by market economies.

IV

AS BELL and Macpherson make clear, the discourse of liberal democracy has been altered decisively by the subordination of the ethical or political elements of the liberal tradition to its acquisitive or economic motif. Because liberalism is the normative tradition in which liberal democracy is grounded and from which it draws its moral force, any significant changes in it are bound to affect liberal democracy itself. Insofar as liberalism has acquired a thorough-going privatistic orientation, the public sphere in which democracy operates and upon which it depends for its vitality has been undermined radically. Citizenship has been assimilated to consumption, albeit of "public goods," and politics has been reduced to a conflict of private interests, no one of which can claim moral superiority over others. As a result, all interests must be satisfied if the legitimacy of political institutions is to remain unquestioned, even if this means that the "public interest" goes unsatisfied.

Both Bell and Macpherson hope that the ethical dimension

of liberalism will be rejuvenated, thereby providing a moral foundation for a "born again" liberal democracy. Indeed, their efforts to recover what has been lost have this as their practical aim. (Macpherson appropriately subtitled his collected essays on democratic theory "Essays in Retrieval.") But neither has provided a convincing argument to the effect that the desired resuscitation of liberalism is realistically possible. Consequently, their recommendations have a utopian ring to them, particularly when we consider other analyses of the crisis of democracy that explicitly deny the possibility of what Bell and Macpherson recommend.

For example, the thesis of one-dimensionality has been applied explicitly to the evolution of ideas about liberal democracy by Jürgen Habermas. His *Strukturwandel der Öffentlichkeit* is an historical study of the emergence and subsequent decline of the public sphere in bourgeois societies. As such it may be interpreted as an attempt to articulate the historical and structural conditions under which the liberal concept of democracy was generated and institutionalized (Cohen 1979).[11]

Habermas contends that the contradiction between democracy and governability identified by the Trilateral Commission is a structural feature of modern societies, especially those of organized capitalism. In order to be legitimate, regimes must respond to the demands of "the democracy." And in order to be effective they must satisfy the interests of those actors, e.g. business, upon whose actions the regime's performance ultimately depends. The conflict between these imperatives is, therefore, an intrinsic feature of liberal democracy, at least insofar as "liberal" refers to a commitment to market economies.

The situation need not be untenable, however. So long as the demands of "the democracy" for more democracy remain at moderate levels, no serious constraints on regimes' ability

[11] This work has not been translated into English. Hohendahl (1979) presents an extended review and commentary.

to make policy exist. Administrative power is democratically legitimated, but not democratically controlled, since enough latitude or "slack in the system" (Dahl 1956) remains for bureaucratic initiatives to be implemented, without running afoul of the nominal overseers of the bureaucracy, the legislature.

Crises arise when citizens' demands on democratic institutions begin to intrude on administrative power. Unless these demands are somehow restrained, the system will be overloaded, its functioning impaired, and its legitimacy called into question. Thus, Habermas concurs with the so-called neoconservatives in their analysis of the decline of the "civic culture." However, he explains this decline with reference to the actions of government itself. The civic culture has been worn steadily away by the stabilization policies of the welfare state as more and more spheres of once-private life have come under direct or indirect purview of government. Incursions into heretofore untouched areas, e.g. education and the workplace, have undermined traditions of privatism, and in the process reduced their efficacy in regulating citizens' demands on the state.

Thus, the "repoliticization" of society by governmental interventions begins to undermine those traditions essential to the "depoliticization" of society from which the latitude for intervention derives (Schroyer 1975).[12] Moreover, no comparable traditions or justifications for self-reliance have emerged, leaving the state as the provider of first *and* last resort. Hence, an apolitical citizenry can no longer be taken

[12] This is a more general statement of Marx's arguments concerning the contradiction between the forces and relations of productions. For Habermas, system imperatives, e.g. stabilization, contradict social imperatives, e.g. legitimation, in organized capitalism. The crisis tendencies of late capitalism are therefore rooted in a structural contradiction between system and society (Habermas 1975). An even more general statement may be found in Habermas's (1979b) work, which construes the evolution of human society in terms of the dialectical interplay between instrumental and practical reason. Marx's forces and relations of production, as well as the current system and society, are therefore but historical contradictions in an ongoing dialectic.

for granted, which limits the state's ability to respond to crisis situations and stabilize economies.

The potential for legitimation crises is apparent. This situation could be defused, however, if it were somehow possible to completely disconnect politics from administration under the guise of technical or economic necessity. Such a situation is of course implicit in a new background ideology of science and technology that reduces political questions to technical problems. This technocratic consciousness eliminates all considerations of what is just or good in favor of what is necessary to stabilize economy and society.

In Habermas's view the absorption of politics by administration constitutes a new and unacknowledged form of political domination. The role of liberal regimes in preserving and promoting the private accumulation of wealth has retreated behind a façade of administrative neutrality. The class-based domination inherent in capitalist formations is insulated from any fundamental scrutiny. In this way, "the conflict still built into the structure of society by virtue of the private mode of capital utilization is the very area of conflict which has the greatest probability of remaining latent" (Habermas 1970, 108).

The "scientization of politics" as evidenced in the Great Society reflects this process. With the assumption by the state of responsibility for economic and social stability, the ideal of a good and just society has been replaced by that of a self-regulating, cybernetic social system. Politics has given way to administration, and policy discussions have been reduced to considerations of economic necessity and technical feasibility. Consequently, the range of perceived and allowable collective action has been considerably reduced, to the point where genuinely ethical and political questions concerning the ends of such action are suppressed. This, Habermas (1970; 1973; 1975) wants to say, is the true crisis of liberal democracy.

Because technocratic consciousness is not based on the element of wish-fulfillment implicit in previous ideologies, it does not appear to be ideological. Nevertheless, it is ideological insofar as it excludes questions of societal organization from political discourse in favor of discussions about improving the performance of *existing* forms of organization. Hence, technocratic consciousness is highly conservative, in the sense that it protects existing power relations from serious scrutiny. The manner in which this is achieved is quite revealing, for

> technocratic consciousness reflects not the sundering of an ethical situation but the repression of "ethics" as such as a category of life. The common, positivist way of thinking renders inert the frame of reference of interaction in ordinary language, in which domination and ideology both arise under conditions of distorted communication and can be reflectively detected and broken down. The depoliticization of the mass of the population, which is legitimated through technocratic consciousness, is at the same time men's self-objectification in categories equally of both purposive-rational action and adaptive behavior. The reified models of the sciences migrate into the socioculture lifeworld and gain objective power over the latter's self-understanding. The ideological nucleus of this consciousness is *the elimination of the distinction between the practical and the technical*. It reflects, but does not objectively account for, the new constellation of a disempowered institutional framework and systems of purposive-rational action that have taken on a life of their own. (Habermas 1970, 112–113)

It is for this reason that Habermas avers that "today the problem of language has replaced the traditional problem of consciousness; the transcendental critique of language supersedes that of consciousness" (McCarthy 1978, 273). The famous "linguistic turn" of critical theory is necessitated by the fact that in organized capitalism the utopian content of past ideologies, including liberal democracy, has been replaced by a technocratic consciousness. Whereas previous

ideological traditions drew their persuasive power from substantive conceptions of the good and just society, technocratic
consciousness does not. Instead, it is defined entirely in procedural terms that reduce politics and political decision-making to administrative activities (Habermas 1970, 111).

V

HABERMAS CONTENDS that liberal democratic norms, which
once offered the possibility of substantive legitimation *and*
immanent criticism, have lost their regulative force in advanced capitalism. He endorses the contention that advanced
capitalist societies have lost their capacity for self-criticism—
they are societies without effective opposition. Indeed, Habermas's version of the one-dimensionality thesis is, if anything, even more thoroughgoing than Marcuse's because he
locates the problem not in false consciousness, but in language, the medium of consciousness.

Habermas, even more than Marcuse, is concerned with the
organization of consciousness, rather than its substantive content. It is his contention that one-dimensional societies, i.e.
societies without opposition, represent communities in which
communicative processes are themselves grossly distorted.
Consequently, consciousness is one-dimensional precisely
because language is systematically distorted by the structures
of domination in which it is embedded. According to this
view, these systematic distortions of communication introduce a "mobilization of bias" into the organization of political
discourse by surreptitiously incorporating relations of power
into the symbolic structures of speech and action. Certain
questions, e.g. those concerning the underlying nature of
economic and political domination, are organized out of politics and consciousness because the symbolic structures that
inform them are misshapen. Thus, systematic distortions of
communication contribute to the reproduction of the patterns
of domination from which they arise (Habermas 1973, 12ff.).

Nevertheless, Habermas's most original contribution involves the insight that the "scientization" of politics and the

concomitant emergence of one-dimensional societies are not irresistible processes. To be sure, the destruction of substantive cultural traditions, i.e. "the repression of 'ethics' as such as a category of life," makes chronic legitimation problems in liberal democracies highly likely. However, Habermas also sees new possibilities for democracy where other critical theorists, e.g. Adorno, saw none. For Habermas, the legitimation crises to which liberal democracies are prone represent occasions for initiating new essential contests on the meaning of democracy in advanced capitalist societies. As such these crises represent significant flaws in the "seamless" web of domination known as technocratic consciousness.

This is because the "depolitization" implicit in technocratic consciousness is difficult to maintain in the face of the "re-politicizing" consequences of increased intervention by the state in once-private affairs. The state has replaced the market as the medium in which class relations unfold in late capitalism. The relations of production, and wage relations in particular, are now mediated by complex systems of industrial relations organized under the auspices of the state (Hanson 1982). The impersonal forces of the market have been replaced by the political forces of industrial relations, though this has not altered the basic pattern of class domination in liberal democracies. Thus, Habermas argues that

> recoupling the economic system to the political—which in a way repoliticizes the relations of production—creates an increased need for legitimation. The state apparatus no longer, as in liberal capitalism, merely secures the general conditions of production . . . but is now actively engaged in it. It must, therefore—like the precapitalist state—be legitimated, although it can no longer rely on residues of tradition that have been undermined and worn out during the development of capitalism. (1975, 36)

Therefore, the state in late capitalism is faced with conflicting imperatives. Intervention in the process of accumulation, even (or especially) when it is undertaken in the interest of "stabilization," is necessarily intervention on behalf of the interests of capital, for stabilization produces what Macpherson (1977) aptly describes as an "equilibrium in inequality." The use of public power and resources to maintain this situation of private advantage generates an increased need to justify or legitimate such actions. To the extent that such justifications are not forthcoming or are unconvincing, the administrative latitude of the state vis-à-vis economic stabilization is reduced.

Consequently, the depoliticizing effects of technocratic consciousness, which other critical theorists thought were inescapable, are, in Habermas's view, at least partially offset by the repoliticizing consequences of state policy-making. It is precisely because the domination of technocratic consciousness is not (yet) total that legitimation crises occur in liberal democracies. Hence, *Legitimation Crisis* must be understood as an attempt to reestablish the possibility of a new discourse on the organization of society.

For this reason, Habermas has tried to formulate a theory of evolution that would permit us to anticipate the range of democratic possibilities that are present in contemporary society, and that would at the same time allow us to identify the conditions under which "progressive" possibilities might be realized. His theory of social evolution is a "philosophy of history with a practical intent" that seeks to reveal possibilities *as* possibilities, and so dissolve the mystification of the present that appears to be beyond our control. For example, Habermas anticipates a more democratic discourse in *Toward a Rational Society*:

> We shall understand "democracy" to mean the institutionally secured forms of general and public communication that deal with the practical question of how men can and want to live under the objective conditions of their ever-expanding power of control. Our problem can then be stated as one of the relation of technology and democracy: how can the power of technical control be brought within

the range of the consensus of acting and transacting citizens? (1970, 57)

The solution to this problem involves "setting into motion a politically effective discussion that rationally brings the social potential constituted by technical knowledge and ability into a defined and controlled relation to our practical knowledge and will" (ibid., 61). Thus, the new discourse on democracy would involve a dialogue on the democratic uses of science and technology. Ideally, it would consist of a reciprocal communication between scientists and politicians, mediated by public opinion. In this way the direction of technical progress might be determined by the practical needs of society, democratically interpreted, i.e. in a democratic manner. At the same time, technical progress "measures and criticizes this self-understanding [of needs] in the light of the possibilities for gratification created by technology" (ibid., 68).

The most radical element of this conception of democratic communication is the assumption that the interpretation of social needs lies at the center of discourse rather than at the margins, as it is in a technocratic society. As Benhabib (1981, 56) observes, needs and their interpretations are not only the subject matter, but also the motivating force in activities oriented toward the transformation of societies in a more humane direction. The process of self-determination is therefore a constitutive aspect of democratic politics.

Of course, this aspiration was itself a central theme of the Enlightenment, particularly among liberal democratic thinkers who saw the social contract as the epitome of practical reason. However, the liberal democratic goal of consensual decision-making was never achieved, according to Habermas, for the concrete institutions of "democracy" always reflected the interests of the dominant class in the societies from which they developed. And as the structure of class domination in liberal societies began to recede behind the façade of technological consciousness, the failure of these societies to live up to their ideals became less and less apparent. With the reduction of politics, which deals with questions about the organization of society, to administration, which proceeds within the confines of a given form of organization, the practical failure of politics is assured—almost.

Thus, Habermas ultimately wants to argue that the commitment to liberal institutions and procedures of "democratic" decision-making can and must be abandoned if liberal democratic principles, especially the avowed commitment to consensual decision-making on collective matters, are to be realized. Consequently, Misgeld is quite right to argue that Habermas's recent work "should be regarded as both coming from within the liberal democratic tradition and indeed articulating its utopian content" (1981, 135). For rational reflection on the events leading up to the crisis of liberal democracy will show that the practical limits of liberal democracy can only be overcome by apprehending the theoretical limits of substantive liberal commitments themselves.

VI

HABERMAS'S RESORT to a critical *theory* of democratic discourse presumes that we now live in "one-dimensional societies" in which substantive democratic ideologies have lost their meaning. The identification and critique of systematically distorted communication by reference to an ideal speech situation is necessary because immanent criticism of political discourse on the basis of stated ideals is no longer possible in the age of science and technology.

However, Habermas may have overstated his case vis-à-vis the destruction of meaningful traditions by technical modes of thinking. He himself alludes to this possibility in *Legitimation Crisis* when he wonders why formal democracy is retained at all in advanced-capitalist societies, particularly insofar as it hinders governability. As he puts it,

If one considers only the functional conditions of the administrative system, it could as well be replaced by variants: a conservative-authoritarian welfare state that reduces political participation of citizens to a harmless level; or a fascist authoritarian state that holds the population by the bit at a relatively high level of permanent mobilization without having to overdraw its account through welfare state measures. (1975, 74)

These possibilities are dismissed by Habermas because they are incompatible with cultural developments that are characteristic of organized capitalist societies: "the socio-cultural system produces demands that cannot be met in authoritarian systems." In particular, the (irreversible) development of a universal political morality, complete with rights and privileges, as well as duties, makes the abandonment of democracy unlikely, if not impossible. These cultural barriers "could be broken through only at the psychological cost of regressions," as in the case of German fascism, but the memory of fascism mitigates against this development (ibid., 84).

The other "solution" to legitimation crises, of course, entails the creation of an entirely new mode of socialization, in which citizens' behavior is programmed without regard to reason. That is, reasons would no longer be necessary to motivate citizens to perform in desired ways. Rather, citizens would simply learn to act appropriately, even in the absence of compelling reasons for doing so. This type of behavioral engineering would mean the "end of individuality" as we know it, since the moral agency of human beings would become irrelevant in this kind of sociopolitical order (ibid., 117).

This possibility cannot be discounted, according to Habermas. However, his theory of social evolution suggests that another alternative is conceivable, namely, the establishment of a new "communicative ethics" on the residues of universal political morality peculiar to late capitalism. However, this is only an abstract possibility, since Habermas's theory cannot identify the dynamic tendencies that might lead to such a result. It only shows that the developmental logic of world views does not in principle *exclude* this possibility (Cohen 1979, 92).

Habermas does not consider a third possible outcome to contemporary legitimation crises, i.e. the reactivation of traditional belief systems that might prove capable of justifying political institutions and practices. Although his earlier work was very much concerned with the identification and resuscitation of traditional democratic norms and ideals, Habermas's later work accepts the thesis of one-dimensionality in a fairly radical form, so that he no longer believes that the decay of traditions is reversible. It can only be transcended by an evolutionary leap to a higher stage of development, as in the case of communicative ethics (ibid.).

Yet Habermas's own argument implies that this possibility must be considered more carefully. Cohen suggests that the persistence of democratic institutions, which Habermas acknowledges and even accords a central role in precipitating legitimation crises, can only mean that democratic ideas still retain normative force in contemporary Western, industrialized nations. Their meaning, and hence their ability to motivate action, has not been totally destroyed. Otherwise, we could not explain why the growth of state power and responsibilities, particularly in the area of welfare, has triggered more demands for democratic participation in decision-making (ibid., 93). In other words, Habermas's hypotheses regarding the decline of bourgeois traditions of privatism may not apply to other cultural traditions involving rights or entitlements to participation. With respect to legitimation crises, it seems as if traditions that restrain participation have been eroded, while those that inspire it have not decayed, so that democratic constraints on policy-makers are indeed pressing. Consequently, the persistence of participatory ideals means that democratic criticism may still be possible, so that resort to abstract, theoretical notions such as the ideal speech situation is not necessary.

Hence, Cohen wonders if substantive democratic traditions might not be reactivated and perhaps radicalized and so turned against contemporary "democratic" discourse. This point is pursued by Mendelson who suggests that a tradition or set of traditions can therefore still serve as a reservoir of slogans, symbols, and ideals which both anticipate a better society and resonate with large numbers of people. If that is the case, then an immanent critique would still seem possible and desireable [*sic*] to a critical theory which took seriously hermeneutic insights into the relation of reflection to tradition, of theoretical to practical reason. (1979, 71–72)

An interrogation of the liberal democratic tradition, informed by a critical interest and perspective, might allow us to identify (and so remove) systematic distortions of communication. It might, in other words, perform the same critical function as Habermas's notion of ideal speech, without becoming so abstract as to be inaccessible to those to whom the analysis is addressed. The "audience problem" of critical theory would thereby be solved by a "critical hermeneutics" that involves "letting the past generate meanings that can show the way to overcome the present for the future" (Benhabib 1981, 58).

Such a critical reinterpretation must focus on the historical liberalization of democracy that has occurred in the U.S., if Macpherson and Habermas are right, for it is their belief that the current crisis of democracy reflects an unhealthy predominance of market institutions and practices over democratic claims. For Macpherson and Habermas, the resolution of this crisis depends on a "democratization of liberalism" that will offset the distorting effects of the liberalization of democracy. This requires abandoning our allegiance to market arrangements that are unnecessarily confining and not necessarily liberal.

Habermas and Macpherson do not see the abandonment of certain liberal institutions and practices, e.g. markets, as a repudiation of liberalism, but rather as a logical consequence of a commitment to liberal principles that are partially, but never completely, embodied in these institutions. According to them, the vitality of liberal democracy depends on the continuous adaptation of institutions and practices to new circumstances. It is this democratic experimentation that is the true legacy of the past, and it is the willingness to engage in further experimentation that represents the means by which the liberal democratic tradition is extended via the transcendence of prior accomplishments. This, and not some unquestioning commitment to the political solutions adopted by preceding generations, is the essence of liberal democracy as Macpherson and Habermas understand it, and it is the failure of the present generation to embrace this tradition of political experimentation that leads them to conclude that the condition of liberal democracy is now critical.

VII

IN A FOURTEENTH-CENTURY account of the stages of Arabic civilization a historian named Ibn Khaldun remarks that the generation of founders knows the costs of what they achieved, because they bore them. The second generation knows the founders, and so presumably knows that a cost was paid, though they may not appreciate its fullness in the way their fathers did. The third generation, which does not know the founders, lives by tradition, while the fourth—and last—generation, in token of decay, knows the cost of nothing and believes that it has everything coming to it (Somkin 1967, 4).

Khaldun was discussing a tradition of what his translator called "prestige," one of the keywords of his culture that denoted a quality essential to the might and greatness of a civilization. His point seems clear enough; prestige does not come to those who, because they expect it, merely wait for its bestowal on them. Prestige is an accomplishment, not a bequest, and each generation must achieve its own prestige in order for a civilization to persist.

Later generations may not always understand this, especially if they confuse those things that are bequeathed to them by their predecessors with their own achievements. They may, for example, take the institutions and practices that embody their ancestors' prestige and revere them, even preserve them, without obtaining prestige of their own. It is only when they emulate their founders' activity under different circumstances, calling for different actions, that their own prestige is secured, and their tradition extended.

Thus, later generations must employ earlier generations' *modes* of problem-solving. They cannot simply copy their predecessors' solutions to historically specific problems. Past solutions not only may not solve present problems, but they may in fact be part of those problems. Those who would extend their tradition must therefore follow the example set by those who went before by reenacting their commitment to solving problems in a certain way, without simply reproducing old solutions.

A historical consciousness of the sense in which generations different from one another may also be part of a common tradition is essential to this enterprise, for it establishes the identity of a community in terms that permit variations on a theme. In the case of the liberal democratic tradition that theme concerns the problematic relationship between liberal values and democratic commitments, and the variations consist of successive generations' efforts to establish a practical accommodation that is appropriate to their circumstances as they understand them. Such accommodations may be passed on to later generations in the form of concrete institutions and practices, but they seldom suffice under new historical circumstances that call for new accommodations.

When later generations fail to respond to that call, or respond merely by reasserting the accomplishments of their forebearers, they actually undermine the vitality of the tradition initiated by their founders. And when this happens repeatedly over successive generations it is not surprising that crises should arise, when the very future of a tradition is called into question.

The "crisis of democracy" in liberal democratic cultures like that of the United States is one such crisis. The once-vital argumentative tradition of liberal democracy is no longer characterized by genuine contestation. The practical commitment to progress through contestation, which lies at the cen-

ter of liberal democratic power talk, has been almost completely eroded by past contests over the meaning of liberal
democracy. With each successive contest, the course of argument has been systematically distorted by efforts to fore-
close discussion of questions which, if discussed seriously,
might undermine the legitimacy of ruling elites. The cumulative effect of these distortions has so circumscribed the
range of debate that the original problem of liberal democracy, namely, the relation between liberalism and democracy, has been suppressed. Hence, neither legitimation nor
criticism is any longer compelling because their mutual reference point has been forgotten.

The extent of this distortion is most apparent in the destruction of democracy as a class concept. Throughout its history democracy has always referred to a specific class in society and to the form of government in which that class
predominated. In the case of liberal democracy, particularly
in the U.S., "the democracy" were members of the productive classes in society, while "the plutocracy" were wealthy
members of the parasitic or nonproductive classes. A democratic republic was, therefore, a republic in which "the democracy" held a preponderance of power, and righfully so, as
they were the "bone and sinew" of the nation, as Andrew
Jackson put it.

An explicit reference to the class structure of society informed virtually all American conceptions of liberal democracy until well into the twentieth century. Even as late as the
New Deal, the notion of democracy as a class concept prevailed among all of the major competing usages of "democracy," *except* for that of the New Dealers themselves. Hence,
the point of contestation was to work out some sort of compromise form of democratic capitalism in which "the democracy" and "the plutocracy" lived in uneasy peace, if not harmony. Naturally, this involved a widespread recognition that
the proper relationship between classes in a democracy *was*
problematic, and in this recognition a practical closure was

achieved. It was this common reference that established a context in which rhetorical arguments found practical closure.

However, beginning with the Progressive era, extending through the New Deal, and culminating in the Great Society, the class connotations of democracy were gradually eliminated in favor of a more "universal" conception of democracy founded on an all-inclusive social class—consumers. As class came to be defined in terms of consumption rather than production, the image of a class-divided society began to fade from American political rhetoric. So, too, did the partisan interpretations of democracy that were grounded in class divisions. The *rhetorical* transcendence of class conflict emptied liberal democracy of its traditional meaning and import and removed the basis of contestation upon which its vitality had heretofore depended.

Once democracy was "declassified," the very idea of democracy as rule by a particular class with substantive interests that were somehow different from or even in conflict with the interests of other classes lost all sense. The idea of democracy as a class concept became irrelevant, and the strategic rationale for partisan interpretations of democracy virtually disappeared in the face of a "consensus" on democratic capitalism. With the emergence of the administrative state and the technocratic takeover of policy-making, the liberal image of a just and moral society was supplanted by a well-regulated, cybernetic system of crisis management (Dickson, 1981). Behind the façade of administrative neutrality and, for a while at least, competence, the class basis of the state vanished from sight, and questions about the organization of power were reduced to considerations of economic necessity and technical efficiency—both defined with reference to existing institutions and practices.

Hence, the relevance of class differences for understanding democracy as a substantive organization of power was destroyed by the rhetorical identification of "democracy" with existing or improved techniques of administration. The point of these administrative institutions and practices was lost as their relationship to the organization of liberal society was obscured, and they became givens in discussions of social goals and organization. The impact of this was, of course, to defuse fundamental criticism of the status quo. Once democracy is understood in terms of specific institutions and procedures, rather than rule by a particular class, criticism of those institutions and procedures for failing to realize class rule is rhetorically irrelevant. They must be accepted or rejected on their own terms, as self-evidently or essentially democratic.

Of course any institutional failures must then be construed as failures of liberal democracy per se, rather than imperfect instantiations of consensual decision-making. This is in fact the gist of the Trilateral Commission's (Crozier 1975) arguments concerning the crisis of democracy—too much democracy yields too little governability. The solution to problems of governability therefore requires some sort of immunization against the "democratic distemper" that afflicts Western liberal democracies.

Alternatively, the problem may be seen as one of too little democracy, wherein unresponsive institutions are to blame (Steinfels 1979). This is usually coupled with a recommendation for new institutions that are "really" democratic, and which are capable of meeting the expectations of citizens in these countries. Between these two alternatives, however, no rational choice can be made, because we have no basis for deciding which arguments are correct, even in a provisional sense. Since we do not know what democracy really is, and since there is no reference to a common enterprise of argumentative inquiry, a choice between them must be strictly partisan.

VIII

THE SUBLIMATION of the class content of liberal democracy is only one aspect of a more general demoralization of American political discourse. During the twentieth century, moral terms have been systematically purged from rhetoric as a more neutral, and hence less divisive, political language has been created. The pace of this development has accelerated since the New Deal. Contemporary discourse is now characterized by a rhetoric of consumption that comprehends all interests by reducing them to a lowest common denominator—their "interest" in consumption under a system of interest-group liberalism.

This is merely another way of saying that American political rhetoric has been thoroughly rationalized under the imperative of growth. Growth has become the unquestioned object of public policy, and political discussion is reduced to a consideration of the best means for realizing it. Such a constraint is politically significant, for it makes "zero-growth" policies virtually incomprehensible. The range of politically viable options is thereby reduced as the need for growth becomes "self-evident." As such, growth needs no special justification, and the reasons why growth is necessary for the survival of liberal democracy are never discussed. No explanations of the imperative status of growth are given, and so the false harmony of interests promoted by consumer democracy goes unquestioned, at least for as long as the system delivers the goods.

When the flow of public goods and services is threatened, however, the superficiality of this harmony of interests is revealed, and the importance of growth affirmed. As Offe notes, under conditions of economic stagnation the machinery of class compromise itself becomes the object of class conflict, as both conservatives and radicals attack the welfare state for failing to satisfy their interests (1981). The welfare state is too democratic and insufficiently liberal for some, and too liberal and insufficiently democratic for others.

The tragedy of consumer democracy is that it has no defense against what republicans called the corruption of politics, i.e. the subordination of public concerns to private interests. Yet this is a natural consequence of a concept of democracy that, in seeking to transcend class differences, seeks to establish the consumption of public goods and services as a common interest. Under consumer democracy people are entitled to these goods and services by virtue of their citizenship, and any restriction of access to them is tantamount to a denial of the rights and privileges of citizenship (Taylor 1981). Consequently, it is difficult, and perhaps impossible, to limit public consumption, even when that appears to be "in the public interest." That certainly does not mean that uneven sacrifices are never imposed; they are an intrinsic feature of class societies. It does mean that these sacrifices may often appear to be unreasonable, and perhaps intolerable, from the standpoint of those upon whom they are imposed. Only growth offers an escape from this situation, for it ostensibly renders sacrifices unnecessary. All interests may be satisfied in a growing economy.

The vulnerability of consumer democracy to stagnation stems from the fact that there is no moral basis for imposing limits on public consumption. This is especially true where the limits are selective. There is no logic or rationale for treating some people differently than others, because the moral distinctions that might support this have been obliterated. William Graham Sumner's attribution of superiority to entrepreneurs, no less than the Jacksonians' association of virtue with producers, drew upon widely accepted moral categories to justify an uneven burden of sacrifice. Among the universal class of consumer citizens, no such distinctions exist, and so it is not possible to provide a convincing justification for unequal treatment vis-à-vis the entitlements of citizenship.

That is why political debate in this country has degenerated so badly in recent years. Under the present circumstances, all our problems, especially those centering on the restoration of growth, entail an unequal burden of sacrifice that cannot be justified in a convincing manner. Hence, politics becomes power politics as various groups defend themselves against the efforts of others to impose special burdens on them. Some groups are much better able to defend their interests, it is true, but the point is that their victory is not *morally* secure; it is recognized as the result of a power play, as the complaints of their victims demonstrate so vividly.

Thus, contemporary discourse consists mainly of rationalizations that fail to disguise the realities of power politics; it is a sham debate that is but a parody of authentic argument. With the destruction of any commitment to arguing well in the name of progress, only the clash of partisan interpretations of liberal democracy now exists. Figures from the past are, of course, invoked: the Founding Fathers and their more notable descendants, e.g. Jackson and Lincoln, are cited approvingly, and their arguments are adopted by those who see themselves as modern-day heirs, or who merely seek the legitimacy that such rhetorical associations afford. Nevertheless, this is incapable of sustaining rational argument in the absence of a common recognition of what the problem is and what sort of response it demands.

In the absence of any recognition that the translation of ideas into practices is politically problematic, the argumentative predicament in which contestants find themselves is dramatically altered. Winning the debate assumes much greater importance, and the commitment to progressive enlightenment through rational disputation becomes less important as the point of disagreement fades from sight. Partisan interpretations then tend to become dogmatic assertions, and the very idea of rational political argumentation is called into question.

IX

BECAUSE WINNING the argument has become the principal objective of those engaged in contemporary arguments about democracy, these disputes lack the moral underpinnings that permitted Gallie to argue that essential contests, though not resolvable on rational grounds, were capable of being *sustained* by rational arguments. In the absence of a commitment to contestation per se, there is no practical closure. As a result, present discussions involve incommensurable uses of "democracy," between which there is no choice, and in fact no common understanding.

Understanding presumes the existence of common meanings at some level of social life. Such common meanings, as Taylor (1971) describes them, are the very basis of community; they constitute the field of meaning in which action unfolds, and without which social life is literally inconceivable. Common meanings are, therefore, the deep structure of social life, and it is only on the basis of them that less fundamental differences of opinion make sense. Without common meanings, differences are just that—differences that do not exist in relation to each other, and so are incommensurable. They make sense only when there exists a medium in which the differences are (or can be made) intelligible as alternative interpretations of social life and its possibilities.

To say that contemporary disputes about democracy lack closure, then, means that they lack common meanings in which disputation might make sense. They are not underpinned by a common commitment that would make different interpretations of liberal democracy understandable as different, but commensurable, opinions on the practical meaning of liberal democracy in the present day and age. Specifically, they lack a commitment to the value of contestation per se, which in the liberal democratic tradition derives from the principle of consensual decision-making. The very idea of consensual decision-making entails a willingness to abide solely by the forceless force of the better argument in coming to agreement on matters of collective importance, for it is only under such circumstances that a genuine meeting of the minds takes place.

Moreover, the importance of consensual decision-making as a principle of social deliberation itself presumes that an accommodation of differences is necessary in order for outcomes to be valid and legitimate. This is the level at which the common meaning that runs through the liberal democratic tradition may be discerned: legitimate differences must be addressed by consensual, not coercive, means. The struggle to translate this ideal into concrete institutions capable of embodying this idea in practice is what constitutes the liberal democratic tradition as an "historically extended argument" (as described in Chapter One).

The commitment to consensual means of resolving differences "closes" liberal democratic debate, therefore, but only if the participants in this debate share this commitment to explore the problem of translating a common idea into political practice. This must be accompanied by a recognition that this translation is problematic: no set of institutional arrangements embodies the essence of consensual decision-making. All such arrangements fall short, to a greater or lesser degree, and so all are susceptible to valid criticism *on liberal democratic grounds*.

This applies not only to rules for making decisions within institutions, but also (and indeed especially) to the constitutional choice between alternative institutions that partially embody the principle of consensual decision-making. No set of institutions, existing or otherwise, is "essentially" democratic; they simply represent particular efforts to realize in practice an ideal that cannot be fully achieved. Consequently, choices among contending conceptions of the appropriate machinery for making collective decisions must themselves be made democratically. The principle of consensual decision-making applies to all levels of social organization in liberal democratic cultures.

The translation of abstract political principles into concrete practices is a task that all political communities must face. Hence, to identify democracy with the system of a free press, competitive elections, or some other set of arrangements, may only be a shorthand expression for reiterating the outcome of this translation process. However, the participants in contemporary politics seldom see this as a process of translating principles into practice. Rather, they tend to reverse this process altogether: principles are derived from existing or possible practices (witness the neoconservative attack on the "deontology of democracy," which was discussed earlier).

Consequently, disputes over the meaning of democracy come to resemble a clash between the advocates of specific institutional arrangements, rather than a collective effort to clarify the meaning of a complex and intrinsically problematic notion via argumentation.

However, the possibilities for criticizing and evaluating *any* set of "democratic" institutions are drastically reduced once democracy is defined solely with reference to concrete arrangements. Gone is the possibility of questioning the extent to which specific institutions and practices embody the principle of consensual decision-making, since principles that are independent of their embodied practices are no longer recognized. All that is left is to argue for and against specific arrangements, with little understanding or sense of what this argument is about. This is because the identification of democracy with specific institutional forms virtually ensures that the resultant contest over the meaning of democracy will involve incommensurable uses of democracy. Each of the contestants will insist that the institutions they advocate are democratic, while those that others advocate are not, or at least are not *as* democratic. And, as in truly genuine contests, no contestant will be able to definitively prove the superiority or correctness of her or his interpretation. However, the tendency in these disputes is to substitute power for power talk, thereby distorting systematically the course of argumentation. Even though this may be accomplished via the imposition of institutions and practices that ostensibly embody the essence of democracy, the principle of consensual decision-making is violated, and liberal democracy compromised.

X

AT THIS POINT it would be tempting to conclude that the crisis of liberal democracy cannot any longer be resolved since the practical closure necessary for sustaining such arguments no longer exists, having been undone by the relentless rationalization of discourse in the twentieth century. However, this conclusion is warranted only if no way of reestablishing practical closure exists, or if the achievement of closure cannot be made democratically, i.e. in accord with distinctively liberal principles of argumentation.

We can do this once we recognize the presence of distorting influences on contemporary discourse, for these distortions are influential mainly to the extent that they remain unacknowledged and invisible. Their effectiveness in "closing" debate depends on their unquestioned acceptance as rules of argumentation. When their status as organizing principles of discourse is made problematic, i.e. questioned, then distortions no longer close debate effectively.

Indeed, their problematic status actually opens debate to new issues and concerns—those having to do with the organization of discourse itself. Consequently, the power of distortions to skew the outcome of rhetorical disputes by restricting the range of issues to be considered is diminished in proportion to our increasing awareness that they have this effect. As we move to reflective levels of argumentation the power of systematic distortions is broken and a truly radical rhetorical exchange becomes possible.

The difficulty, of course, lies in the invisibility of systematic distortions that make genuine contestation impossible. These distortions cannot be identified with reference to ostensibly "progressive" interpretations of liberal democracy. Any characterization of liberal democracy in terms of appropriate institutional arrangements merely expands the conflict of interpretations that now exists. For that reason, any designations of alleged systematic distortions that originate in "objective" models of liberal democratic argumentation will be treated as partisan complaints by those who hold different interpretations of liberal democracy. Under these circumstances, distortions will not be acknowledged as distortions by other participants in the dispute, and so of course the power of distortions will remain intact, if they in fact exist.

Nor will the injection of moralistic interpretations of democracy do much to undo the demoralization of political discourse in this country. That, too, would only expand the number of participants in an incommensurable dispute without really altering the practices that underpin and organize that contest. It is the very organization of our power talk that is now problematic, and for that a much more radical solution is needed in order for progress out of the crisis of democracy to be made.

What is needed is a rediscovery of the ethics of communication that identifies liberal democratic power talk *as* liberal democratic power talk. We must move to a reflective level of argumentation in which not only the content of liberal democratic discourse but also the practices by which it is conducted are the subject of conversation. Specifically, this new radical discourse must be allowed to range freely over issues and concerns that have previously been excluded from political debate because they seemed to contradict ostensibly liberal democratic institutions. The commitment to liberal democratic *principles* of political argumentation requires that we abandon our allegiance to certain "liberal democratic" institutions and practices that no longer, or perhaps never did, embody those principles very well. We must remain committed to liberal democracy as an open discourse in which substantive conclusions are not predetermined, but are uncovered in the process of argumentation itself.

Progress in liberal democratic problem-solving does not depend only or even mainly upon victories by progressive forces, therefore. Victory is not a guarantee of progress, no matter which force gains it. If that were so, liberal democracy would not be problematic; the only difficulty would be in identifying which side was "right" or "progressive." Power talk would then become a matter of clarifying right views and rectifying wrong ones, rather than a collective effort to solve genuine problems having to do with the tension between liberalism and democracy.

Hence, would-be liberal democrats cannot bring about progress by triumphing in political discourse. This does not mean that would-be liberal democrats ought to stop advancing concrete interpretations of liberal democracy that they claim are progressive. It simply means that *by themselves* these new interpretations will not bring about the desired problem-shift. That requires something else altogether. It requires a transcendence of partisanship and a commitment to the clash of interpretations as progressive in and of itself.

It is in that sense that liberal democrats who reflect on their tradition and its meaning are bound to undertake actions in the name of progress. The root principle of liberal democracy—the commitment to consensual decision-making—is truly radical, and those who trace their roots are obliged to be radical, too. Ironically, the conservation of the liberal democratic tradition may demand the rejection of institutions and practices that no longer embody the principles of our tradition, if indeed they ever did. Nevertheless, it is only in this limited sense that progress in our story is possible. Precisely because liberal democracy is a form of power talk oriented toward consensual decision-making, its conclusions vis-à-vis the conduct of politics in everyday life must not be predetermined by the machinery for making collective decisions. The abandonment of closed institutions in favor of more open political practices is, therefore, progress, in liberal democratic terms.

Our responsibilities as liberal democrats are therefore quite momentous. We must act to bring about progress, since that is the only sensible course open to us in the traditional drama we are engaged in. Moreover, we must do so in the absence of certain knowledge about what progress means. That is why open contestation is so valuable: it clarifies the meaning of progress for us, and so allows us to see what is to be done.

CHAPTER TWELVE

History and Liberation

I

WE HAVE NOW returned to the question with which we began in Chapter One: Is the liberal democratic tradition any
longer viable? Habermas claims it is not and urges us to seek
a new kind of discourse based on a rational ethics of communication. Bell and Macpherson, on the other hand, hope
that our tradition may yet be extended into the future, but
even these partisans of liberal democracy are concerned
about the prospects of reviving the ethical dimension of liberal democracy in an age that prides itself on putting an end
to ideology.

This suggests that we must concern ourselves with the recoverability of political traditions in general, and the liberal
democratic tradition in particular. The "remembrance of
things past" is therefore the subject of this chapter.[1] The
claim I advance and defend may be succinctly summarized:
Those who would make their own history must understand it
as well. They must remember the past in order to repudiate
the present in the name of the future. Only in this way can
history be truly made. By this I do not mean simply that
historical knowledge is a useful weapon in the arsenal of revolution, although that may be true. Rather, my argument is
that the future is only conceivable in light of the past, and
conversely that the past is only intelligible in light of the fu-

[1] I use the common English translation of Marcel Proust's great novel *A
la recherche du temps perdu*, which really ought to be translated *Remembrance of Times Lost*, since *perdu* means lost, as well as past. Then the
significance of recovering time—both past and future—would be made apparent.

ture. Between past and future there exists an essential continuity that is forged in the present by those who struggle against past and future and in so doing participate in the making of history.

Hence, when I speak of the recoverability of political traditions I am referring to the recovery of history, not as something that lies only in the past, but as something that lies in the future as well. For the future represents the potentiality of the present, which in turn is an outgrowth of the past. Political traditions stretch from the past into the future, and their recovery in the present is simultaneously a remembrance of things past and a retrieval of future possibilities. Remembrance restores the possibility of liberation as present action oriented toward the future.

In order to substantiate this claim, I shall review the debate between Gadamer and Habermas over the possibility of a critical hermeneutics.[2] The main issue in this debate centers on the way in which we understand the present. For Gadamer, the present must be understood primarily with reference to its past, since the very categories with which we approach the present (or the future, for that matter) are themselves conditioned by the past. Habermas, on the other hand, argues that this concedes too much to the authority of the past over the present, and that we must anticipate the future in order to realize the latent possibilities of the present. Thus, the standpoint from which we understand the present and its possibilities for liberation is in question in this exchange.

After presenting the debate in somewhat stylized form, I propose a reconciliation of these two points of view. In essence I argue that both past and future perspectives on the present are necessary in order to grasp our situation and act upon it. I suggest that such a synthesis depends on locating

[2] This debate is contained in Gadamer (1960), which is reviewed in Habermas (1977), to which Gadamer (1976) responds. (These are the English translations, which appeared out of chronological order.)

the present in a narrative framework that tells the story of a tradition as it unfolds in those actions that embody it. These actions are "always already" bound by tradition and so reflect the authority of the past over the present. At the same time, they are oriented toward the future insofar as these actions extend the life of traditions and move the story forward. When this future orientation becomes an explicit part of the "story of a tradition," i.e. when it becomes the motivating force behind the actions of those who are the bearers of tradition, liberating episodes in history become possible.

However, this liberation from the past is not, nor can it be, an escape from tradition. Liberation only adds more episodes to our story, which has no end that is not also an end for us.

II

THE CONCEPT of tradition refers to the relationship between past and present. "Tradition" is from the Latin root *tradere*, to hand over or deliver.[3] It is usually understood as the handing down of certain practices from one generation to another, often with connotations of respect for tradition and its authority. The liberal democratic tradition, for example, is a particular way of conducting politics that has been passed down from generation to generation of citizens in Anglo-Saxon countries and their colonies. Like other political traditions, the liberal democratic tradition binds generations to one another, overcoming (at least partially) their separation in time. It is a source of continuity in the history of certain political communities.

However, the persistence of traditions depends as much on the taking up of the practices in question by their heirs as it does upon the bequest by forebears. Unless the handing down of traditions is met with an embrace by subsequent generations, traditions will surely die. The reception of a political tradition by the members of a political community is therefore a remembrance of things past. This act of remem-

[3] Cf. n. 6 below.

brance recalls, i.e. calls to mind again, the past in its relationship to the present. It recollects the meaning of a tradition for the members of the present generation of a political
community. Hence, the remembrance of things past renews
the membership of a current generation in the tradition.

Remembrance is the process by which a political community *identifies* itself in relation to its past. Remembrance is
the recollection of *our* past, of a past that we make ours in
some way. For that reason we do not seek to understand the
past as past, but only in relation to the present. We strive to
see the past in the present, so to speak, and on the basis of
that partial identification we try to understand the significance of the past for the present.

This "fusion of horizons," to use Gadamer's terminology, is
something that we *must* seek, if we are to understand at all.
It is necessary for us to answer the call *for* understanding in
order *to* understand.[4] The call itself arises out of the fact that
meaning is never simply given to us. Its existence is in some
sense always problematic, because our present situation,
though it is affected by the past, is never identical to it. To
the extent that our present situation differs from the past, the
relevance of past interpretations or meanings is not and cannot be presumed. It must be made apparent by the search
for understanding, which strives to overcome the nonidentity
of past and present on the basis of their *partial* identity, i.e.
the "presence" of the past in the present. Consequently,
interpretation is action oriented toward reaching an under-

---

[4] Gadamer's argument here is ontological: because we *are* in time we must
understand ourselves *in* time. For us there is no other way to achieve understanding; we cannot escape the finitude of the hermeneutic situation of
being in time. With respect to the problem of understanding, it is "not what
we are doing, not what we ought to be doing but what happens with us
beyond our wanting and doing" that is in question (Gadamer 1976, xi).
Hence, "tradition is not simply a precondition into which we come, but we
produce it ourselves, inasmuch as we understand, participate in the evolution of tradition and further determine it ourselves. Thus the circle of understanding is not a 'methodological' circle, but describes an ontological
structural element in understanding" (Gadamer 1960, 261).

standing, and it is the practice in which meaning itself is constituted.

What is true of contemporary interpretations is also true of all past interpretations. They too represent efforts of past generations to place *their* past in intelligible relation to *their* present. A tradition is, therefore, a continuous process of showing the relevance of the past to the present. It is a never-ending effort to make sense out of that which is necessarily puzzling, but which can be resolved in the act of interpretation itself.

III

As each generation returns time and again to its past and recognizes it as such, the past is extended into the present. By the very act of interpreting its past in relation to its present situation, a generation enters "into the happening of a tradition in which past and present are constantly mediated," according to Gadamer (Habermas 1977, 356). Hence, traditions are reproduced by efforts to understand their meaning in circumstances that have changed and rendered their significance unclear or problematic.

This means that historical understanding does not involve going back in time so that somehow people from the present are able to experience life as did those about whom history is written. Historical understanding is not, and cannot be, achieved via "objective" methods of interpretation that allow us to understand past events in the same way that those who lived those events did. That kind of hermeneutics is literally impossible, because it disregards the way in which the past influences the present and so *allows* us access to the past.

It is precisely because history is *effective* history that an understanding of the past from the standpoint of the present is possible (Gadamer 1976).[5] History is not simply an archive

---

[5] "A proper hermeneutics would have to demonstrate the effectivity of history within understanding itself. I shall refer to this as 'effective-history.' Understanding is, essentially, an effective-historical relation" (Gadamer 1960, 267).

or repository of human artifacts that may become the object of interpretation. History acts upon the present from a distance, as it were, by virtue of the way in which it constitutes the present. The past is present in our understanding of the present because "our consciousness is determined by a real historical process, in such a way that we are not free to juxtapose ourselves to the past." Hence, Gadamer says that "we must always become conscious afresh of the action which is thereby exercised over us, in such a way that everything past which we come to experience compels us to take hold of it completely, to assume in some way its truth" (Ricoeur 1981, 73–74).

Because the past is present we gain access to it insofar (and only insofar) as we become conscious of the effectiveness of history. We become aware of the past and understand its meaning for us when we become conscious of the impact of the past on the present and our understanding of the present. That impact is objectively mediated by the chain of preceding interpretations by which past events and their significance are transmitted to us in the present and so affect our understanding of them. When we reflect on this sedimentation of meaning we are reflecting on the historical conditions of our present understanding of the past, so that the effectiveness of history is revealed to us.

The return *to* the past entailed by remembrance is therefore a return *from* the present. Moreover, remembrance culminates in a return to the present by way of the past that is contained therein. Historical understanding is achieved in this "eternal re-turning" in time, by which we overcome the temporal separation of past and present. In the so-called hermeneutic circle the horizons of past and present are fused, and understanding is reached.

This process of mediation in which traditions are reconstituted also explains the remarkable fecundity of traditions. Since interpretation involves a "fusion of horizons" it necessarily produces meaning. Interpretation does not simply convey meanings from the past; it creates meaning by establishing the significance of the past for the present. But the present is not the end of time, it is only a point in time. The present is always becoming past and the future is always becoming present. This means that new interpretations are always possible, and indeed necessary for the survival of traditions. Thus, the recovery of traditions is a continuous process. Because our present vantage point, from which we interpret the past, is historically situated, both our vantage point and those things that it overlooks are constantly unfolding before us.

Hence, our understanding of the past and its significance for the present must be continuously revised and reinterpreted. The process of revision and reinterpretation is, therefore, an essential aspect of living history. This, as Habermas (1977, 351) observes, is Gadamer's real achievement: the rehabilitation of the concept of a tradition embodied in a language that is unavoidably transmitted from generation to generation. Each generation necessarily appropriates the meaning of the past in reference to its current situation, and in so doing extends or renews the tradition of which it is a part.

The fact that we share a language with those in our past ensures that we can understand the past in its relation to the present by working through that language. The past speaks to us in a language that we can understand if we open ourselves to the question that animates the past, as Heidegger would put it. The participation in language that binds generations to one another establishes traditions *on an objective basis*, since it is in language that we live and become conscious of our being in the world of language. Language is, therefore, the medium of history.

This point must be emphasized: Language is for Gadamer constitutive of human being. It is not merely a distinctive feature of human life, it is a *constitutive* feature of it. Language defines us in an active way:

> In all our knowledge of ourselves and in all knowledge of the world, we are *always already* encompassed by the lan-

guage that is our own. We grow up, and we become acquainted with men and in the last analysis with ourselves when we learn to speak. Learning to speak does not mean learning to use a preexistent tool for designating a world already somehow familiar to us; it means acquiring a familiarity and acquaintance with the world itself and how it confronts us. (Gadamer 1976, 62–63; my emphasis)

The relationship between effective history and language should be obvious. We are affected by language, not in accidental ways, but in a fundamental manner. To learn a language is to grant the authority of the past over the present, insofar as what we learn is the past in the present. This authority can never be completely repudiated without losing our identity. However, we can become conscious of effective history by becoming aware that we are "always already" encompassed by language.

In that sense there is no escape from language, only the recognition of its unavoidable presence. Correspondingly, there is no escaping tradition. To be is to be in a language that has been, and it is to reproduce and extend that language in encounters with the world. Being is becoming in language.

IV

TRADITIONS THAT LINK generations also bind them; that is, the *authority* of tradition over the present makes it impossible to criticize or even repudiate that tradition, since it is only on the basis of tradition that we understand at all. We may become conscious of the effectiveness of history, but even the knowledge that our understanding of the past is grounded in a present that is itself the product of past understandings is not enough to free us from the influence of traditional ways of understanding. As Habermas says, Gadamer's hermeneutics "bangs helplessly, so to speak, from within against the walls of tradition" (Gadamer 1976, 31). The finitude of the hermeneutic situation cannot be transcended.[6]

[6] Williams (1976, 269) observes that *tradition* can also mean "hand over" in the sense of betrayal or surrender. Hence, *extradition* refers to the sur-

For Habermas that is not enough, because hermeneutics can only recognize the partiality of its understanding, without being able to criticize that partiality. That would require "a reference system that goes beyond the framework of tradition as such; only then can tradition also be criticized" (Habermas 1977, 358). Only from a vantage point outside of tradition can tradition per se be appropriated in its totality.

Such a vantage point is needed in order to complete our understanding of the present in light of the past because the language of tradition is not a neutral medium. Traditional meanings appear to be authoritative because the grounds for their authority or legitimacy cannot be questioned. These grounds remain submerged, and hence unexamined, because the process of interpretation is systematically distorted by relations of power. These relations of power incorporate a mobilization of bias into language itself, thereby precluding any genuine understanding of a situation by the actors involved. Hence, the authority of tradition is in actuality but a mask behind which domination conceals itself, so that the appropriation of a tradition in its totality requires that we comprehend its ideological aspect in order to understand its relevance to the present. Habermas's point is this:

> It makes good sense to conceive of language as a kind of metainstitution on which all social institutions are dependent; for social action is constituted only in ordinary language communication. But this metainstitution of language as tradition is evidently dependent in turn on social processes that are not reducible to normative relationships. Language is *also* a medium of domination and social power; it serves to legitimate relations of organized force. Insofar as the legitimations do not articulate the power relations whose institutionalization they make possible, insofar as these relations merely manifest themselves in the legitimations, language is *also* ideological. Here it is a question

---

render of a prisoner by one authority to another. Here the surrender is to the authority of the past by the sovereignty of the present.

not of deceptions within a language but of deception with language as such. Hermeneutic experience that encounters this dependency of the symbolic framework on actual conditions turns into critique of ideology. (ibid., 360)

Whence can the critique of the ideological aspect of tradition be launched, and on what is this critique founded, if not tradition itself? What is the reference system that goes beyond the framework of tradition and permits us to appropriate the meaning of tradition in its totality?

According to Habermas, a critical vantage point can only be secured in a "philosophy of history with a practical intent" (ibid., 361). Such a philosophy situates the present not only in relation to its past, but also in relation to its future. It does this by considering the present with reference to what it might become, once the possibilities that are latent within it are recognized, acted upon, and hence *realized*. The orientation of this philosophy is, therefore, practical: it is concerned with praxis—in this case history-making.

A "philosophy of history with a practical intent" concedes the effectiveness of history for human life, and hence the impossibility of discovering a vantage point outside of history from which the significance of events in history may be evaluated and judged. That much of Gadamer's argument is accepted by Habermas. However, he opposes a notion of an "effective future," as it were, to Gadamer's concept of history as an effective past. Since the future, too, is *in* history, it can provide a reference point for understanding our present situation, in the same way that the past does. By anticipating what we might become, we may understand that which we have not yet become because of the distorting influence of tradition, which reconciles us to what we are. The tension between what we are and what we may become establishes a distance that only practice can overcome, as we strive to become that which we are not, but which is possible for us to become.

The possibility of such action depends on the distance between present and future, and upon our recognition that this is a distance that calls for action, since it can only be overcome by "becoming." It is Habermas's philosophy of history with a practical intent that creates this possibility by enabling us to envision a future that is ours to make, albeit within certain limitations, for it allows Habermas to outline the conditions under which humans can become aware of the possibilities for making history that are "present" in the present.

Not surprisingly, the particular version of a philosophy of history with a practical intent adopted by Habermas is a reformulation of Marx's historical materialism. It was Marx, after all, who wrote that "men make their history, but they do not make it just as they please; they do not make it under circumstances chosen by themselves, but under circumstances directly found, given and transmitted from the past. The tradition of all the dead generations weighs like a nightmare on the brain of the living" (Marx and Engels 1972, 437).

Precisely for this reason the task of a philosophy of history with a practical intent must aim at dispelling this nightmare. It must be oriented toward the critique of tradition in its ideological aspect, so that the future can be restored to the present as a human possibility.[7] Habermas represents, therefore, the latest in a long line of exponents of what Ricoeur (1981, 34) calls a "hermeneutics of suspicion" oriented toward demystifying tradition. That is the Enlightenment project, whereas Gadamer espouses a "hermeneutics of faith" that forms the romantic antithesis of the enlightenment.

The critical moment of Habermas's "hermeneutics of sus-

[7] Lest I be misunderstood here, let me emphatically deny any sympathy with a crude determinism. The material conditions of our existence are the circumstances, not of our choosing, in which we must act. Once we realize that these conditions "determine" our existence only insofar as we fail to change them (within historical limits), they lose their power. Once we realize that the conditions of our existence are *social* conditions that are subject to human action, revolutionary action is possible. That is the whole point of historical materialism, which, in contradistinction to Feuerbach's contemplative materialism, aims to realize the truth of Camus's insight that "crushing truths perish from being acknowledged" (1955, 90).

picion" originates in a foreground of anticipation. The universal foreground, where *fore* means before in a transcendental sense, of all communication is the ideal speech situation, upon which unavoidable fiction the possibility of understanding rests. This ideal speech situation permits us to reconstruct historical discourse as it would have proceeded in the absence of any distortions introduced by inequalities of power. In so doing it allows us to identify systematic distortions of communication embedded in traditions. The partiality of traditions is thereby exposed and recognized *as* partiality, and at the same time is criticized *for* its partiality. Hence, a tradition may be appropriated in its entirety, and thereby transcended, insofar as the power of tradition over the present is broken by this critical reflection on it.

Gadamer's "hermeneutics of faith," on the other hand, raises a foreground of interpretation that is not universal, but situated in time. The *fore* here means before in a historical sense. *Every* interpretation is limited by its history and is specific to a time and place in history. Though new interpretations are possible, and indeed necessary for traditions to persist in time, they, too, will be time-bound. Hence, there is no escape from the hermeneutical situation, only a recognition of its necessity.

V

A HERMENEUTICS of suspicion requires a vantage point upon which its suspicions may be founded. Whence can this critique of ideology be launched if not from the world of our experience, i.e. the tradition-bound situation in which hermeneutics operates? Habermas's answer is derived from his theory of communicative competence, which is an attempt to understand what, practically speaking, must be assumed in order for an understanding to be reached. That is, it seeks to identify the minimal conditions that must be satisfied before an understanding can be achieved.

Gadamer, it will be remembered, construes hermeneutics as action oriented toward reaching an understanding. Habermas's strategy for criticizing the inadequacy of this approach is to observe that this conception of the hermeneutic enterprise *presumes* an idea of understanding that is largely unexplicated in Gadamer's own work. By trying to understand what is necessarily implied in the very idea of understanding, Habermas hopes to arrive at some basis for distinguishing instances in which a genuine "meeting of the minds" has been achieved from those that present only the appearance or semblance of understanding. Obviously, such a benchmark would vindicate Habermas's claim that a true or genuine understanding of a tradition depends on its critical appropriation as a whole, in which the ideological dimension of the tradition is laid bare.

The essence of this critical vantage point is summarized in the notion of an ideal speech situation. The ideal speech situation is one in which only the forceless force of persuasion is involved in bringing about an agreement or consensus among those trying to arrive at an understanding. This situation, in which reason rather than authority determines the outcome of efforts to achieve agreement, provides a regulative ideal that governs communicative action. It governs or regulates communication insofar as all action oriented toward reaching an understanding anticipates an exchange among equals free from the distortions of power and influence. Indeed, this and only this anticipation provides a rationale for participating in discourse in the first place, since an obviously closed discourse would induce few to participate in a process whose outcome was predetermined.[8]

---

[8] Formally, the ideal speech situation is characterized by symmetry. In an ideal speech situation communicative processes are undistorted because the participants sincerely engage in discourse freed from the constraints of action, i.e. from the context of power, which distorts ordinary discourses. Moreover, the play of discourse proceeds via argumentative give-and-take in which all possible participants enjoy equal chances of initiating conversation, advancing claims, challenging others' claims, and recommending suitable norms for making practical decisions. Cf. White (1980) for a summary of these conditions and an explanation of the function of ideal speech in Habermas's overall project.

To be sure, the conditions that define an ideal speech situation are never realized in practice.[9] Still, the anticipation of it is an "unavoidable fiction [upon which] rests the humanity of intercourse among men who are still men" (McCarthy 1973, 140). Ideal speech is a pragmatic assumption, not an empirical account, of communicative action. Without it, the very idea of understanding would be unintelligible.

How can the ideal speech situation be used to destroy the effectiveness of the authority of tradition over the present? According to Habermas, reflection on ideal speech provides a way of revealing the systematic distortions of communication that are embedded in a tradition and that lend it ideological force. The power (not the authority) of traditions is a function of the invisibility of these distortions. Once they are made visible, i.e. raised to consciousness, they lose their ability to distort communication. They are then susceptible to criticism from the standpoint of ideal speech.

However, as we saw in Chapter One, this does not mean that we simply compare ideal with real discourse and measure the extent of distortion. Rather, it requires that we reconstruct historical discourse in order to arrive at some understanding of how that discourse *would* have proceeded *in the absence of systematic distortions*. The orienting question in this reconstructive effort is this:

How would the members of a social system, at a given stage in the development of productive forces, have collectively and bindingly interpreted their needs (and which norms would they have accepted as justified) if they could and would have decided on organization of social intercourse through discursive will-formation, with adequate knowledge of the limiting conditions and functional imperatives of their society? (Habermas 1975, 113)

---

[9] Nevertheless, Habermas (1979a) argues that situations in which one or another condition is not satisfied may (only) be understood as deviations from their ideal.

Thus, the notion of ideal speech cannot be applied in unmediated form. It must first be translated into concrete form, i.e. a form within history. Once this counterfactual situation has been created, it is then compared with the actual discourse as it took place. To the extent that the actual discourse diverges from the reconstructed discourse, systematic distortions are presumed to be operating.

Ideal speech does not provide a "blue print" for future society; it has no utopian content. Instead it makes permanent the possibility of criticizing our understanding of the present and its possibilities by establishing a purely negative reference point. The formal conditions identified with the ideal speech situation can never be fulfilled; attempts to realize them will always fall short. Consequently, there will always be a difference betwween what we are and what we might become, a difference that calls for action oriented toward the future. In this way the "unavoidable fiction upon which human society" rests constitutes an *effective future* that may be used to destroy the effectiveness of the past over the present.

VI

THE DEPLOYMENT of counterfactual dialogues against the past and present in order to grasp the ideological aspect of tradition is an exercise in critical hermeneutics. As Benhabib describes it, this involves "letting the past generate meanings that can show the way to overcome the present for the future" (1981, 58).

This can only be done within a framework that explodes the contradictions that are present in the thematic universe of our experience. A thematic universe is a complex of "generative themes" according to which the members of a given culture understand the world and their relation to it. These themes are a defining feature of reality, since it is in and through them that the members of society apprehend reality. Of course, in defining or constituting reality these generative themes also define the possibilities for change that are present in "reality." That is why Freire (1970) calls them generative themes—they generate possibilities for action, once it is understood that reality is a social construction, and not something that is objectively given to human beings.

Because of the generative powers of such themes, any pedagogy of the oppressed must strive to activate them by raising them to consciousness. If this can be done without manipulation, "reality" will appear as something problematic, i.e. as a problem to be solved in praxis, as a drama to be concluded in action. Properly conceived, a pedagogy of the oppressed eventuates in an experiment in remaking reality, not just in theory, but in practice as well. It constitutes an episode in the unfolding of human action on the future.

How can these themes be activated? Freire seems to imply that a given thematic universe may be unlocked by certain keywords, out of which the themes are constructed, as it were. Such words are, according to Williams (1976, 13), significant and binding in certain activities and their interpretation, and they are significant, indicative words in certain forms of thought. The investigation of a culture's vocabulary of keywords is therefore an analysis of particular formations of meaning.

Keywords have special political import, because control over their meaning represents control over cultural perceptions of reality and its unrealized potential. Because of their thematic centrality, keywords are at once words of domination and liberation, depending on how they are used and by whom. When oppressed people use their oppressors' keywords uncritically, they literally inhabit a world that is defined *for* them. But when oppressed people use keywords authentically to define their world for themselves, they have liberated themselves in a quite decisive way. They have rebelled against their oppression, and if those who hold power over them are to retain that power, they must re-press the rebels.

Thus, the experimental use of keywords is necessarily a threat to existing patterns of domination. Precisely because of the practical consequences of such experimentation, the conquest of keywords is always an important part of the function of reigning ideologies. By the same token, the repossession of keywords by the oppressed is almost always rightly seen as an act of defiance and rebellion, especially by those engaged in the experimental use of keywords. "Renaming the world" is not merely a symbolic act, but a substantive challenge to power.

This is especially true when the keywords in question are fundamental to the political identity of a society. That is why it makes sense to argue, as I did in Chapter One, that a political tradition consists of "an historically extended, socially embodied argument, and an argument precisely in part about the goods which constitute that tradition" (MacIntyre 1981, 207). Such arguments are an important part of the struggle to control the meaning of keywords and the thematic universe they constitute. In that sense the semantic history of keywords is a political history, insofar as it requires reference to the political struggle over semantics, i.e. the meaning of words.

However, semantic history is political in another, more important sense. By portraying meaning as a historical artifact it also reminds us that we, too, must establish the meaning of keywords like democracy *for ourselves*. The meaning of democracy is just as problematic for us as it was for our historical predecessors. Its meaning is not given to us, but must be taken by us, as we seek to understand the world and its human possibilities.

To portray the meaning of keywords like "democracy" as politically problematic is necessarily to view them historically. It is to represent their meaning as something that is created and recreated during the course of political struggles to understand the world. This becomes obvious when we examine the history of past generations' efforts to define the meaning of democracy and establish institutions, practices, and policies that embodied their ideals. This history reminds us that we are a part of this ongoing argument over the meaning of democracy, and that our actions will have a decisive bearing on the longevity of the tradition that engulfs us.

Consequently, this history is generative by virtue of its call to us to participate in the argument about democracy, and so overcome the "culture of silence" that is the one-dimensional society. The retelling of this story is a pedagogical act; once we rediscover that the meaning of democracy is highly partisan, then the contemporary crisis of democracy can be seen as an opportunity to continue the experimental use of "democracy." And once democracy is taken to be problematic, and this is understood to be our heritage, we actually enter into the happening of the liberal democratic tradition as we engage it argumentatively.

This type of history accomplishes two things. First, it challenges conventional wisdom, which depicts the present as either having no history, or as representing the culmination or end of history. In so doing this conventional wisdom denies the future; more to the point, it denies us any role in making the future. Semantic history exposes this denial by showing human institutions for what they are—human creations that, because they are human creations, are subject to recreation. In the words of Jack Lawson, it shows that "*our institutions have not yet arrived*" (Warpole 1981, 25; my emphasis). Second, the type of consciousness that semantic history propagates presents the future not only as a possible arena of action, but as a necessary one as well. It does this by reminding us that our "lives are connected with the lives, struggles and understandings of previous generations" and that because of this there is "a common moral responsibility inherent in the historical process, both backwards to our parents' and grandparents' generations, and forwards to our children and those who come after them" (Warpole 1981, 25).

Thus, a subversive consciousness of history—of our place in the story—involves us in a way that requires us to continue the story in a certain direction, or at least with a certain intention.[10] Theory returns to practice by way of historical reflection on the story that is ours.

[10] The close connection between doing history, in the sense of telling a story about events in the world, and making history, in the sense of partici-

The fight between an effective past and an effective future is therefore an essential contest between a hermeneutics of faith and one of suspicion. At times one or the other seems to have a decisive advantage, only to be put on the defensive when the individuals of the present make their intentions known to these "theoretical antagonists." That, in fact, is what a political tradition is: a shifting battleline between past and future that is the present.

For this reason we may tell the political story of certain keywords by recounting past struggles to control their meanings. This story is at once a history of political traditions and a political history that enters into and extends the life of those traditions, for it presents the political world as a human creation. If the meaning of keywords is that their meaning is worked out among contending parties, then their meaning for us is never something that is given, but must be taken, as it were. By recalling this to mind, by remembering the history of the political traditions that engulf us, we may reawaken those traditions and ignite new discourses on the meaning of keywords *for us*. In the next section I suggest how this might be done.

VII

BY CONSTRUING traditions as more or less continuous essential contests over the meaning of the keywords that constitute those traditions, we may inspire action oriented toward the future. If we tell the story of traditions by remembering the essential contests that make up the various episodes in their histories we are also implicitly suggesting that future episodes depend on our actions. Certainly, we cannot act just as we please, but the fact remains that the meaning that the future holds *for* us must be made *by* us in the course of contests over the meaning of the keywords that constitute our political

---

pating in the events that are narrated, is evident in the double meaning of *history*. *History* means both the telling and the making of a story, as many interpreters have noted.

universe. By telling the story from this point of view, we call for action that will continue the story and so will extend the life of a tradition into the future.

Thus, the narrative structure of our history directs our attention toward the future, a future whose meaning is ours to make, but only by extending, and perhaps changing, our past. Remembrance of times lost, both past and future, is the unifying act by which we make our history. Without remembrance, there is neither past nor future, but only a dispossessed present of aimless searching, for as Tocqueville (1969) observed, where the past throws no light on the future, the human spirit wanders in darkness.

By the same token, where the future holds no attraction for those who live in the present, no future exists for the present. When a political community identifies itself exclusively with its past, forgetting its future, it has no future of its own. It has only the past and a present that is continually receding into the past.

Where either past or future are lost to the present, then, there can be no real identity for a political community.[11] Hence, there can be no question of a choice between past and future in order to act in the present. There must be some point of contact between the hermeneutics of faith and the hermeneutics of suspicion that will fuse not only past and present but present and future in an unbroken horizon of history. As Ricoeur says, the "choice" between an ontology of prior understanding and the project of freedom is a false antinomy: "Eschatology is nothing without the recitation of acts of deliverance from the past" (1981, 100).[12] That is, the

[11] Identity is a relational concept. It presumes the existence of a difference that can be shown or made a "nondifference," or at least made inessential. When a political community remembers its past or future, the separation in time of the generations in question is overcome. Without that separation or difference, however, the concept of identity loses all sense, for then there is nothing with which to identify. We identify with others, not with ourselves.

[12] We may carry the religious theme a bit further: Would the Christian doctrine of salvation be as powerful as it is without the Incarnation of the

power of ideal speech to expose authority for what it is, namely domination, and to inspire action oriented toward overcoming domination depends on a creative renewal of cultural heritage. This is because

> distortions can be criticized only in the name of a *consensus* which we cannot anticipate merely emptily, in the manner of a regulative ideal, unless that ideal is exemplified; and one of the very places of exemplification of the ideal of communication is precisely our capacity to overcome cultural distance in the interpretation of works received from the past. He who is unable to reinterpret his past may also be incapable of projecting concretely his interest in emancipation. (ibid., 97)

This raises the question of the appropriate form of language in which critical theory must be expressed if it is to become a material force in the world, i.e. a force that motivates action on the future that is present as potential.[13] For critical theory to "seize the masses" and hence become a material force in the world it must first and foremost be expressed in a language that can be grasped by the audience of critical theory. I have elsewhere discussed this issue in terms of the rhetorical adequacy of critical theory and the restrictions on rhetorical strategies that are necessary if critical theory is to be educative rather than manipulative (Hanson 1983, 383ff.). Here I shall concentrate on the form of language that is best suited for inspiring action oriented toward liberation.

That form is, I submit, the narrative, for it is narration that establishes the basic framework in which we understand the present in relation to its past and to its future, too.[14] For the

---

Word in the life of Christ? One need only compare the Judaic tradition, with its *promise* of a Messiah, with its Christian offspring in order to appreciate the profound impact that remembrance has on eschatology.

[13] "The weapon of criticism cannot replace the criticism of weapons, material force must be overthrown by material force; but theory, too, becomes amaterial force *once it seizes the masses*." (O'Malley 1970, 137; my emphasis).

[14] Habermas (1979b, 40–41) argues that a critical theory of evolution

structure of a narrative is the structure of our experience in time *as we understand it*: "We are members of the field of historicity *as* storytellers, *as* novelists, *as* historians. . . . The game of telling is included in the reality told" (Ricoeur 1981, 294; my emphasis).

It is not simply that the narrative form is a useful way of understanding human events. It is indispensable because it constitutes the structure of our experience: "In other words, *the form of life to which narrative discourse belongs is our historical condition itself*" (ibid., 288). Consequently, the relationship between historicity and narration is fundamental; historicity is the form of life correlative to the language-game of narrating (ibid., 289).

Thus, we understand ourselves in narrative terms by placing ourselves and those with whom we interact in the context of an unfolding plot. Our lives are embedded within a story line that stretches from the actions that have led to the present to those that may follow. That story renders intelligible our relation to the past by referring to its continuation in the future. It is toward the future that a plot progresses, and it is the future that acts as a pole of attraction in the whole process (ibid., 277).

Nevertheless, the conclusion of this process can be neither deduced nor predicted from the plot line: "There is no story unless our attention is held in suspense by a thousand contingencies. Hence we must follow the story to its conclusion. So rather than being *predictable*, a conclusion must be *acceptable*" (ibid., 277). Or rather, it must be *intelligible*. As MacIntyre (1981, 201) observes, there are an indefinite number

---

"needs no further narrative reshaping, [and] cannot even be brought into narrative form" without leading to a "theory of development claiming to be a theory of history [that] makes us the unfulfillable offer of predicting historical processes and accepting the role of prophecy." This depends on an implausible distinction between theory and history, as McCarthy (1978) shows. A theory of *social* evolution is unavoidably a history of the human species, even though it proceeds at a more abstract level of explanation.

of conclusions that will make sense of a story, even though
not every conclusion will do so.

It may be useful here to think of a musical analogy to this
unfolding of action. A jazz improvisation elaborates on what
went before in the play of music, and it may do so in any
number of ways. Each elaboration leads to further elaborations, and so on until a virtually endless improvisation may
be conceived, if not actually played. Nevertheless, the indeterminacy of this process does not mean that it is unconstrained. Not just anything counts as an elaboration, and
some elaborations lead nowhere. Moreover, the whole improvisation builds on what went before.

In the same way, the story that we live and about which
we weave our own narratives is affected by actions that have
gone before—history *is* effective. Hence, we "act out" our
lives "upon a stage which we did not design and we find
ourselves part of an action that [is] not of our making" (ibid.,
199). Still, the outcome of the story remains in doubt, since
it depends in part on the way in which we, the *dramatis
personae*, perform roles that remain to be written by us. Insofar as we are able to grasp our present situation and the possibilities contained therein, and then act upon those possibilities, the story may continue indefinitely and unpredictably.

Indeed, the value of Habermas's attempt to establish a negative reference point lies precisely in the permanent tension
it establishes between present and future. We do not move
toward ideal speech and its realization at some point in the
future, at which point our story ends. Rather, we improve
our present situation by recognizing its openness to action.
We anticipate the future, improvise our story, and so carry
the plot ever forward in time.

VIII

BECAUSE OUR HISTORY is narratively structured, it points
toward the future: "History is only present to us in light of
our futurity. Here we have all learned from Heidegger, for
he exhibited the primacy of futurity for our possible recollec-

tion and retention, and for the whole of our history" (Gadamer 1976, 9).[15]

If futurity is the condition of memory, memory is the safeguard of futurity.[16] Precisely because the circumstances in
which men and women act are not of their choosing, effective
action, i.e. action oriented toward changing the world, depends on an understanding of those circumstances and the
limits they impose upon action.[17] Without this understanding, action is ineffective, for unless we understand the present in terms of what it has been and what it can become, we
will fail to make history. We will run up against the objective
limits to action that are present in *any* historical situation.
Indeed, it is precisely this realistic understanding of possibilities that are latent in society that distinguishes Marx's and
Engel's scientific socialism from its utopian counterfeit, which
strives to realize what cannot be realized.

[15] Despite the importance of the concept of futurity in philosophical hermeneutics, Gadamer, by his own admission, remains a partisan of the past:
"I shall not deny, however, . . . that I have emphasized the element of the
assimilation of what is past and handed down." This is because Gadamer
believes that a corrective is needed to the one-sidedness of the modern attitude toward making, producing, and constructing, an attitude that down-
plays questions about the feasibility or possibility of such practices. Hence,
"the hermeneutic consciousness, which must be awakened and kept awake,
recognizes that in the age of science the claim of superiority made by philosophic thought has something vague and unreal about it. But it seeks to
confront the will of man, which is more than ever intensifying its criticism
of what has gone before to the point of becoming a utopian or eschatological
consciousness, with something from the truth of remembrance: with what is
still and ever again real" (Gadamer 1960, xxv–xxvi).

This distinction between willing and remembering or thinking is, of
course, a central theme in Hannah Arendt's *The Life of the Mind* (1978).

[16] "Memory, in the sense of human thinking that recalls, dwells where
everything that gives food for thought is kept in safety . . . [it] consists in
the 'keeping' of what is most thought-provoking. Keeping is the fundamental
nature and essence of memory" (Heidegger 1968, 150–151).

[17] I read the eleventh of Marx's "Theses on Feuerbach" to mean that a
contemplative understanding of the world is alienating, and that understanding the world *in order to* change it is inadequate praxis. Rather, we must
understand the world *as* something to be changed, *as* a problem to be
solved, *as* a world to be created and recreated in action.

To see the world as a contradiction of our humanity is, therefore, to see it as something to be dissolved by action, rather than as something to which we must reconcile ourselves in thought. Thus, successful action oriented toward liberation presumes historical knowledge. But there is another and perhaps more fundamental connection between remembrance and liberation. It involves the inspiration to act, to make history, that sometimes comes from an appreciation of history. History is, after all, a reminder that human beings can, under certain conditions, make history. They can make the future present, and the present past by realizing one or another of the possibilities that are "present" in the present through effective action. For that reason would-be revolutionaries of all stripes call upon history to motivate people to act in the spirit of past revolutionaries and forebears.

At times this invocation leads to the results anticipated by Marx in *The Eighteenth Brumaire of Louis Bonaparte*, where he comments that "Hegel remarks somewhere that all great, world-historical facts and personages occur, as it were twice. He has forgotten to add: the first time as tragedy, the second as farce" (Marx and Engels 1972, 436). The first revolutionaries make history by transforming their present into its future. But the second or third generation revolutionaries who conjure up the dead return the present to a caricatured version of its past.[18] They produce a Louis Bonaparte for Napoleon, a Louis Blanc for Robespierre. Hence, they do not make history, but only parody it. That is why Marx insisted that "the social revolution of the nineteenth century cannot draw its poetry from the past, but only from the future" (ibid., 439). True revolutionaries must break with the past in order to achieve their liberation. They must write their own history, rather than engage in a romantic remembrance of things past.

---

[18] Revolutions that seek their legitimacy in the authority of the past "revolve" in time, while those that seek it in the promise of the future "break" with time, exhibiting the two main senses of *revolution*.

Marx's advice certainly seems sound, insofar as remembrance replaces action on the future in the present. Reveries do not make revolutions; they do not liberate us from the material conditions of our existence. However, certain types of remembrance have a different relation to action. They constitute effective action by reminding us that the future is ours. They recall to mind the historicity of our present, which is not the end of time, but only a moment within it. They recollect past presents that *became* past through the action of men and women who saw the futures that were present for them, and whose deeds realized those futures, i.e. *made* them present.

This sort of remembrance, in which all things pass, and in which history is made in the passing, is revolutionary. It restores to us our capacity to act effectively by reminding us of our agency. When we recall, not revolutionary personages or their specific deeds, but the *examples* of making history that constitute our past (and present, as well), remembrance and liberation are joined in the present.

My claim here is not merely that history can sometimes be inspiring, leading us to make history. Rather, it is that this sense of our own historicity that remembrance provides is indispensable to effective action, or liberation. To make history *presumes* that we are historical agents and that we are conscious of that "ontological vocation" that is ours by virtue of that fact (Freire 1970, 12). The experience of our own historicity is essential to that realization. Remembrance, understood a certain way, is therefore liberation, since it frees us to act within the confines of a given historical situation.

This is not merely a philosophical point. As soon as we lose sight of our ontological vocation, we can no longer make our history, for then we have forgotten our agency. We become the bearers of history, rather than its makers. Unless we can remember times lost, we will lose time altogether. We will be dispossessed of both future and past, and our children will be born in political exile (LeGuin 1974, 72).

IX

TO FOLLOW A HISTORY is to follow the plot of the story, so to speak, which requires us to anticipate a final course or outcome, without being able to predict that outcome with certainty. This anticipation allows us to see the significance of a chain of events in terms of the outcome to which it leads, while the chain of events leads us to correct our anticipation as we follow its links.

In that sense every history is told from a future point of view. Telling history from the standpoint of the future is not something we choose to do; it is something we must do. As Habermas (1977, 350) observes, "Every historian is in the role of the last historian" since the writing of history necessarily proceeds on the basis of certain expectations about the future and its conclusion. All historians, insofar as they are *historians*, anticipate "the end of history" from which history may be told. It is only from such a standpoint that the significance of various episodes in history emerge: they lead to a certain conclusion, and that is why they are deemed significant.

Hence, to tell our own story we must anticipate what we *may* become. We cannot be certain of what we *will* become, but it is only in light of our possibilities as we presently understand them that we will be able to recount our history. Otherwise, we would not be able to see the significance of the events in our past—we would not be able to say where these events lead, or what lends them significance.

Thus, we understand ourselves in historical terms by placing ourselves and those with whom we interact in the context of an unfolding plot. Our lives are embedded within the story line that stretches from the actions that have led to the present and to those that may follow. The story renders intelligible our relation to the past by referring to its continuation in the future because it is toward the future that a plot progresses, and it is the future that acts as a pole of attraction in the whole process (Ricoeur 1981, 277).

Our anticipation of the future, of what we may become, can only be hypothetical, and subject to correction on our part as further "surprises" unfold. We must view it practically, i.e. as a project. This means that we must adopt certain practices vis-à-vis a future that is not known and indeed cannot be. We must project ourselves into the future as we understand it and orient our actions "in the here and now" accordingly. At the same time, however, we must remain open to the future: we must be willing and able to adjust our expectations in light of any surprises that might come our way.

Of course, by projecting ourselves into the future we are identifying that future as ours in some way. It is a future that we imagine, and that we implicitly seek to realize in the actions that we undertake on the basis of this image. Consequently, the future is something that we call into existence as we "enter into the happening of a tradition" and try to extend it.

It is for this reason that remembrance is liberating, in the sense that I argued in the last section. It is also for this reason that remembrance is obliging, in the sense of recalling our responsibility to us. Because we are actors in a drama not of our making, we cannot be held accountable for failing to perform our appointed role if we do not understand our place in the drama. However, once we remember how we came to be where we are today, our place in the liberal democratic tradition becomes evident, and so, too, do our responsibilities as liberal democrats. We must conduct ourselves in a manner that is consistent with the constitutive ideas of liberal democracy, so that the story may continue to unfold in an intelligible direction.

We cannot avoid this responsibility. Whether we will it or not, we are liberal democrats by virtue of our historical situation. We cannot escape the weight of tradition. However, by remembering our place in the story, we may recall what has to be done in order to extend our tradition in a progressive direction.

Would-be liberal democrats *must* assume that progress is

possible; there really is no choice for them. To choose other-wise would deny the value of contestation itself, since it is in and through arguments over the meaning of liberal democ-racy in concrete situations that progress occurs. The commit-ment to progress via arguments over the meaning of liberal democratic progress is therefore a constitutive feature of lib-eral democratic power talk. Without this commitment liberal democratic discourse cannot persist. Participants would no longer have any reason to engage in disputation. They would be confronted by the choice between withdrawing from the argument altogether, or enforcing their interpretation on others who do not share it. In either case, liberal democratic power talk, properly speaking, would cease to exist.

Liberal democrats who assume that progress is possible, and that it can be achieved through argumentative exchanges oriented toward collective problem-solving, do not do so be-cause they know what the future holds. Knowledge of the future is, after all, impossible. We may have certain hy-potheses about what the future holds, but these hypotheses remain untested until the future actually takes place. To be sure, some of our hypotheses may seem more plausible than others. We may, for example, anticipate what is to come on the basis of what has already been. History may lead us to expect certain things from the future, and our reading of his-tory may sustain our hope for progress. However, we cannot write a history of the future until it happens, and so our un-derstanding of the future and its possibilities remains essen-tially incomplete.

Not even theories of evolution can provide us with knowl-edge of the future. Whereas history is always retrospectively oriented, and so cannot tell us much about the future, theo-ries of evolution, which are prospectively oriented, cannot tell us which way history *will* unfold. They may tell us a great deal about what will not or cannot happen, and they may even tell us something about the range of possible outcomes that might occur, but they cannot tell us which of several possibilities will actually be realized (Habermas 1979b). To the extent that they try to do so, they deny history and our agency within it, because the future is determined for us.

Thus, liberal democrats confront the future without knowledge of what it holds for them. Their attitude toward the future, therefore, must be *practical*; it cannot be theoretical. For liberal democrats, as we have seen, this entails a commitment to keeping the future forever open. Progress is an indefinite possibility, so long as the shape of the future is determined only by the "forceless force of the better argument."

Hence, undistorted communication is the practical hypothesis that liberal democrats make vis-à-vis the future and its determination, and that allows them to anticipate the future as one of permanent possibilities for progress. The ideal speech situation, in which only the forceless force of persuasion is involved in bringing about an agreement or consensus among those trying to arrive at an understanding, provides a constitutive ideal that governs liberal democratic power talk. It governs or regulates communication insofar as all action oriented toward reaching an understanding anticipates an exchange among equals free from the distortions of power and influence. Indeed, this and only this anticipation provides a rationale for participating in discourse in the first place, since an obviously closed discourse would induce few to participate in the process whose outcome was predetermined.

Liberal democratic power talk involves agreeing to disagree, not only in the sense of tolerating alternative interpretations of liberal democracy, but of engaging them argumentatively. Disagreement is essential, insofar as it is through disagreements that new interpretations of liberal democracy are produced. Seen in this light, liberal democratic discourse makes progress when disagreements are tolerated, expressed, and engaged, and when disagreement itself is valued above the peace that victory brings. Only when the commitment to pro*gress*, understood as an intransitive verb, underpins discussions of specific notions of progress, understood as a noun, is coherent discourse possible.

Political opposition to this kind of discourse is quite substantial and powerful. To paraphrase Lakatos (1970), every challenge to reigning interpretations of liberal democracy is born refuted by the status quo, and when these challenges involve radical reinterpretations, they face great opposition indeed. Hence, those who would be liberal democrats are in an unenviable, but hardly unique, position. They must act so as to initiate a new essential contest over the meaning of liberal democracy, and they must do so under circumstances that seem to auger against the success of their efforts. Even worse, their failure, should it occur, may eventuate in a more sinister form of power talk, if today's confusion is replaced by the coherence of a totally closed universe of discourse. Further degeneration is conceivable, after all, once the contest is reopened—albeit in hopes of progress.

That is a risk that liberal democrats must take, in my judgment. Any historical situation that is open to progressive actions is also open to regressive ones, and the latter may occur even if the former are not undertaken. In that sense those who hope for progress have no choice but to act upon that hope, if only to guard against further regression. If they do not act on that hope, no progress (as liberal democrats understand it) will be forthcoming. The future does not come to those who wait; it answers the call of those who summon it.

REFERENCES

Ackerman, Bruce A. 1980. *Social Justice and the Liberal State*. New Haven: Yale University Press.

Adair, Douglass. 1957. " 'That Politics May be Reduced to a Science': David Hume, James Madison and the Tenth *Federalist*." *Huntington Library Quarterly* 20 (August):343–360.

———. 1974. "Fame and the Founding Fathers." In *Fame and the Founding Fathers: Essays by Douglass Adair*, ed. H. Trevor Colbourn, pp. 3–26. New York: W. W. Norton.

Adams, W. Paul. 1970. "Republicanism in Political Rhetoric before 1776." *Political Science Quarterly* 85 (September):397–421.

Addams, Jane. 1960. *Jane Addams: A Centennial Reader*. New York: Macmillan.

Allen, Devere. 1935. "The Conquest of Democracy." *American Socialist Quarterly* 4 (March):3–14.

American Review: A Whig Journal Devoted to Politics and Literature. January 1845; September 1847; September 1851; February 1852.

Ames, Fisher. [1854] 1971. *Works*. Edited by Seth Ames. 2 vols. New York: Burt Franklin Publishers.

Apel, Karl-Otto. 1980. *Towards a Transformation of Philosophy*. Translated by Glyn Adey and David Frisby. London: Routledge & Kegan Paul.

Appleby, Joyce. 1982. "What Is Still American in the Political Philosophy of Thomas Jefferson?" *William and Mary Quarterly* 39 (April):287–309.

Arendt, Hannah. 1958. *The Human Condition*. Chicago: University of Chicago Press.

———. 1978. *The Life of the Mind*. New York: Harcourt Brace Jovanovich.

Auer, John Jeffrey, ed. 1963. *Antislavery and Disunion, 1858–1861; Studies in the Rhetoric of Compromise and Conflict*. New York: Harper & Row.

Bachrach, Peter. 1967. *The Theory of Democratic Elitism: A Critique*. Boston: Little, Brown.

Bailyn, Bernard. 1967. *The Ideological Origins of the American Revolution*. Cambridge: Harvard University Press.

Ball, Terence. 1978. "Two Concepts of Coercion." *Theory and Society* 5 (January):97–112.

———. 1979. "Interest Explanations." *Polity* 12 (Winter):187–201.

———. 1983. "The Ontological Presuppositions and Political Consequences of a Social Science." In *Changing Social Science: Critical Theory and Other Critical Perspectives*, ed. Daniel R. Sabia and Jerald Wallulis, pp. 31–52. Albany: State University of New York Press.

Banner, James M., Jr. 1970. *To the Hartford Convention: The Federalists and the Origins of Party Politics in Massachusetts, 1789–1815*. New York: Alfred A. Knopf.

Banning, Lance. 1978. *The Jeffersonian Persuasion: Evolution of a Party Ideology*. Ithaca: Cornell University Press.

Barbour, D. Christine. 1980. "Virtue and the Founding Fathers: The Ideological Underpinning of American Politics." Photocopy. Bloomington: Department of Political Science, Indiana University.

Barker, Ernest, ed. and trans. 1975. *The Politics of Aristotle*. New York: Oxford University Press.

Bay, Christian. 1981. *Strategies of Political Enlightenment*. Notre Dame, IN: University of Notre Dame Press.

Beard, Charles. 1965. *An Economic Interpretation of the Constitution of the United States*. New York: Free Press.

Beer, Samuel H. 1965. "Liberalism and the National Idea." In *Left, Right and Center: Essays on Liberalism and Conservatism in the United States*, ed. Robert A. Goldwin, pp. 142–169. Chicago: Rand McNally.

———. 1978. "In Search of a New Public Philosophy." In *The New American Political System*, ed. Anthony King, pp. 5–44. Washington, D.C.: American Enterprise Institute for Public Policy Research.

Bell, Daniel. 1962. *The End of Ideology: On the Exhaustion of Political Ideas in the Fifties*. New York: Crowell-Collier Publishing, Collier Books.

———. 1976. *The Cultural Contradictions of Capitalism*. New York: Basic Books.

Bellamy, Edward. 1917. *Looking Backward, 2000–1887*. New York: Random House.

———. 1968. *Equality*. Upper Saddle River, NJ: Gregg Press.

Benhabib, Seyla. 1981. "Modernity and the Aporias of Critical Theory." *Telos* 49 (Fall):39–60.

Bennett, David H. 1969. *Demagogues in the Depression: American Radicals and the Union Party, 1932–1936*. New Brunswick, NJ: Rutgers University Press.

Benson, Lee. 1961. *The Concept of Jacksonian Democracy: New York as a Test Case*. Princeton: Princeton University Press.

Berlin, Sir Isaiah. 1958. *Two Concepts of Liberty*. Oxford: Clarendon Press.

Bernstein, Richard J. 1978. *The Restructuring of Social and Political Theory*. Philadelphia: University of Pennsylvania Press.

Berthoff, Rowland. 1979. "Independence and Attachment, Virtue and Interest: From Republican Citizen to Free Enterpriser." In *Uprooted Americans: Essays to Honor Oscar Handlin*, ed. Richard Bushman, Neil Harris, David Rothman, Barbara Miller Solomon, and Stephen Thernstrom, pp. 97–124. Boston: Little, Brown.

Bezold, Clement, ed. 1978. *Anticipatory Democracy: People in the Politics of the Future*. New York: Random House.

Biemiller, Andrew. 1934. "Socialism and Democracy." *American Socialist Quarterly* 3 (Spring):20–28.

Blau, Joseph L. 1954. *Social Theories of Jacksonian Democracy: Representative Writings of the Period 1825–1850*. New York: Liberal Arts Press.

Bloom, Alan, trans. 1968. *The Republic of Plato*. New York: Basic Books.

Boase, Paul H., ed. 1980. *The Rhetoric of Protest and Reform, 1878–1898*. Athens: Ohio University Press.

Boorstin, Daniel. 1969. *An American Primer*. New York: New American Library.

Bouchier, David. 1979. *Idealism and Revolution: New Ideologies of Liberation in Britain and the U.S.* New York: St. Martin's Press.

Breines, Paul, ed. 1970. *Critical Interruptions: New Left Perspectives on Herbert Marcuse*. New York: Herder & Herder.

Brinkley, Alan. 1982. *Voices of Protest: Huey Long, Father Coughlin and the Great Depression*. New York: Random House, Vintage Books.

Brown, Robert E. 1968. *Middle-Class Democracy and the Revolu-*

tion of Massachusetts, 1691–1780. New York: Russell & Russell Publishers.

Brown, Roger H. 1964. *The Republic in Peril: 1812*. New York: Columbia University Press.

Brownson, Orestes Augustus. 1840. "The Laboring Classes." Parts 1, 2. *Boston Quarterly Review* 3 (July, October): 358–395, 420–512.

————. 1865. *The American Republic: Its Constitution, Tendencies and Destiny*. New York: P. O'Shea.

————. 1882–1887. *The Works of Orestes Brownson*. Edited by Henry F. Brownson. 20 vols. Detroit: Thorndike Nourse.

Buel, Richard, Jr. 1964. "Democracy and the American Revolution: A Frame of Reference." *William and Mary Quarterly* 21 (April): 165–190.

Buhle, Mari Jo. 1983. *Women and American Socialism, 1870–1920*. Urbana: University of Illinois Press.

Buhle, Mari Jo, and Buhle, Paul. 1978. *The Concise History of Woman Suffrage: Selections from the Classic Works of Stanton, Anthony, Gage, and Harper*. Urbana: University of Illinois Press.

Burgess, Parke G. 1969. "The Rhetoric of Black Power: A Moral Demand?" In *The Rhetoric of Our Time*, ed. J. Jeffrey Auer. New York: Appleton-Century-Crofts.

Butterfield, Herbert. 1951. *The Whig Interpretation of History*. New York: Charles Scribner's Sons.

Calhoun, John C. 1883. *Works*. Vol. 1. Edited by R. K. Cralle. New York: D. Appleton & Co.

————. [1853] 1978. *A Disquisition on Government and Selections from the Discourse*. Ed. C. Gordon Post. Indianapolis, IN: Bobbs-Merrill Co.

————. 1980. " 'Remarks on Receiving Abolition Petitions,' in the U.S. Senate, February 6, 1837." In *The Papers of John C. Calhoun*, ed. Clyde N. Wilson, vol. 13, pp. 391–398. Columbia, SC: University of South Carolina Press.

Calvert, Greg. 1967. "Participatory Democracy, Collective Leadership and Political Responsibility." *New Left Notes*, December 18, pp. 1, 8.

Calvert, Greg, and Neiman, Carol. 1971. *A Disrupted History: The New Left and the New Capitalism*. New York: Random House.

Camus, Albert. 1955. *The Myth of Sisyphus and Other Essays*. New York: Random House, Vintage Books.

Campbell, Bruce A., and Trilling, Richard J., eds. 1980. "Toward a Theory of Realignment: An Introduction." In *Realignment in American Politics: Toward a Theory*. Austin: University of Texas Press.

Cantor, Milton. 1978. *The Divided Left: American Radicalism, 1900–1975*. New York: Hill & Wang.

Care, Norman S. 1973. "On Fixing Social Concepts." *Ethics* 84 (October):10–21.

Carey, George W. 1978. "Separation of Powers and the Madisonian Model: A Reply to the Critics." *American Political Science Review* 72 (March):151–164.

———. 1980. "Comment: Constitutionalists and the Constitutional Tradition: So What?" *Journal of Politics* 42 (February):36–46.

Carmichael, Stokely, and Hamilton, Charles V. 1967. *Black Power: The Politics of Liberation in America*. New York: Random House, Vintage Books.

Cash, W. J. 1941. *The Mind of the South*. Garden City: Doubleday, Anchor Books.

Chesneaux, Jean. 1978. *Pasts and Futures, or What Is History For?* London: Thames & Hudson.

Chinard, Gilbert. 1939. *Thomas Jefferson: The Apostle of Americanism*. 2d ed. Ann Arbor: University of Michigan Press.

Churchill, Winston. 1947. "Speech before the House of Commons on the Parliament Bill." November 11. *Parliamentary Debates* (Commons), 5th ser., 444:204–321.

Clecak, Peter. 1973. *Radical Paradoxes: Dilemmas of the American Left, 1945–1970*. New York: Harper & Row, Torchbooks.

Cohen, Jean. 1979. "Why More Political Theory?" *Telos* 40 (Summer):70–94.

Colborne, H. Trevor. 1965. *The Lamp of Experience: Whig History and the Intellectual Origins of the American Revolution*. Chapel Hill: University of North Carolina Press.

Collingwood, R. G. 1939. *An Autobiography*. Oxford: Oxford University Press.

———. 1956. *The Idea of History*. London: Oxford University Press.

Colton, Calvin. 1974. *The Junius Tracts and the Rights of Labor*. Edited by Michael Hudson. New York: Garland Publishers.

Connerton, Paul. 1980. *The Tragedy of Enlightenment*. Cambridge: Cambridge University Press.

Connolly, William E. 1974. *The Terms of Political Discourse*. Lexington, MA: D. C. Heath.

——. 1979. "Appearance and Reality in Politics." *Political Theory* 7 (November):445–468.

——. 1981. "The Politics of Reindustrialization." *Democracy* 1 (July):9–21.

Coughlin, Charles E. 1933. *Driving Out the Money Changers*. Royal Oak, MI: Radio League of the Little Flower.

——. 1934. *Eight Lectures on Labor, Capital and Justice*. Royal Oak, MI: Radio League of the Little Flower.

——. 1935. *A Series of Lectures on Social Justice*. Royal Oak, MI: Radio League of the Little Flower.

——. 1938. *Sixteen Radio Lectures: 1938 Series*. Royal Oak, MI: Charles E. Coughlin.

Croly, Herbert. 1910. *The Promise of American Life*. New York: Macmillan.

——. 1914. *Progressive Democracy*. New York: Macmillan.

Crozier, Michel, Huntington, Samuel P., and Watanuki, Joji. 1975. *The Crisis of Democracy: Report on the Governability of Democracies to the Trilateral Commission*. New York: New York University Press.

Curry, Richard O. 1974. "The Civil War and Reconstruction, 1861–1877: A Critical Overview of Recent Trends and Interpretations." *Civil War History* 20 (September):215–238.

Dahl, Robert A. 1956. *A Preface to Democratic Theory*. Chicago: University of Chicago Press.

Davis, David Brion. 1962. "The Emergence of Immediatism in British and American Antislavery Thought." *Mississippi Valley Historical Review* 49 (September):209–230.

——. 1966. *The Problem of Slavery in Western Culture*. Ithaca, NY: Cornell University Press.

——. 1975. *The Problem of Slavery in the Age of Revolution, 1770–1823*. Ithaca, NY: Cornell University Press.

Dekema, Jan D. 1981. "Incommensurability and Judgment." *Theory and Society* 10 (July):521–546.

Destler, Chester M. 1946. *American Radicalism 1865–1901*. New London: Connecticut College.

Desvernine, Raoul E. 1936. *Democratic Despotism*. New York: Dodd, Mead.

Dewey, John. 1963. *Liberalism and Social Action*. New York: Paragon Book Reprint Corp.

Dickson, David. 1981. "Limiting Democracy: Technocrats and the Liberal State." *Democracy* 1 (January):61–79.

Dubofsky, Melvyn. 1969. *We Shall Be All: A History of the Industrial Workers of the World*. New York: New York Times Book Co.

Dunn, John. 1974. "Democracy Unretrieved, or the Political Theory of Professor Macpherson." *British Journal of Political Science* 4 (October):489–499.

Dwight, Theodore. 1970. *History of the Hartford Convention: With a Review of the Policy of the United States Government Which Led to the War of 1812*. New York: Da Capo Press.

Elliott, E. N. 1860. *Cotton is King, and Proslavery Arguments*. Augusta, GA: Pritchard, Abbott & Loomis.

Emerson, Ralph Waldo. 1965. *The Portable Emerson*. Edited by Mark van Doren. New York: Viking.

———. n. d. *The Works of Ralph Waldo Emerson*. 4 vols. New York: Tudor Publishing Company.

Evans, Sara. 1978. *Personal Politics: The Roots of Women's Liberation in the Civil Rights Movement and the New Left*. New York: Alfred A. Knopf.

Farry, Joseph P. 1984. "The Bill of Rights and the Anti-Federalists' Theory of Republicanism." Paper presented at the annual meeting of the Midwestern Political Science Association, April 12–14, Chicago.

Ferkiss, Victor Christopher. 1957. "Populist Influences on American Fascism." *Western Political Quarterly* 10 (June):350–373.

Fine, Sidney. 1956. *Laissez Faire and the General-Welfare State*. Ann Arbor: University of Michigan Press.

Fischer, David H. 1965. *The Revolution of American Conservatism: The Federalist Party in the Era of Jeffersonian Democracy*. New York: Harper & Row.

Fitzgerald, Frances. 1979. *America Revised: History Schoolbooks in the Twentieth Century*. Boston: Little, Brown.

Fitzhugh, George. [1854] n.d. *Sociology for the South, or the Future of Free Society*. New York: Burt Franklin Publishers.

———. [1857] 1960. *Cannibals All! or Slaves Without Masters*. Edited by C. Vann Woodward. Cambridge: Harvard University Press, Belknap Press.

Flexner, Eleanor. 1974. *Century of Struggle: The Woman's Rights Movement in the United States*. New York: Atheneum.

Foner, Eric. 1970. *Free Soil, Free Labor, Free Men: The Ideology of the Republican Party before the Civil War*. New York: Oxford University Press.

———. 1976. "Tom Paine's Republic: Radical Ideology and Social Change." In *The American Revolution: Explorations in the History of American Radicalism*, ed. Alfred F. Young. DeKalb, IL: Northern Illinois University Press.

———. 1980. *Politics and Ideology in the Age of the Civil War*. New York: Oxford University Press.

Foner, Philip S. 1964. *History of the Labor Movement in the United States*. Vol. 3. New York: International Publishers.

———. 1976. *The Democratic-Republican Societies, 1790–1800: A Documentary Sourcebook of Constitutions, Declarations, Addresses, Resolutions and Toasts*. Westport, CT: Greenwood Press.

Forcey, Charles. 1961. *The Crossroads of Liberalism: Croly, Weyl, Lippmann, and the Progressive Era*. New York: Oxford University Press.

Formisano, Ronald P. 1971. *The Birth of Mass Political Parties: Michigan, 1827–1861*. Princeton: Princeton University Press.

———. 1974. "Deferential-Participant Politics: The Early Republic's Political Culture." *American Political Science Review* 68 (June):473–487.

Freehling, William W. 1965. "Spoilsmen and Interests in the Thought and Career of John C. Calhoun." *Journal of American History* 52 (June):25–42.

———. 1966. *Prelude to Civil War: The Nullification Controversy in South Carolina, 1816–1836*. New York: Harper & Row.

Freire, Paulo. 1970. *Pedagogy of the Oppressed*. Translated by Myron Bergman Ramos. New York: Seabury Press, Continuum Books.

Freneau, Philip M. 1929. *Poems of Freneau*. Edited by Harry Hayden Clark. New York: Hafner Publishing.

Gadamer, Hans-Georg. 1960. *Truth and Method*. Edited by Garret Barden and John Cummings. New York: Seabury Press, Continuum Books.

————. 1976. *Philosophical Hermeneutics*. Translated and edited by David E. Linge. Berkeley and Los Angeles: University of California Press.

Galbraith, John Kenneth. 1952. *American Capitalism: The Concept of Countervailing Power*. Boston: Houghton Mifflin.

Gallie, W. B. 1955–1956. "Essentially Contested Concepts." *Proceedings of the Aristotelian Society*. 56:167–198.

————. 1964. *Philosophy and the Historical Understanding*. London: Chatto & Windus.

Garver, Eugene. 1978. "Rhetoric and Essentially Contested Arguments." *Philosophy and Rhetoric* 11 (Summer):156–172.

Geertz, Clifford. 1964. "Ideology as a Cultural System." In *Ideology and Discontent*, ed. David E. Apter, pp. 47–76. New York: Free Press.

Genovese, Eugene. 1967. *The Political Economy of Slavery*. New York: Random House, Vintage Books.

George, Henry. [1879] 1948. *Progress and Poverty*. New York: Robert Schalkenbach Foundation.

Gettleman, Marvin E., and Mermelstein, David. 1967. *The Great Society Reader: The Failure of American Liberalism*. New York: Random House, Vintage Books.

Gilbert, James. 1972. *Designing the Industrial State: The Intellectual Pursuit of Collectivism in America*. Chicago: Quadrangle Books.

Gilder, George. 1981. *Wealth and Poverty*. New York: Bantam Books.

Gill, Robert M. 1983. "*The Degradation of the Democratic Dogma*: Henry Adams and the Death of the Democratic Ideal." In *The Constitutional Polity: Essays on the Founding Principles of American Politics*, ed. Sidney A. Pearson, Jr., pp. 103–123. Washington, D.C.: University Press of America.

Ginger, Ray. 1965. *Age of Excess: The United States from 1877–1914*. New York: Macmillan.

Gitlin, Todd. 1967. "Potentials of the Poor." *New Left Notes*, June 26, pp. 13–19.

Goldman, Eric. 1956. *Rendezvous with Destiny*. New York: Random House, Vintage Books.

Goldwin, Robert A., ed. 1971. *How Democratic is America? Responses to the New Left Challenge*. Chicago: Rand McNally.

Goodman, Paul. 1967. "The First American Party System." In *The American Party Systems: Stages of Political Development*, ed. William Nisbet Chambers and Walter Dean Burnham, pp. 56–89. New York: Oxford University Press.

Goodwyn, Lawrence. 1976. *Democratic Promise: The Populist Moment in America*. New York: Oxford University Press.

———. 1981. "Organizing Democracy: The Limits of Theory and Practice." *Democracy* 1 (January):41–60.

Gray, John. 1977. "On the Contestability of Social and Political Concepts." *Political Theory* 5 (August):331–348.

———. 1978. "On Liberty, Liberalism and Essential Contestability." *British Journal of Political Science* 8 (October):385–402.

Grob, Gerald N. 1969. *Workers and Utopia: A Study of Ideological Conflict in the American Labor Movement 1865–1900*. New York: New York Times Book Co.

Grønbjerg, Kirsten A. 1977. *Mass Society and the Extension of Welfare 1960–1970*. Chicago: University of Chicago Press.

Haber, Samuel. 1964. *Efficiency and Uplift: Scientific Management in the Progressive Era*. Chicago: University of Chicago Press.

Habermas, Jürgen. 1970. *Toward a Rational Society: Student Protest, Science and Politics*. Translated by Jeremy J. Shapiro. Boston: Beacon Press.

———. 1973. *Theory and Practice*. Translated by John Viertel. Boston: Beacon Press.

———. 1975. *Legitimation Crisis*. Translated by Thomas McCarthy. Boston: Beacon Press.

———. 1977. "A Review of Gadamer's *Truth and Method*." In *Understanding and Social Inquiry*, ed. Fred R. Dallmayr and Thomas A. McCarthy, pp. 335–363. Notre Dame, IN: University of Notre Dame Press.

———. 1979a. *Communication and the Evolution of Society*. Translated by Thomas McCarthy. Boston: Beacon Press.

———. 1979b. "History and Evolution." *Telos* 39 (Spring):5–44.

———. 1981. "New Social Movements." *Telos* 49 (Fall):33–37.

Hammond, Bray. 1957. *Banks and Politics in America from the Revolution to the Civil War*. Princeton: Princeton University Press.

Hanson, Russell L. 1982. "Labor and Legitimacy under Organized Capitalism." Paper presented at the annual meeting of the Western Political Science Association, March 25–27, San Diego, CA.

————. 1983. *The Democratic Imagination in America: Conversations with Our Past*. Ph.D. dissertation, University of Minnesota.

Hansot, Elizabeth. 1974. *Perfection and Progress: Two Modes of Utopian Thought*. Cambridge, MA: MIT Press.

Hart, Vivien. 1978. *Distrust and Democracy: Political Distrust in Britain and America*. Cambridge: Cambridge University Press.

Hartz, Louis. 1955. *The Liberal Tradition in America*. New York: Harcourt, Brace & World.

Hatch, Nathan O. 1977. *The Sacred Cause of Liberty: Republican Thought and the Millennium in Revolutionary New England*. New Haven: Yale University Press.

Hayek, Friedrich A. 1944. *The Road to Serfdom*. Chicago: University of Chicago Press.

Hays, Samuel P. 1980. *American Political History as Social Analysis*. Knoxville, TN: University of Tennessee Press.

Heidegger, Martin. 1968. *What Is Called Thinking?* Translated by J. Glenn Gray. New York: Harper Colophon Books.

Held, David. 1980. *Introduction to Critical Theory*. Berkeley and Los Angeles: University of California Press.

Hibbing, John R., and Alford, John R. 1981. "The Electoral Impact of Economic Conditions: Who Is Held Responsible?" *American Journal of Political Science* 25 (August):423–439.

Hibbs, Douglas A., Jr. 1982. "The Dynamics of Political Support for American Presidents among Occupational and Partisan Groups." *American Journal of Political Science* 26 (May):312–332.

Hicks, John D. 1936. *The Populist Revolt: A History of the Farmers' Alliance and the People's Party*. Lincoln: University of Nebraska Press.

Higham, John. 1955. *Strangers in the Land: Patterns of American Nativism, 1860–1925*. New Brunswick, NJ: Rutgers University Press.

Hirschman, Albert O. 1977. *The Passion and the Interests: Political Arguments for Capitalism before Its Triumph*. Princeton: Princeton University Press.

Hofstadter, Richard. 1948. *The American Political Tradition and the Men Who Made It*. New York: Random House, Vintage Books.

————. 1955. *The Age of Reform: From Bryan to FDR*. New York: Random House, Vintage Books.

Hofstadter, Richard. 1968. *The Progressive Historians: Turner, Beard, Parrington*. New York: Alfred A. Knopf.

———. 1969. *The Idea of a Party System: The Rise of Legitimate Opposition in the United States, 1780–1840*. Berkeley and Los Angeles: University of California Press.

———. [1965] 1979. *The Paranoid Style in American Politics: And Other Essays*. Chicago: University of Chicago Press.

Hohendahl, Peter U. 1979. "Critical Theory, Public Sphere and Culture: Jürgen Habermas and His Critics." *New German Critique* 16 (Winter):89–118.

Hole, Judith, and Levine, Ellen. 1971. *Rebirth of Feminism*. New York: Quadrangle Books.

Hoover, Herbert. 1972. *American Ideals Versus the New Deal*. St. Clair Shores, MI, Scholarly Press.

Horkheimer, Max. 1972. *Critical Theory: Selected Essays*. Translated by Matthew J. O'Connell et al. New York: Seabury Press, Continuum Books.

Howe, Daniel Walker. 1980. *The Political Culture of the American Whigs*. Chicago: University of Chicago Press.

Howe, Irving, and Coser, Lewis. 1957. *The American Communist Party: A Critical History (1919–1957)*. Boston: Beacon Press.

Howe, John R., Jr. 1966. *The Changing Political Thought of John Adams*. Princeton: Princeton University Press.

Hoye, Timothy. 1984. "A Republic in Time: The Scottish Enlightenment and the American Founding." Presented at the annual meeting of the Midwest Political Science Association, April 11–14, Chicago.

Huntington, Samuel P. 1975. "United States." In *The Crisis of Democracy: Report on the Governability of Democracies to the Trilateral Commission*, ed. Michel Crozier, pp. 59–118. New York: New York University Press.

———. 1981. *American Politics: The Promise of Disharmony*. Cambridge: Harvard University Press.

Ickes, Harold L. 1934. *The New Democracy*. New York: W. W. Norton.

Inglehart, Ronald. 1977. *The Silent Revolution: Changing Values and Political Styles among Western Publics*. Princeton: Princeton University Press.

Isaac, Rhys. 1976. "Dramatizing the Ideology of Revolution: Popular

Mobilization in Virginia, 1774 to 1776." *William and Mary Quarterly*, 33 (July):357–385.

Jacobson, Norman. 1963. "Political Science and Political Education." *American Political Science Review* 57 (September):561–569.

Jay, Martin. 1973. *The Dialectical Imagination: A History of the Frankfort School and the Institute of Social Research, 1923-1950*. Boston: Little, Brown.

Jenkins, William Sumner. [1935] 1960. *Proslavery Thought in the Old South*. Gloucester, MA: Peter Smith.

Jentz, John B. 1977. "Artisans, Evangelicals, and the City: A Social History of the Labor and Abolitionist Movement in Jacksonian New York." Ph.D. dissertation, Graduate Center, City University of New York.

Johnson, Richard; McLennan, Gregor; Schwarz, Bill; and Sutton, David, eds. 1982. *Making Histories: Studies in History Writing and Politics*. Minneapolis: University of Minnesota Press.

Judd, Dennis R. 1979. *The Politics of American Cities: Private Power and Public Policy*. Boston: Little, Brown.

Kātz, Barry. 1982. *The Art of Liberation: An Intellectual Biography of Herbert Marcuse*. London: New Left Books.

Katznelson, Ira. 1981. *City Trenches: Urban Politics and the Patterning of Class in the United States*. Chicago: University of Chicago Press.

Kekes, John. 1977. "Essentially Contested Concepts: A Reconsideration." *Philosophy and Rhetoric* 10 (Spring):71-89.

Kelley, Robert. 1969. *The Transatlantic Persuasion: The Liberal Democratic Mind in the Age of Gladstone*. New York: Alfred A. Knopf.

———. 1979. *The Cultural Pattern in American Politics: The First Century*. New York: Alfred A. Knopf.

Kenyon, Cecelia. 1955. "Men of Little Faith: The Anti-Federalists on the Nature of Representative Government." *William and Mary Quarterly* 12 (January):3–43.

———. 1962. "Republicanism and Radicalism in the American Revolution: An Old-Fashioned Interpretation." *William and Mary Quarterly* 19 (April):153–182.

———, ed. 1966. *The Anti-Federalists*. Indianapolis, IN: Bobbs-Merrill Co.

Kerber, Linda. [1970] 1980. *The Federalists in Dissent: Imagery and Ideology in Jeffersonian America*. Ithaca: Cornell University Press.

Kipnis, Ira. 1952. *The American Socialist Movement, 1897–1912*. New York: Columbia University Press.

Kolko, Gabriel. 1963. *The Triumph of Conservatism: A Reinterpretation of American History, 1900–1916*. New York: Free Press.

Kraditor, Aileen S. 1965. *The Ideas of the Woman Suffrage Movement, 1890–1929*. Garden City, NY: Doubleday, Anchor Books.

———. 1981. *The Radical Persuasion: Aspects of the Intellectual History and the Historiography of Three American Radical Organizations*. Baton Rouge: Louisiana State University Press.

Kramnick, Isaac. 1982. "Republican Revisionism Revisited." *American Historical Review* 83 (June):629–664.

Kuhn, Thomas. 1962. *The Structure of Scientific Revolutions*. Chicago: University of Chicago Press.

Lakatos, Imre. 1970. "Falsification and the Methodology of Scientific Research Programmes." In *Criticism and the Growth of Knowledge*, ed. Imre Lakatos and Alan Musgrave, pp.91–196. London: Cambridge University Press.

Latner, Richard B. 1977. "The Nullification Crisis and Republican Subversion." *Journal of Southern History* 63 (February):19–38.

Laudan, Larry. 1977. *Progress and Its Problems: Towards a Theory of Scientific Growth*. Berkeley and Los Angeles: University of California Press.

Lears, T. J. Jackson. 1983. "From Salvation to Self-Realization: Advertising and the Roots of the Consumer Culture." In *The Culture of Consumption: Critical Essays in American History, 1880–1980*, ed. Richard Wightman Fox and T. J. Jackson Lears, pp. 1-38. New York: Pantheon Books.

LeGuin, Ursula K. 1974. *The Dispossessed*. New York: Avon Books.

Leiss, William. 1974. *The Domination of Nature*. Boston: Beacon Press.

Lester, Julius. 1969. *Look Out, Whitey! Black Power's Gon' Get Your Mama!* New York: Grove Press.

Leuchtenburg, William E. 1963. *Franklin Roosevelt and the New Deal*. New York: Harper Torchbooks.

Levitan, Sar A. and Robert Taggart. 1976. *The Promise of Greatness*. Cambridge: Harvard University Press.

Lewis, R.W.B. 1955. *The American Adam: Innocence, Tragedy and*

Tradition in the Nineteenth Century. Chicago: University of Chicago Press.

Lienesch, Michael. 1980. "The Constitutional Tradition: History, Political Action and Progress in American Political Thought, 1787–1793." *Journal of Politics* 42 (February):1–30, 47–48.

Lincoln, Abraham. 1965. *The Lincoln-Douglas Debates of 1858*. Edited by Robert W. Johannsen. New York: Oxford University Press.

Lindblom, Charles E. 1977. *Politics and Markets: The World's Political-Economic Systems*. New York: Basic Books.

Link, Eugene P. 1942. *The Democratic-Republican Societies, 1790–1800*. New York: Octagon Books.

Lippmann, Walter. 1922. *Public Opinion*. New York: Macmillan.

———. 1925. *The Phantom Public*. New York: Macmillan.

Lloyd, Henry Demerest. 1894. *Wealth against Commonwealth*. New York: Harper and Brothers.

Long, Huey Pierce. 1934. *Share Our Wealth*. Washington, D.C.: U.S. Government Printing Office.

———. [1935] 1972. *My First Days in the White House*. New York: Da Capo Press.

Lowi, Theodore. 1969. *The End of Liberalism*. New York: W. W. Norton.

Lukács, Georg. 1971. *History and Class Consciousness: Studies in Marxist Dialectics*. Translated by Rodney Livingstone. Cambridge, MA: MIT Press.

Lukes, Steven. 1973. *Individualism*. Oxford: Basil Blackwell.

———. 1979. "The Real and Ideal Worlds of Democracy." In *Powers, Possessions and Freedom*, ed. Alkis Kontos, pp. 139–152. Toronto: University of Toronto Press.

Luraghi, Raimondo. 1972. "The Civil War and the Modernization of American Society: Social Structure and Industrial Revolution in the Old South before and during the War." *Civil War History* 18 (September):230–250.

Lutz, Donald S. 1980. "From Covenant to Constitution in American Political Thought." *Publius* 10 (Fall):101–134.

McCarthy, Thomas A. 1973. "A Theory of Communicative Competence." *Philosophy of the Social Sciences* 3:135–156.

———. 1978. *The Critical Theory of Jürgen Habermas*. Cambridge, MA: MIT Press.

McCormick, Richard P. 1967. "Political Development and the Second Party System." In *The American Party Systems: Stages of Political Development*, ed. William Nisbet Chambers and Walter Dean Burnham. New York: Oxford University Press.

McCoy, Drew. 1980. *The Elusive Republic: Political Economy in Jeffersonian America*. Chapel Hill: University of North Carolina Press.

McDonald, Forrest. 1958. *We the People: The Economic Origins of the Constitution*. Chicago: University of Chicago Press.

———. 1965. *E Pluribus Unum: The Formation of the American Republic, 1776–1790*. Boston: Houghton Mifflin.

———. 1980. "Comment on Constitutional Tradition." *Journal of Politics* 42 (February):31–35.

MacIntyre, Alasdair. 1973. "The Essential Contestability of Some Social Concepts." *Ethics* 84 (October):1–9.

———. 1978. *Against the Self-Images of the Age: Essays on Ideology and Philosophy*. Notre Dame, IN: University of Notre Dame Press.

———. 1981. *After Virtue: A Study in Moral Theory*. Notre Dame, IN: University of Notre Dame Press.

Mackenzie, William L. 1846. *The Life and Times of Martin Van Buren*. Boston: Cooke and Co.

Macpherson, C. B. 1966. *The Real World of Democracy*. Oxford: Oxford University Press.

———. 1973. *Democratic Theory: Essays in Retrieval*. Oxford: Clarendon Press.

———. 1977. *The Life and Times of Liberal Democracy*. Oxford: Oxford University Press.

———. 1984. "Democracy, Utopian and Scientific." In *After Marx*, ed. Terence W. Ball and James F. Farr. Cambridge: Cambridge University Press.

Madison, James. 1900–1910. *The Writings of James Madison*, 9 vols. Edited by Gaillard Hunt. New York: G. P. Putnam's Sons.

———. 1966. *Notes of Debates in the Federal Convention of 1787*. Edited by Adrienne Koch. New York: W. W. Norton.

Mandel, Ernest. 1976. *Late Capitalism*. London: New Left Books.

Mann, Arthur. 1962. "The Progressive Tradition." In *The Reconstruction of American History*, ed. John Higham. London: Hutchinson.

Mannheim, Karl. 1936. *Ideology and Utopia*. New York: Harcourt, Brace & Co., Harvest Books.

Marcuse, Herbert. 1955. *Eros and Civilization: A Philosophical Inquiry into Freud*. Boston: Beacon Press.

———. 1958. *Soviet Marxism: A Critical Analysis*. London: Routledge & Kegan Paul.

———. 1964. *One-Dimensional Man: Studies in the Ideology of Advanced Industrial Society*. Boston: Beacon Press.

———. [1965] 1968. "Repressive Tolerance—with a Postscript." In *A Critique of Pure Tolerance*, by Robert Paul Wolff, Barrington Moore, Jr., and Herbert Marcuse, pp. 81–123. Boston: Beacon Press.

———. 1969. *An Essay on Liberation*. Boston: Beacon Press.

Marshall, Lynn L. 1969. "Opposing Democratic and Whig Concepts of Party Organization." In *New Perspectives on Jacksonian Parties and Politics*, ed. Edward Pessen, pp. 38–68. Boston: Allyn & Bacon.

Marty, William Ray. 1968. *Recent Negro Protest Thought: Theories of Nonviolence and "Black Power."* Ph.D. dissertation, Duke University.

Marx, Karl. 1967. *Capital*, 3 vols. Edited by Frederick Engels. New York: International Publishers.

Marx, Karl, and Engels, Frederick. 1968. *Selected Works*. New York: International Publishers.

———. 1972. *The Marx-Engels Reader*. Edited by Robert C. Tucker. New York: W. W. Norton.

Marx, Leo. 1964. *The Machine in the Garden: Technology and the Pastoral Ideal in America*. New York: Oxford University Press.

Matusow, Allen J. 1971. "From Civil Rights to Black Power: The Case of SNCC, 1960–1966." In *Conflict and Competition: Studies in the Recent Black Protest Movement*, ed. John H. Bracey, Jr., August Meier, and Elliot Rudwick, pp. 135–156. Belmont, CA: Wadsworth Publishing.

Mayer, Margit, and Fay, Margaret A. 1977. "The Formation of the American Nation-State." *Kapitalistate* 6 (Fall):39–90.

Meek, Ronald L. 1976. *Social Science and the Ignoble Savage*. Cambridge: Cambridge University Press.

Mendelson, Jack. 1979. "The Habermas/Gadamer Debate." *New German Critique* 18 (Fall):44–74.

Merleau-Ponty, Maurice. 1969. *Humanism and Terror*. Translated by John O'Neill. Boston: Beacon Press.

Merrill, Edward H., ed. 1964. *Responses to Economic Collapse: The Great Depression of the 1930s*. Boston: D.C. Heath.

Merriman, W. Richard, and Parent, T. Wayne. 1981. "Big Brother and Brotherly Love: The Dilemma of Government Race Policy and the Market Mentality." Photocopy. Department of Political Science, Indiana University.

Meyers, Marvin. 1957. *The Jacksonian Persuasion: Politics and Belief.* New York: Random House, Vintage Books.

Miller, Perry, ed. 1954. *American Thought: Civil War to World War I.* San Francisco: Rinehart Press.

————, ed. 1957. *The American Transcendentalists: Their Prose and Poetry.* Garden City, NY: Doubleday, Anchor Books.

Misgeld, Dieter. 1981. "Science, Hermeneutics, and the Utopian Content of the Liberal-Democratic Tradition. On Habermas' Recent Work: A Reply to Habermas." *New German Critique* 22 (Winter):123–144.

Mitchell, Neil J. 1983. "U.S. Corporate Self-Images and Social Policy: A Political Theory of Private Enterprise." Ph.D. dissertation, Indiana University.

Moody, J. Carroll. 1973. "The Transformation of the American Economy, 1877–1900." In *The Reinterpretation of American History and Culture,* ed. William H. Cartwright and Richard L. Watson, Jr., pp. 401–424. Washington, D.C.: National Council for the Social Studies.

Moon, J. Donald. 1980. "Political Ethics and Critical Theory: On the Logic of Legitimation Problems." Photocopy. Department of Political Science, Wesleyan University.

Moore, Glover. 1953. *The Missouri Controversy 1819–1821.* Lexington: University of Kentucky Press.

Morantz, Regina Ann Markel. 1971. " 'Democracy' and 'Republic' in American Ideology, 1787–1840." Ph.D. dissertation, Columbia University.

Morgan, Robin, ed. 1970. *Sisterhood Is Powerful: An Anthology of Writings from the Women's Liberation Movement.* New York: Random House, Vintage Books.

Mowry, George. 1958. *The Era of Theodore Roosevelt, 1900–1912.* New York: Harper & Row.

Nash, Gary. 1979. *The Urban Crucible: Social Change, Political Consciousness and the Origins of the American Revolution.* Cambridge: Harvard University Press.

Nelson, William N. 1980. *On Justifying Democracy.* London: Routledge & Kegan Paul.

Noble, David W. 1958. *The Paradox of Progressive Thought*. Minneapolis: University of Minnesota Press.

North, Douglass C. 1966. *The Economic Growth of the U.S., 1790–1860*. New York: W. W. Norton.

Nugent, Walter T. K. 1963. *The Tolerant Populists: Kansas Populism and Nativism*. Chicago: University of Chicago Press.

———. 1967. *The Money Question during Reconstruction*. New York: W. W. Norton.

———. 1968. *Money and American Society, 1865–1880*. New York: Free Press.

Oakeshott, Michael. 1975. *On Human Conduct*. Oxford: Clarendon Press.

O'Connor, James. 1973. *The Fiscal Crisis of the State*. New York: St. Martin's Press.

Offe, Claus. 1972. "Political Authority and Class Structures—an Analysis of Late Capitalist Societies." *International Journal of Sociology* 2 (Spring):73–108.

———. 1981. "Some Contradictions of the Modern Welfare State." *Praxis International* 1 (July):219–229.

O'Malley, Joseph, ed. 1970. *Karl Marx's Critique of Hegel's Philosophy of Right*. Cambridge: Cambridge University Press.

Oneal, James. 1934. "To Comrade Thomas." *The New Leader*, June 23, pp. 3, 8.

Oppenheim, Felix E. 1971. "Democracy—Characteristics Included and Excluded." *The Monist* 55 (January):29–50.

Orwin, Clifford. 1983. "Welfare and the New Dignity." *The Public Interest* 71 (Spring):85–95.

Paine, Thomas. 1942. *The Rights of Man*. New York: Willey Book Company.

Palmer, Bruce Edward. 1972. "The Rhetoric of Southern Populists: Metaphor and Imagery in the Language of Reform." Ph.D. dissertation, Yale University.

Palmer, R. R. 1934. "Notes on the Use of the Word 'Democracy'." *Political Science Quarterly* 68 (June):203–226.

Panken, Jacob. 1934. "Panken Sees Disaster If Members Adopt Document." *The New Leader*, June 23, pp. 3, 6.

Parenti, Michael. 1978. *Power and the Powerless*. New York: St. Martin's Press.

Parrington, Vernon L. 1954a. *The Colonial Mind (1620–1800)*. Vol.

1 of *Main Currents in American Thought*. New York: Harcourt, Brace and World, Harvest Books.

———. 1954b. *The Romantic Revolution in America (1800-1860)*. *Main Currents in American Thought*, vol. 2. New York: Harcourt, Brace & World, Harvest Books.

———. 1958. *The Beginnings of Critical Realism in America. Main Currents in American Thought*, vol. 3. New York: Harcourt, Brace & World, Harbinger Books.

Pease, William H., and Pease, Jane H., eds. 1965. *The Antislavery Argument*. Indianapolis, IN: Bobbs-Merrill Co.

Perelman, Chaim, and Olbrechts-Tyteca, L. 1969. *The New Rhetoric: A Treatise on Argumentation*. Translated by John Wilkerson and Purcell Weaver. Notre Dame, IN: University of Notre Dame Press.

Piven, Frances Fox, and Cloward, Richard A. 1971. *Regulating the Poor: The Function of Public Welfare*. New York: Random House, Vintage Books.

———. 1982. *The New Class War: Reagan's Attack on the Welfare State and Its Consequences*. New York: Pantheon.

Pocock, J.G.A. 1965. "Machiavelli, Harrington and English Political Ideologies in the Eighteenth Century." *William and Mary Quarterly*, 22 (October):549–583.

———. 1975. *The Machiavellian Moment: Florentine Political Thought and the Atlantic Republican Tradition*. Princeton: Princeton University Press.

Pole, J. R. 1962. "Historians and the Problem of Early American Democracy." *American Historical Review* 67 (April):626–646.

———. 1966. *Political Representation in England and the Origins of the American Revolution*. New York: St. Martin's Press.

———, ed. 1967. *The Advance of Democracy*. New York: Harper & Row.

Pollack, Norman, ed. 1967. *The Populist Mind*. Indianapolis, IN: Bobbs-Merrill Co.

Potter, David M. 1976. *The Impending Crisis, 1848–1861*. New York: Harper & Row.

Przeworski, Adam. 1980. "Material Bases of Consent: Economics and Politics in a Hegemonic System." *Political Power and Social Theory* 1:21–66.

Putnam-Jacobi, Mary. [1894] 1915. *"Common Sense" Applied to Woman Suffrage*. 2d ed. New York: Knickerbocker Press.

Redstockings of the Women's Liberation Movement. 1978. *Feminist Revolution: An Abridged Edition with Additional Writings*. New York: Random House.

Reich, Charles A. 1970. *The Greening of America*. New York: Random House, Vintage Books.

Revel, Jean-François. 1971. *Without Marx or Jesus: The New American Revolution Has Begun*. New York: Dell Publishing.

Ricoeur, Paul. 1978. *The Philosophy of Paul Ricoeur: An Anthology of His Work*. Edited by Charles E. Reagan and David Stewart. Beacon Press.

———. 1981. *Hermeneutics and the Human Sciences*. Edited and translated by John B. Thompson. Cambridge: Cambridge University Press.

Risjord, Norman K. 1965. *The Old Republicans: Southern Conservatism in the Age of Jefferson*. New York: Columbia University Press.

Robbins, Caroline. 1947. "Algernon Sidney's *Discourses Concerning Government*: Textbook of Revolution." *William and Mary Quarterly* 4 (July):267–296.

———. 1968. *The Eighteenth-Century Commonwealthman: Studies in the Transmission, Development, and Circumstances of English Liberal Thought from the Restoration of Charles II until the War with the Thirteen Colonies*. New York: Atheneum.

Roche, John P. 1961. "The Founding Fathers: A Reform Caucus in Action." *American Political Science Review* 55 (December):799–816.

Rosenblum, Nancy C. 1978. *Bentham's Theory of the Modern State*. Cambridge: Harvard University Press.

Ross, Dorothy. 1979. "The Liberal Tradition Revisited and the Republican Tradition Addressed." In *New Directions in American Intellectual History*, ed. John Higham and Paul K. Conkin. Baltimore: Johns Hopkins University Press.

Rossiter, Clinton S., ed. 1961. *The Federalist Papers*. New York: New American Library, Mentor Book.

Rostow, W. W. 1960. *The Stages of Economic Growth: A Non-Communist Manifesto*. Cambridge: Cambridge University Press.

Roszak, Theodore. 1969. *The Making of a Counterculture: Reflections on the Technocratic Society and Its Youthful Opposition*. Garden City, NY: Doubleday, Anchor Books.

Roszak, Theodore. 1973. *Where the Wasteland Ends*. Garden City, NY: Doubleday, Anchor Books.

Rotunda, Ronald D. 1968. "The 'Liberal' Label: Roosevelt's Capture of a Symbol." *Public Policy* 17:377–408.

Rozwenc, Edwin C., ed. 1963. *The Meaning of Jacksonian Democracy*. Boston: D.C. Heath.

Rutland, Robert A. 1983. "Madison: The Fourth President and the Press." *Media History Digest* 3 (Spring):20–25.

Safire, William. 1968. *The New Language of Politics: An Anecdotal Dictionary of Catchwords, Slogans, and Political Usage*. New York: Random House.

Sale, Kirkpatrick. 1973. *SDS*. New York: Random House.

Sartori, Giovanni. [1962] 1973. *Democratic Theory*. Reprint. Westport, CT: Greenwood Press.

Schattschneider, E. E. 1975. *The Semisovereign People: A Realist's View of Democracy in America*. Hinsdale, IL: Dryden Press.

Schlesinger, Arthur M., Jr. 1939. *Orestes A. Brownson: A Pilgrim's Progress*. Boston: Little, Brown.

———. 1945. *The Age of Jackson*. Boston: Little, Brown.

Schmitter, Philippe C. 1974. "Still the Century of Corporatism?" *Review of Politics* 36 (January):85–131.

Schroyer, Trent. 1973. *The Critique of Domination: The Origins and Development of Critical Theory*. Boston: Beacon Press.

———. 1975. "The Re-politicization of the Relations of Production: An Interpretation of Jürgen Habermas' Analytic Theory of Late Capitalist Development." *New German Critique* 5 (Spring):107–128.

Scott, William B. 1977. *In Pursuit of Happiness: American Conceptions of Property from the Seventeenth to the Twentieth Century*. Bloomington, IN: Indiana University Press.

Seaman, John W. 1982. "On Retrieving Macpherson's Liberalism." Paper presented at the annual meeting of the American Political Science Association, September 2-5, Denver, Colorado.

Shalhope, Robert E. 1972. "Toward a Republican Synthesis: The Emergence of an Understanding of Republicanism in American Historiography." *William and Mary Quarterly* 29 (January):49–80.

———. 1982. "Republicanism and Early American Historiography." *William and Mary Quarterly* 39 (April):334–356.

Shannon, David A. 1955. *The Socialist Party of America: A History*. New York: Macmillan.

Shapiro, Jeremy J. 1972. "The Dialectic of Theory and Practice: Marcuse and Habermas." In *The Hidden Dimension: European Marxism Since Lenin*, ed. Dick Howard and Karl Klare. New York: Basic Books.

Shefter, Martin. 1983. "Regional Receptivity to Reform: The Legacy of the Progressive Era." *Political Science Quarterly* 98 (Fall):459–483.

Shoemaker, Robert W. 1966. " 'Democracy' and 'Republic' as Understood in Late Eighteenth Century America." *American Speech* 41 (May):83–95.

Shumer, S. M. 1979. "Machiavelli: Republican Politics and Its Corruption." *Political Theory* 7 (February):5–34.

Skinner, Quentin. 1978. *The Foundations of Modern Political Thought*, 2 vols. Cambridge: Cambridge University Press.

Skocpol, Theda. 1980. "Political Response to Capitalist Crisis: Neo-Marxist Theories of the State and the Case of the New Deal." *Politics and Society* 10:155–201.

Skowronek, Steven. 1982. *Building a New American State: The Expansion of National Administrative Capacities, 1877–1920*. New York: Cambridge University Press.

Sombart, Werner. 1976. *Why Is There No Socialism in the United States?* Translated by Patricia M. Hocking and C. T. Husbands. White Plains, NY: M. E. Sharpe.

Somkin, Fred. 1967. *Unquiet Eagle: Memory and Desire in the Idea of American Freedom, 1815–1860*. Ithaca, NY: Cornell University Press.

Stagg, J.C.A. 1983. *Mr. Madison's War: Politics, Diplomacy and Warfare in the Early American Republic, 1783–1830*. Princeton: Princeton University Press.

Stanton, Elizabeth Cady. [1894] 1977. *Suffrage a Natural Right*. Microfilm. New Haven, CT: Research Publications.

Statistical Abstract of the U.S. 1970. Washington, D.C.: Bureau of the Census, U.S. Department of Commerce.

Stave, Bruce M., ed. 1975. *Socialism and the Cities*. Port Washington, NY: Kennikat Press.

Steinfels, Peter. 1979. *The Neoconservatives*. New York: Simon & Schuster.

Storing, Herbert J. 1981. *What the Anti-Federalists Were For*. Edited by Murray Dry. Chicago: University of Chicago Press.

Stourzh, Gerald. 1970. *Alexander Hamilton and the Idea of Republican Government*. Stanford, CA: Stanford University Press.

Sumner, William Graham. 1940. *Essays of William Graham Sumner*, 2 vols. Edited by Albert C. Keller and Maurice R. Davie. New Haven: Yale University Press.

―――. [1883] 1974. *What Social Classes Owe to Each Other*. Caldwell, ID: Caxton Printers.

Sundquist, James. 1973. *The Dynamics of the Party System: Alignment and Realignment of Political Parties in the United States*. Washington, D.C.: Brookings Institution.

Takaki, Ronald T. 1971. *A Proslavery Crusade: The Agitation to Reopen the African Slave Trade*. New York: Free Press.

Taylor, Charles. 1971. "Interpretation and the Sciences of Man." *Review of Metaphysics* 25 (September):3–51.

―――. 1981. "Growth, Legitimacy and the Modern Identity." *Praxis International* 1 (July):111–125.

Thomas, Norman. 1934a. "Proposals for Action at Detroit." *The World Tomorrow* 17 (April 26):206–208.

―――. 1934b. "What About Democracy?" *The New Leader* (July 7):12.

Thompson, John B., and Held, David. 1982. *Habermas: Critical Debates*. Cambridge, MA: MIT Press.

Thompson, William Irwin. 1971. *At the Edge of History: Speculations on the Transformation of Culture*. New York: Harper Colophon Books.

Thurow, Lester. 1980. *The Zero-Sum Society: Distribution and the Possibilities for Economic Change*. New York: Basic Books.

Tindall, George B., ed. 1966. *A Populist Reader: Selections from the Works of American Populist Leaders*. New York: Harper & Row.

Tocqueville, Alexis de. 1948. *Democracy in America*. Henry Reeve text as revised by Francis Bowen. Further corrected and edited with Introduction, Editorial Notes, and Bibliographies by Phillips Bradley. New York: Alfred A. Knopf.

―――. 1969. *Democracy in America*. Translated by George Lawrence and edited by J. P. Mayer. New York: Doubleday, Anchor Books.

Toffler, Alvin. 1971. *Future Shock*. New York: Bantam Books.

————. 1978a. "Introduction on Future Conscious Politics." In *Anticipatory Democracy: People in the Politics of the Future*, ed. Clement Bezold, pp. xi–xxii. New York: Random House, Vintage Books.

————. 1978b. "What Is Anticipatory Democracy?" In *Anticipatory Democracy: People in the Politics of the Future*, ed. Clement Bezold, pp. 361–365. New York: Random House, Vintage Books.

Tugwell, Rexford G. 1935. *The Battle for Democracy*. New York: Columbia University Press.

Unger, Irwin. 1964. *The Greenback Era: A Social and Political History of American Finance, 1865–1879*. Princeton: Princeton University Press.

United States Magazine and Democratic Review. January 1838.

Van Buren, Martin. 1867. *Inquiry into the Origin and Course of Political Parties in the United States*. New York: Hurd & Houghton.

Van Deusen, Glyndon G. 1959. *The Jacksonian Era: 1828–1848*. New York: Harper & Row.

Von Wright, Georg Henrik. 1971. *Explanation and Understanding*. Ithaca, NY: Cornell University Press.

Wagstaff, Thomas, ed. 1969. *Black Power: The Radical Response to White America*. Beverly Hills, CA: Glencoe Press.

Wallace, Michael. 1968. "Changing Concepts of Party in the United States: New York, 1815–1828." *American Historical Review* 74 (December):453–491.

Walters, Ronald G. 1977. *The Antislavery Appeal: American Abolitionism After 1830*. Baltimore: Johns Hopkins University Press.

————. 1978. *American Reforms, 1815–1860*. New York: Hill & Wang.

Ward, Lester F. 1967. *Lester Ward and the Welfare State*. Edited by Henry Steele Commager. Indianapolis, IN: Bobbs-Merrill Co.

Ware, Cellestine. 1970. *Woman Power: The Movement for Women's Liberation*. New York: Tower Publications.

Warpole, Ken. 1981. "A Ghostly Pavement: The Political Implications of Local Working-Class History." In *People's History and Socialist Theory*, ed. Raphael Samuel, pp. 22–31. London: Routledge & Kegan Paul.

Warren, Frank A. 1974. *An Alternative Vision: The Socialist Party in the 1930s*. Bloomington: Indiana University Press.

Webster, Noah. 1953. *The Letters of Noah Webster*. Edited by Harry R. Warfel. New York: Library Publishers.

Weinberg, Albert K. 1935. *Manifest Destiny: A Study of Nationalist Expansionism in American History*. Baltimore: Johns Hopkins Press.

Weinstein, James, 1968. *The Corporate Ideal in the Liberal State: 1900–1908*. Boston: Beacon Press.

Weinstein, James, and Eakins, David W., eds. 1970. *For a New America: Essays in History and Politics from 'Studies on the Left' 1959–1967*. New York: Random House, Vintage Books.

Westbrook, Robert. 1983. "Politics as Consumption: Managing the Modern American Election." In *The Culture of Consumption: Critical Essays in American History, 1880–1980*, ed. Richard Wightman Fox and T. J. Jackson Lears, pp. 143–174. New York: Pantheon Books.

Weyl, Walter. 1912. *The New Democracy: An Essay on Certain Political and Economic Tendencies in the United States*. New York: Macmillan.

White, Stephen K. 1980. "Reason and Authority in Habermas: A Critique of the Critics." *American Political Science Review* 74 (December):1006–1018.

White, William A. 1910. *The Old Order Changeth: A View of American Democracy*. New York: Macmillan.

Wiebe, Robert H. 1967. *The Search for Order, 1877–1920*. New York: Hill & Wang, American Century Series.

———. 1973. "The Progressive Years, 1900–1917." In *The Reinterpretation of American History and Culture*, ed. William H. Cartwright and Richard L. Watson, Jr., pp. 425–442. Washington, D.C.: National Council for the Social Studies.

Williams, Raymond. 1976. *Keywords: A Vocabulary of Culture and Society*. New York: Oxford University Press.

Williams, T. Harry. 1960. "The Gentleman from Louisiana: Demagogue or Democrat?" *Journal of Southern History* 26 (February):3–21.

Williams, William Appleman. 1966. *The Contours of American History*. Chicago: Quadrangle Books.

Williamson, Chilton. 1960. *American Suffrage: From Property to Democracy, 1760–1860*. Princeton: Princeton University Press.

Wills, Garry. 1979. *Inventing America: Jefferson's Declaration of Independence*. New York: Random House, Vintage Books.

———. 1981. *Explaining America: The Federalist*. Garden City, NY: Doubleday.

Wilson, Christopher P. 1983. "The Rhetoric of Consumption: Mass Market Magazines and the Demise of the Gentle Reader, 1880–1920." In *The Culture of Consumption: Critical Essays in American History, 1880–1980*, ed. Richard Wightman Fox and T. J. Jackson Lears, pp. 39–64. New York: Pantheon Books.

Wilson, Major L. 1967. "The Concept of Time and the Political Dialogue in the United States, 1828–48." *American Quarterly* 19 (Winter):629–644.

———. 1977. "What Whigs and Jacksonian Democrats Meant by Freedom." In *The Many-Faceted Jacksonian Era: New Interpretations*, ed. Edward L. Pessen, pp. 192–211. Westport, CT: Greenwood Press.

———. 1984. *The Presidency of Martin Van Buren*. Lawrence: University of Kansas Press.

Wilson, Woodrow. 1914. *The New Freedom: A Call for the Emancipation of the Generous Energies of a People*. New York: Doubleday, Page & Co.

Winch, Peter. 1958. *The Idea of Social Science and Its Relation to Philosophy*. New York: Humanities Press.

Wittgenstein, Ludwig. 1958. *The Blue and Brown Books*. New York: Harper & Row, Colophon Books.

Wolfe, Alan. 1977. *The Limits of Legitimacy: Contradictions of Contemporary Capitalism*. New York: Free Press.

Wolfskill, George. 1962. *The Revolt of the Conservatives: A History of the American Liberty League, 1934–1940*. Boston: Houghton Mifflin.

———. 1969. "New Deal Critics: Did They Miss the Point?" In *Essays on the New Deal*, ed. Harold M. Hollingsworth and William F. Holmes, pp. 49–68. Austin: University of Texas Press.

Wolin, Sheldon S. 1981a. "The People's Two Bodies." *Democracy* 1 (January):9–24.

———. 1981b. "The New Public Philosophy." *Democracy* 1 (October):23–36.

Wood, Gordon. 1972. *The Creation of the American Republic, 1776–1787*. New York: W. W. Norton.

Woodward, C. Vann. 1960. Introductory essay in *Cannibals All! or*

Slaves Without Masters, by George Fitzhugh. Cambridge: Harvard University Press, Belknap Press.

Yarbrough, Jean. 1979a. "Republicanism Reconsidered: Some Thoughts on the Foundation and Preservation of the American Republic." *The Review of Politics* 41 (January):61–95.

———. 1979b. "Representation and Republicanism: Two Views." *Publius* 9 (Spring):77–98.

Yates, Gayle Graham. 1975. *What Women Want: The Ideas of the Movement*. Cambridge: Harvard University Press.

Young, Alfred F., ed. 1976. *The American Revolution: Explorations in the History of American Radicalism*. DeKalb: Northern Illinois University Press.

Young, Nigel. 1977. *An Infantile Disorder? The Crisis and Decline of the New Left*. London: Routledge & Kegan Paul.

Ziff, Larzer. 1981. "Landlessness: Melville and the Democratic Hero." *Democracy* 1 (July):123–139.

Zinn, Howard. 1970. *The Politics of History*. Boston: Beacon Press.

Zvesper, John. 1977. *Political Philosophy and Rhetoric: A Study of the Origins of American Party Politics*. Cambridge: Cambridge University Press.

abolitionists: antislavery splits
American Whig party, 164; Fitz-
hugh's attack upon, 170; invoke
Declaration of Independence,
162, 170, 179, 180; political ac-
tion and party realignment, 163;
portray slavery as a national
problem, 161; religiously in-
spired, 159; varieties of, 162-163;
women's suffrage and, 159, 236.
See also antislavery, political op-
position as a basis for; Garrison,
William L.; moral sense doctrine
Adams, Henry: *Democracy* and *The
Degradation of the Democratic
Dogma*, 207n; on the American
Whig party, 142
Adams, John, 74n
Adams, John Quincy, 142, 145,
148; criticizes Paine, 79; election
of 1828, 119, 126; supports
American System, 119, 126,
139n, 145
Addams, Jane, 232
Adorno, Theodor, 335, 381
Albany *Argus*, 112, 114, 115
Albany Regency, 111, 156. *See also*
Bucktails; Van Buren, Martin
Alien and Sedition Acts, 87, 103n
Allen, Devere, 289-291
American Bankers Association, 220
American Labor Party, 291
American Liberty League, 258,
266; allies of Republicans, 265;
constitutional democracy pre-
ferred by, 260, 263-264; opposes
democratic despotism, 261-262
American Review, 123, 138n, 140,
141, 144
American Revolution, 62, 64

American System, 124-127; J. Q.
Adams supports, 119, 126, 139n,
145; defended as republican, 143-
147; denounced as a "corrupt
bargain," 127, 130; theological
backing, 146; waning appeal, 148;
Whigs' program, 119, 125, 138.
See also American Whig party;
Clay, Henry
American Whig party:
advocates American System of
improvements, 119, 125, 138
denounces King Andrew, 140;
opposes manifest destiny, 143-
144
disintegrates, 165; Conscience
and Cotton Whigs, 164; election of 1844, 164; silence on
slavery, 155, 157
ideology of: interpretation of civic
virtue, 138n; understanding of
"improvement" and progress,
143-148; view of liberty, 125,
138
origins of name, 140n; Country
party roots of American Whigs,
142
seeks to reclaim democratic label,
141
See also Brownson, Orestes; Colton, Calvin; and Jacksonian
Democrats
Ames, Fisher, 85, 86, 95
anarchism, 351-353
anticipatory democracy. *See* democracy, interpretations of; Toffler,
Alvin
Antifederalists, 54, 58, 64, 66, 75,
77, 78
Articles of Confederation and, 65

oppose War of 1812 and victimization of New England, 99-103
seek to reclaim republican discourse, 85, 98-99
See also Antifederalists; Democratic-Republican Societies; Hamilton, Alexander; Hartford Convention; Jeffersonian Republicans; Madison, James
Federal Reserve Act, 221, 246, 273
Federal Reserve Board, 221
female liberation. See women's liberation
female suffrage. See women's suffrage
Fessenden, Thomas G., 98
Feuerbach, Ludwig, 9, 412n
Fillmore, Millard, 179
Fire-Eaters, 173
Firestone, Shulamith, 312, 316
Fitzhugh, George, 161n; attacks abolitionists, 170; *Cannibals All!*, 166; Free Society of North criticized by, 169-171; "Greek democracy" in the South, 171, 182; industrialization of South endorsed by, 169; natural rights derided by, 166; plantation economy idealized by, 167-168; *Sociology for the South*, 166
Fortune, 343n
Frankfurt School, 335
Freedmen's Bureau, 268n
Freedom Democratic party, 321
Freedom Summer, 321
free enterprise and civic virtue, 128-129
free labor ideology: Gompers and, 188-189, 192n; free soil movement, 176-177; National Labor Union and the Knights of Labor, 187; racism and, 186; Socialist critique fails, 187n, 188; trade unionism replaces, 187

Free Silver campaign, 280
Free Society, 331. *See also* Movement; Students for a Democratic Society
Free Society of the North, 166, 169-171, 182. *See also* Brownson, Orestes; Fitzhugh, George
free soil movement, 176-177
Free Soil party, 165, 173, 177. *See also* free labor ideology; Wilmot Proviso
Frémont, John C., 178
French Revolution, 79, 83n
Freneau, Philip, 80
frontier, 139, 176, 187

Gadamer, Hans-Georg, 403, 425n; effectiveness of history, understanding the, 406-407; hermeneutics of faith, 412; interpretation as "fusion of horizons," 405, 407, 421; language as tradition, 408-409. *See also* critical hermeneutics; Habermas, Jürgen; tradition
Gag Rule, 157. *See also* Southern Slave Power
Gallatin, Albert, 143
Garrison, William Lloyd: Constitution as "covenant with death," 162; criticizes labor movement, 174-175; *The Liberator* founded by, 159; review of Gamaliel Bailey, 160
Genêt, Jean, 84
George, Henry, 196n
Gerry, Elbridge, 77n
Gewiner, Holt, 266
Gilded Age, 183, 184, 200, 255
Gillette, King, 242n
Gitlin, Todd, 303, 305n, 308
Glass, Carter, 221
Goldwater, Barry, 297, 298
Gompers, Samuel, 188, 189, 192n
Goodman, Paul, 297

LIBRARY OF CONGRESS CATALOGING IN PUBLICATION DATA

HANSON, RUSSELL L., 1953-
THE DEMOCRATIC IMAGINATION IN AMERICA.

ORIGINALLY PRESENTED AS THE AUTHOR'S THESIS
(PH.D.—UNIVERSITY OF MINNESOTA, 1982)
BIBLIOGRAPHY: P.
INCLUDES INDEX.
1. POLITICAL SCIENCE—UNITED STATES—HISTORY.
2. UNITED STATES—POLITICS AND GOVERNMENT.
3. DEMOCRACY. I. TITLE.
JA84.U5H36 1985 320.5'0973 85-42687
ISBN 0-691-07690-1 (ALK. PAPER)
ISBN 0-691-02238-0 (PBK.)